FINDING ROOM:
OPTIONS FOR A CANADIAN RENTAL HOUSING STRATEGY

Finding Room is the first Canadian book to focus solely on the question of how to provide affordable rental housing for low-income households. Two dozen authors – from business leaders to university researchers to representatives of the Aboriginal community – address this question.

The contributors offer analyses of the economics of low-rental housing; commentary on the relationship between housing and human rights; social perspectives on the lives and health of low-income renters; overviews of how the current system developed; suggestions for housing innovations; recommendations for all levels of government; and insights into the roles of public, private, and non-profit s⌐

Finding Room is intended⌐ ⌐y options for affordable housing by prov⌐ ⌐om experts in the topic. The contributions⌐ ⌐out the need for certain policy changes, a⌐  ⌐ areas remain.

The book is a resource for community leaders, policy makers, researchers, and students. It includes a glossary, key documents relating to housing rights in Canada, and background on the economic and political context written in non-academic language.

Finding Room is published by the Centre for Urban and Community Studies at the University of Toronto.

EDITORS

J. David Hulchanski is director of the Centre for Urban and Community Studies and professor of housing and community development in the Faculty of Social Work, University of Toronto. His research and teaching focuses on housing policy, social welfare, community development, and human rights. In the 1980s he was a professor in the School of Community and Regional Planning at the University of British Columbia and Director of the UBC Centre for Human Settlements. He has a M.Sc. and Ph.D. in urban planning and is a member of the Canadian Institute of Planners. In 1997 he was appointed to the only endowed chair in housing studies in North America, the Dr. Chow Yei Ching Chair in Housing.

Michael Shapcott is co-chair and a founding member of the National Housing and Homelessness Network and a founding member of the Toronto Disaster Relief Committee, the Toronto Coalition Against Homelessness, and the Bread Not Circuses Coalition. He is the coordinator of the Community/University Research Partnerships (CURP) program at the Centre for Urban and Community Studies, University of Toronto. See: www.urbancentre.utoronto.ca/curp.html

Edited by J. David Hulchanski and Michael Shapcott

Finding Room:
Options for a Canadian Rental Housing Strategy

CUCS Press
Centre for Urban and Community Studies
University of Toronto

ISBN 0-7727-1433-9

Printed by University of Toronto Press Incorporated
Cover design by Ireland + Associates, Toronto
Cover illustration by Tim Zeltner / i2i Art, Toronto
Editing by Philippa Campsie, Toronto
Printed in Canada

CUCS Press
Centre for Urban and Community Studies
University of Toronto
455 Spadina Avenue, Suite 400
Toronto, Ontario, Canada M5S 2G8
www.urbancentre.utoronto.ca

Printed on acid-free paper

Library and Archives Canada Cataloguing in Publication

Finding room : options for a Canadian rental housing
strategy / edited by J. David Hulchanski and Michael Shapcott.

ISBN 0-7727-1433-9

1. Rental housing – Canada. 2. Housing policy – Canada.
I. Hulchanski, John David II. Shapcott, Michael III. University of
Toronto. Centre for Urban and Community Studies.

HD7288.85.C2F44 2004   363.5'0971   C2004-903000-0

The University of Toronto's Centre for Urban and Community Studies acknowledges
with thanks the financial support of the TD Bank Financial Group and Canada Mortgage and Housing Corporation. The analysis and interpretations provided in this book
are those of the individual contributors and do not necessarily represent the views of the
financial contributors or of the Centre for Urban and Community Studies.

Contents

Part II. Perspectives on the Current Situation

Part III. Options for an Affordable Housing Strategy

Appendix

Acknowledgements

In June 2003 the Centre for Urban and Community Studies hosted a Policy Forum on a new national rental housing strategy. Participants included community-based housing and homeless advocates, as well as policy analysts and researchers from the private sector, government, and universities.

We asked participants to suggest practical strategies that would help to solve Canada's affordable rental housing crisis. We set a very specific target: the poorest half of Canadian renter households. Renters whose income is below the median pay a huge percentage of their income on rent. Some become homeless because they cannot continue to pay rent. The market cannot supply new housing for this group – half of Canada's renter households. Existing lower-rent housing is aging, and many units are being demolished, converted to condominium ownership, or rehabilitated and offered at much higher rents. The challenge for housing developers and for public policy is how best to deliver new rental housing at rents these households can afford.

This book grows out of the discussions that took place at the 2003 forum. Part I, Setting the Context, provides a critical overview. It begins with a major research study from TD Economics, which was presented in draft form at the Forum. Part II, Perspectives on the Current Situation, includes edited presentations from key participants at the Forum. No discussion of the affordable housing crisis is complete without examining the policy options, which are set out in Part III.

As we write these acknowledgements, the debate in Canada appears to be shifting from the question of whether we need a new national housing strategy with a focus on affordable rental housing supply to a more specific query: What are the key elements of a national rental housing strategy? We believe this book provides some answers, thanks to the excellent contributions from many people and organizations.

We want to begin by thanking the many participants in the 2003 Forum, in particular, the keynote speaker Don Drummond, and other presenters whose contributions appear in Part II of this book: Elyse Allan, Steve Pomeroy, Elisabeth Arnold, Jim Lanigan, Greg Suttor, and Jon Harstone.

We also want to thank the other contributors: Derek Burleton, Toba Bryant, Merrill Cooper, Joe Darden, George Devine, Allan Gilbert, Mark Goldblatt, Stephen W. Hwang, Gillian Manning, Robert Murdie, Sylvia Novac, David Peters, Bruce Porter, Anne-Marie Séguin, and John Stapleton.

Several organizations also made invaluable contributions, including the City of Toronto Urban Development Roundtable, the Toronto Board of Trade, and the National Housing and Homelessness Network.

Funding for the forum, and for the production of this book, was provided by the TD Bank Financial Group, Canada Mortgage and Housing Corporation (CMHC), and the Centre for Urban and Community Studies. We are particularly grateful for the financial support of the TD Bank Financial Group and CMHC. Without their contribution the production of a book this size would not have been possible.

Special thanks go to the person who laboured behind the scenes at the forum, and for many months afterwards. Philippa Campsie, our editor and advisor, had the unenviable job of taking the earnest prose from researchers, practitioners, policy analysts, and community leaders and shaping it into the very readable book that you hold in your hands. Thank you, Philippa, for the consistently high quality of your work and for the significant contribution that you have made to this debate.

Opinion polls consistently show that most Canadians want to see solutions to our nationwide affordable rental housing crisis. Thanks to the efforts of all the contributors, this book will help provide some of the tools we need to better understand both the scale of the problem and the range of policy and program options.

Affordable rental housing is not merely a subject for scholarly debate. We hope that everyone who reads this book will work towards practical solutions in their communities and in the country. Plenty of organizations and associations are part of the solution – and they would benefit from your active involvement.

An informed and active public is a necessary step in the realization of our shared goal: adequate and affordable housing for all.

J. David Hulchanski
Michael Shapcott

Toronto, July 2004

Foreword

DAVID MILLER
Mayor, City of Toronto

Home is the place where, when you have to go there,
They have to take you in.
—Robert Frost, *The Death of the Hired Man*

When politicians talk about Canada's housing crisis, we tend to speak of waiting lists, funding sources, and divisions of responsibility among the three orders of government. These issues are important, but they don't get at the thing that makes our current situation so outrageous: the fundamental need of every human being to have a place to call home.

Home isn't where you *want* to go, it's where you *have* to go; it's a right, not a privilege. Somewhere along the line in Canada, we've allowed this to be forgotten. Policies and priorities changed, housing money disappeared, and politicians began to accept a fundamentally unacceptable situation. There are hundreds of Canadians who cannot afford to rent or buy a home. This defies both logic and morality. It is an unsustainable situation.

In Toronto, the problem has been building for more than twenty years. Today, Toronto's homeless have become a routine part of the city backdrop. We should never have let things get to this point. Our city is far from unique. Every major urban centre in Canada faces housing challenges that are similar in nature, if not in degree, to those of Toronto.

While the state of affordable housing in Canada is deplorable, there are also good reasons to be hopeful. This crisis has come to the fore at the very moment that we have a rare opportunity to solve it. This opportunity can be described in many ways, but what it boils down to – as with so many seemingly intractable issues – is that the political will now exists to do something about it. Not only do politicians at every order of government recognize the value of fixing this problem, but ordinary Canadians also understand the necessity.

In early 2004, shortly after I was elected Mayor of Toronto, City Council tried a new experiment in community engagement, designed to help chart a course for the future of our city. City Council wanted to know what residents envisioned for their city before we debated the municipal budget on the floor of council. In a series of highly successful public meetings known collectively as *Listening to Toronto,* we asked Torontonians about their priorities for City Council's budget. All over Toronto, people told us the same thing: our number one job has to be to ensure all residents have an affordable place to live. Our mandate is clear.

When we work to address the issue of affordable housing, it accomplishes two important goals. First, it enables people to exercise their inalienable right to have a home. Second, investing in affordable housing ensures the economic well-being of the city. Given that cities are the economic engines of our country, when Toronto and other cities thrive, the country itself thrives. The political will to address this issue comes from both recognition of our responsibilities, and from an understanding of the benefits we will reap.

To stop the decay of the affordable housing issue, and to build for the future, we need to face this issue head on with vision, creativity, and boldness. For me as Mayor of Toronto, that means everything from spearheading negotiations with the other orders of government for resources and decision-making power, to small symbolic projects that help us build and keep our momentum.

One such project that means a great deal to me has to do with a Habitat for Humanity project in downtown Toronto. In 2004, Toronto City Council made a small but important gesture by providing the financial support for one extra home on this site – an unprecedented initiative. That single home makes only a tiny difference, but the act itself exemplifies the exact kind of commitment and creativity that will allow us to forge solutions for the big picture.

In February of that same year, I hosted an affordable housing summit at Toronto City Hall. More than 350 people from all walks of life attended. The resulting report is a tremendous source of optimism and inspiration. The ideas that emerged from this meeting of minds have become the driving force behind Council's actions as well as those of the many community organizations, businesses, and volunteer groups that are working together on the housing front.

One of City Council's most important jobs involves our ongoing negotiations with the provincial and federal governments to secure long-term stable funding for affordable housing. And just like the Habitat for Humanity project, the governmental solution requires not just new funds, but new ideas. We are seeking support for a range of initiatives, including everything from the creation of supportive housing for people who need help with day-to-day tasks, to better control over the demolition of rental properties. We also need to limit the conversion of rental properties into condominiums that are affordable only to people with large incomes.

There is much more. In Ontario, we need the province to honour its commitments to fund affordable housing, and to provide desperately needed rent supplements. The province must also re-invest in existing and new supportive housing. We also need a federal government that will fund affordable housing programs that actually result in new affordable housing.

Nobody can do more to help the other orders of government come up with a workable plan than Toronto City Council and other city councils across the country. That is why, in addition to seeking new sources of housing funding, cities are asking for a "seat at the table" with the other orders of government. City governments have a presence on the streets and in the neighbourhoods where you can really see the problems associated with affordable housing. Our unique understanding of the issues helps us assess needs and direct resources in ways that will have maximum impact. But our insight into city issues will only be effective if we have a say in housing policy from the very start. Not only would it cost the other governments nothing to give cities a seat at the table, it would mean we could do much, much more with our current resources.

I am confident that we will strike a new deal with the other orders of government that will allow us to find sustainable sources of revenue to create and maintain housing, and that will see us sit down together to settle policy matters. With a minority federal government, we've never had a better opportunity for boldness and creativity in the way governments do things.

I am also aware, though, that we can't just wait around while negotiations for a new deal for cities play out. We have to get keys into the hands of people who need homes, and we have to do it this year, not next year, or the year after that.

Toronto is Canada's largest city, drawing people from across the country and around the world. We feel the housing crunch particularly acutely. Toronto has a responsibility to show leadership on this issue. That is why City Council has included $14 million in new funding in our municipal budget for affordable housing and why we are turning that money into new homes as quickly as we can. We also are committed to accelerating projects that are already in the works.

We are also addressing affordable housing as we move forward on redeveloping our waterfront. The waterfront is the key to so much of Toronto's – and by extension Canada's – future. We are transforming our 46 kilometres of shoreline from old industrial space into new, sustainable neighbourhoods. We have a bold plan for the waterfront, including at least 40,000 new homes with ready access to public parks and public transit. Like the rest of Toronto, these communities will be rich and vibrant in their diversity. One of the ways we will promote that diversity is to work with the other orders of government to ensure that at least a quarter of the homes – a full 10,000 – will be affordable housing.

There is every reason to be confident that Canadians have the will to find the resources to meet this country's housing needs. But bricks and mortar are not the entire solution. The other half of the equation involves assessing and addressing the needs of low-income families who require affordable housing. It also involves those least fortunate Canadians who have no homes at all.

The causes of poverty and homelessness are complex and subtle. Our response to them must be equally nuanced and multi-faceted, not to mention humane. Outreach initiatives must integrate many kinds of assistance: needs assessment, referral to shelter, transportation, access to housing, storage of personal belongings, applications for financial assistance, and help for people who want to return to their home community.

Canada has difficult issues to address in this community, such as the fact that shelters, which are designed for short-term, emergency situations, have become long-term residences for many people who simply have nowhere else to go. This is bad for them, and it creates an extra financial burden for cities. In Toronto, for instance, fully 17 percent of long-term hostel residents use 46 percent of hostel resources.

We have to be innovative with our existing resources in order to meet this challenge. Toronto has launched a pilot project using a provincial rent supplement program that will help many long-time shelter residents move into their own homes. We started with 200 such supplements, but this program will ultimately make a huge difference, and relieve a great deal of the pressure on the shelter system.

Addressing the affordable housing crisis in Canada is an onerous job; we have our work cut out for us. For years, cities have been starved of the funds and resources they need to provide adequate housing for their residents. Now, we have to rectify the problems wreaked by long-term underfunding, while finding new, constructive ways move forward. It's a daunting process, but we have to remain undaunted. Our response has to be as overwhelming and as multi-faceted as the problem itself.

Here are five fundamentals that should serve as guides as we move forward on these issues:

- Programs must be individualized to suit varied needs throughout the country.
- Municipal governments must be given a seat at the table with the other orders of government when housing policy is created.
- The federal government must provide long-term funding for affordable housing.
- The provincial and territorial governments must take immediate action to complement federal initiatives.
- Municipalities must show leadership on the ground, where money and ideas get turned into dwellings.

The current unity of resolve among the three orders of government, private and non-profit organizations, and the people of Canada will not last forever. We need to take action now, while this rare alignment of priorities exists. It's only by turning ideas into action, commitments into policy, and dollars into houses, that we can ensure that every family and individual has a place they can afford to call home.

When it comes down to it, we have no option but to overcome the obstacles to a sound affordable housing policy. With apologies to Robert Frost, when a Canadian has to go home, we have to be there to take them in.

Mayor David Miller was a Toronto city councillor for nine years before being elected mayor in November 2003. As a city councillor, he chaired the Charter City Reference Group, sat on the committee on the future role of municipal government at the Federation of Canadian Municipalities, and was a director of Metropolis, an international organization of cities with more than a million inhabitants. Soon after becoming mayor, he organized a big city mayors' conference to promote a national urban agenda and held an open forum that allowed Torontonians to suggest ways of increasing the stock of affordable housing in the city. Mayor Miller has a degree in economics from Harvard and a law degree from the University of Toronto. Before running for public office, he was a partner at the Toronto law firm Aird & Berlis.

FINDING ROOM:
OPTIONS FOR A CANADIAN RENTAL HOUSING STRATEGY

Chapter 1

Introduction: Finding Room in the Housing System for *All* Canadians

BY J. DAVID HULCHANSKI AND MICHAEL SHAPCOTT

> Decent housing is important both to individual households and to economic growth. It impacts on individuals' disposable income, their ability to access employment, their health, and their inclusion in society. This is why the Government is committed to ensuring that everyone should have the opportunity of a decent home and is setting itself targets to improve the condition of both the social and private sector housing stock, and to achieve a more sustainable balance between housing availability and the demand for housing ... and the sustainability of existing towns and cities.

Many Canadians wish that this statement had come from a recent Canadian federal budget. It is, instead, taken from the United Kingdom's July 15, 2002, *Spending Review* (the equivalent of the national budget). The U.K. government announced a new funding package for municipalities, housing supply and rehabilitation, and community planning. The minister responsible told the House of Commons that "anyone looking at the record over past decades will recognise that all governments have failed to meet the housing needs of our people." He noted the "continuing decline in the provision of all houses – social and private," and stated that the "situation will get worse unless we take radical action now."[1] This statement applies equally to the affordable rental housing situation in Canada – the focus of this book.

The lack of federal and provincial commitment to housing for all Canadians during the past 15 years contrasts not only with housing policies in most other Western nations, but also with the philosophy of successive Canadian governments from the 1960s to the mid-1980s. Problems associated with urbanization, including the creation of affordable housing, were the focus of significant policy and program attention. There were very few homeless people and few, if any, homeless families in Canada before the mid-1980s.

After 50 years of federal involvement in housing programs, the housing situation in Canada is described as follows in the interim report of the Task Force on Urban Issues:

> The shortage of affordable housing is one of the biggest challenges affecting economic competitiveness and quality of life. Municipal governments and housing providers cannot meet the demand for affordable housing and emergency shelter. As more and more people migrate to cities, the pressure to find suitable accommodation has a ripple effect on society as a whole. As competition for existing housing stock intensifies, tenants at the lower end of the market increasingly have no choice but to turn to shelters or remain in already overcrowded conditions.[2]

While we focus on the remaining part of Canada's housing problem, we cannot lose sight of the tremendous progress that has been achieved for most Canadian households. Unlike citizens in many other countries around the world, the vast majority of Canadians are well housed. Average Canadian housing standards are equal to or better than those of any other nation. The federal government helped make this possible, partly through the Canada Mortgage and Housing Corporation, established in 1946, which focused on making the amortized mortgage market work. The government engaged in direct mortgage lending for many years, and in 1954 introduced mortgage insurance to protect lenders. Although much of the housing built after the war was unplanned tract housing and most experts agree that even the "planned" subdivisions of recent decades are an environmental problem given their low densities, this focus of the Canadian government on the homeownership sector was, and is, successful.

In the rental housing part of Canada's housing system, however, the record is not as good. From the late 1940s until 1985 several programs promoted the construction of private-sector rental housing. These included the Limited Dividend Program, the Assisted Rental Program, the Multiple Unit Residential Building (MURB) tax shelter, and the Canada Rental Housing Supply Program. These former programs had mixed results, depending on the subsidy formula. Few units remained "affordable" for very long. Those with lower rents tended to be in poor-quality buildings in poor locations.

While most Canadians have adequate housing, about 8 percent live in dwellings that require major repairs and about 5 percent in housing that is overcrowded. When we take a more detailed look at this information, we find that almost 20 percent of renters, compared to 10 percent of homeowners, live in housing that is in need of major repairs or is over-crowded. Although the average household spends 21 percent of its total income on housing, homeowners spend 18 percent, compared to 28 per-cent for tenants.

The data on Canadian housing conditions reveal that Canadians are divided into two very different groups according to housing tenure. Owners are not only wealthier, but have twice the income of renters. Although there is only one housing market, there are two pools of hous-ing consumers with dramatically different incomes and assets.

If housing all Canadians adequately is a prerequisite for a sustainable social fabric, and we know that it is, the toughest part of the problem is how to house people with moderate and low incomes when the market mechanism is the main provider and allocator of housing. Although the problem of affordable housing and homelessness is not exclusively urban, in a nation that is 80 percent urbanized, in which half the popula-tion lives in the four largest metropolitan areas, the majority of the most severe need for affordable housing is concentrated in the expensive, big-city housing markets.

Housing is the most expensive single item in the household budget, yet the wide gap between the highest and lowest income levels means that more and more people are excluded from the housing market – and some are left completely unhoused. Though Canada has permitted a huge and growing income and wealth gap as one of the defining charac-teristics of our country, there is only one housing market and one price structure for land and housing.

Although many Canadians refer to the health care *system* or the social welfare *system*, few refer to the housing *system*. Most people talk only of the housing *market*. Homeowners are happy when they hear that prices in the housing market are going up; renters who can afford a house or a condominium watch interest rates in the mortgage market carefully. Few people, however, pay close attention to the rental market. Yet Can-ada does have a housing *system*, a set of institutions that allocates, or fails to allocate, adequate housing to Canadian households. Canada's housing system is out of balance. It is designed to function smoothly, and provide a great deal of choice, for those who have sufficient income. It is out of balance in that it is discriminatory in the way it treats the ownership and rental sectors. Interventions are continually made to ensure that the market mechanism of supply and demand works for the ownership sector but little, almost nothing, is being done about market failure in the rental sector. Canada has an increasingly *exclusive* housing system in the sense that some Canadian households are excluded from access to any housing.

As a result of the housing policy changes over the past two decades, Canada's housing system is now the most private-sector market-based of any Western nation, including the United States (where intervention on behalf of homeowners is extensive). A 1996 Cambridge University study that compared the housing systems and housing policies of 12 Western nations found that, compared to all the other countries, "Canada has an essentially free market approach to housing finance. Owner-occupation has the advantage of not paying capital gains tax whilst there is very little support for investment in the private rental sector and tenants receive very little support in paying rents."[3] Canada also has the smallest social housing sector of any major Western nation, except for the United States.

Over recent decades, therefore, the growing gap between rich and poor Canadians has increasingly manifested itself in the housing system. There is a great deal of *social need* for housing, but the households in need lack the money to generate effective *market demand*. Public policy decisions since the mid-1980s have exacerbated the problem and have failed to respond to several harmful trends.

The most extreme manifestation of the housing and income inequity problem in Canada is homelessness. Homelessness is not *only* a housing problem, but it is *always* a housing problem. The central observation about the diverse group of Canadians known as "the homeless" is that they are people who once had housing but are now unhoused. Canada's housing system once had room for virtually everyone; now it does not.

The housing system is a socially created institution. It is a mix of public, private, and non-profit actors. Over the past two decades the public and private actors in the system have increasingly left more and more people without housing. Homeless-making processes are now a part of Canada's housing and social welfare systems. Moreover, homelessness does not occur by itself. As Jahiel notes:

> The events that make people homeless are initiated and controlled by other people whom our society allows to engage in the various enterprises

that contribute to the homelessness of others. The primary purpose of these enterprises is not to make people homeless but, rather, to achieve socially condoned aims such as making a living, becoming rich, obtaining a more desirable home, increasing the efficiency of the workplace, promoting the growth of cultural institutions, giving cities a competitive advantage, or helping local or federal governments to balance their budgets or limit their debts. Homelessness occurs as a side effect.[4]

Having no place to live means being excluded from all that is associated with having a home, a neighbourhood, and a set of established community networks. It means being exiled from the mainstream patterns of day-to-day life. Without a physical place to call "home" in the social, psychological, and emotional sense, the hour-to-hour struggle for physical survival replaces all other possible activities.

The "dehousing" processes operating in society are producing a diaspora of the excluded. Up to a quarter of the homeless people in some Canadian cities are Aboriginal and about 15 percent of Toronto's hostel users are immigrants and refugees.[5] Race is still a barrier to equal treatment in Canada's housing and job markets. Families are now the fastest-growing group among the homeless. Some landlords refuse to rent apartments to families with children, single mothers, or to people on social assistance.[6] Many community-based services that used to help these families have lost their government funding. Federal and provincial human rights codes are well-intentioned but often toothless documents with weak enforcement mechanisms. Budget cuts have also slowed progress in combating discrimination.

The policy options for addressing these problems in the immediate future are neither complex nor particularly innovative. There is a great deal of experience to draw on. Western nations have had at least 50 years of experience with measures aimed at meeting housing needs.

This book is about solutions to the toughest part of Canada's housing problem: how to house people with moderate and low incomes in a country where the market mechanism is the main provider and allocator of housing, and where the price structure for residential land is driven by the ownership market. Out of the mixture of strategies and instruments governments can deploy to meet housing policy objectives (e.g., negotiation, moral suasion, direct expenditure, tax expenditures, taxation, public enterprise, partnerships, and regulation), there is no escaping the need for significant federal and provincial expenditures.

In his 1948 book *Houses for Canadians*, Humphrey Carver ended with a chapter called "The Ultimate Housing Problem." He defined the ultimate objective of national housing policy as "the provision of a decent dwelling for every Canadian" and the ultimate test of the effectiveness of housing policy as "the condition of the worst housed families in our communities." The "ultimate housing problem" itself is the supply of low-rent housing. "Unless a balance in the ratio between incomes and housing costs can be established," he noted, "the shortage [of low-rent housing] will continue to stack up against families in the lower-income ranges."[7]

This is indeed what has happened. There is not only a huge income and wealth gap, but also a huge and widening gap between the cost of housing and the income of many Canadians. In the 1960s the income gap between homeowners and renters was about 20 percent. That is, homeowners had, on average, incomes that were about 20 percent higher than those of renters in the province. There could be – and there was – private-sector construction of rental housing during the 1960s. Many tenants could afford what was being built. Developers could make money by building for renters. Vacancy rates in existing rental housing were consistently high enough to allow the rental market to function as a market (i.e., supply and demand). The federal government was also building public housing for families and the elderly. The social housing stock increased from about 12,000 units in 1963 to about 200,000 by 1975 (another 300,000 or so units were added between the mid-1970s and 1993).

Condominiums have compounded the problem of providing new rental housing. In 1970 legislation allowing condominium ownership was introduced, which meant that apartments could be owned. Before that time, residential land was zoned either for homeowners (low-density areas) or renters (areas where higher-density apartment buildings were allowed). There was a great deal of real estate speculation in the 1970s as the baby boomers entered the housing market, forcing up urban land and house prices. It was also a time of dramatic swings in interest rates (mortgage interest rates peaked at 21 percent in August 1981).

There is no shortage of reports on what should be done. There was a national task force in 1990, the National Liberal Caucus Task Force on Housing, chaired by Paul Martin and Joe Fontana, that provided a detailed and comprehensive set of housing recommendations (see table on following page). The co-authors, opposition MPs at the time, noted that:

Liberal Task Force on Housing, May 1990: Ten Key Recommendations

All Canadians have the right to adequate housing	That the issue of housing rights be placed on the list of items to be discussed at the next First Ministers' Conference.
Cuts to transfer payments for provincial social assistance programs be restored	That cuts in transfer payments to the provinces for social assistance be restored and that negotiations be initiated with the provinces to increase the shelter component of provincial social assistance allowances.
An income supplement be provided for the working poor	That the federal and provincial governments establish a new social program providing an income supplement for workers whose earnings from employment leaves them below the poverty line.
A national conference on homelessness be convened	That a National Conference on the Homeless be immediately convened to set real objectives and policy responses for the eradication of homelessness in Canada.
Eliminate all sub-standard on-reserve housing	That the federal government set the year 2000 as the target for the elimination of sub-standard on-reserve housing and allocate the necessary funds to accomplish this objective.
Funding for the Federal Co-op Housing Program be restored	That funding for the Federal Co-operative Housing program and the Rent Supplement Program be increased to allow for the construction of 5,000 new co-operative housing units annually.
Provide affordable housing for all Canadians with special needs	That the federal government ensure that an adequate supply of affordable housing units be made available for individuals with special needs.
Develop a new community housing investment mechanism	That the federal government immediately develop new community and housing investment mechanisms that facilitate the supply of affordable housing through public-private and non-profit-private partnerships.
Review all forms of taxation on housing	That the federal government convene a special meeting with the Federation of Canadian Municipalities to review the full range of consequences of housing taxation at all three levels of government.
Develop a National Housing Policy	That the federal government convene at the earliest possible date a National Housing Forum to discuss the development of a national housing policy and related strategies such as municipal infrastructure, aimed at alleviating the housing crisis in Canada

Source: Martin and Fontana, 1990. See www.housingagain.web.net. There were a total of 25 recommendations.

The federal government has abandoned its responsibilities with regards to housing problems ... The housing crisis is growing at an alarming rate and the government sits there and does nothing ... The federal government's role would be that of a partner working with other levels of government, and private and public housing groups. But leadership must come from one source; and a national vision requires some national direction.[8]

The report called for "the development of a national housing policy and related strategies" and named specific categories of housing programs that ought to be federally funded. These observations are still relevant and can be used as an outline for moving forward. Yet, the fact that during the 1990s the Liberal government failed to implement them shows the lack of political will to build an inclusive housing system.

Will Canadians see a change in federal housing policy? Or will conditions continue to worsen for some people? Will the federal government once again coordinate and expand its spending in urban areas? Will provincial governments join in or, indeed, help lead the way? This book is intended to inform the discussion of policy options for affordable rental housing. It is intended as a resource – a source of both information as well as analysis from a broad range of housing policy expertise.

Part I of the book sets the context by explaining the nature and scope of the problem and issues that an affordable housing policy must address.

In Part II, specific housing needs and policy options are presented by individuals from different backgrounds, representing different organizations.

Part III presents specific policy and program advice for Canada as a whole, and for Canada's largest metropolitan area. Although the focus of the book is on a national affordable rental housing strategy, there is a secondary focus on Toronto, the country's biggest city, where the problems are particularly acute. Toronto serves as an example for testing solutions that can help inform both national policy and define a more effective municipal role.

All the chapters, to varying degrees, help answer the main question: how can we house people with moderate and low incomes in a country where the market mechanism is the main provider and allocator of housing? The following key sub-questions are also addressed throughout the book:

• How should new housing and services be structured to make sure that they are cost-effective and accountable, and provide the best quality of service?

- What role can various sectors (non-profit, volunteer, co-operative, government, for-profit) perform in a comprehensive national housing strategy?
- What types of innovative housing solutions are available for the "affordable" part of the rental housing sector?
- Which types of housing and related services have been successful in Canada and elsewhere in meeting the housing needs of low-income households?

The individuals and organizations invited to contribute to this book have been deeply engaged in policy work on issues related to affordable housing. Their contributions to this book reveal a growing consensus about certain policy responses, as well as providing a better framing of the debate over some of the remaining controversial policy choices.

J. David Hulchanski is director of the Centre for Urban and Community Studies. His research and teaching focuses on housing policy, social welfare, community development, and human rights. In the 1980s he was a professor in the School of Community and Regional Planning at the University of British Columbia and Director of the UBC Centre for Human Settlements. He has a M.Sc. and Ph.D. in urban planning and is a member of the Canadian Institute of Planners. In 1997 he was appointed to the only endowed chair in housing studies in North America, the Dr. Chow Yei Ching Chair in Housing.

Michael Shapcott is co-chair and a founding member of the National Housing and Homelessness Network and a founding member of the Toronto Disaster Relief Committee, the Toronto Coalition Against Homelessness, and the Bread Not Circuses Coalition. He is the coordinator of the Community/University Research Partnerships (CURP) program at the Centre for Urban and Community Studies, University of Toronto (see: www.urbancentre.utoronto.ca/curp.html).

Endnotes

1 United Kingdom, *Spending Review, 2002*. London, Chapter 9.
2 Judy Sgro, *Interim Report*, Ottawa, April 2002: 17–18.
3 Freeman, A.J.M., A.E. Holmans, and C.M.E. Whitehead, "Is the UK Different? International Comparisons of Tenure Patterns." London: Council of Mortgage Lenders, a study carried out by the Property Research Unit of Cambridge University, 1996.
4 Rene I. Jahiel, "Homeless-Making Processes and the Homeless-Makers." In R.I. Jahiel, ed., *Homelessness: A Prevention-oriented Approach*. Baltimore: Johns Hopkins University Press, 1992.

5 Toronto, Mayor's Homelessness Action Task Force, *Taking Responsibility for Homelessness: An Action Plan for Toronto.* City of Toronto, January 1999, p. 19.

6 Ken Dion, "Immigrants' Perceptions of Housing Discrimination in Toronto: The Housing New Canadians Project." *The Journal of Social Issues* vol. 53, no. 3 (2001), pp. 523–539; Sylvia Novac, Joe Darden, David Hulchanski, and Anne-Marie Seguin, *Housing Discrimination in Canada: The State of Knowledge.* Ottawa: Canada Mortgage and Housing Corporation, February 2002.

7 Humphrey Carver, *Houses for Canadians.* Toronto: University of Toronto Press, 1948, pp. 123–24.

8 Paul Martin and Joe Fontana, *Finding Room: Housing Solutions for the Future, Liberal Task Force on Housing.* Ottawa, 1990. See http://www.housingagain.web.net

Part I
Setting the Context

Chapter 2

Affordable Housing in Canada: In Search of a New Paradigm

DON DRUMMOND, DEREK BURLETON, GILLIAN MANNING

Housing is a necessity of life. Yet many households in Canada cannot afford acceptable shelter. In fact, at last count, roughly one in five Canadian households were considered to be in this situation. Even more troubling, ten years of economic expansion have barely put a dent in the problem. As Canadian households struggle to find shelter and still make ends meet, their plight is spawning a series of related social problems in communities all across the country – making the shortage of affordable housing one of the nation's most pressing public policy issues today.

This study represents the fourth in a series of TD Economics reports addressing the challenges Canada's urban areas face. In April 2002, the Bank released *A Choice Between Investing in Canada's Cities or Disinvesting in Canada's Future*. This was followed by two reports that focused on specific issues within the Greater Toronto Area (May 2002) and the Calgary-Edmonton Corridor (April 2003). These studies were undertaken on the heels of a number of speeches in 2001 and 2002 by A. Charles Baillie, former TD Bank Financial Group Chairman and CEO, who focused on the need to raise Canada's standard of living above U.S. levels within 15 years. Mr. Baillie cited improving living conditions in metropolitan areas, where an increasing share of Canadians are both working and playing, as vital to achieving this ambitious goal.

The public policy case for addressing the problem of affordable housing could not be more transparent. Given that shelter is a necessity of life, we tend to be less tolerant of huge disparities in housing arrangements than we are of income and other disparities. But, there are also a number of obstacles – created by current government policy and by the market itself – that prevent the creation of an adequate housing supply in the price range that lower income households can afford.

We are used to thinking of affordable housing as both a social and a health issue. That makes considerable sense. First, a large portion of residents of social housing receive their main source of income from government transfers, such as welfare, Old Age Security (OAS) and the Guaranteed Income Supplement (GIS). Since public subsidies of rental accommodation can be seen as a complement to, or substitute for, social assistance payments, affordable housing should be viewed as only one piece – albeit a key one – of the social policy universe in Canada. Second, public health authorities have long recognized good quality, affordable housing as a basic determinant of health, with many studies showing a strong correlation between neighbourhoods with poor housing and lower health outcomes.

However, working to find solutions to the problem of affordable housing is also smart economic policy. An inadequate housing supply can be a roadblock to business investment and growth. And, a high cost of housing certainly plays into immigrants' decisions of where to locate. This is not to mention the negative impact on overall quality of life that would come from an eroding housing stock. Hence, implementing solutions to resolve this issue ties in well with the TD goal of raising Canadian living standards.

This is not a report on homelessness per se. However, it is important to recognize that a significant number of homeless people in Canada are without shelter because they cannot afford it – our report very much does address this aspect of the problem. Clearly, any successful efforts to alleviate the problem of insufficient income and/or increase the supply of affordable housing will help relieve the growing problem of homelessness – particularly those cases involving either the working poor or people who have the capacity to work but cannot find employment. At the same time, there are other people who are homeless because they are struggling with mental illness, addiction or other serious challenges. These individuals are often in need of supportive housing, but they also require other services, and accordingly, encompass a dimension of the affordable housing problem that is beyond the scope of this report.

Quantifying the Problem

Defining the terms of the debate

As part of its mandate – to be "committed to housing quality, affordability and choice for Canadians" – Canada Mortgage and Housing Corporation (CMHC), the country's national housing agency, has developed a measure of housing conditions that reflects prevailing societal norms about what constitutes acceptable housing in Canada. The measure is called "core housing need," and it is assessed in relation to the three standards of adequacy, suitability, and affordability. Adequacy refers to the physical condition of a dwelling; a dwelling is deemed to be inadequate if it needs major repairs or lacks proper plumbing facilities. Suitability pertains to the size of a dwelling – chiefly, whether or not the number of bedrooms is sufficient for the size and composition of the occupant household. Affordability refers to the cost of a dwelling as a share of household income; the rule of thumb – a familiar benchmark in household budgeting – is that households should not have to spend 30 percent or more of their pre-tax income to obtain shelter that is adequate and suitable.[1]

1996 Census Results

- 6.7 million households (68 percent): dwellings are adequate, suitable and affordable
- 1.4 million households (14 percent): dwelling fails at least one test, but could be rectified without spending more than 30 percent
- 1.7 million households (17 percent) are in core housing need
- 656,000 households (7 percent) spend more than 50 percent on shelter costs, up from 422,000 households (5 percent) in 1991

CMHC deems a household to be in core housing need if its dwelling fails to meet one of these three standards and the household would have to spend 30 percent or more of its income to pay the median market rent for alternative local market housing that does. In other words, the assessment is a two-step process. First, households' dwelling situations are evaluated against each of the three standards separately. Then, if a household is found to have fallen below at least one of the standards, a means test is applied to determine whether or not the household could find an acceptable alternative for less than 30 percent of its before-tax income. If not, the household is said to have fallen into core housing need.

CMHC does not have an official category for households that pay at least half of their income to fix the problem, but they have conducted research on this segment of the population, which is generally considered to be "severely burdened."[2] And, while there has been some debate as to whether the 30-percent cut-off is a reasonable threshold –

given, say, differences in geographical locations, family structures, and stages in the life cycle – there is no doubt that at 50 percent, a household would be extremely squeezed financially. Households paying 50 percent or more of their income on housing are almost certainly living from pay cheque to pay cheque or from transfer payment to transfer payment and are unlikely to have a pool of savings built up. Any interruption in their income flow would put them at high risk of becoming homeless.

The process of determining core housing need is a complicated one. CMHC submits its tests for housing standards to Statistics Canada, which combines those tests with its own data on household income and shelter costs to obtain an estimate of the number of households in core housing need. Major surveys are done every five years, using the extensive household income and expenditure data collected by Statistics Canada in the national Census. Given the time lag required for Statistics Canada to re-tabulate CMHC's housing standards against the new Census database, an updated report on core housing need as of the 2001 Census is not yet available. However, 2001 Census figures on income and housing costs – while not presenting the full picture – provided some insight as to likely trends in core housing need as the 1990s drew to a close.

What is the situation in Canada today?

The good news is that, as of the 1996 Census, the lion's share of Canadian households were properly housed, which is not altogether surprising in light of Canada's status as an advanced industrialized economy, which has ranked near the top of the United Nations human-development survey for the past several years. According to CMHC, roughly two-thirds of households surveyed (6.7 million) lived in dwellings that were adequate, suitable, and affordable. Moreover, although an additional 1.4 million households resided in dwellings that did not meet all three standards, they had the financial means to rectify the situation by moving to alternative housing in their local market.[2]

However, that still leaves a substantial 1.7 million households – or about one in five of the Canadian total – that were deemed to be in core housing need. That is, they were already earmarking 30 percent or more of their pretax income for adequate and suitable housing, or would have had to spend 30 percent or more of their income to fix any adequacy and/or suitability problem by relocating.

Either way, the problem for these households was overwhelmingly a financial or affordability problem. And, in a still-significant number of cases, the picture is particularly dire. In fact, CMHC found that 656,000 households in core need – or 7 percent of total Canadian households – spent at least half of their before-tax household income on shelter (i.e., were severely burdened) in 1996, compared with 422,000 households, or 5 percent, in 1991.[3]

Who is experiencing affordability problems?

In its research, CMHC found that the incidence of core housing need is highest among specific groups. About two-thirds of low-income households (those earning less than $20,000 per year) were affected – not surprising, given the primary role affordability plays in driving core housing need. Moreover, while making up only 35 percent of all households, 68 percent of those struggling to pay the housing bill were renters of accommodation. At the same time, individuals living alone – notably young adults and elderly females – as well as lone-parent families with children – especially female-headed lone parent families – made up a disproportionate share of those who pay an unacceptably high proportion of their incomes on housing. Lastly, roughly 1 in 3 off-reserve, non-farm native households – almost twice the national average – were in core housing need.[4]

2001 Census shows a hint of improvement

The 2001 Census figures on income and housing costs provided a smattering of good news regarding the proportion of Canadian households in core housing need, but certainly not enough to warm the heart. After rising sharply in the first half of the 1990s, the percentage of households spending 30 percent or more of their income on shelter declined between 1996 and 2001. And, even more notably, the downward movement was led by a 3.5-percentage-point decline in the renters' share. Both trends also obtained for households spending more than 50 percent of their income on shelter. Still, both the overall ratio and that for renters remained well above the levels recorded in 1990. Moreover, as we will discuss in more detail later in this report, income growth at the lower end of the spectrum was minimal, at best, during the latter half of the 1990s. At the same time, data from CMHC show that rental rates rose during this period – all of which suggests that we should be cautious about proclaiming a turning point in the problem of core housing need in Canada.

Proportion of Households with an Affordability Problem*

	Census Years		
	1991	1996	2001
Owners & Renters			
30% or more	22.7	26.6	24.1
50% or more	9.4	12.0	10.6
Owners			
30% or more	15.4	16.9	6.0
50% or more	5.4	6.5	6.2
Renters			
30% or more	34.8	43.2	39.6
50% or more	16.0	21.6	19.0

Proportion of household income devoted to shelter costs. Shelter costs refer to gross rent for renters and owner's major payments for owners. Source: Statistics Canada (1991, 1996 & 2001 Census), TD Economics.

No magic from 1990s expansion

Economic developments in Canada go a long way in explaining the recent – albeit limited – improvement in the overall proportion of households suffering from an affordability problem in the second half of the 1990s. In contrast to the first half of the decade – which began with a severe recession in the 1990–91 period and was then followed by a limp recovery in 1993–95 – job market conditions in Canada finally began to heat up in the 1996–2000 period, sending the nation's unemployment rate tumbling to a 24-year low of 6.8 percent by 2000. Personal income promptly followed suit. Still, given the slow start to the 1990s economic expansion, real personal disposable income (PDI) per capita had posted only a modest increase over its 1990 level as of 2000 – the latter year coinciding with the collection of the 2001 Census data.

Furthermore, affordability in the home-ownership market remained extremely favourable in the second half of the 1990s. Inflation stayed subdued, which paved the way for interest rates to remain extremely low. With affordability levels for home purchases holding at close to his-torical highs, many middle-to-lower income families were lured into the housing market, pushing up home-ownership rates to record levels across the country. At the same time, developers stepped up their pace of building in order to satisfy the growth in demand for single-detached homes and condominiums.

Seniors Suffer Especially from Affordable Housing Problem

- Seniors are 21 percent of households, and 26 percent of those in core housing need.
- But, seniors are 17 percent of those in severe core housing need (i.e., paying more than 50 percent of their income on shelter)

A two-sided challenge

Undeniably, the favourable mix of a strong economy and low interest rates since the mid-1990s has delivered significant benefits to the average Canadian household. But, therein lies a problem – most Canadian households are not "average." And, hence, interpreting these results at face value can lead to a distorted picture. For many – especially the vulnerable groups identified above – two important developments put a damper on the progress achieved in the second half of the 1990s:

- Most low-income families continued to fall further behind during the second half of the 1990s. Although total family income in real terms for the lowest 20 percent of income earners began to grow again in the 1996–2000 period (by 0.5 percent per year) after falling by an annual average rate of 0.8 percent in the 1991–95 period, these gains were one-quarter of that chalked up by the average Canadian family. And, for those who did fare better, rising incomes were often outstripped by rent-cost increases.
- The overall supply of rental housing has stagnated in recent years, and has actually been receding at the lower end of the rent range – which is the segment of the market where lower-income households with affordability problems are concentrated – causing rents in this spectrum to jump accordingly.

Variations exist across Canadian markets

Just as it is important not to put too much weight on "average" tallies, painting with one brush the affordable housing situation facing Canada's regions is also a dicey game. In examining the regional dimension, we focus our discussion on nine of Canada's large urban markets – Vancouver, Calgary, Edmonton, Regina, Winnipeg, Toronto, Ottawa, Montreal and Halifax – which were chosen on the basis of size, as well as good regional representation. (For summary statistics for Canada and these metropolitan areas, see the Appendix beginning on page 40.)

A shortage of affordable housing is commonly thought to be predominantly a problem affecting large urban centres. This is not just because disadvantaged individuals from other parts of the country tend to migrate to cities. It is also because the limited availability of land near employment centres in cities drives up overall real estate costs and rents relative to incomes. So, it is perhaps not surprising to see that, among the nine Census Metropolitan Areas (CMAs) we studied, the three largest – Vancouver, Toronto and Montreal – finished one, two and three, respectively, in terms of having the highest percentage of households (owners and renters combined) experiencing affordability problems in 2000.

However, a closer look shows the extent to which almost every community is grappling with the need for affordable housing, and especially on the rental side. For example, when CMAs are ranked based on the share of renter households suffering from an affordability problem, Halifax – one of the smaller metropolitan areas on the list – jumps into first place ahead of Toronto, and Regina places third, while Montreal and Ottawa are home to the lowest share of renter households experiencing financial difficulties. In fact, shelter-cost ratios for renter households in non-CMAs were roughly on a par with those in CMAs. But, wherever you live, if you rent, you have a much higher risk of facing affordability problems. Indeed, as the tables above make clear, roughly one in five or six renter households across Canada is experiencing a severe affordability problem – that is, paying 50 percent or more of their income for shelter.

In the sections that follow, we will delve more deeply into the two drivers of the affordable housing crisis – the failure of groups at the lower end of the income scale to do better, and the reality of a shrinking supply of lower-priced housing.

A problem of low income

The release of income statistics from the 2001 Census on May 13, 2003, revealed that pre-tax median family income in Canada – after adjusting for inflation – rebounded in the second half of the 1990s, but still ended the decade only a shade above its 1990 level. Regionally, the picture was similar across major markets, with most experiencing weak showings in the 1990–95 period and then recoveries in the 1996–2000 period. However, Calgary was the only market that managed to chalk up growth in real median family income in both the first and second halves of the decade. In contrast, four CMAs – Vancouver, Toronto, Montreal and Halifax – saw incomes fall during the decade.

Is there evidence that a rising tide lifts all boats?

While the data on median income tallies on balance give little cause for celebration, a more important question from the standpoint of the housing affordability problem is whether the rewards of robust economic growth in recent years have made their way down to those Canadians households most in need.

There is no short answer to this question. On an aggregate basis, the bottom 20 percent of families enjoyed a modest rebound in real total income in the 1996–2000 period. But, at 0.5 percent per year, this growth rate paled in comparison to the 2-percent annual rate of growth recorded by Canadian families on average. Moreover, the fastest rate of real income growth was posted by the top 20 percent of earners (2.7 percent per year). And, while a breakdown of income gains is not available by CMA, provincial figures show that income performances for those in the bottom 20 percent of the spectrum lagged behind province-wide averages in all regions except Newfoundland and Labrador, with the largest gaps in New Brunswick, Alberta and British Columbia. While the second lowest quintile of families recorded income increases in the 1996–2000 period more in line with their higher-income counterparts, they still fell well short in all provinces except New Brunswick, Nova Scotia, and Newfoundland and Labrador.

Given the disappointing showing of low-income earners relative to their higher-income counterparts, Canada's low-income rate (i.e., the proportion of individuals with incomes below Statistics Canada's Low Income Cutoff) tipped the scales at a still sizeable 14.6 percent in 2000, the same level where it stood in 1990.[5] Among the markets, Vancouver, Halifax and Ottawa-Hull saw low-income rates increase between 1990 and 2000, while Calgary was the only market to experience a sizeable improvement.

Lone-parent families and seniors doing better...

Not all the news flowing from recent income data has been discouraging. Notably, two of the most vulnerable groups in society – lone-income families and seniors living alone – actually posted increases in real median income above the national average and declining low-income rates. Single elderly females, who record among the lowest of median incomes across demographic types, experienced increases from coast to coast. And, while the drop in seniors' low income rate may be largely a function of the stockmarket bubble in the late 1990s – one that has since fizzled – the improvement in the lone-parent category provides compelling evidence that many struggling households are benefiting from the buoyant conditions in the nation's job market. What's more, gains in lone-parent family incomes were reasonably broadly based across the country, although certainly in cities where job markets outperformed – namely Calgary, Toronto and Ottawa-Hull – the tallies were the most impressive. And, with the job market remaining hot overall in the 2001–02 period, there is good reason to believe that this trickle-down effect has continued from coast to coast into the new millennium.

Another bright spot was the fact that median incomes of renter households, after losing ground to owners in the 1990–95 period, actually rose faster during the second half of the 1990s. Growth in renter incomes was especially strong in Calgary, Edmonton and Montreal, although all markets examined turned in healthy showings on this front.

...but new immigrants fall further behind...

Unfortunately, progress on these fronts was counterbalanced by news that other groups continued to fall further behind in the second half of the 1990s. Although Statistics Canada has not released the full set of Census income data by family type, it has reported that new immigrant households continued to record among the weakest income gains and sharpest increases in low-income rates during the late 1990s. And, with immigrants comprising an increasing share of Canada's population growth, the rising low-income rate among newcomers was a key reason why Canada did not record more success in reducing poverty during the 1996–2000 period.

...and homelessness still pervasive

Estimating the number of homeless in Canada with precision is no easy task. Since Census counts assume individuals have a fixed address – rendering them useless in this respect – projections are heavily sensitive to how homelessness is defined. Applying a narrow definition to the term – such as "those using emergency shelters and those sleeping on the street" – yields estimates in the 35,000–40,000 range on an average night in Canada.[6] But, given that homelessness is often episodic, with individuals cycling between having shelter and not, there is good reason to believe that the number of people experiencing homelessness at one time or another over the course of a year is several times that level. In any event, most observers agree that, even as the Canadian economy expanded in the late 1990s, a growing number of Canadians found that tough income and rental market conditions virtually slammed the door on their hopes of finding any shelter, whatsoever.

Indeed, contrary to popular belief, low income is a major driver of homelessness. In the 1998 Pathways study of homelessness in Toronto, researchers at the Clarke Institute of Psychiatry, the Queen Street Mental Health Centre and Wellesley Hospital conducted clinical assessments over the course of a year with a representative sample of approximately 300 people in downtown Toronto.[7] Respondents cited the following reasons for being homeless:

- job loss, inadequate income, or eviction (45 percent)
- abuse and/or divorce (26.7 percent)
- drug or alcohol addiction (17.7 percent)
- mental illness (3.7 percent)

As Dr. Don Wasylenki, one of the principal investigators noted, "If you read studies in the mental health literature, they tend to repeat that 30–50 percent of people who are homeless have a mental illness, and that mental illness must be a major causative factor of homelessness. What our findings say is that mental illness is not a major precipitating cause of homelessness in metro Toronto."[8] A study done by Marybeth Shinn et al., on predictors of homelessness, reached similar conclusions. After following 568 families in the New York City hostel system over a five-year period to determine what helped them achieve stable housing, the authors concluded that "subsidized housing is a necessary and sufficient condition to 'cure' homelessness for families."[9] Clearly, there is a significant segment of the homeless population whose problems are related to low income and inadequate housing supply, and in Canada, their situation worsened in the 1990s.

In sum, the evidence that a rising tide lifts all boats is spotty at best – though, certainly, it is superior to a situation where all the boats are sinking.

Supply of Affordable Rental Units Under Pressure

As the preceding discussion makes clear, low income is the main driver of demand for affordable housing in Canada. But, the problem is also one of supply. There are not enough dwellings available for Canadian households today at a price they can afford on their current income – and, that is at least partly because the rent that lower income households can afford to pay is not high enough to elicit new private-sector supply or refurbish existing stock. In this section, we will examine the factors that have led to the current shortage of affordable housing.

Rash of new supply targeted at homeowners

It is not as if there has been a dearth of new overall housing supply on the market. Supported by a healthy economic climate and low borrowing costs, residential developers have been breaking ground at a feverish clip in recent years, with the number of new residential starts soaring to 13-year highs. In fact, total starts have been trending up in all major markets over the past 5–10 years, pushing the total stock of housing from 10.0 million units in 1991 to 11.6 million units in 2001.

That's the good news. The bad news is that Canada's stock of rental housing – which is the segment of the market wherein those in core need are largely situated – has been shrinking for years. New private sector rental construction began tapering off in the 1970s, and the stock of rental housing in Canada has virtually stagnated since the mid-1990s. What's worse, the lower end of the market – which is to say, affordable rental housing, as measured by rent levels – has been particularly hard hit in most of Canada's major cities.

Why has rental supply hit the wall?

Clearly, the dwindling share of rental housing owes something to the strong allure of homeownership in Canada. But, this is not the only factor. There have also been significant changes in the policy landscape over the last several decades that have progressively weighed on supply, in both the private and publicly funded rental markets.

Declining government support

Beginning in the 1970s, the federal government introduced a series of tax reforms that made the tax treatment of rental properties less favourable for investors. As the economics of rental construction worsened, developers turned toward more lucrative segments of the market – chiefly, higher-end rental properties, owner-occupied units, and commercial real estate.[10] The problem was compounded in the 1990s, when the federal and provincial governments took aggressive steps to eliminate deficits. This affected the supply of affordable rental housing in two ways.

First, the onset of federal and provincial belt-tightening, which began in the mid-1980s, resulted in significant cuts to government support for rental housing. Historically, the bulk of the affordable rental housing built in Canada in the post-war period has been subsidized by the government.[11] That support has been delivered in three forms: direct spending on government-owned public housing; subsidies to non-profit organizations and cooperatives; and subsidies to private developers to build affordable rental housing, mainly in the form of grants and interest-free loans.[12] All three types of funding were slashed in the mid-1980s and mid-1990s.

After peaking in the 1980s, federal funding for housing began to decline, and the federal government withdrew all funding for new assisted housing in 1993 (though it continued to provide almost $2 billion per year in interest subsidies for the existing stock). And, as the accompanying chart shows, about half the provinces – Alberta, Ontario, Newfoundland & Labrador, Nova Scotia, and New Brunswick – slashed spending on housing between fiscal 1993–94 and 2000–01, while only two provinces – British Columbia and Prince Edward Island – increased spending significantly. The statistics on social housing tell the tale. With the notable exception of Vancouver, virtually no new social housing has been built in Canada's largest CMAs since 1995. However, since fiscal 2000–01, some provinces have reinvested modest amounts in housing.

Second, the 1990s were marked by a period when Canadian municipalities were required to take on new spending demands in a raft of areas. Notably, the federal and provincial governments downloaded responsibility for a number of new services directly (in Ontario's case, this included housing) or indirectly, by vacating certain fields. While Ontario's municipalities received some property tax room as part of the downloading exercise, in most cases, there was no commensurate increase in municipal governments' revenue-raising abilities – a problem we discussed in two major reports on Canada's cities last year. This placed corresponding upward pressure on non-residential property taxes and development charges, which further increased the costs to developers of building new units.

CMHC tightens policies

Another factor that depressed private sector rental construction in the 1990s was a change in CMHC's mortgage underwriting practices for rental housing projects. In Canada, chartered banks are prohibited by federal statute from offering mortgages worth more than 75 percent of a property's estimated value. To lend more than this amount – a so-called "high-ratio" mortgage – banks have to insure themselves against the risk that a borrower may default on a mortgage.[13] There are only two providers of mortgage default insurance in Canada – CMHC and General Electric Mortgage Insurance Canada (GEMICO) – and only CMHC offers insurance for rental projects.

For decades after their introduction, the availability of CMHC-insured high-ratio mortgages for rental housing projects played a significant role in stimulating new rental construction in Canada. However, after sustaining heavy losses in the 1980s and 1990s, as rising interest rates led to an increase in defaults, CMHC hiked insurance premiums and applied more conservative estimates of capitalization rates for new projects.[14] The first measure made mortgage insurance more costly. The second reduced the size of the mortgage borrowers could obtain, by lowering the base lending value of the prospective project – thereby increasing the initial equity investment required. Together, the two measures cut back the supply of financing available for rental construction. In 1998, CMHC eased mortgage insurance terms for existing rental properties, making them a more attractive investment for pension funds and real estate investment trusts, and it changed the criteria for new rental units – where capital was really needed – in 2001.

Rent controls an obstacle

An additional factor that weighed on rental market supply to differing degrees across the country was the existence of provincial rent controls and other regulations. In the mid-1970s, all provinces had adopted rent controls as part of a fight against rising inflation. At the same time, many lacked any kind of controls on the demolition and conversion of existing rental properties. As we noted earlier, the worsening climate for private-sector rental investment induced many developers to maximize the return on their urban properties by converting them into higher-end, owner-occupied units and/or non-residential units. Indeed, gentrification pressures caused by demolitions and conversions have been behind much of the decline in affordable rental housing supply in many Canadian CMAs.

While a number of provincial jurisdictions have since amended their legislation to lessen restrictions on rent increases (notably, Ontario's *Tenant Protection Act* of 1997), many still have rent restrictions in place in some shape or form. That is a concern, because the legacy of rent controls on private investment can last for years to come. The public typically focuses on how lifting rent controls boosts rents, hurting low-income tenants. But, the corollary is just as important – i.e., that rent controls discourage new construction, and encourage demolitions and/or conversions of existing rental stock into owner-occupied units. As the chart above shows, both rental supply and rents have risen in Toronto since rent control legislation was eased in 1997.

Secondary rental market provides some solace

One factor that has helped ease tight rental market conditions across the country over the past year is the increasing size of the "secondary" rental market. This market comprises basement apartments, apartments over storefronts, flats in single- and semi-detached homes and row houses, and rented condominiums. Unfortunately, data on existing stock of non-conventional units are scarce, so it is difficult to discern trends in supply. That is partly because some units are illegal – for example, basement flats – so owners do not report their existence.

Still, inferences can be made about the size of the secondary market by comparing Census data on the total rental stock, which includes non-conventional units, with CMHC data on the public and private rental stock, which does not. As the chart below demonstrates, the secondary market makes up a large share of the overall rental market in most CMAs – from one-fifth in Winnipeg to a high of one-half in Vancouver. And, anecdotal reports suggest that – with the important exception of the condominium segment – it is an especially important source of supply at the lower end of the income scale.

According to a recent report on the secondary market in Toronto by the Starr Group, it has represented an effective "safety valve."[15] However, the report also cautions that most forms of secondary rental housing are "highly elastic." As such, the supply tends to fluctuate with economic conditions and can't be counted on for a stable long-run supply. For example, homeowners may rent out a self-contained flat in their home during difficult economic times, but withdraw it from the market when conditions improve and they no longer need the rental income.

Moreover, it seems reasonable to deduce that the construction and subsequent renting out of new condominiums is behind much of the growth in secondary market supply of late. Given that these types of rental units tend to be priced at or above market levels, this would not be expected to boost the supply of genuinely affordable rental housing. So, it is perhaps not surprising to see that vacancy rates remain below 2 percent in the lower rental quintiles in most urban markets, indicating that supply remains tight.

Adding it all up

To quantify the impact of the decline in private- and public-sector rental market construction on the supply of affordable rental housing, we obtained data from CMHC on rental market conditions in the nine CMAs previously cited, as well as Canada overall. Many of the figures referred to are shown in the summary tables pertaining to housing in the Appendix on page 41. An exhaustive review of the results is beyond the scope of this report, but a few key details are worth noting:

• The strength in the owner-occupied housing market cited earlier – reflecting strong personal disposable income growth at the upper end of the income scale, as well as rising housing affordability – led to a shift in the composition of the housing stock in Canada throughout the last decade. In every CMA we studied, the stock of rental housing either expanded at a slower pace than the stock of owner-occupied housing, or actually declined outright, as existing rental units were demolished or converted into owner-occupied housing.

• Between 1996 and 2001, the total number of rental units (including secondary apartments, such as basement units) rose by a scant 2,000 units across Canada, following growth of 186,000 units during the previous 5-year period. Only Vancouver, Edmonton, Montreal, Ottawa, and Halifax recorded any increase in rental supply between 1996 and 2001, while the number of units dropped in Calgary, Regina, Winnipeg, and Toronto, with the latter losing more than 17,500 units.

• Over the same 1996–2001 period, the total number of primary 1-bed-room and 2-bedroom rental units in Canada rose by almost 13,000 units, but the increase was concentrated in the most expensive units by rent range (top 20 percent). In contrast, the bottom 20 percent of the rental market experienced a decline of 1,300 rental units.

- Not surprisingly, rental vacancy rates plummeted across the country in the late 1990s. In Canada as a whole, the vacancy rates for 1-bedroom and 2-bedroom units dropped to 2.3 percent and 2.0 percent, respectively, in 2001, less than half the levels recorded in the early 1990s. (In contrast, most estimates of a "balanced" market are in the 2.5–3.0 percent range.) The drop in vacancy rates has been most pronounced at the lowest end of the rental spectrum.

- In 2001, the tightest rental markets, where overall vacancy rates slipped to 1 percent or lower for 1- and 2-bedroom units, were found in Montreal, Ottawa, Toronto, Edmonton, and Vancouver. At the lower end of the market, rates in all of these CMAs except Vancouver were also sub-1 percent in 2001. In contrast, overall vacancy rates in Regina and Halifax were the highest, although at 2.0–3.5 percent they remained low.

- The rental market crunch may have reached a nadir in 2001. In most markets, vacancy rates rebounded noticeably in 2002, suggesting that the affordability crisis may have eased slightly last year. And, new rental construction starts have crept up in recent years, likely prompted by low vacancy rates and rising rents – indicating that the private sector is not completely unresponsive to the laws of supply and demand.

- Montreal stands out as experiencing the most significant tightening in rental market supply in recent years – with its vacancy rates falling from roughly 9 percent in 1992 to 0.5–1 percent in 2001.

- Predictably, tight supply has put upward pressure on rents, particularly since 1998. Between 1998 and 2001, the average rent for a 2-bedroom apartment in Canada has risen at a compound annual rate of 2.9 percent, yielding 2.0 percent per year for the decade as a whole. The average rent for a 1-bedroom apartment climbed even faster, rising by 3.7 percent per year – or 2.1 times the rate of inflation.

- At 6 percent per year in the 1998–2001 period, rent increases have been particularly pronounced in Edmonton, Toronto, and Ottawa, although above-average gains have also been chalked up in Calgary. And Regina has seen the largest rent increases for units in the bottom 20 percent of the rent range.

- However, overall vacancy rates across all the major markets remained below 3 percent in 2002 (with Montreal's mired at a strikingly low 0.7 percent). And the average vacancy rate in Canada for rental units in the bottom 40 percent of the rent spectrum continued to slip compared to 2001, highlighting the fact that much of the improvement in rental market conditions reflects rising vacancy rates at the higher end of the rental spectrum. Moreover, the slight easing in rental market pressure overall did not stop rents from climbing even further in 2002. Rents for 1- and 2-bedroom apartments rose by more than 3 percent on average, and closer to 4 percent in the bottom 20 percent of the rent range. In Edmonton, Montreal, and Halifax, rent increases for a 2-bedroom apartment were above 4 percent in 2002.

TD Economics estimates the shelter gap

Thus far, we have studied the two main drivers of the housing afford-ability problem in isolation – first, examining trends in income, and then looking at trends in the supply of affordable rental housing. Here, we link the demand and supply sides of the problem, in an effort to quan-tify just exactly what the shortage of affordable housing means for lower-income households in dollar terms.

An idea of the gap between what poorer Canadians can afford to pay for shelter and the price of the available stock is useful context for the debate on the affordable housing problem. This gap is often portrayed as the difference between what the poor can afford and either average rents or the cost of building new units. As would be expected, the gap is very substantial. This may not be a realistic portrayal of the situation, however. As discussed above, society is rightly troubled by the notion that there is a huge disparity in the quality of the shelter that various segments of Canadian society can afford. Yet while it is a laudable objec-tive to ensure that the poor have adequate shelter, striving for the aver-age rental unit seems unrealistically ambitious.

We present two alternative funding gaps here. For each of the large urban markets, the first compares what the poorest 20 percent of Cana-dians can "afford" (taken to be 30 percent of gross household income) with two-thirds of the average rent. On average, the funding gap is $2,503 per household on an annual basis. The gap varies widely across the country from roughly $1,700 in Edmonton, Winnipeg, and Montreal to a high of around $4,000 in Vancouver and Toronto, with Ottawa not too far behind. The disparities across the country arise because incomes at the low end of the distribution tend to be more evenly spread than rents (because so much of this income comes from government transfer payments, including Old Age Security and the Guaranteed Income Sup-plement, which are constant regardless of location).

The second funding gap compares the average income of the bottom 40 percent of the income distribution with three-quarters of the average rent in each market. The Canada-wide funding gap is reduced to $801. Edmonton (negative), Regina, Winnipeg, and Montreal do not have significant gaps. However, at around $2,000 per household per year, the calculation still paints a troubling picture for Vancouver, Toronto, and, to a lesser degree, Ottawa.

Recent Affordable Housing Initiatives

As the 1990s drew to a close, declining rental vacancy rates and rising rents saw Canadian governments come under pressure to tackle the shortage of affordable housing, and poverty more generally. The momentum has gained pace in the last two years, spurred by two reports – from the Federation of Canadian Municipalities (FCM) in 2000, and the Prime Minister's Task Force on urban issues in 2001 – calling on the federal government to move back into the housing arena by developing a national strategy.[16]

And, the urgency with which advocacy groups have pursued their campaign reflects not just the severity of the problem today, but also expectations that the need for affordable housing will only grow more acute in the coming years. At last count, CMHC had projected that 45,000 new rental units would be required annually this decade – and, based on current trends, at least half of these new renter households will be low-income households in need of affordable units.[17] Advocacy groups foresee even greater demand. To put a real dent in the problem, the FCM has called for a 10-year program that would provide 20,000 new or acquired affordable units per year, 10,000 rehabilitated affordable units per year, and enough income rent assistance to 40,000 incremental households per year to make their units affordable.[18] The FCM estimates the total cost of their recommendations at $1.6 billion per year, while the One Percent Solution, conceived by Michael Shapcott and David Hulchanski, of the University of Toronto's Centre for Urban & Community Studies, calls for all governments to double their spending on housing, which would effectively boost the share that housing commands in government budgets by one percentage point – hence, the "One Percent" moniker.[19] The resulting $2 billion in additional federal spending would bring spending on new housing units back to where it was in the late 1980s.

Governments are beginning to respond

The need to address the problem of affordable housing has not fallen on completely deaf ears. The federal government has since announced a new cost-sharing program with the provinces aimed at boosting supply of rental housing, as well as new amounts for homelessness and the renovation/rehabilitation of existing housing stock. Moreover, the federal government has reduced the Goods and Services tax payable on the development of affordable rental housing. And, after studying the issue at length, several provinces and municipalities have forged ahead with some new programs of their own, especially in the regions that face the gravest difficulties with respect to affordable housing. Still, as the following review of recent policy initiatives reveals, there is much work to be done.

Income support measure: Raising the Canada Child Tax Benefit

In the 2003 budget season, there were some new measures aimed at helping the working poor and those on welfare. Most notably, armed with a large surplus, the federal government will gradually increase benefits under the Canada Child Tax Benefit (CCTB) program over the next few years, providing an additional $965 million annually to low-income families in 2007. And it has offered up an additional $900 million over the next five years to assist provinces and territories in improving access to quality child care and early learning opportunities, as well as an additional $35 million for First Nations children, primarily on reserve. The federal government has already provided $2.2 billion over five years under the September 2000 Early Childhood Development Agreement. To the extent that these measures deliver direct benefits to lower-income households in Canada, they represent an important step toward helping to ease the affordability problem. However, most of the provincial announcements were modest in scope, and most did not take any action whatsoever on assisting low-income families. Instead, new investments in health care, education, and infrastructure dominated the list of new measures.

Measures to spur rental supply

Governments Agree on an Affordable Housing Framework (AHF)

In November 2001, the Federal, Provincial and Territorial Ministers agreed on a five-year $680 million framework – formally named the Affordable Housing Framework (AHF) – within which bilateral agreements on affordable housing programs can be negotiated. Since the

AHF is designed as a cost-sharing program with the provinces and territories (who have primary responsibility for housing), the federal government has entered into negotiations with each jurisdiction to reach bilateral agreements over the past year and a half. British Columbia and Quebec were first to sign on in December 2001, and all provincial and territorial governments are now on board. The main criteria of the AHF are as follows:

• The maximum federal contribution is $25,000 per unit over the duration of the program.
• Provinces and territories have to match the federal contributions overall in the form of capital or noncapital assistance, through cash, or in kind. Contributions may also be made by a third party (i.e., municipalities, not-for-profit, and/or for-profit entities).
• The initiative must create affordable housing for low- to moderate-income households.
• Units created under the program must remain affordable for a minimum of 10 years. The agreement sets the average market rent in each market as the benchmark for affordability.
• Depending on each federal-provincial agreement, initiatives may extend to renovation (beyond the existing RRAP program), rehabilitation, conversion, home ownership, supportive housing programs, and rent supplements.

Federal-Provincial Affordable Housing Framework (AHF)

• Established in 2001
• $1 billion in federal investment by 2007–08
• Matching funds required by provinces and territories
• Housing must be affordable for at least 10 years
• As many as 35,000 units could be created

In its 2003 budget, the federal government increased its investment in the AHF by an additional $320 million over five years, yielding a total outlay of $1 billion by fiscal 2007–08. The government has estimated that as many as 30,000–35,000 units could be created over the life of the program across Canada, depending on the overall amount of capital contributions.

The AHF is the first major initiative on the affordable housing front in several years, but already, it has drawn criticism. First and foremost, the criterion for affordability is average market rents. As our shelter gap calculations demonstrate, these rents are currently far from affordable for low-income households. By choosing this benchmark, the program fails to target the needs of low-income households specifically. Second, apart from a few notable exceptions, most provinces have either been slow to act on the new program, or have used provisions within the agreement to avoid anteing up their share of the funding – for example, identifying municipal resources as part of their contribution. That is not a problem if the resources represent new municipal funding, but this has not always been the case. And, third, even if the AHF achieves its target of creating 35,000-odd units, this new supply will still fall well short of the number of Canadians households already in severe core housing need, quite apart from any new cases that may emerge over the program's five-year life.

Finally, the AHF agreement overlooks a significant demographic group. Aboriginal people are over-represented among the homeless and those at risk of homelessness in most parts of Canada. Yet, as the National Aboriginal Housing Association and other aboriginal housing and service providers have pointed out, the AHF does not contain any specific targets for off-reserve aboriginal housing. The federal affordable housing program that was cancelled in 1993 had an Urban Native Housing strategy built into it, and several provinces had targeted programs, as well. Currently, there are some 10,000 units of off-reserve aboriginal housing in Canada under aboriginal control, but that number falls short of the actual need.[20] In its Speech from the Throne and 2003 budget, the federal government highlighted Aboriginal concerns, but there has been no recognition of the need to restore a targeted off-reserve Aboriginal housing program under aboriginal control.

Homelessness Strategy Extended For Three Years

In 1999, the federal government introduced a three-year $753 million strategy to combat homelessness, the National Homelessness Initiative (NHI). The main pillars of the program were $135 million per year for the Supporting Communities Partnership Initiative (SCPI), which includes measures to stem homelessness, and $128 million annually under the Residential Rehabilitation Assistance Programs (RRAP), to provide support to all existing housing types from owner-occupied homes to rooming houses.

Both programs have given rise to multiple new projects aimed at providing services to the homeless. A smaller tranche – $10 million over three years – was allocated to the Surplus Federal Real Property for

Homelessness Initiative (SFRPHI), which transfers federal properties to nonprofit organizations or lower levels of government for the purpose of assisting homeless people. Under this program, several former Department of National Defence properties have been turned over for affordable housing.

Although these programs had been due to expire on March 31, 2003, the federal government elected in its 2003 budget to keep the programs running for at least another three years, maintaining funding at its previous levels. However, agencies that provide services to homeless people in a number of communities have noted that, even though new money has been promised, the new funding has not materialized. And, as of late May 2003, there were reports that a number of agencies had either laid off or were about to lay off as many as 300 frontline workers in Montreal and a number of other communities. The City of Toronto has offered a limited form of bridge funding to help homeless service providers in that city stay open for the summer, but concern regarding the transition remains.

And, the needs of urban aboriginals appear to have been overlooked here, as well. While the original 1999 NHI strategy included enhanced funding for the Urban Native Program – an existing federal program for shelter and services for off-reserve Aboriginal people – this enhancement was not renewed as part of the extension accorded SCPI in the 2003 federal budget. That means that funding under this program will fall back to 1999 levels.

Federal Homelessness Strategy

- Established in 1999
- Original 3-year, $753 million initiative renewed for 3 years in the 2003 federal budget
- $135 million per year for the Supporting Communities Partnership Initiative (SCPI)
- $128 million per year for the Residential Renovation Assistance Program (RRAP)

PROVINCIAL AND MUNICIPAL HOUSING INITIATIVES

Over and above their participation, or lack thereof, in the AHF, provincial governments – especially in central and western Canada, where the rental situation is worst – have been making or looking at changes aimed at boosting the supply of affordable housing. Provinces have been focusing their attention on implementing regulatory changes. These range from improving the overall private investment climate for housing – for example, by scaling back regulations on rent increases – to "watering down" legislation to protect the existing rental stock. Moreover, some provinces have also handed over increased powers to local governments so that they could implement policy changes themselves, such as altering provincial building codes. For example, in Ontario – the only province that has downloaded responsibility for social housing to municipalities, as part of its Local Services Realignment – the provincial government introduced changes to the Ontario *Municipal Act* that will allow municipalities to provide "bonusing" or special tax incentives as a lure to the private sector.

Not all provincial jurisdictions have shied away from introducing affordable housing programs in recent years. Three in particular – Quebec, Manitoba, and Saskatchewan – have designed and administered new programs aimed at preserving existing stock.[21] Quebec, faced with a relatively low ownership rate compared to other provinces, has offered financial incentives to encourage tenant residents to convert existing rental stock into owner-occupied condominium buildings. Manitoba has established "Neighbourhoods Alive," which is targeted specifically towards inner-city neighbourhood housing and affordable housing, as well as the Winnipeg Housing and Homelessness Initiative, a tripartite agreement between the federal, Manitoba and City of Winnipeg governments that, at last count, had produced 700 housing units. Finally, Saskatchewan has set up two innovative programs targeted at ensuring the maintenance of quality and affordable rental stock in its four largest cities.

Confronted with increased cost pressures and weak growth in their revenue base, municipalities in Canada have been forced to be innovative in tackling affordable housing programs on their front doorstep. Many have either adopted, or are increasingly looking at, a number of options to make rental housing development more attractive to the private sector, many of which are being used south of the border. These include:[22]

- Waiving or reducing development charges, fees and property taxes in return for approval of affordable housing construction.
- Establishing direct capital assistance funds to provide grants to housing providers.
- Providing land at a reduced cost through sale or long-term land lease.
- Reviewing zoning by-laws and standards governing secondary suites,

and often relaxing them, and establishing by-laws to encourage the retention of existing affordable rental housing.

- Allowing "alternative development standards," like lot sizes and right of way widths, without compromising safety, and reducing the length of approvals.
- Using "inclusionary" housing policies, such as density bonusing, to encourage more rental properties.

CMHC INCREASING INSURANCE FLEXIBILITY

CMHC recently announced that effective June 2003, it will offer increasing flexibility in its underwriting practices to spur new affordable housing production in both the rental and owner-occupied markets. These changes include allowing larger rental loans, reducing mortgage insurance premiums, and providing greater flexibility related to cash flow requirements, loan advancing, and repayment terms. For example, over the next three years, a borrower will now be able to obtain a loan of up to 95 percent of the project's underlying value, if the project will provide affordable rents. CMHC will also offer increased financial assistance to potential housing providers who are in the very early stages of developing an affordable housing proposal, as well as increased training and consultation services. Some housing advocates have further called on CMHC to re-invest the Corporation's "operating surplus" in new affordable housing projects, but as we discuss below, this suggestion fails to recognize CMHC's new mandate to conduct its insurance and securitization operations on a more commercial basis.

Provincial and Municipal Initiatives

Provincial:
- Participation in the Affordable Housing Framework
- In some provinces:
  - measures to improve business climate
  - restrictions eased on rent increases
  - more flexibility granted to municipalities to
  - provide incentives or alter regulations

Municipal:
- Adopting policies to spur rental supply, such as:
  - waiving/reducing property taxes, fees and charges
  - providing public land at lower cost
  - offering "density bonuses"
  - improving zoning by-laws

A New Affordable Housing Paradigm

The Conceptual Framework

It is encouraging to see the attention now being paid to the affordable housing problem in Canada. Governments are beginning to act and various advocates have recommended further measures. However, in our view, some of the approaches are not grounded in a proper analysis of the problem. Accordingly, we will begin Part Two of this report by taking a step back from the mass of data and the whirl of recent policy developments to examine the foundations of affordable housing policy in Canada.

Conventional analyses of the problem of housing affordability in Canada rest on similar foundations. The problem is commonly diagnosed as one involving an inadequate supply of housing priced at a level that lower-income households can afford. The solution typically recommended is to employ one or more of a vast array of subsidies to stimulate construction of new multiple-unit properties.

We believe this approach is flawed in three important respects. First, it treats income levels as given. Second, it focuses primarily on supply-side measures, and emphasizes those aimed at increasing rental housing supply overall – which has only a minimal impact at the affordable end of the scale. And, third, many of the measures recommended as a means of stimulating this new supply (whether expenditure-based or tax-based) are inefficient, which is to say they entail a high public cost per new unit of affordable housing created.

Below, we will suggest an alternative paradigm for affordable housing – one that situates the problem in its larger economic and social context. This broader perspective makes it clear that a comprehensive solution to the affordable housing problem will require a two-pronged approach to address the demand and supply sides of the equation.

TD Diagnosis

There are too many low-income households in Canada. Market-generated incomes at the low end are not rising quickly enough, and transfers have been only partially successful in alleviating this problem.

TD Proposal

The ultimate solution is to raise market incomes over the long term and develop a more effective and equitable income transfer regime to help lower-income households avoid the perils of the proverbial low-income trap. As these are necessarily longer-term objectives, complementary actions will be required in the interim to:

- improve supports for lower-income individuals;
- address the current supply shortage;
- remove market imperfections that contribute to that supply shortage.

The rationale behind this formulation of the problem

The first criticism we levelled at the conventional model of affordable housing was that it treats income levels as given. Indeed, much of the existing literature on affordable housing assumes a priori the existence of a stratum of low-income individuals who are perpetually in need of assisted housing. Rather than accepting this as inevitable, we argue that a comprehensive affordable housing strategy should seek to ameliorate this underlying cause of the problem. This is the only way to achieve a permanent reduction in the need for affordable housing.

The conventional perspective on income issues is to be concerned by the income distribution. That is, how the groups at the bottom end of the distribution are faring relative to the higher-income groups. That is not the relevant issue here. Unfortunately, someone will always be at the bottom end of the distribution. Our concern should be with the absolute welfare of those groups. The goal should be to lift the incomes of the poorest Canadians.

Ideally, the incomes of the poorest Canadians should be raised through market mechanisms – more and better paying jobs. Realistically, the income transfer regime will always be required to play an important, supportive role. That transfer regime has already accomplished a great deal. Old Age Security, the Guaranteed Income Supplement and the Canada and Quebec Pension Plans have done a great deal to alleviate poverty among the elderly. The Canada Child Tax Benefit is doing the same for families with children. However, the regime still leaves much to be desired. In its present form, the system is inadequate to meet the needs of many lower-income households; it is inequitable, in that it treats households with similar incomes unequally; and, it is inefficient, in that it often creates a low-income trap with a dependency upon social assistance because very little financial incentive is provided to households to improve their situation through increasing their market incomes or savings.

Why interim measures are needed

Ultimately, addressing the plight of lower-income households is about tackling the problem of poverty. However, the measures needed to address that problem – more funding for education, reform of the tax and transfer systems, and social policy initiatives targeted at vulnerable populations – involve complex changes that cannot be implemented overnight. We will discuss these measures in more detail below, but given the lengthy timetable involved, progress in achieving the ultimate goal of poverty reduction will likely be measured in years, if not generations.

In the interim, measures must be taken to ease the burden for low-income households. We identify three such measures. The first – enhancing income subsidies – is the medium-term corollary of the longer-term focus on poverty reduction. Lower-income households need improved income supports today to help them bridge the gap between their total income – their market income plus the transfer payments they receive from the government – and their shelter costs. And, as with the transfer system overall, reforms to the income subsidy system must be informed by the principles of efficiency and equity. That is, income subsidies need to be targeted more carefully, to ensure that they go to those genuinely in need, and that they fully meet that need. This will require striking a delicate balance, because providing subsidies to selected groups means those left unsubsidized will be relatively worse off. As we note below, subsidies tend to fuel rent inflation in the short term, as subsidized tenants use the additional income to enhance their ability to compete for a fixed supply of rental properties. That leaves tenants not receiving a subsidy relatively worse off. This does not mean that targeted subsidies are a bad idea – just that they need to be used with care and deliberation.

At the same time, measures to boost income cannot be introduced in isolation. Because of the time lag involved in bringing new supply onto the market, the benefits of income subsidies often filter upward to the landlord initially because of competition among tenants for the existing supply of units. Accordingly, income supports must be accompanied by measures to enhance supply. This brings us to the other two criticisms we levelled at the conventional paradigm – that the supply-side measures it favours are inefficient, both with respect to their stated goal and their cost-effectiveness. The conventional paradigm calls for measures to stimulate construction of rental housing in general. Theoretically, the argument goes, any increase in the supply of rental housing is desirable, even at the higher end of the rental spectrum, because some households occupying existing units will move into the new, higher-quality units. That will free up space at the lower end of the rental scale, as well as relieve the upward pressure on rents overall that bite hardest at the lower end of the income scale. However, in practice, the "trickle down" benefits for lower-income households from the production of higher-end rental units have been limited.

If the objective is to stimulate production of affordable rental housing, doing so indirectly, via measures to boost the supply of rental housing overall, is an inefficient – not to mention costly – way to proceed. The supply of new affordable housing units created relative to the total number of new units is small, and the per-unit cost is higher. Instead, a more sensible approach would be to target the construction of affordable rental housing, specifically, and take steps to preserve the existing stock of affordable rental housing – a far less costly approach than building brand new supply.

Finally, our exhortations to provide demand- and supply-side supports should not be interpreted as an excuse to leave existing market imperfections in place. As a general rule, measures that distort the market should be eliminated, wherever possible. But doing so will sometimes entail a cost to the public treasury. Given the reality of scarce resources (i.e., limited public funds), if the principal goal is to produce more affordable housing, we would argue that removing market distortions that are only tangentially related to this segment of the market may not represent the most efficient use of public funds.

With this new paradigm in mind, we will now take a closer look at the affordable housing environment in Canada, evaluating current policies in relation to what our model would suggest are the key areas requiring action.

1. The ultimate solution: Raising market incomes at the lower end

GETTING THE MACROECONOMIC CONTEXT RIGHT

Over the past few years, Canadian governments have been successful in implementing policies that have placed the country on a more competitive footing internationally. In aggregate, Canada's governments have reined in $66 billion in deficits since fiscal 1993–94, and Canada is now the only nation among the G-7 major industrialized countries to be paying down debt. The ensuing fiscal dividend has allowed personal and business income tax rates to be cut over the past half decade, and governments have made significant investments in productivity-enhancing health care, R&D and infrastructure. These efforts have played a positive role in fuelling economic growth in Canada since the mid-1990s. At the same time, the Bank of Canada's success in quelling inflation has led to a prolonged period of comparatively low interest rates.

The combined effects of robust economic growth, low inflation, and low interest rates have boosted the fortunes of Canadian households across the income spectrum. The benefits have been particularly apparent in the housing market. Reductions in the cost of homeownership have enticed a lot of renters into becoming property owners, increasing rental vacancy rates across the country and containing pressures on rents. While vacancy rates have risen most at the high end of the rental spectrum, there has unquestionably been some improvement in the affordable rent range as well. As we discussed in Part One, the filtering down of the overall economic growth to the lower end of the income distribution has been somewhat spotty. There is considerable debate as to whether a rising tide lifts all boats. Still, it is undeniable that nobody is lifted when the tide runs out. The conclusion should be that getting the macroeconomic context right is a necessary but not sufficient condition for easing the affordable housing problem.

TD Recommendation

Continue to put a high priority on maintaining a strong and stable economic environment characterized by low inflation, which permits low interest rates.

BUILD SAFEGUARDS AGAINST A LOW-INCOME TRAP

Why have lower-income Canadians failed to make up any ground? Three main factors appear to be at play:

First, over the past decade, disparities in earnings from employment have widened in tandem with the changing structure of Canada's economy. New job creation has been concentrated in a number of highly skilled professional occupations, with educational requirements rising in lockstep. At the same time, globalization has seen lower-wage occupations shift to developing countries. This has widened skills differentials across job types, reduced opportunities for low-skilled workers, and increased returns from postsecondary education relative to high school.

Second, federal and provincial governments have implemented steep cuts in transfer payments since the 1990s, resulting in a significant difference between pre-tax and after-tax incomes for low-income families. Notably, eligibility requirements have been tightened and benefit levels frozen, not only for programs such as provincial welfare and federal employment insurance, but also for a number of other subsidies that have assisted low-income households, including child care and shelter programs. Although gains in market income have actually more than offset cuts to transfer payments over the last five years, after-tax incomes for the bottom 20 percent have actually fallen, dealing a harsh blow to the working poor. This is because market income is taxable, whereas transfer payments are tax-free. And, for those who have remained reliant on transfer payments (and particularly the lowest 10 percent of working-age families) the past half decade has been particularly rough.

Third, the Canadian population and work force have become increasingly reliant on new immigrants to Canada, who, in turn, are struggling the most to realize their true potential. Paradoxically, immigrants – and primarily the 25 percent brought into Canada under the economic class – tend to be among the best-educated members of the population. Yet language barriers and problems with foreign credential recognition continue to prevent these individuals from finding higher-paying jobs.

Together, these three roadblocks are effectively limiting any potential widespread improvement at the low end of the income scale. In her report, "Smart Social Policy – Making the Work Pay," Judith Maxwell of Canadian Policy Research Networks highlights the risk to Canada's economy from large numbers of workers in Canada trapped in a so-called low-wage "ghetto."[23] That is, people working for $8 to $10 per hour in many sales and service occupations, who, because of huge barriers to improving their income prospects, will likely remain in low-paying jobs. The barriers she cites are Canada's punishingly high marginal effective tax rates, which penalize individuals at the lower end of the spectrum by scaling back their social benefits in line with any incomes gains they secure, and high out-of-pocket costs for quality child care and supplementary health insurance. Furthermore, individuals in low-wage employment face major obstacles to acquiring new skills, since employers are reluctant to pay for training, while programs offered by federal and provincial governments are usually restricted to the unemployed.

These kinds of inequities and inefficiencies contribute to the formation of a welfare/poverty wall, which many households are finding it increasingly difficult to scale. Removing these barriers is essential if lower-income Canadians are to have a genuine opportunity to improve their situation. At the October 2002 TD Forum on Canada's Standard of Living, we compiled a list of recommendations for reforms to the social policy and income transfer system that would deliver significant benefits to vulnerable populations. Here, we reiterate our top four recommendations for the federal and provincial governments.

TD Recommendations

- Adjust the design of federal and provincial tax systems to "make work pay" by reducing the rate at which benefits for low-income households under programs such as the National Child Benefit Supplement (NCBS) portion of the Canada Child Tax Benefit (CCTB) are taxed back. In many respects, the federal government's CCTB program and the joint federal-provincial National Child Benefit (NCB) initiative, introduced five years ago, is a "landmark in Canadian social policy."[24] First, by combining income support with social services, including child care, early childhood services, and drug and health benefits, it addresses many of the roadblocks faced by the working poor. And, second, the CCTB represents an example of effection collaboration between the federal and provincial governments. While the jury remains out on its long-term effectiveness, we recommend ongoing federal and provincial support for this program to assist low-income individuals in their quest to improve their financial prospects.
- It would be ideal if the incomes of the elderly cohort were raised over time by people setting aside greater savings over their lifetime. Yet that is not feasible under the current incentives for retirement savings. In fact, low-income households could actually be left worse off in retirement if they set aside savings. Extreme sacrifices are required for low-income households to save, but the tax benefits they receive at the time the savings are set aside could be swamped by the ultimate loss of government benefits – income and in-kind – if they retire with

a higher private income. In the February 2003 Budget, the federal government said that it was studying a complementary form of retirement income incentives to address this disincentive. There is considerable merit to a system where, instead of providing a tax benefit at the time the savings are generated, there is an exemption from taxes for the ultimate return on the savings.

- Consider best practices that aim to move individuals off social assistance or raise their earning prospects. U.S. governments are currently experimenting with programs, including "living wage" requirements (which place the onus on the private sector to pay reasonable wages in return for public subsidies) and individual development accounts (which encourage people to save by offering matching deposits).[25]
- Recognize the critical role that education plays in helping all Canadians participate in the "knowledge" economy. Although most provinces increased funding for education in their latest budgets, educational institutions across the country are still reeling from the cutbacks in the mid-to-late 1990s. At the postsecondary level, tuition fees have been on a steep upward trend in most parts of the country, leaving students with huge debt levels upon graduation. The rising cost of education has reduced its accessibility to many Canadians from low-income families, and made it more difficult to break the generational cycle of poverty. Interestingly, even small steps on the educational front can make a big difference. Studies suggest that a high school education provides the biggest marginal benefit. Against that backdrop, Canada's low literacy rate – astonishingly low for a developed country – and high secondary school drop-out rate are disturbing signs.
- Improve immigration-settlement services for new Canadians, and continue to work with bodies to speed up foreign-credential recognition.

2. Interim complementary actions

INCOME SUBSIDIES TO PLUG THE GAP IN THE SHORT TERM

Working to lift market incomes at the low end will take time. In the interim, shelter subsidies represent an efficient way to assist households in core housing need. There are two types of subsidies – rent supplements and shelter allowances. We assess the pros and cons of each as a way to help low-income households plug the shelter gap.

Rent supplements involve an arrangement between the government (through a public financing agency) and a landlord, whereby the latter agrees to provide rental units for low-income tenants. In most cases, the tenant is required to pay what he can afford, or a "rent-geared-to income" (RGI). A number of provinces – British Columbia, Manitoba, Quebec, New Brunswick, and Nova Scotia – currently have limited rent supplement programs in place, with many targeted to special-needs groups such as the disabled. Some experts – including Steve Pomeroy of Focus Consulting Inc. – point out that public rent supplement programs have had a less-than-stellar track record in Canada.[26] In particular, the administrative burden and restrictions on rent associated with rent-supplement arrangements have resulted in low landlord demand, or in many private landlords opting out at renewal time, leaving tenants in limbo. Other housing advocates counter that rent supplements provide protections for tenants – namely, that landlords must avoid predatory rent practices and maintain proper building standards. And they note that with rental vacancy rates beginning to creep up again, especially at the higher end of the rental spectrum, landlords may be more willing to enter into this kind of arrangement.

The other kind of shelter subsidy is a shelter allowance. In contrast to rent supplements, these are direct payments to the tenant, and accordingly, get around the need to negotiate agreements with landlords. The shelter allowance concept, supported by the FCM, is akin to the U.S. Section 8 Voucher. We tend to favour this option, because it is less disruptive to the market and provides individuals with freedom of choice. For example, shelter allowances preserve mobility, allowing individuals to move elsewhere if job opportunities change. In addition, the structure of the assistance formula takes into account both income and market rent for a unit, and thus can be better targeted to a selected definition of need. Lastly, they can be designed to keep costs down not only because benefit limits can be imposed per family, but also because they are primarily applied to rents on existing units, which tend to be cheaper than new units.

Still, shelter allowances have their flaws. In an environment of tight supply, the benefits generally flow upward to the landlord in the short-to-medium term, as low-income tenants use the subsidy to compete for a fixed supply of rental units. That drives up rents across the board – and, if the income support system privileges some groups at the expense of others, the latter can end up worse off in relative terms, as well. In the long run, higher rents should stimulate the creation of new supply – but, in practical terms, this can take a very long time to occur. In the interim, the "trickle-up" economics of income subsidies can actually worsen the affordability problem, as tenants bid up the rents of existing units beyond the amount of their subsidy.

Moreover, simply providing households in need with income support is no guarantee that they will use that support to obtain adequate housing. Some segments of the population – people suffering from mental illness, people coping with drug or alcohol addiction, or adolescents living on the street – may be unable to make responsible decisions about income. In some cases, these problems can be addressed through public trusteeships or "rent direct" arrangements, whereby the shelter portion of an existing shelter allowance subsidy or income transfer is paid directly to the landlord. But other individuals and households may divert income subsidies to other uses out of necessity – for example, because they do not have enough money left over after covering their shelter costs to pay for other essentials, like food. Either way, the result – pockets of severe poverty and urban decline – creates problems for everyone in the community. As we will argue in the next section, this is why it is essential to combine income subsidies with measures to boost supply.

Virtually all provinces use rent supplements and shelter allowances in some form, but there are a number of improvements that could be made to the system to target the needs of lower-income households more efficiently.

TD Recommendations

- Most shelter allowance programs are currently restricted to welfare recipients. Some housing pundits have advocated a transitional benefit for welfare households, to assist welfare recipients acquire skills and work experience to make the transition back to work.[27] Currently, welfare recipients lose their shelter benefit as they begin to earn market income.
- Another problem with the current design is that little effort is made to align the welfare shelter benefit with the cost of market rents. Take Ontario, for example. Welfare families in Kingston receive the same shelter allowance as families in Toronto, despite a wide gap in rent rates. This should be addressed.
- Just as the affordability burden varies by region, so too does it disproportionately affect certain demographic groups – such as senior citi-

zens living alone, particularly women. A large proportion of female seniors do not qualify for the same CPP benefits as their male counterparts because of their history of lower workforce participation. As such, benefits under the OAS and GIS programs, which are a maximum of just under $1,000 per month, constitute total household income for many seniors. It is time to re-evaluate the adequacy of these benefit programs. As with the working poor, seniors at top end of the low income threshold are hit with extremely high tax rates, as additional investment income is clawed back from public pensions they would otherwise have received. They may also suffer considerable financial hardship upon the death of a spouse. When one spouse passes away, the cost of living for the surviving one does not drop by half – more likely, it declines to 65–75 percent of its previous level. Yet public income support is cut in half, as is support from a private pension plan, should seniors have one.

Measures to Enhance Supply

As we have already discussed, the potentially inflationary impact of income subsidies in an environment of tight supply means that income supports must be complemented by measures to boost supply. Given the extent of the shortage of affordable rental housing today – as we documented so starkly in Part One – those measures will have to include efforts to bring new supply onto the market. But it is equally important that steps be taken to forestall any further loss of existing stock. A comprehensive supply-side solution to the affordable housing problem should encompass both of these objectives.

Creating new supply

Changes to federal, provincial and municipal taxes are often recommended as part of an approach to increase the supply of affordable housing. A number of reports provide detailed descriptions of the provisions most directly affecting the supply of rental housing and how they could be changed.[28] We will not replicate this level of detail, but rather focus on some basic questions.

The main goal of taxation should be to raise revenues for governments. Taxes should do this with the least distortion to economic activity. So the first question must be:

Are there tax changes that would correct market distortions, or do the recommendations largely amount to an alternative form of housing subsidy?

Many of the studies that advocate tax changes have as their clear mandate increasing the supply of rental accommodation. They are not directly focused on affordable housing, although they note that by increasing the overall supply, some benefits will flow to the lower-cost end of the rent spectrum. Hence our second question is:

How effective would tax changes be in improving the situation for affordable housing? Effectiveness encompasses not only the likely supply response of affordable housing, but also the net cost to governments. Do tax changes give the biggest "bang for the buck" to affordable housing?

To the extent that tax changes are a form of housing subsidy, they must be evaluated by the following criterion:

How effective would tax changes be relative to alternative forms of subsidies to improve the affordable housing situation?

First, we will briefly describe the main tax changes that have often been recommended. Many of the recommendations amount to reinstating provisions that existed prior to 1972, when the federal government began to eliminate various items they argued unduly assisted higher-income investors. Of course, the coincidence in timing of these tax-tightening measures with the decline in the supply of rental housing has been cited by those advocating the measures be reversed. Further ammunition is drawn from the observation that some of the U.S. tax provisions for real estate are similar to those in place in Canada prior to 1972.

(a) Give Corporations With Fewer Than 6 Employees Access to the Small Business Deduction
   • The lower small business corporate income tax rate is not available to corporations engaged in the rental of real property if they have fewer than six full-time employees. This rule flows from the decision to classify rental housing as a "passive investment," which also denies landlords access to the $500,000 small business lifetime capital gains exemption.
(b) Allow Capital Cost Allowances (CCA) Losses to be Deducted Against Other Income

- Individuals and non-real estate companies cannot apply CCA losses against income from other sources.

(c) Allow "Pooling" of CCA Across Buildings
  - Rental properties cannot be pooled to recapture CCA on the sale of a building – hence capital gains taxes have to be paid when one building is sold and another is purchased. Pooling is allowed in the U.S., and capital gains are deferred where a property of equal or greater value is bought.

(d) Enrich the Rate of CCA for Rental Buildings
  - Some have argued that the 4 percent annual tax depreciation rate for rental buildings should be increased to the 5 percent rate that was in place prior to 1988.

(e) Allow Immediate Deductibility of all "Soft Costs"
  - In recent decades, tightening provisions have been put in place for those not in the business of real estate, dictating that certain costs, such as legal and accounting fees, promotion costs, etc., must be capitalized and depreciated over the life of the building rather than written off for tax purposes immediately.

(f) Eliminate Capital Taxes (or Exempt Rental Housing)
  - Capital taxes are levied on the asset value of the building regardless of any income that flows.
  - In recognition of the distortions they cause, the federal government, in its 2003 budget, is legislating the elimination of its capital tax over 5 years, and a number of provinces have either already dropped theirs or have promised to do so.

(g) Lower or Eliminate the GST on Rental Properties
  - As of 2000, rental units qualify for the same GST rebate as owner-occupied housing, implying an effective rate of around 4.5 percent. Finance Canada argues that this puts roughly the same tax burden on real estate as under the pre-1991 Manufacturers Sales Tax. Some advocates do not accept this and argue for a lower effective rate. Others argue that the GST should be entirely removed from new rental housing.
  - As residential rents are GST-exempt, landlords cannot claim a GST input tax credit on their taxable purchases.

(h) Equalize Property Taxes on Multiple-Unit and Owner-Occupied Housing
  - In many municipalities, property taxes can be several times higher on rental properties. There are some ad hoc attempts to deal with this – such as in Ontario, where municipalities now have the right

to bring the property tax rates on new rental housing down to the owner-occupied level for up to 35 years.

- Property taxes remain much higher on existing rental buildings than for owner-occupied housing.

(i) Introduce New Tax-Related Incentives to Encourage Rental Housing

- The U.S. Low-Income Housing Tax Credit (LIHTC) is often the focus of such recommendations. Created in 1986, the program is one of the main tools for developing affordable housing in the United States. Under the LIHTC, U.S. states are authorized to issue federal tax credits for new construction, or the acquisition and rehabilitation of affordable rental housing. The credits are typically shared among equity investors brought together by syndicators. They can be used by property owners to offset taxes on other income or sold to outside investors to raise funds for a new project. Depending on the property, tax credits can generate 50 to 60 percent or more of the cost of development. The rest of the funding typically comes from market-rate first mortgages and low- or no-interest second mortgages. To qualify, a certain number of units must be set aside for low-income households. The program is called a tax credit, but in essence, it operates very much like a grant.
- Create a new tax credit modelled after the Labour Sponsored Venture Capital Corporations, whereby investors would receive a tax credit for putting their money into rental housing.
- Provide a tax exemption for bonds used to finance rental housing. This would be along the lines of the tax-free municipal bonds in the United States. The rate on the bonds could be below market values because bondholders would be exempt from income taxes. (The current Ontario Opportunity Bonds do not include housing.)

In assessing the relative merits of the above proposals, a priority should be assigned to changing those tax measures that are highly distortionary. Capital taxes would be high on this list. As mentioned, many Canadian governments have recognized this and are acting accordingly. The others should quickly follow suit. The much higher property taxes on rental as opposed to owner-occupied housing are also highly distortionary. As soon as feasible, more comprehensive solutions than the availability of time-limited corrections in some markets should be implemented.

The suggestions of new tax breaks for rental housing do not address existing tax-related distortions. For all intents and purposes they are tantamount to grants or subsidies. Therefore, they should be evaluated on whether they are efficient in achieving the goal – improving the situation for affordable housing. Of course, direct spending programs and subsidies are not 100 percent efficient, either. They have administrative and other overhead costs that reduce the funds actually applied to affordable housing. Still, the question is where the degree of leakage is worst.

On this score, there is no compelling reason to think that tax breaks would work more effectively than grants targeted at affordable housing. While the Low-Income Housing Tax Credit does channel substantial assistance to low-cost housing, studies have documented that a good part of the U.S. government support delivered under the program is diluted before it gets to affordable housing, as discounts are applied in selling the credits and syndicators charge a fee.[29] Programs such as labour sponsored venture capital funds do elicit private-sector involvement, but since much of the financing is ultimately from the forgone revenue collections of governments, they have some attributes of grants. In the case of tax-free bonds, the lower borrowing cost is roughly equivalent to the forgone income taxes. In fact, the U.S. experience is that the savings fall short of the forgone taxes; in other words, investors get a higher rate of return on tax-free bonds than on taxable bonds. It is argued that this gap would be even larger in Canada because foreigner investors are influential in setting Canadian bond prices and they would pay tax on them. Finally, some of the benefits are lost to transaction fees paid to brokers and bond traders.[30]

Interestingly, the call to increase the rate of depreciation on rental housing is seldom accompanied by any evidence that this is warranted on the basis of the useful life of the buildings. In fact, the economic depreciation rate on multiple-unit buildings is most likely below the current 4 percent tax depreciation rate. As such, the recommendation to raise the 4 percent rate to 5 percent does seem like a plea for a subsidy, which again should be viewed in the context of its relative efficiency compared to grants.

Judging whether the other common tax changes address distortions is a bit more subjective. For example, if one accepts the notion that rental income is "passive" and should be treated differently from "active" business income, then many of the current tax provisions can be defended. Questions could be raised around this notion, however.

There is no doubt that the tightening of the tax provisions on rental housing has lowered the rate of return to developers and investors. Hence, there has been a curtailment of supply. However, this alone is not enough to justify going back to the old tax regime. There would be a cost to the federal and provincial treasuries, so the question must be asked as to whether these tax changes would be an efficient way to deliver support to affordable housing.[31]

Virtually any action on the tax side would have only an indirect and modest impact on affordable housing. It is very difficult to tailor tax incentives to particular needs.

The tax measures would support all forms of rental housing – indeed, in some cases, all multiple-unit housing, including condominiums. It is true that a healthier supply of multiple-unit housing would bring benefits throughout the range of rents, but the impact at the low end would be muted relative to the total cost of the measure. As such, the biggest "bang for the buck" would come from directing the support to affordable housing.

Of all the tax recommendations cited above, only the U.S. Low-Income Housing Tax Credit is targeted at affordable housing. As explained above, while described as a tax program, it is really the equivalent of a grant. And a substantial part of the government support is diluted through the syndication process. Indeed, in his assessment of the LIHTC, McClure asserts that "the most efficient mechanism for providing government aid to the development of low-income housing ... is a capital grant."[32]

It has been argued that an advantage in the Canadian context of using tax measures is that they largely avoid the need for formal federal-provincial agreements – which, as in the case of the AHF, tend to be tricky. There is some, but only limited, merit to this notion. Technically, if the federal government changes something in the tax base, then the change automatically applies to the taxes of provinces in the Tax Collection Agreement. For personal income tax changes, that would exempt only Quebec from the federally-imposed change. However, for corporate income tax changes, Quebec, Ontario, and Alberta would all be exempted. Further, while provinces under the Tax Collection Agreement do not have a veto on federally imposed changes, in recent years there has been an increasing understanding that the tax base is to be commonly managed. Therefore, federal-provincial dynamics would not be avoided by using the tax system to stimulate housing. That is not to say that all provinces would object to some of the tax recommendations cited above. Indeed, some have been pushing for several of these items. There may be a fiscal angle to this tactic. Whereas the provinces are typically required to ante up 50 percent of any expenditure program, their share of the cost of tax measures is considerably lower.

In conclusion, tax changes are unlikely to bring the biggest "bang for the buck" to affordable housing. Some of the provisions, such as the capital tax and the distortion between property taxes on rental and owner-occupied housing, should be fixed for their broad merits. The other recommendations would no doubt increase the supply of rental housing, but the benefits would be diluted across the full spectrum of housing and have a limited "trickle-down" effect to affordable housing. A greater benefit-cost ratio could be realized through initiatives to directly target the lower-cost segment of the market.

Preserving existing stock

In Part One of this report, we cited the worsening climate for private-sector investment in rental properties as one of the factors behind the dearth of new privately initiated rental construction in Canada. This factor has also been responsible for the loss of existing rental units, as owners and developers have found that they can earn a better return on their investment by replacing older properties with new, higher-end rental or owner-occupied units. Thus the shrinking supply of affordable rental housing in Canada is a function not just of a lack of new construction, but also of the erosion of existing stock. And with the share of rental housing in Canada in need of major repairs still on the rise – a natural corollary of the aging of the housing stock – the prospect of more demolitions and/or conversions poses an ongoing threat to affordable housing supply.

There are significant gains to be realized from halting or slowing this process. As numerous housing advocates have noted, creating new affordable housing supply by refurbishing existing stock offers a number of advantages over new construction:[33]

- Renovating an existing building is generally more cost-effective than new construction, with some estimates suggesting that existing units can be converted into affordable housing for 40 to 50 percent of the cost of building from scratch – meaning funding could be stretched almost twice as far.
- Converting or rehabilitating existing properties can be done more quickly than building new properties from the ground up.

- For abandoned and derelict buildings, their renovation and rehabilitation into affordable housing has the salutary side effect of contributing to urban renewal and revitalization.

- For properties already functioning in some capacity as rental housing, facilitating their purchase by a non-profit provider who will convert the property into affordable housing units can run into less resistance from neighbours than launching a new social housing venture. And, if the property in question is already occupied, it may be possible to preserve a greater mix of tenants than is typically the case with social housing projects.[34]

The Residential Rehabilitation Assistance Program (RRAP) – funding for which was renewed in the 2003 federal budget – has been one of the chief instruments through which existing housing stock has been renovated and transformed into affordable housing. The RRAP program does not actually target the problem of housing affordability directly. Rather, it was conceived in the 1970s as a means of addressing the problem of sub-standard housing in Canada – housing that fell short of the adequacy dimension of core need we described in the opening section of this report. While adequacy is not the main driver of core housing need in Canada, a significant number of low-income households occupy dwellings that are considered physically sub-standard in some respect, and they face a greater risk of health and safety problems as a result.

Accordingly, RRAP was introduced to help households bring their dwellings up to standard, and it has since grown to encompass individual programs aimed at addressing specific objectives. For example, Rental RRAP and Rooming House RRAP provide assistance for affordable housing landlords and rooming house owners to pay for repairs to units occupied by low-income tenants. These programs help prevent further loss of existing affordable housing stock. Meanwhile, RRAP for Conversions provides assistance for converting commercial or industrial buildings into affordable housing, which has allowed some synergies to be realized in the domain of boosting affordable housing supply. RRAP for Conversions offers funds to private entrepreneurs, non-profit corporations and First Nations groups to convert and rehabilitate non-residential properties into affordable rental housing or bed-units for low-income tenants.

As Focus Consulting's Steve Pomeroy has noted, the involvement of non-profit corporations is a particularly attractive option. Because their operating charter commits them to keeping units affordable over the long term, affordable housing projects created under their auspices tend to remain affordable – which has not always been the case with social housing programs in Canada in the past. Pomeroy cautions that there are limits to the volume of new housing that can be generated by non-profits. Indeed, non-profit corporations have been involved in the provision of social housing in Canada for decades, but even at their height, they produced only 25,000–30,000 units annually – as compared with a population of households in core housing need that numbers more than a million.[35]

But what this approach lacks in quantity, it may more than make up for in quality. Because of their roots in the community, non-profit corporations are uniquely placed to develop housing solutions that are tailored to communities' distinct needs. Recognizing these distinct needs is a critical aspect of a comprehensive affordable housing solution. As our analysis of rental markets indicated in Part One, housing markets differ markedly from one city to the next in Canada. Different problems require different solutions, and non-profits can play a valuable role in crafting those distinctive solutions, as a recent report from the Canadian Housing and Renewal Association (CHRA) makes clear. It documents numerous cases of non-profits using funding programs like RRAP and the Supporting Communities Partnership Initiative (SCPI) to develop innovative ways to preserve existing stock and/or develop new affordable housing based on communities' individual needs.[36]

At a minimum, renovation and rehabilitation can help preserve the existing stock of affordable rental housing, thereby stemming any further loss of supply. Whether it can also contribute to the creation of new affordable housing supply will likely vary from one municipality to the next.

Converting buildings into new affordable housing implies the initial purchase of a property, which can be an expensive proposition in cities where land and property values are high – Toronto springs to mind. But, in other Canadian cities – notably, in the Prairie provinces – lower property values have made conversions a viable option.[37] Although this will never substitute for new construction, given the magnitude of the supply shortage at present, more attention to existing stock is a key component of any strategy for enhancing the supply of affordable housing.

TD Recommendations

- Eliminate tax provisions that are genuinely distortionary. At the top of this list are capital taxes and the inequities in the property tax system that privilege owner-occupied housing at the expense of rental housing.

- Given the high degree of leakage associated with most tax policy changes, focus on capital grants targeted toward the production of affordable housing, specifically. This is a more efficient way to deliver support to the low end of the rental spectrum.
- Promote the renovation and rehabilitation of existing rental properties as a cost-effective strategy for preserving and maintaining affordable housing supply.

REMOVING MARKET IMPERFECTIONS

Given the severity of the affordable housing crunch in Canada today, it is clear that significant new funding will be required to plug the supply shortfall. But it is also important to ask whether more can be done to address the root causes of that shortfall – the various market imperfections that prevent the creation of an adequate supply of housing at a price lower-income households can afford in the first place. These imperfections – the last element of our new affordable housing paradigm – include everything from property tax biases, to rent controls, to a lack of available land in reasonable-cost locations, to low density zoning that prevents low-cost construction.

We have discussed a number of these imperfections elsewhere in this report. In our evaluation of the relative merits of tax breaks and capital grants as a means of boosting affordable housing supply, we urged governments to eliminate capital taxes and redress imbalances in the property tax system that create disincentives for the production of rental housing. And, in our review of recent developments on the policy front, we noted that provinces and municipalities are becoming more proactive about addressing market imperfections that impede the production of affordable housing. Provincial governments are scaling back regulations on rent increases – trading off some pain for lower-income tenants in the short run to achieve an improved climate for private-sector rental construction that will help boost supply over the long run. Similarly, municipalities have begun to recognize that land costs and development charges are so high in the downtown core that developers cannot earn an acceptable return on properties aimed at lower-income tenants, while non-profit housing providers are simply priced out of the market. Accordingly, they have begun providing land at a reduced cost and waiving or reducing development fees and charges for providers willing to produce new affordable housing. To this list, we would add the suggestion that provincial and municipal governments resist the urge to regulate secondary market units – the often-illegal flats and base- ments apartments that are an important source of supply at the lower end of the rental scale. Informal secondary units are the lowest-cost form of affordable rental housing to create, even cheaper than renovat- ing or rehabilitating existing stock. However, introducing legislation governing their existence – even legislation legalizing them in jurisdic- tions where they are currently prohibited – could spawn a new set of regulations that would greatly diminish the cost advantages they cur- rently offer.[38]

In many cases, the regulations listed above were introduced to correct some other market distortion, only to become distortionary influences themselves. Zoning requirements present another interesting case of a market-distorting measure that may be doing more harm than the prob- lem it was intended to solve. A common tool for dealing with housing affordability externalities – namely, dilapidated buildings and pockets of urban poverty – zoning restrictions may be ruling out an important housing option for affordable housing consumers.

One Size Doesn't Fit All

In Canada, housing policy has generally been informed by the principle of equity – the idea that all individuals and households, regardless of their income level, should have access to housing that meets certain basic standards. For the most part, this has resulted in a boilerplate approach to producing new affordable housing, with government-subsidized housing being built to conventional rental market standards of size and quality, and studies of affordable housing measuring supply pressures in relation to conditions in the rental market as a whole.

But housing affordability is not a problem that affects all households in Canada equally. It is overwhelmingly a problem for individuals at the lower end of the income spectrum – and, by definition, these individuals are not average. They earn below-average incomes, likely drive below- average cars (if they have a car), and have below-average expenses – except when it comes to the share of their household budget they have to devote to shelter, in which case they are often alarmingly "above- average." Given that low-income individuals and households are clearly not average in so many other respects, is it reasonable to expect that they should be able to achieve average housing conditions?

In a completely free market, lower-income households would seek below-average accommodations, and the market would provide that housing. In Canada, however, as in many advanced, industrialized countries, governments – uncomfortable with the notion of segments of the population being forced to live in sub-standard housing because of insufficient income – have using zoning restrictions to control the supply of this kind of housing. But the process may have gone too far – as governments tried too hard, perhaps, to deliver an average standard of housing to Canadian households who have not yet achieved "equality of condition" in other respects.

At a recent conference on affordable housing, a survivor of the mental health system who is currently living in a social housing unit that does not conform to conventional standards of size and design described herself as having housing "wants," but no longer having housing "needs." If affordable housing consumers are prepared to accept this distinction, perhaps providers should be, too.

In this respect, one housing option that can play an important role for very low-income individuals and/or people transitioning out of the shelter system is the rooming house or single-room occupancy (SRO) unit. Because of their smaller size – generally, 150–300 square feet, as compared with bachelor or studio apartments, which are usually 350–400 square feet in size – rooming houses and SROs can be built at a lower cost. A 1999 study for the Ontario government found that suites could be developed in large urban centres for 40–50 percent of the cost of a typical new one-bedroom unit.[39] They are suitable for single individuals, who make up a large share of the households in core housing need, and because many of the residents do not own a car, parking requirements are minimal.[40] And, while they are most common in urban centres, as long as they are in an area served by public transportation, they need not be situated right in the downtown core, where land costs are highest.

Of course, rooming houses and SROs are not without their problems. In some units, kitchens and bathrooms are shared, reducing privacy and safety for tenants, and necessitating a fairly high operating budget to ensure that shared quarters are properly maintained. And, in the broader community, rooming houses and SROs carry a social stigma, often due to a well-earned reputation for being poorly maintained, overcrowded and/or home to an "undesirable" element of the population. As a result, NIMBY (not in my backyard) sentiment can make it difficult to remove restrictions on this kind of housing from municipal development codes.

However, there has been some progress on this front. The Residential Rehabilitation Assistance Program (RRAP) provides support to all existing housing types, and CMHC's new flexibilities, which specifically target units of modest size and design, include rooming houses and SROs. Since many properties of this sort are older and/or in a state of disrepair, increasing funding for renovation and rehabilitation will help address some of the problems that have prompted governments to restrict their supply.

At the same time, more could be done to improve conditions in this kind of housing by bringing enhanced income supports into the mix – in particular, allowing welfare households to maintain their shelter benefits as they transition back into the workforce. This was one of the recommendations of a study done by the University of Winnipeg's Institute of Urban Studies, following a lengthy series of interviews with rooming house tenants in Winnipeg. In "Out of the Long Dark Hallway: Voices from Winnipeg's Rooming Houses," the authors suggest that income subsidies would help plug the shelter gap for rooming house tenants newly employed in part-time or low-paying work, thereby reducing the "revolving door" reality of this kind of housing.[41] Rooming houses and SROs may never be a popular option, either with tenants or the surrounding community, but for very low-income individuals, they can make the difference between being housed and being homeless. As such, they represent an important element in a comprehensive affordable housing strategy.

TD Recommendations

- Provincial and municipal governments should step up their efforts to eliminate regulations that distort the proper functioning of the housing market. At the top of the priority list, regulations on rent increases should be steadily phased out, and, as we have already stated previously, imbalances in the property-tax system should be redressed and capital taxes should be eliminated.
- Municipal governments should take a closer look at zoning restrictions to determine if they are squeezing out an important affordable housing solution.

What Governments Need to Do

The market imperfections that contribute to the shortage of affordable housing implicate all levels of government, which means that any effort to remove them will be part of the broader web of intergovernmental relations. That is quite appropriate, because a solution to the affordable housing problem will clearly require the full cooperation of all three levels of government.

Provinces Need to Step up to the Plate

Over the last two years, as federal-provincial negotiations under the AHF agreement have gotten under way, a number of provincial governments have been dragging their feet. Following the April 2003 federal-provincial-territorial housing ministers' meeting in Winnipeg, federal housing minister David Collenette appeared to sound a warning signal in this regard, suggesting that the federal government would consider bypassing recalcitrant provinces and dealing directly with willing municipalities and other housing providers. Certainly, there is nothing to stop the federal government from taking such an action – and it might help expedite affordable-housing development, especially in the short run. But, without a key funding partner, it would certainly reduce the scale of the overall program. Thus, while we recognize the fiscal strains the provinces are under, it is vital that they step up their efforts, and become a leading contributor within the AHF.

Municipalities Need a New Funding Arrangement

At the same time, municipalities, which must be a key ingredient in any solution to the affordable housing crisis, are in no position to live up to their side of the bargain. On the one hand, new responsibilities have been laid at their doorstep by the provincial and federal governments as a result of downloading and offloading in recent years. Yet, on the other hand, municipalities currently have few revenue tools to draw on beyond the slow growing (and somewhat flawed) property tax. This has placed them at a disadvantage compared to their federal and provincial counterparts with respect to their ability to meet taxpayer needs. As a result, we now echo a call we have made in our earlier reports on urban issues that municipalities need to be given a more sustainable funding arrangement, one that will arm them with increased flexibility to tackle their own individual needs. In particular, municipalities should be given the power to levy their own municipal excise taxes, provided that the federal and provincial governments agree to free up the room by lowering their corresponding levies.

In and of itself, the idea of downloading programs from the federal and provincial governments to the municipal level makes a lot of sense – assuming commensurate funding is provided – since services can be better tailored for communities' unique needs. However, in areas where there are income-distributive aspects and/or where targeted recipients tend to be highly mobile – certainly the case with affordable housing – programs may be more effectively run under the auspices of provincial governments. As a result, we see a need for the Ontario government to consider taking back funding responsibility for housing, as well as other social services. Nonetheless, there is a good argument that municipalities should continue to be involved in the actual delivery of social services.

TD Recommendations

• Give municipalities a wider array of revenue sources – notably, the flexibility to levy their own excise taxes.
• Upload responsibility for social housing from the municipal level back up to the level of the provincial government in Ontario.

Conclusion

With Canadian governments still in the early stages of developing a new strategy to combat the affordable housing problem, the time is ripe to re-think the premises of that strategy. We have argued in this report that the conventional affordable housing paradigm is flawed and have proposed an alternative paradigm that we believe would provide a better solution to the problem. That paradigm suggests that the optimal policy for addressing the affordable housing problem is a combination of demand- and supply-side measures. Over the long term, a key goal must be to raise market incomes at the bottom end of the scale, but in the interim, governments need to provide adequate support at the lower end of the income scale. In the interim, these efforts must be complemented by measures to boost income subsidies and rectify the shortage of supply – by funding new supply, preserving existing stock, and removing market imperfections that contribute to shortages.

Interestingly, almost all of the literature on affordable housing focuses on supply side subsidies. Most authors try to break down the required subsidies into so many elements – tax and expenditure. Is that necessary or even desirable? We think not. For the most part, capital grants are probably the most efficient way to go on the supply side. And we would add that the focus should be directly on affordable rental housing, rather than the rental market more generally. There is no doubt that housing affordability would improve if the rental market as a whole worked better – certainly, higher overall supply would be unequivocally a good thing. But for this to make an appreciable difference to the supply of affordable rental housing relies heavily on a belief in "trickle-down" economics, for which the historical record provides little empirical support. In fact, for every dollar of public support for the overall market, the impact at the bottom end will be marginal. Accordingly, while market imperfections that hold back the general market should be removed, subsidies should be targeted at the bottom end for efficiency. That conclusion takes off the books a large number of recommendations from other studies – such as almost all of the tax recommendations, which do not address particular market failures and do not concentrate benefits at the affordable end.

This report is also available online at:
http://www.td.com/economics/special/house03.jsp

Don Drummond *is Senior Vice President and Chief Economist of the TD Bank Financial Group;* **Derek Burleton** *is Senior Economist and* **Gillian Manning** *is an Economist at the TD Bank Financial Group.*

Endnotes

1 Canada Mortgage and Housing Corporation, "Special Studies on 1996 Census Data: Canadian Housing Conditions," Socio-economic Series, Issue 55–1.

2 Canada Mortgage and Housing Corporation, "Special Studies on 1996 Census Data: Canadian Households in Core Need and Spending at Least Half Their Income on Shelter," Socio-economic Series, Issue 55-7.

3 Ibid.

4 Ibid. For the data on off-reserve, non-farm aboriginal households, see Canada Mortgage and Housing Corporation, "Special Studies on 1996 Census Data: Housing Conditions of North American Indian, Metis and Inuit Households in Canada," Socio-economic Series, Issue 55-10.

5 LICOs (Low Income Cutoffs) are popularly described as the income level where a family will tend to spend a significantly higher proportion of its income on food, shelter and clothing than the average family. When this measure was first developed using 1959 Family Expenditure Survey data, the average household spent 50 percent of its pre-tax income on food, shelter and clothing. Twenty percentage points were added to this figure, on the rationale that a family spending over 70 percent of its

income on essentials could be regarded as being in "straitened circumstances." This 70 percent threshold was then converted to a set of Low Income Cutoffs that vary by family size and community size. Citation from Maryanne Webber, Income Statistics Division, "Measuring Low Income and Poverty in Canada: An Update," Catalogue No. 98-13, Statistics Canada, May 1998, p. 1.

6 Barbara Murphy, *On the Street: How We Created Homelessness*, J. Gordon Shilling-ford Publishing Inc., 2000, p. 12.

7 Unpublished transcript, "Mental Illness and Pathways into Homelessness Confer-ence," January 16, 1998, p. 6.

8 Ibid., p. 5.

9 Mary Beth Shinn, Beth C. Weitzman, Daniela Stojanovic, James R. Knickman, et al., "Predictors of Homelessness Among Families in New York City: From Shelter Request to Housing Stability," *American Journal of Public Health*, vol. 88, no. 11, pp. 1651–1657.

10 Beginning in 1972, the federal government introduced a series of reforms that changed the treatment of rental housing under the tax code. The changes were intro-duced to dampen speculation in real estate markets, which was rife at the time, but their impact was more far-reaching. The principal reforms affected the tax deduct-ibility of depreciation on rental properties. Prior to 1972, all investors in rental hous-ing were permitted to treat depreciation on a building – often referred to as a capital cost allowance (CCA) – as an expense that could be deducted from their taxable income. And, when the sale of a property triggered the recapture of this deprecia-tion, investors could avoid the tax penalty if they applied the proceeds of the sale toward the purchase of another property of equal or greater value – a feature known as "pooling." After 1972, the use of "pooling" was prohibited for all investors in rental housing, and only principal business corporations were eligible to use depreci-ation as a deductible expense. Other changes followed, including new restrictions on the use of "soft costs" incurred during the construction, renovation, or alteration of a rental building as a deductible expense (essentially, costs not related to the acquisi-tion of land, building or equipment), and the introduction of capital gains taxes on rental properties. These reforms reduced the appeal of investing in rental properties for all investors, but especially for "casual" ones – investors not principally in the real estate business. And the combined effect was not limited to quelling speculative buying and selling of existing rental properties – it also dampened construction of new properties for decades to come. For more information, see Housing Supply Working Group, "Affordable Rental Housing Supply: The Dynamics of the Market and Recommendations for Encouraging New Supply," Interim Report, May 2001, pp. 19–21; also, see Clayton Research Associates Limited, "The Rental Housing Problem in Ontario and What To Do About It," prepared for The Fair Rental Policy Organization, September 2000, p. 5.

11 Ibid., p. 7.

12 At the federal level, the 1974 Assisted Rental Program (ARP) gave developers grants, and later interest-free loans to build new rental housing. The Canadian Rental Sup-

ply Plan (CRSP) provided interest-free loans where payments were not required for 15 years to developers between 1981 and 1983. The Multiple Unit Residential Building (MURB) program allowed owners of newly constructed multi-unit buildings to claim losses resulting from capital cost depreciation (the capital cost allowance referred to in endnote 10, above) against other income between 1974 and 1981. Strictly speaking, it was a tax incentive program to support affordable housing, but many MURB projects were partially financed through ARP, making it difficult to disentangle the two. See Clayton Research Associates, "The Rental Housing Problem in Ontario," p. 6 and footnote; J. David Hulchanksi, "Housing and a Sustainable Social Fabric," Review Draft, CPRN Project F-83, p. 7; Michael Shapcott, "Housing for All Canadians: A Nationwide Crisis Requires a National Solution," submission to the TD Forum on Canada's Standard of Living, August 28, 2002, p. 2.

13 Several major changes were introduced. First, CMHC doubled the premium for a high-ratio mortgage, from 2.5 percent to 5 percent. Second, it applied a minimum 9 percent capitalization rate to new projects, instead of the prevailing market rate – which, typically, varies by projection to reflect different local market conditions and perceived risk. This reduced the base lending value of the property, thereby reducing the size of the available mortgage. Third, it required a minimum 1:1 debt-coverage ratio for all new mortgages, based not on prevailing mortgage rates, but mortgage payments assuming a 9-percent mortgage rate amortized over 35 years. While not particularly onerous initially, these criteria became progressively more burdensome over the ensuing years, as falling capitalization and mortgage rates in the broader market opened up an ever wider gap with CMHC's fixed terms. See Greg Lampert and Steve Pomeroy, "Promoting a Positive Mortgage Insurance Environment for New Rental Construction," prepared for the Research Subcommittee of the Housing Supply Working Group, Ontario Ministry of Municipal Affairs and Housing, March 2002, pp. 5–10.

14 Ibid.

15 The Starr Group Inc. "Secondary Rental Market Study," prepared for the Ontario Ministry of Municipal Affairs and Housing & CMHC, April 2000.

16 Federation of Canadian Municipalities, "A National Affordable Housing Strategy," October 2000; Prime Minister's Task Force on Urban Issues, "Canada's Urban Strategy: A Blueprint for Action," Final Report released November 2002.

17 Federation of Canadian Municipalities, "A National Affordable Housing Strategy," Section 3.

18 Ibid.

19 Shapcott, "Housing for All Canadians," pp. 7–8.

20 Congress of Aboriginal Peoples website, section on Urban Native Housing Program, at http://www.abo-peoples.org/programs/ housing.html.

21 Canadian Housing and Renewal Association, "Municipal Initiatives: Stemming the Loss of Rental Stock," October 2002.

22 See Canada Mortgage and Housing Corporation website, "Improving Housing Quality and Affordability," at www. cmhcschl.gc.ca.

23 Judith Maxwell, "Smart Social Policy – Making Work Pay," submission to the TD Forum on Canada's Standard of Living, August 28, 2002, Executive Summary, p. 2.

24 Ibid., p. 11.

25 Ibid., pp. 11–12.

26 Steve Pomeroy, "Toward a Comprehensive Affordable Housing Strategy for Canada," Caledon Institute of Social Policy, October 2001, pp. 18–21.

27 Ibid., p. 21.

28 Examples include "An Evaluation of Housing Taxation Measures," Canada Mortgage and Housing Corporation, and Housing Supply Working Group, "Affordable Rental Housing Supply."

29 See, for example, Kirk McClure, "The Low-Income Housing Tax Credit as an Aid to Housing Finance: How Well Has It Worked?" Fannie Mae Foundation, 2000.

30 These arguments against tax-free bonds are summarized in, Jack Mintz, "Why Tax-Exempt Municipal Bond Financing is Bad Policy," *National Post*, May 14, 2002.

31 Indeed, some argue that the tax loss would be minimal and that under some assumptions of the supply response, governments might not lose any tax revenue and could even be fiscal winners. A healthy dose of skepticism should be applied to such claims – they were very common in the era when governments were building up massive deficits. Unless the tax change addressed a market distortion, it can be argued that if governments fully recovered the direct revenue loss, the tax change was not needed at all – private market participants would likely have come together to bring about the new activity on their own.

32 McClure, "The Low-Income Housing Tax Credit," p. 111.

33 Ontario Non-Profit Housing Association, "Response to CMHC Public Consultation on Housing Renovation Programs," August 2002, p. 5.

34 Steve Pomeroy, "Toward a Comprehensive Affordable Housing Strategy for Canada," p. 17.

35 Ibid., p. 11.

36 See Canadian Housing and Renewal Association, "Municipal Initiatives: Stemming the Loss of Rental Stock."

37 Steve Pomeroy, "Toward a Comprehensive Affordable Housing Strategy for Canada," p. 16.

38 For an excellent defence of this proposition, see Michael Poulton, "Affordable Homes at an Affordable (Social) Price," in *Home Remedies: Rethinking Canadian Housing Policy, The Social Policy Challenge*, eds. John Richards and William G. Watson, C.D. Howe Institute, Renouf Publishing Company Limited, 1995, pp. 50–122.

39 Ibid.

40 Ibid.

41 Jino Distasio, Michael Dudley, and Mike Maunder, "Out of the Long Dark Hallway: Voices from Winnipeg's Rooming Houses," Institute of Urban Studies, University of Winnipeg, November 2002, p. 58.

Chapter 3

The Right to Adequate Housing in Canada

BRUCE PORTER

The Gap Between International Commitments and Domestic Reality

At the international level, Canada has long been an advocate for social and economic rights and for the right to adequate housing. Canada ratified the International Covenant on Economic, Social and Cultural Rights (ICESCR) in 1976.

Unfortunately, the image projected by Canada internationally is increasingly at odds with domestic policy and legislation. There is no evidence of any commitment on the part of the federal government or provincial governments in Canada to give effect to the right to adequate housing. Nor is there any explicit recognition of the right to adequate housing anywhere in Canadian law. The policy direction in recent years in Canada has been toward the withdrawal of commitments to ensure access to adequate housing and meaningful security of tenure.

Since Canada ratified the ICESCR in 1976, violations of the right to adequate housing have reached unprecedented proportions. Dozens of people die on the streets of Canada's cities every winter. About 30,000 individuals use shelters for the homeless in the City of Toronto every year, including more than 6,000 children. Aboriginal people living on reserves endure housing conditions described as "intolerable" by a Royal Commission on Aboriginal Peoples.

The Canadian government is fond of telling UN treaty monitoring bodies that Canadians enjoy one of the highest standards of housing in the world: 64 percent of Canadians own their own homes with, on average, more than seven rooms and an average 1996 value of $150,000

(Cdn). Almost three-quarters of a million households own an additional vacation home in the country. In the context of such affluence, violations of the right to adequate housing in Canada among those who are disadvantaged are clearly the result of explicit legislative choices rather than a lack of resources.

Forced Evictions and Security of Tenure

During the late 1960s and 1970s, tenants across Canada fought for and won important protections of security of tenure, requiring landlords to go to court to terminate a tenancy. Previously, these issues had been resolved primarily outside of the judicial system, and in the words of one government member introducing new legislation in Ontario, "the landlord ruled like a medieval baron over his tenant." By the time Canada ratified the ICESCR, legal security of tenure had become a reality for many residential tenants.

Increasing numbers of households in Canada, however, do not enjoy statutory protections of security of tenure because of their housing situation. Many low-income tenants share a kitchen or bathroom with an owner and are usually denied the protection of both landlord and tenant and human rights legislation. Increasingly, low-income families with children live in small motel units that are rented by the week and are also generally exempt from security of tenure provisions. Even in apartments protected by security of tenure legislation, women and children may be forced from their home after a male partner whose name was on the lease or who usually paid the rent vacates for some reason.

Tenants who enjoy the legal protection of security of tenure find that this right is increasingly reduced to procedures designed to provide expeditious eviction for landlords, without any recognition of the substantive right to adequate housing.

Revised landlord and tenant legislation in Ontario, for example, permits landlords to evict tenants if, after five days of receiving a notice of termination of tenancy from the landlord, tenants do not file a written notice of intent to dispute. Not surprisingly, most tenants do not manage to file a written notice and most evictions in Ontario occur without a hearing.

Tenants are routinely evicted for minimal arrears of rent. About 80 percent of applications to evict for arrears in Toronto, where homelessness is a serious risk for any evicted household, are for amounts of less than an average month's rent. In many cases, households may be evicted when the landlord actually owes the tenant money, because the arrears are less than the initial deposit the tenant paid the landlord to cover the last month's rent.

In many countries, poor and homeless people tend to be located in particular communities, often as squatters occupying particular tracts of land. In these situations the term "forced evictions" is associated with entire communities being evicted. In Canada, this pattern of forced relocation of entire communities has characterized some of the violations of the right to adequate housing of Aboriginal people. These include displacement and relocation through the destruction of habitat and resources, massive flooding for hydroelectric projects, or deliberately engineered "relocations" for administrative or developmental purposes. Forced evictions of communities of homeless people from squatter communities in Canada has also occurred.

Most evictions leading to homelessness in Canada, however, occur in individual households. If Ontario's 60,000 evictions a year were imposed on a single community with bulldozers, they would attract the attention of the international community. Yet these evictions derive as much from deliberate government choice as the forced evictions of squatter communities elsewhere. A single mother in Toronto relying on social assistance, unable to pay the rent with a shelter allowance that covers only half of the average rent, is, like her counterparts in other countries, forcibly removed and left on the street with her belongings and a crying child. No one – from the tribunal adjudicator to the sheriff who carries out the eviction – is likely to inquire if she and her child have a place to go. The weather may be frigid and the shelters may be full. Yet hundreds of these evictions occur every day in Canada and are accepted as part of the "rule of law" in a country that prides itself in its human rights record.

The Right to Housing and Canadian Law

Rights recognized in international human rights treaties ratified by Canada are not enforceable by domestic courts unless they are incorporated into Canadian law by parliament or provincial legislatures. Nowhere in Canada's domestic law is there any explicit recognition of the right to adequate housing – not in the twenty-year-old *Constitution Act, 1982*, including the Canadian Charter of Rights and Freedoms, nor in provincial or federal human rights legislation, national, provincial or territorial housing legislation, or federal-provincial agreements.

When the Charter was drafted, food banks did not exist in Canada and the term "homelessness" referred to a small number of transient men living in rooming houses. Jean Chrétien, then Minister of Justice, noted during debates on the Charter that Canada was committed to implementing the ICESCR and did not need to list specific economic and social rights in the Constitution. Section 36 of the Constitution contains a joint commitment of federal and provincial/territorial governments to "promote the well-being of Canadians and to provide essential public services of reasonable quality to all Canadians."

Ten years later, after the severe housing shortage of the 1980s made homelessness and food banks a reality, a Liberal Housing Task Force, co-chaired by Paul Martin, recommended amending the Charter to include the right to adequate housing. The recommendation was never followed up.

The following year, during constitutional discussions leading to the failed Charlottetown Constitutional Accord, the provincial government of Ontario proposed the inclusion of a "social charter" in the constitution. However, despite a strong lobby from human rights groups across the country for an alternative social charter that would have included enforceable social and economic rights, the First Ministers in Charlottetown adopted a different approach. As noted subsequently by the UN Committee on Economic, Social and Cultural Rights (CESCR), the proposed text of the revised Constitution would have reduced fundamental human rights such as the right to adequate housing to unenforceable "policy objectives" of governments. The Charlottetown Accord was defeated in a referendum, after women's groups and other human rights groups argued that its provisions would weaken rights in the Charter of Rights and Freedoms.

Quebec's Charter of Human Rights and Freedoms is the only human rights legislation in Canada that refers to social and economic rights. It does not explicitly mention the right to adequate housing, but it guarantees to every person in need "the right for himself and his family to measures of financial assistance and to social measures provided for by law, susceptible of ensuring such person an acceptable standard of living."

A consistent recommendation of the CESCR in its most recent reviews of Canada has been that human rights legislation in other Canadian jurisdictions be amended to include social and economic rights.

The Right to Housing in the Interpretation of Canadian Law

Given the absence of explicit provisions in Canadian law guaranteeing the right to adequate housing, the interpretation of the open-ended provisions of the Canadian Charter of Rights and Freedoms is critical for giving domestic effect to this right in Canada.

The CESCR notes, "Domestic law should be interpreted as far as possible in a way which conforms to a State's international legal obligations." The Supreme Court of Canada has affirmed that this "interpretive presumption" must apply when Canadian courts interpret laws and when administrators exercise discretion.

Denial of the right to adequate housing to marginalized, disadvantaged groups in Canada clearly assaults fundamental rights in the Canadian Charter of Rights and Freedoms, even if the Charter does not explicitly refer to the right to adequate housing.

The right to equality in section 15 of the Charter and the right to "life, liberty and security of the person" in section 7 are of particular importance in giving domestic effect to the right to adequate housing.

The Supreme Court of Canada has referred to the ICESCR in interpreting provisions of the Charter. It has been careful to distinguish "corporate-commercial economic rights" (which were deliberately excluded from the Charter when "property rights" were rejected) from "such rights, included in various international covenants, as rights to social security, equal pay for equal work, adequate food, clothing and shelter." It is thus reasonable to assume that at least some components of the right to adequate housing will be protected under the rubric of "life, liberty and security of the person" in section 7 of the Canadian Charter of Rights and Freedoms, and the right to equality in section 15.

In fact, in its Second Periodic Review under the ICESCR in 1993, the Government of Canada informed the CESCR that the protection of "life, liberty and security of the person" in the Charter at least guarantees that people are not to be deprived of basic necessities such as food, clothing, and housing.

The Supreme Court of Canada has adopted a "substantive" approach to interpreting the right to equality, which includes positive obligations to provide the resources necessary for disadvantaged groups to enjoy the equal benefit of government programs and maintain human dignity.

While reacting positively to these developments at the Supreme Court of Canada, the CESCR has been harshly critical of government pleadings and lower-court decisions in a number of Charter cases addressing the right to adequate housing. The CESR noted that "provincial governments have urged upon their courts in these cases an interpretation of the Charter which would deny any protection of Covenant rights" and that the courts had "opted for an interpretation of the Charter which excludes protection of the right to an adequate standard of living and other Covenant rights."

Of particular concern to the Committee were the cases of Gosselin in Quebec, Fernandes in Manitoba, and Masse in Ontario. In all of these cases, failure to provide adequate financial assistance resulted in the violation of the right to adequate housing. In the Masse case, uncontested evidence showed that the 22 percent cut to social assistance payments in Ontario would force 67,000 single mothers and their children from their homes. Yet in all three cases, lower courts found that the Charter does not guarantee a right to adequate housing or to adequate financial assistance to cover the cost of housing.

Although claims to a level of financial assistance sufficient to provide for adequate housing have met stiff resistance from lower courts in Canada, important advances have been made in other types of equality claims. For example, before 1993, public housing tenants in three provinces were denied the protection of landlord and tenant law. A significant victory was won under section 15 of the Charter in 1993 when Irma Sparks, a black single mother living in public housing in Nova Scotia, successfully challenged this exclusion as discrimination against racialized minorities, single mothers, and people living in poverty.

A form of discrimination in housing that has been the subject of extensive litigation in Ontario and Quebec under provincial human rights legislation is landlords' use of "minimum income criteria" to disqualify low-income applicants for apartments. Many landlords disqualify applicants who would be paying more than 30 percent of income on rent, even though all social assistance recipients and most single mothers, young families, young people, and newcomers to Canada must spend much more than this on rent.

Landlords argue that such policies are a reasonable way to assess the risk of rental default, but low-income tenants have successfully challenged income requirements as discriminatory and have disproved the stereotype that low-income applicants are more likely to eventually default on rent. Tribunal and court decisions in these cases are the first in Canada and internationally to establish that discrimination in housing because of poverty constitutes discrimination on the basis of sex, race, citizenship, and other prohibited grounds.

Reviews by the CESCR

Over the last decade, housing rights advocates have made extensive use of the treaty monitoring process to create a solid jurisprudence on violations of the right to adequate housing in Canada.

In 1993, as Canada's second review under the ICESCR approached, several Canadian NGOs wrote to the CESCR asking for permission to appear before the Committee. The Committee agreed to try out a new procedure, unprecedented at the time in the UN treaty monitoring system, allowing for oral submissions on behalf of domestic NGOs at the beginning of its session. This process has greatly enhanced the Committee's credibility and influence in Canada and elsewhere.

The 1993 CESCR review noted the evidence of homelessness and inadequate living conditions in Canada, high rates of poverty among single mothers and children, and evidence of families being forced to relinquish their children to foster care because of inability to provide adequate housing or other necessities. The review also covered inadequate welfare entitlements, growing reliance on food banks, evidence of widespread discrimination in housing against families with children, and inadequate protection of security of tenure for low-income households.

Despite unprecedented media coverage and parliamentary debate of the CESCR's Concluding Observations, Canadian governments did not address any of the Committee's concerns. On the contrary, in the five-year period between Canada's second review in 1993 and its third review in 1998, retrogressive measures were taken in all of the critical areas identified by the Committee relating to the right to adequate housing.

The federal government froze its social housing budget and eliminated further funding for new social housing from 1994 on, with the exception of on-reserve Aboriginal housing. Between 1985 and 1997, provincial spending on housing was cut by more than 90 percent to about $100 million.

The year after the federal freeze on social housing, the federal government introduced a bill that represented an unprecedented attack on the right to adequate housing in Canada. Without any public consultation or warning, the federal government revoked the Canada Assistance Plan Act (CAP) as of April 1, 1996. CAP had been a central pillar of the right to an adequate standard of living, ensuring that those in need received enough financial assistance to cover the cost of necessities such as housing. The adequacy requirements under CAP were enforceable, not only by the federal government, but also by affected individuals. If rates were inconsistent with basic requirements (allowing for some provincial flexibility), the court could order that federal transfer payments be withheld until the province complied with the requirements of CAP.

Under the new block funding arrangement that replaced CAP, the requirement of an adequate level of assistance to cover the cost of housing and other necessities and the mechanism for providing legal remedies when such assistance was not provided were eliminated.

In May 1995, a delegation of Canadian NGOs appeared before the CESCR in Geneva to outline the implications of the bill to revoke CAP. The Committee responded by sending a letter to the Canadian government, reminding the government of its obligations under the ICESCR, and requesting that a report on the legislation be included in Canada's third periodic report, due later that year. The federal government proceeded to revoke CAP.

This move led to dramatic cuts in benefits by several provinces and a growing gap between the assistance available and the money needed for adequate housing. In Ontario, social assistance rates were cut by 22 percent in October 1995, forcing an estimated 120,000 households from their homes. Since that time, rents have risen and benefit levels have remained frozen. In its third periodic review of Canada, the CESCR noted, "The replacement of the Canada Assistance Plan (CAP) by the Canada Health and Social Transfer (CHST) entails a range of adverse consequences for the enjoyment of Covenant rights by disadvantaged groups in Canada."

In its recommendations, the CESCR suggested that new federal, provincial, and territorial agreements for social programs clarify the legal obligations of provincial governments. However, the Social Union Framework Agreement signed by the federal government and all provinces except Quebec three months later contained no legally enforceable rights and did not refer to governments' obligations under the ICESCR or other human rights treaties. It contained only a commitment to the "principle" of "meeting the needs of Canadians," including ensuring access "to essential social programs" and providing "appropriate assistance to those in need."

A year after CAP was revoked, the federal government implemented dramatic changes to Canada's unemployment insurance system. Since most tenant evictions for rent arrears result from unexpected job loss or reduction of income, protection from income loss is a critical component of security of tenure in Canada. The changes put in place in 1997, however, disqualified many of those who were vulnerable to homelessness, making it much more difficult for part-time workers, 80 percent of whom are women, to qualify for benefits.

In 1998, the federal and provincial governments reached an agreement on a supplementary child benefit for low-income families that, under the terms of the agreement was to be "clawed back" from social assistance recipients with children. All but three provinces decreased social assistance payments for families with children by the amount of the benefit. As a result of this "clawback" of the National Child Benefit, many of the poorest families at greatest risk of homelessness are disqualified from a benefit they desperately need to pay the rent. The CESCR recommended amending the National Child Benefit scheme to prevent provinces' deducting the benefit from social assistance, but this recommendation has not been acted upon.

In 1998, the CESCR also noted that there had been "little or no progress" in alleviating social and economic deprivation among Aboriginal people. Many Aboriginal communities lacked even safe drinking water and a quarter of dwellings were in need of major repairs and lacking basic amenities.

In summary, the CESCR found in 1998 that in virtually every respect, governments in Canada had taken unprecedented, and arguably deliberate, retrogressive measures undermining the right to adequate housing.

Reviews under the ICCPR and CEDAW

Three months after Canada's review by the CESCR and a month before Canada was scheduled for its fifth periodic review by the Human Rights Committee (HRC), Lynn Maureen Bluecloud, a homeless, pregnant Aboriginal woman, died of hypothermia within sight of the Parliament Buildings in Ottawa. Her death helped convince the HRC to put aside some of the traditional divisions between civil and political rights and social and economic rights to address the implications of Canada's failure to relieve poverty and homelessness as a potential violation of rights in the International Covenant on Civil and Political Rights (ICCPR).

The direct link between governments' failures to address homelessness and the right to life, protected in article 6 of the International Covenant on Civil and Political Rights, had become particularly stark in a country with so cold a climate. For the first time, the HRC stated in its 1999 concluding observations on Canada that "positive measures" to address homelessness are required to comply with the right to life under the ICCPR.

The HRC's concluding observations in 1999 echoed a number of the other concerns of the CESCR about the effect of social program cuts on women and the children in their care. The HRC also joined the CESCR in condemning the discriminatory clawback of the National Child Benefit from families on social assistance and calling for the implementation of the recommendations of the Royal Commission on Aboriginal Peoples.

The degree to which the reviews of Canada by the CESCR and the HRC converged on critical issues of poverty and homelessness sent a strong message to the international community that the right to adequate housing is a fundamental right that is inextricably linked to the right to dignity and security at the heart of international human rights law. Relieving affluent countries of responsibility for violations of the right to adequate housing damages the integrity and universality of the right and violates the international rule of law.

The Committee on the Elimination of All Forms of Discrimination Against Women (CEDAW) reviewed Canada in 1997. It noted that Canada's domestic policies seem to be at odds with its leadership role on women's issues internationally, so that on the one hand Canada is promoting equality for women internationally but on the other, it is pursuing economic policies that relegate increasing numbers of women to homelessness and poverty, not only in Canada, but in all countries.

A Global Pattern

Although Canada represents one of the starkest examples of unnecessary violations of the right to adequate housing in the midst of plentiful resources and a robust economy, what has occurred in Canada is part of a larger global pattern.

A confidential letter to Canada's Finance Minister, Paul Martin, from the International Monetary Fund (IMF), written in December 1994, recommended that the federal government reduce spending on social housing and social programs, restrict eligibility for unemployment insurance, limit its regulatory role over social policies, and revoke the Canada Assistance Plan in favour of a system of block funding with no built-in rights or entitlements. Nearly all the drastic measures that have led to the violation of the right to adequate housing in Canada in the last decade were encouraged and recommended by the IMF. Its list of "recommendations" was virtually identical to the CESCR's list of "concerns" – and it is obvious which document got more attention from the Finance Minister.

Responses and the Way Forward

A few days before Canada was to appear before the HRC in April 1999 in New York, the Prime Minister appointed a cabinet minister to coordinate the federal response to homelessness and formed a National Secretariat on Homelessness. The Secretariat has tended to focus on providing support services and emergency shelter. Despite this and similar initiatives by provincial and municipal governments to help homeless people survive Canada's winters, there has been no dramatic reduction in deaths on the streets.

But neither the CESCR nor the HRC recommended that Canada merely do a better job of preventing homeless people from dying. Both committees stated that effective, positive measures were needed to redress imbalances in the allocation of available resources and the devastating consequences of social program cuts, to ensure that disadvantaged households have access to adequate income and housing.

Although to date, the federal and provincial governments have acted on only a few recommendations made by the CESCR and the HRC, the reviews by the two committees have nevertheless had a significant impact. Advocates for the right to adequate housing in Canada continue to place considerable emphasis on the treaty monitoring process because we derive from it a new paradigm of human rights, one that fills out the substance of rights in domestic law and challenges structural changes that systematically violate the fundamental rights of many disadvantaged constituencies. A more global perspective has challenged the arrogant complacency of a country that prides itself on its high average standard of living, while choosing to deny increasing numbers access to the dignity and security of adequate housing.

Housing rights advocates in Canada will continue to work to strengthen international mechanisms that enforce the right to adequate housing, while pressing for more effective domestic protection of this right. These two areas of activity are interconnected – advances must be made simultaneously on both the domestic and international fronts if Canadians are to move forward in claiming and enforcing the right to adequate housing.

Bruce Porter has been promoting the right to adequate housing and other social and economic rights in Canada and internationally for 20 years. He was executive director of the Centre for Equality Rights in Accommodation (CERA) from 1987 to 2002 and has been coordinator of the Charter Committee on Poverty Issues since 1994. He lives in Muskoka, Ontario, coordinating national and international initiatives to promote social and economic rights. He is currently director of the Social Rights Advocacy Centre. Some of his writings are available at http://www.equalityrights.org/cera/index.cfm?nav=reso&sub=charter
E-mail: bporter@socialrightsadvocacy.ca

Chapter 4

A Tale of Two Canadas: Homeowners Getting Richer, Renters Getting Poorer

J. DAVID HULCHANSKI

Renters Concentrated in High-cost Metropolitan Areas

One third of all Canadian households live in the three largest metropolitan areas: Toronto, Montreal and Vancouver. Canada's renting households are even more concentrated. Just over 40 percent of all renters live in those three cities.

About 60 percent of Canada's households are homeowners; the other 40 percent rely mainly on the private rental sector. Only 5 percent of Canadian households live in non-market social housing (in contrast to much of Europe, where the average is 20 percent). The Montreal metropolitan area has the highest concentration of renters (54 percent) compared to about 45 percent in Toronto and Vancouver. (See Table 1.)

A major problem in all three metropolitan areas, and in much of urban Canada, is the inability of the private sector to provide new rental housing. Very little unsubsidized rental housing has been built since the early 1970s. In explaining the lack of rental housing starts, housing analysts usually focus on rent controls, municipal regulations, and taxes.

Few, however, have examined the ability of the potential consumer – the renter household – to pay the rents developers would require to make rental investment sufficiently profitable. In the late 1960s, when a great many rental apartments were built in urban Canada, the gap between the income of owners and renters was relatively small – about 20 percent. Today that gap has widened.

Although some people rent housing only when they are young, others will need rental housing throughout their lives. They will never be able to afford homeownership and will always depend upon the private

Table 1: Canada's Three Largest Metropolitan Areas

Number of Households by Tenure, 1999

Metropolitan Area	Owners	Renters	Total	% Renters
Toronto	940,000	780,000	1,720,000	45%
Montreal	690,000	820,000	1,510,000	54%
Vancouver	450,000	390,000	840,000	46%
3 Metro Areas Total	2,080,000	1,990,000	4,070,000	
Canada – Total	7,375,000	4,840,000	12,215,000	40%
Three Metropolitan Areas as a % of Canada	28%	41%	33%	

rental and social housing sectors. These life-time renters are at a particular disadvantage.

In 1984 and 1999 Statistics Canada carried out a detailed survey of household income and wealth, called the Survey of Financial Security. Initial results from the 1999 survey were published in March 2001 as *The Assets and Debts of Canadians* (www.statcan.ca/cgi-bin/downpub/research.cgi).

This chapter reports on a further analysis of the 1984 and the 1999 financial security data. Special tabulations were obtained from Statistics Canada with a focus on housing tenure: the income and wealth of owners compared to renters. All dollar amounts have been inflation-adjusted by Statistics Canada to 1999, allowing a comparison of the two periods (15 years apart).

A National Overview of Income and Wealth

Canada has two distinct groups of housing consumers, and the income gap between the two has been increasing by about 1 percent per year.

Between 1984 and 1999, the income and wealth of Canada's home-owners increased dramatically and that of renters decreased.

Income and wealth of homeowners up, renters down

- **Income.** Over the 15-year period, the median income of homeowners increased by $2,100 (5 percent) while the income of renters decreased by $600 (–3 percent).

Table 2: Comparison of Income and Wealth of Owner and Renter Households

Canada, Toronto, Montreal and Vancouver, 1984 and 1999
(1984 $ adjusted to 1999 $)

		Median Income		Median Net Worth	
		Owners	Renters	Owners	Renters
Canada	1984	$41,380	$21,554	$116,845	$3,985
	1999	$43,478	$20,947	$145,200	$2,060
	change	$2,098	–$607	$28,355	–$1,925
	% change	5%	–3%	24%	–48%
Toronto	1984	$48,821	$24,212	$174,254	$4,291
	1999	$53,563	$27,039	$248,400	$3,300
	change	$4,742	$2,827	$74,146	–$991
	% change	10%	12%	43%	–23%
Montreal	1984	$44,266	$23,389	$107,174	$4,291
	1999	$43,944	$19,605	$142,291	$2,112
	change	–$322	–$3,784	$35,117	–$2,179
	% change	–1%	–16%	33%	–51%
Vancouver	1984	$49,982	$24,407	$192,340	$5,574
	1999	$47,310	$21,897	$243,550	$5,000
	change	–$2,672	–$2,510	$51,210	–$574
	% change	–5%	–10%	27%	–10%

Source: Statistics Canada, Survey of Financial Security, 1984, 1999.

- **Wealth.** The median net worth of homeowners in 1999 was $145,000, an increase of $28,400 (24 percent) over 1984. For renters, the trend was the opposite: median net worth decreased by $1,900 (–48 percent), from $4,000 in 1984 to $2,100 in 1999.

The income and wealth gap is huge and growing

- **Income Gap:** The gap between the median income of homeowners and renters grew by 16 percent (from $19,800 in 1984 to $22,500 in 1999). In 1984, homeowners had almost double the income of renters (192 percent). By 1999, the gap had increased to more than double (208 percent). This represents an average growth in the income gap between owners and renters of about 1 percent a year.

- **Wealth Gap**: The gap in the median net worth of homeowners and renters increased from $112,900 in 1984 to $143,100 in 1999. Home-owners' wealth increased from being 29 times that of renters in 1984 to 70 times that of renters in 1999. Statistics Canada reports that the most important non-financial asset of Canadians, accounting for 38 percent of household wealth, is the owner-occupied house. Home-ownership is, therefore, a major (but not the only) reason for the large gap in wealth between owners and renters.

Trends in Toronto, Montreal, and Vancouver

Income: Up in Toronto, down in Montreal and Vancouver

In Toronto, the median income of homeowners and renters increased, whereas in Montreal and Vancouver it decreased. (See Table 2.)
- **Toronto.** The median income of owners and renters rose at about the same rate between 1984 and 1999: 10 percent for owners and 12 percent for renters. In 1999 the median income was $54,000 for owners and $27,000 for renters.
- **Montreal.** The median income of owners remained about the same over the 15-year period (a 1 percent decrease) while the income of renters declined sharply, by 16 percent. The median income of Mont-real homeowners in 1999 was $44,000 and that of renters was $20,000.
- **Vancouver.** The median income of owners and renters decreased between 1984 and 1999: 5 percent for owners and 10 percent for rent-ers. In 1999, the median income of owners was $47,000 and that of renters was $22,000.

Wealth: Owners up and renters down in all three cities

In Toronto and Vancouver, the average net worth of homeowners is about the same (about $250,000). This is about $100,000 higher than the average net worth of Montreal homeowners. The increase in net worth for homeowners was greatest in Toronto ($74,000), followed by Van-couver ($51,000) and Montreal ($35,000).

The net worth of renter households ranged from a high of $5,000 in Vancouver to a low of $2,200 in Montreal. Between 1984 and 1999, household net worth decreased dramatically for renters in all three met-ropolitan areas: in Montreal by 51 percent, in Toronto by 23 percent, and in Vancouver by 10 percent.

- **Toronto.** The median net worth of owners increased by 43 percent while that of renters decreased by 23 percent. The median net worth of owners was $248,000 (up $74,000) and $3,300 for renters (down by $1,000).
- **Montreal.** The median net worth of owners increased by 33 percent and that of renters decreased by 51 percent. The median net worth of owners was $142,000 (up $35,000) and $2,100 for renters (down by $2,200).
- **Vancouver.** The median net worth of owners increased by 27 percent and that of renters decreased by 10 percent. The median net worth of owners was $244,000 (up $51,000) and $5,000 (down by $600) for renters.

Discussion

What are the policy implications of these trends in household income and wealth?

Two Canadas: Owners and renters

There are two very different types of Canadian households in terms of income and wealth – and housing tenure represents the divide between the two. The gap between owners and renters, in terms of both income and wealth, has grown over the 15-year period. The quality of the housing and of the neighbourhoods they live in has also changed.

Homeowners receive a tax subsidy to assist in their accumulation of household wealth. Capital gains from the sale of a principal residence are not taxed and first-time house buyers can use their tax-sheltered registered retirement savings as a down payment. There are no housing-related tax concessions for renters.

One residential land and housing market

Although there are two Canadas in terms of income and wealth, there is only one residential land and housing market. Owners and potential owners (higher income and upwardly mobile renters) have the ability to outbid renters for residential land (that is, building sites). In order to compete with condominium developers for land, rental housing developers would have to set rents too high for most tenants. A thriving supply/demand market exists in the homeownership sector, but only demand and social need – without new supply – exists in the rental sector.

The growing gap between owners and renters

The gap between owners and renters has increased by an average of about 1 percent a year. Canada's population is, therefore, even more polarized by income and wealth than in the past. This fact has serious implications for rental housing supply. There has been virtually no unsubsidized new supply in recent years – nor will there be as long as this polarization continues. The low income and wealth levels relative to homeowners means that many tenants have a social need for adequate and affordable housing. They do not have enough money to generate effective market demand.

The "dehousing" trend: More homelessness

The gap between the incomes and wealth of owners and renters means that more and more renters are likely to have severe problems remaining housed. Canada's housing system has no mechanism to ensure that their need for adequate housing is met. Families are the fastest-growing group among the homeless, mainly because of a lack of affordable housing. This trend is likely to continue until much more housing at lower rent levels becomes available.

Fewer renters will be able to become homeowners

About 40 percent of all of Canada's renters live in the high-cost housing markets of Toronto, Montreal, and Vancouver. For homeowners, high and increasing house costs contribute to their lifelong accumulation of wealth. For renters, it is the opposite. High housing costs make it difficult, if not impossible, for them to accumulate assets (such as the amount needed for a down payment) resulting, for many, in lifelong impoverishment.

An aging stock of rental housing; the need for new units at modest rents

During the past decade, the federal government has not added to the stock of social housing units. Most provinces do not have social housing supply programs (Quebec is an exception). The private sector has not built significant numbers of new rental apartment buildings for at least two decades. Unlike the situation in the homeownership construction market (condos and suburban tract housing), investors cannot build rental housing and make money. The costs are too high, given the lower income profile of renters. Also, condos compete with high-end rental units.

Policy Implications

The household income and wealth of renters is dramatically below that of owners, and the gap is growing. Renter households may find it increasingly difficult to move into homeownership. Government policies that focus on incentives for homeownership (such as tax-exempt savings plans or the Ontario government's waiver of land transfer taxes) do not address the housing needs of the vast majority of renter households. The federal government has not provided new social housing for low- and moderate-income renters since 1993.

A comprehensive national housing policy, with complementary regional policies, must address the very low income and wealth of renters. Canada, more than most Western nations, relies on the private sector to provide housing. Renters must find adequate housing in housing markets in which prices are driven by the income and wealth levels of homeowners.

Social policies and traditional income assistance programs (social assistance, unemployment, disability pensions, and so forth) must better address the growing income inequality between owners and renters.

Federal and provincial/territorial housing policies must recognize that very few renters have incomes high enough to pay the rent levels required by unsubsidized new construction. Increased supply – the construction of new rental housing – is the only answer to low vacancy rates. Given the income and wealth profile of Canada's renters, only significant public-sector intervention will increase the supply of affordable rental housing.

In summary, there is a growing social need for affordable housing among renters. As the data from the Statistics Canada survey of financial security demonstrates, there is very limited market demand. The income and wealth levels of most renter households are much too low – and continuing to fall relative to homeowners.

This report is available online at:
www.urbancentre.utoronto.ca/pdfs/researchbulletins/02.pdf

J. David Hulchanski *is director of the Centre for Urban and Community Studies. His research and teaching focuses on housing policy, social welfare, commu-*

nity development, and human rights. In the 1980s he was a professor in the School of Community and Regional Planning at the University of British Columbia and Director of the UBC Centre for Human Settlements. He has a M.Sc. and Ph.D. in urban planning and is a member of the Canadian Institute of Planners. In 1997 he was appointed to the only endowed chair in housing studies in North America, the Dr. Chow Yei Ching Chair in Housing.

Chapter 5

Housing Affordability: A Children's Issue

MERRILL COOPER

Introduction

In recent years, children's well-being has been identified by Canadian governments as a policy and spending priority. In 1997, the federal, provincial, and territorial governments endorsed the development of a National Children's Agenda (NCA), and released framework documents for public discussion in May 1999. The NCA is described as "a comprehensive strategy to improve the health and well-being of Canada's children." The four goals of the NCA are to promote children's health, safety and security, success at learning, and social engagement and responsibility.

Despite these commitments, over the past decade, some government decisions – no doubt, unintentionally – have served to undermine, rather than further, the goals articulated in the National Children's Agenda. High on this list are decisions about the role of government in the field of public and social housing.

At present, Canada is the only industrialized country without a national housing strategy. There is now ample evidence of the centrality of housing to the achievement of positive child outcomes and to meeting the four goals of the NCA (see box on next page). If the objectives of the NCA are to be achieved, housing issues must be addressed within a larger policy framework relating to children's well-being. To date, however, housing has never been a key feature of children's policy initiatives, nor have the interests of children been well reflected in Canadian housing policy, which itself has been "disappearing."

Goals of the National Children's Agenda

As a nation, we aspire to have children who are:

1. *Healthy – Physically and Emotionally.* Children who are as physically and emotionally healthy as they can be, with strong self-esteem, life skills and enthusiasm. Children who are physically and mentally active, live healthy lifestyles, are free of preventable disease and injury, and enjoy healthy environments.

2. *Safe and Secure.* Children whose basic needs are met, including love, shelter, food, clothing, recreation and play. Children who are protected from abuse, neglect, exploitation and dangerous environments, and who are given support by caring adults.

3. *Successful at Learning.* Children who achieve physical, emotional and social development, language skills, literacy, numeracy and general knowledge to the best of their capabilities. Children who are ready for learning throughout their lives so they can gain abilities they need for present and future fulfilment.

4. *Socially Engaged and Responsible.* Children who can form stable attachments to nurturing adults when they are young and develop supportive relationships within and outside their families. Children who value Canada's cultural heritage and diversity, and who develop an understanding of the rights and responsibilities of belonging to a wider society. Children who respect themselves and others through being respected, and understand the personal and social consequences of their choices.

(Federal-Provincial-Territorial Council on Social Policy Renewal, A National Children's Agenda: Developing a Shared Vision, Ottawa: 1999)

One result is that while Canadians are well-housed in comparative international terms, there are several indicators of increasing difficulties in meeting housing needs:

- 1.7 million Canadian households are in "core housing need." That is, they fall below the standards set by Canada Mortgage and Housing Corporation (CMHC) for adequacy, suitability, and affordability. Moreover, they would have to spend more than 30 percent of their household income to pay the average rent in their local housing market to secure adequate housing.
- 1.15 million households consist of tenants who pay an average of 47 percent of their income on rent.

- Between 1991 and 1996, the number of renter households paying 50 percent or more of their income on rent rose by 43 percent to 843,000 households, of which 289,000 are families with children.
- In 1989, there were close to 10,000 social housing units developed across Canada while, in 1998, only 1,500 social housing units were completed.[1]

Such patterns are not the result of chance or even of markets. It is true that building fewer rental units (and certainly fewer low-cost rental units) as well as condominium conversions have had effects on reducing supply and raising costs. However, government policy has also affected the situation.

In Ontario, for example, the erosion of rent controls, dramatic declines in funding for social housing, and the reduction of social assistance rates have had major consequences for many families. While the average Toronto family spends 17 percent of its income on housing, there has been an increase of almost 50 percent since 1991 in the households with children that spend more than half their income on housing. The rate is now 16 percent of all families. As well, in December 1998, there were 40,500 children on waiting lists for subsidized housing, and over 1,000 children were living in hostels for the homeless.

Obviously, this is not a situation about which Canadians can be proud. Indeed, in 1998, the United Nations Committee on Economic, Social and Cultural Rights recommended that Canada's federal, provincial, and territorial governments view homelessness and the shortage of affordable housing as urgent national problems. Since then, Ottawa has announced an initiative on homelessness, which would provide support for organizations making emergency shelter available to the homeless. However, as the profile presented above indicates, homelessness is only the tip of a very large iceberg – the lack of reasonably priced housing.

This paper will document the ways in which stable, safe, and secure housing is vital to all aspects of children's health and development, based on the following premise:

> The lack of adequate and reasonably priced housing greatly reduces the chances of achieving the federal and provincial goals for all children identified in the NCA.

Achievement of each of the four NCA goals is intrinsically related to housing, and housing intersects with other factors that bear on good child outcomes. Such links have emerged in research produced from the

National Longitudinal Survey of Children and Youth (NLSCY), a joint project of Statistics Canada and Human Resources Development Canada.

Findings from the NLSCY and other research clearly demonstrate that stable, safe, and secure housing is vital to children's healthy growth and development. It is one key component of both the physical and social environments in which children live, and plays both a direct and indirect role in the achievement of desired outcomes in the areas of health, safety, education, and social engagement. The quality of the dwellings in which children reside is one factor affecting these outcomes. Other critical factors include housing costs, tenure, and stability.

Three Enabling Conditions for Child Well-being

Adequate Income: Adequate family income is needed to meet the physical needs of children for food, shelter, and clothing. Beyond these basic needs, however, adequate income is needed to promote the social development of children by including them in community life, nurturing their talents, and ensuring they can participate with their peers in healthy and stimulating activities.

Effective Parenting: Parents struggle to schedule quality time with their children, concerned that without parental nurturing, children may develop behavioural problems or fall behind in school. Many parents squeeze in more time for their children by giving up on other activities related to work, in the community, with their partners and friends, and for themselves.

Supportive Community Environments: Neighbourhood affluence, which is associated with greater neighbourhood safety, is beneficial to children. Children living in unsafe neighbourhoods are at greater risk of having low scores for both cognitive and behavioural competence. Neighbourhood safety is enhanced where communities share values and common expectations.

The neighbourhoods and communities in which children and families reside are also factors that correlate with child outcomes. Indeed, some recent studies have succeeded in isolating housing, neighbourhoods, and communities as distinct factors affecting healthy child development. However, housing, communities, and neighbourhoods cannot be considered in isolation from the other social, economic, family, and educational factors that affect children's well-being. An abundance of research demonstrates the importance of good parenting, supportive communities, and adequate income for healthy child development.

In a 1999 paper, *What Is the Best Policy Mix for Canada's Young Children?*, the Canadian Policy Research Networks (CPRN) identified adequate income, effective parenting, and supportive community environments as three enabling conditions required to ensure children's well-being and healthy development.

The NLSCY follows a large, representative sample of Canadian children from birth to 25 years of age, with a view to measuring the well-being and development of Canada's children and youth into adulthood. Data collection began in 1994 and continues at two-year intervals. Researchers have analyzed early findings to produce papers on the biological, social, and economic characteristics influencing child outcomes.

NLSCY data and research have greatly enhanced our knowledge about the conditions in which Canadian children live and the ways in which we can improve children's well-being.

Poor Housing Puts Children at Risk

Extensive research has revealed that adequate, stable housing in safe, supportive neighbourhoods and communities is correlated with positive child outcomes in the areas of health, development, and well-being. These inter-relationships are complicated and, because of the confounding effects of other factors, it can be difficult to identify causal relationships between factors. Far more research has been conducted on the relationships between the physical characteristics of housing and child health than on the connections between housing and social, economic, and cultural factors, or on how the cost, quality, and location of housing is related to child development and well-being.

As pointed out by Hwang[2] and Dunn,[3] among others, even the relationship between health and the physical characteristics of housing is confounded by other variables, such as socioeconomic status. For example, Hwang observes that individuals' health can affect the type of housing they live in, and higher-income, well-educated people may have more resources to address identified health risk factors. Moreover, Dunn notes that there has been "relatively little research that examines the intersection of socioeconomic inequalities in health and inequalities generated by the operation of social relations pertaining to housing."

Despite difficulties associated with the identification of causal relationships, recent studies provide evidence of what has long been intuitively known by experts in child health and development. Four aspects of housing – affordability, conditions, stability, and neighbourhood – are directly and indirectly related to each of the four NCA goals of health, safety, education, and social engagement. These housing components and the NCA goals both affect and are influenced by what the Canadian Policy Research Networks has identified as the three enabling conditions that lead to positive outcomes for children: adequate income, effective parenting, and supportive community environments.

Housing affordability

Lack of reasonably priced housing in and of itself poses risks to positive outcomes for children, primarily via the enabling condition of adequate income. It also has indirect relationships with the other two enabling conditions. Parents stressed by overcrowding, for example, may not parent as well as they might if conditions were more favourable. Similarly, neighbourhoods in which poor housing is the norm are also likely (but not necessarily) neighbourhoods with few services, higher than average levels of violence, and so on. It is important to examine affordability, therefore, both as a consequence of inadequate income and for its effects on the three enabling conditions of positive child outcomes.

Where housing is allocated purely on a market basis, "people with low incomes are restricted to the bottom end of the housing market. This segment of the housing market may be cheaper precisely because of its poor physical quality or because its surroundings have environmental problems detrimental to physical and mental health."[4]

Low-income families are spending more money and a greater proportion of their incomes for basic shelter needs and, therefore, less income is available for the other necessities essential to child health and development, including food. Studies in both Canada and the United States have determined that the high costs of shelter contribute to the creation of emergency food needs. For example, a survey on hunger conducted in 21 American cities found the most frequently cited causes for hunger were low-paying jobs and high housing costs.[5]

The link to effective parenting also emerges in the data. Families who are preoccupied with finding the financial resources for shelter and to meet their children's other basic needs experience acute stress and have less time to spend with their children.

In general, Canadian parents are working longer hours and reporting high levels of personal stress. A study for the Vanier Institute of the Family found that 50 percent of working mothers and 36 percent of working fathers report having difficulty managing their family time. These problems are often more prevalent among low-income parents. NLSCY data show that low-income parents are four times more likely to feel chronically stressed than parents with high incomes. Not having enough money to buy household essentials was one of the main stressors. According to the Canadian Council on Social Development, "parents experiencing chronic stress are far more likely to be distracted, hostile and abusive towards their children than are parents who feel happy and in control of their lives."[6] Chronic stress is also related to parental depression, which itself is associated with emotional and conduct disorders among children.

The third enabling condition is supportive community environments. Evidence of links between housing problems and child neglect, and between neighbourhood characteristics and rates of reported abuse and neglect, was found in a number of studies conducted the 1970s and 1980s. More recently, in 1995, Cohen-Schlanger reported a relationship between housing problems and the temporary placement of children into the care of child welfare authorities.[7]

The interrelationships of the three enabling conditions become evident when child protection is addressed. To put it starkly, lack of adequate housing results in children being in taken into care when they might otherwise have remained with their families. For example, a survey of family service workers at the Children's Aid Society of Metropolitan Toronto revealed that, while housing problems alone are not sufficient grounds to find a child in need of protection, in 18 percent of cases, the family's housing situation was one of the factors that resulted in the temporary placement of a child into government care. Of children who were apprehended, the family's housing situation was identified in a large number of cases as a factor preventing or delaying the child's return home. Cohen-Schlanger concludes that housing support may reduce the number of admissions to care, stabilize the family's living situation in ways that promote children's well-being, and reduce housing-related delays in the return of children to their parents. Also, it is possible that the number of children removed from their families could be reduced if more families had access to reasonably priced, appropriate, and adequate housing.

The most extreme consequence of shortages of reasonably priced housing is homelessness. Two of the enabling conditions of positive child outcomes are clearly missing – adequate income and supportive community environments. While homeless parents may struggle to be effective parents, they are fighting incredible odds.

In Canada, one of the most significant demographic changes among the homeless has been the rapid growth in the number of homeless women and children. In Toronto, for example, the number of families admitted to hostels increased by 76 percent between 1988 and 1996, and in 1996, over 5,000 children were homeless in that city alone.[8] The consequences of homelessness can be devastating to children's physical, intellectual, and emotional development.

Although there are few Canadian data on the health and development of homeless children, extensive American studies reveal a high incidence of asthma and other respiratory problems, trauma-related injuries such as burns, lead poisoning, chronic diarrhea, delayed immunizations, tooth decay, ear and skin infections, and conjunctivitis. In addition, the rate of developmental delay is two to three times higher among homeless children than among other poor children, and visual and neurological deficits are also more prevalent.[9]

Significant numbers of homeless children experience chronic hunger, although obesity is also common. Both under-fed and over-fed children suffer from poor nutrition and, consequently, from problems with their health, growth, and development. Compared with poor, housed children, homeless children experience more anxiety, depression, and behavioural problems, and lower educational attainment.

Insufficient housing

Insufficient housing is defined as shelter that is both crowded and in need of major repair. The physical characteristics of dwellings have been related to child outcomes in the areas of health and safety, educational attainment, and social engagement. In most instances, parental income and community characteristics play a role in these relationships, with health and safety risks being clearly specific to housing structure and living conditions. In other words, the goals of the NCA – promoting health, safety and security, success at learning, and social engagement and responsibility – are all put into question when housing is insufficient, as the next sections will document.

RISKS TO HEALTH

Connections between housing, health, and income are well established, while parents' knowledge about risks to their children is also correlated with their education. Therefore, people with low socioeconomic status are more likely than those with higher status to be exposed to housing health risks, less likely to be aware of risks posed by factors such as lead and asbestos, and less able to take steps to redress problems. In addition, poverty interacts with housing to exacerbate some negative outcomes. For example, poorer children are more likely to suffer from poor nutrition, and children with poor nutritional status absorb higher quantities of lead at every level of exposure.

But the problem is one of housing quality much more than one of knowledge, and housing quality is related to parental income. Housing occupied by low-income people "is often inadequate due to its age, chronic poor maintenance and faulty design, leading to a variety of indoor air quality hazards including mould growth or the presence of toxic substances such as lead paint or asbestos." As well, "children living in families with low incomes are more likely to live in older houses with exposure to high lead paints, damp walls and ceilings, crumbling foundations, and corroded pipes. The CMHC categorizes such houses as in need of major repair. Unsafe housing of this nature poses increased threats to healthy child development."[10]

Nowhere are threats to health and safety felt more acutely than within the Aboriginal population. Studies have demonstrated that the high rates of illness and death that occur within the Aboriginal population are integrally related to poor water and sewage systems.[11] Although these problems are not prevalent among other parts of the population, exposure to particular physical, chemical, and biological substances poses serious threats to many Canadian children. For example, NLSCY data show that only 82 percent of children aged four to 11 who lived in insufficient housing had never had asthma, compared to 88 percent of children living in adequate housing.[12] Contaminants such as mould, lead, and asbestos are found more frequently in insufficient housing, placing children at risk of acute and chronic respiratory problems. Old furnishings and carpets may contain large concentrations of lead, pesticides, and other toxic chemicals.

In some studies, household overcrowding has been associated with increases in the number of respiratory infections and reductions in air quality. Both a large family and a small living space have been independently associated with higher incidence of asthma. In Aboriginal communities in Canada, crowded housing "has been identified as a causative factor in the spread of disease which is often a cause of long-term disability."[13]

Analysis of NLSCY data reveals that only 72 percent children aged 0 to 11 years who lived in insufficient dwelling conditions (i.e., shelter that is crowded and in disrepair) had overall excellent health as compared with fully 89 percent of children who lived in adequate housing.

RISKS TO SAFETY AND SECURITY

With respect to this second goal of the NCA, "studies have demonstrated a close correlation between the number of home accidents and socioeconomic conditions such as income and class. In substandard housing, there may be an association between accidents and the greater number of hazards present. There may also be an association between accidents and a reduced understanding of hazard risks."[14]

Home injuries generally occur as the result of falls, poisonings, and burns. Young children are particularly vulnerable. Insufficient housing is often inadequately heated, and just being cold is a health risk, particularly for children. Faulty heating systems have also been associated with carbon monoxide poisoning. In addition, attempts to heat substandard dwellings with kerosene and electric heaters or wood burning stoves have been associated with burns and house fires. Other primary causes of house fires and child burn injuries are floor furnaces, unprotected radiators and pipes, smoking materials, and tapwater temperatures, which cannot always be controlled by apartment tenants. Within Aboriginal communities, a strong link has been identified between heating and electrical deficiencies, and accidents and deaths due to fire.

EDUCATION AND SOCIAL ENGAGEMENT

Achievement of the third and fourth goals of the NCA is also closely related to the quality of housing. NLSCY data demonstrate a correlation between educational attainment and housing conditions. Specifically, only 68 percent of children aged four to 11 years living in insufficient housing do well in school, as compared with three of every four children in adequate housing.

These same data reveal significant differences between well- and poorly-housed children on some measures of social engagement. Research has suggested a link between insufficient housing and the increased commission of property crimes by children living in such conditions. Likewise, there is an association between insufficient housing and aggressive behaviour. Among children in insufficient housing, 33 percent exhibited some degree of directly aggressive behaviour and 20 percent exhibited some degree of indirectly aggressive behaviour, versus 12 and 11 percent respectively of children who lived in adequate housing. While analysis of these data is limited by a small sample size and the configuration of some of the variables, the findings raise issues of concern and are incentives to undertake future studies.

In other research, the Royal Commission on Aboriginal Peoples found that Aboriginal people identified good housing as something that helps children by providing "the opportunity for children to get a good education in a stable environment, that is, not having to change schools frequently." Moreover, insufficient housing has been linked to the extremely high violence-related injury and death rates among Aboriginal people.

Housing tenure and stability

An important issue in the analysis of housing is the form of tenure. Parental income often determines if and where a family can afford to purchase a home. Homeownership is a significant means of accumulating wealth and can also affect the frequency of family moves.

HEALTH AND SAFETY

There has been little investigation of possible relationships among homeownership, housing stability, and child health and safety, although there is some evidence that the health needs of children who move frequently may go undetected by health service providers.[15]

In addition, as reported by Hwang et al., a United Kingdom study published in 1998 found that significantly higher rates of problems were recorded on a range of health-related variables for those living in rented property compared with homeowners. As well, a Swedish study found a relationship between tenure and increased mortality risk at all ages. However, it is also important to note that, in each of these studies, the association may be spurious given the relationship between housing tenure and socioeconomic status.

EDUCATION AND SOCIAL ENGAGEMENT

Analysis of data from the 1983 Ontario Child Health Study and the NLSCY revealed that levels of child problem behaviour are lower in families who own their dwellings, but the amount of homeownership in neighbourhoods is not associated with the problem behaviour. About two-thirds of the benefits associated with homeownership were accounted for by socioeconomic differences (income, education, occupation, family structure, and length of residency) between owners and renters. The author states that there may be other influencing factors not accounted for in the study, but concludes that there is still enough evidence to suggest that "home ownership may provide a means for addressing some of the adverse effects on children associated with living in socioeconomically disadvantaged neighbourhoods."[16]

There is extensive evidence supporting a connection between housing instability, poor school performance, and behavioural problems among children. An analysis of NLSCY data on 10- and 11-year-old children found that, "in general, results for total moves revealed an increased risk of problems at three or more moves, with almost no difference in risk observed between non-movers and those having moved once or twice." The authors speculate that high numbers of moves may be associated with poverty, confounding the connection between residential instability and problem behaviours. They also suggest that moving may intensify other problems in a family, or that frequent moves are a "marker" for dysfunctional families that are also characterized by child behavioural problems.[17]

Neighbourhoods and communities

Lower-income families tend to reside in less affluent neighbourhoods in which, not surprisingly, some neighbourhood characteristics place children's health and safety at risk. Perhaps more surprising is the way in which neighbourhood or community factors interact with other variables – such as effective parenting and family socioeconomic status – to influence other aspects of child development.

HEALTH AND SAFETY

Poor children often live in social and low-rent housing located in inner cities, close to major traffic arteries. In these locations, children risk higher exposure to benzene, a known carcinogen found in gasoline and automobile exhaust fumes, and are more likely to be injured in a traffic accident.

As well, many poor children also reside in neighbourhoods near industrial areas and sites previously used for waste disposal. Contaminated soil is a major source of lead poisoning. Studies have shown a correlation between the age and condition of housing in a community and the concentration of lead in the soil.

NLSCY data reveal that many children in low-income households are living in "problem neighbourhoods," which pose additional risks. The NLSCY defines problem neighbourhoods as "those where negative activities occur, such as drug use and drug dealing, excessive public drinking, burglaries, unrest due to ethnic or religious differences, where groups of young people cause trouble, and where garbage and broken glass litter the street." Also, 47 percent of children in households with incomes under $30,000 live in problem neighbourhoods; 26 percent of parents in households within this income bracket (compared with 8 percent of more affluent parents) felt it was unsafe to walk alone after dark and unsafe for children to play outside or in local parks and playgrounds during the day. The data also show that 24 percent of low-income families expressed reservations about the helpfulness and friendliness of their neighbours, compared to only about 8 percent of families with incomes of at least $50,000.[18]

EDUCATION AND SOCIAL ENGAGEMENT

It is well documented that children in low-income families who have poorly educated parents tend to have a higher prevalence of emotional problems, poor academic achievement, and behavioural problems compared to children from affluent families. These problems are sometimes associated with neighbourhood social environments, such as the presence of crime, drug dealing, gangs, prostitution, and concentrated poverty. Researchers who analyzed NLSCY data also found that conduct problems, hyperactivity, or emotional problems are more likely if children come from a neighbourhood with a high percentage of single-parent families. However, neighbourhood alone accounted for only a small part of the differences among child outcomes. Rather, the strongest predictors of problems were a one-parent family structure and family socioeconomic status.[19]

Using NLSCY data, researchers also found that school readiness was influenced by neighbourhood affluence, employment rates, and safety and cohesion, along with family characteristics including income level and parental education.[20]

The Sorry State of Children's Housing

According to CMHC, 1996 census data reveal that most of Canada's children live in shelter environments that meet or exceed adequate housing standards. However, 15 percent of households with children (516,000) live in core housing need, meaning that either: (1) the housing requires major repairs; (2) it has insufficient bedrooms; or (3) shelter costs including utilities consume more than 30 percent of before-tax household income and the household would have to spend 30 percent or more of its income to pay the average rent of alternative local markets. Eight percent of households with children live in dwellings in need of major repair.

Indeed, increases in both housing shortages and deficiencies have led to a growing number of Canadian families living in core housing need or in insufficient housing (meaning both crowded and in need of major repair). Excluding Aboriginal people living on reserves, about 1.15 million tenant households, including those without children, were in core housing need in Canada in 1996, a 33 percent increase since 1991.

Of households with children, the majority of those living in core need were renters, rather than homeowners. Among core need households, lone-parent tenant households were the largest group (39 percent), followed by two-parent tenant households (26 percent), and two-parent owner households (23 percent). From another perspective, 57 percent of lone-parent renter households with children were in core housing need. The proportion of children in two-parent families that are living in owner-occupied dwellings has remained relatively constant over the past 25 years. However, the percentage of children in lone-parent families who rent their dwellings increased from 59 percent in 1976 to 67 percent in 1996, and, in addition, fewer of these children were living in single detached units. Whether they rented or owned their homes, both lone-parent and two-parent households in core need spent about half of their income on shelter costs.

Both lone- and two-parent households with children living below the affordability threshold had about half the incomes of those living above it. Households below the affordability threshold actually spent more on shelter (29 percent more for two-parent households and 12 percent more for lone-parent households) than those above the threshold, and less on other household expenditures: 25 percent less on food, 41 percent less on transportation, 54 percent less on insurance and pensions, 47 percent less on recreation, 29 percent less on education and reading, and 58 percent less on child care.

NLSCY micro-data from 1994–95 highlight the connection between household income and the housing conditions in which children live. Children aged 4 to 11 years in two-parent, low-income families were more than twice as likely to live in substandard housing than were children in high-income families. Sixty-three percent of children living in households with an income less than $40,000 lived in substandard housing, compared to only 15 percent of children in households with an income of $80,000 or more. Substandard housing is defined as dwellings that have problems such as poor plumbing; unsafe electrical or heating systems; uneven, cracked or damp walls and ceilings; sagging floors; crumbling foundations; and broken light fixtures or windows.

The situation among Aboriginal children is particularly difficult. In 1996, 38 percent of all Aboriginal children lived in core housing need, more than double the percentage of other Canadian children. Among tenant households, this figure rose to 51 percent and to 54 percent in urban tenant households. Not only are more Aboriginal children in core housing need than other Canadian children, the conditions in which they live are vastly inferior.

Data from the CMHC and the Department of Indian Affairs and Northern Development reveal that, in 1991, more than half of all Aboriginal households lived in dwellings that were far below one or more core housing need standards. Specifically, 26 percent of dwellings were in need of major repairs, 14 percent had no indoor plumbing, and 11 percent had insufficient bedrooms to accommodate the number of occupants. Forty-nine percent of off-reserve households were below at least one housing standard and 32 percent were in core housing need. Conditions are worse on reserves where, in 1991, almost two-thirds of households were below at least one housing standard and 25 percent of all households lacked full, operational bathroom facilities. Problems related to water supplies, heating, and electricity were common. Problems are most pronounced among Inuit households residing in northern regions (i.e., in the Yukon and Northwest Territories, Labrador, and northern Quebec). In 1991, 45 percent of Inuit households were in core housing need, and 84 percent of all Inuit households had children.[21]

Between 1986 and 1991, 60 percent of the Aboriginal population in Canada changed residence at least once. Mobility rates are almost twice as high in major urban areas as they are in rural areas or on reserves and, among lone-parent families in some cities, these rates exceed 80 percent. Of all residential moves, those made to improve housing conditions accounted for 51 percent, and involuntary or forced moves (e.g., fire, eviction) accounted for 9 percent. Most of these households did not move into new housing that met accepted standards.[22]

Given these housing conditions – exacerbating the effects of poverty, low income, and perhaps racism – one is led to ask questions about the long-term effects of both inadequate housing and housing that is too expensive, diminishing the outcomes that will affect children's development now, as well as their futures into adolescence and beyond.

The Challenges

The need to explore the relationship between housing affordability and children's well-being is urgent. Economic, social, demographic, and policy shifts over the past decade have both contributed to current housing problems and complicated the possible solutions. Federal spending restrictions, including the cap on the Canada Assistance Plan (CAP) in 1991, followed by its replacement with the Canada Health and Social Transfer in 1995, drastically cut the money available to the provinces for health, education, and social welfare spending.

Such changes to government programs, along with economic restructuring and a changing labour market, contributed to a decline in real family incomes, particularly among young families with children and female lone-parent families. It is only recently that this decline has been halted, but poverty rates remain higher than they were in previous decades.

Even as the poverty rate declines slightly, the income polarization between lower- and upper-income Canadians will likely continue. At the same time, tax cuts have become a priority on many national and provincial agendas, undermining the possibility of renewed, large-scale social spending. As well, to a large extent, responsibility for the well-being of society's less fortunate is being shifted from government to the voluntary sector.

In 1993, the federal government altered its housing policy significantly. It reduced the role of the Canada Mortgage and Housing Corporation, froze expenditures for social housing at 1993 levels, and began the process of transferring responsibility for the administration of social housing to the provinces. Few provinces have chosen to fill the federal void. Most are themselves withdrawing from the provision of social and public housing by further cutting expenditures and devolving housing responsibilities to the municipalities. As a result, since 1994, federal and provincial funding for social housing has declined by $500 million.

Government withdrawal from the social housing field left a gap that has not been met by the private sector. In the 1990s, the quantity of low-cost rental housing stock steadily declined as a result of gentrification, demolition, and conversion to condominiums. Private developers assume the lead role in the construction of new housing, but they have little incentive to build affordable family homes, particularly rental accommodation or housing in rural areas. New rental construction has been targeted to upper-income households, but the assumption that these households would vacate more affordable units, thereby increasing the number of units available for lower-income families, has proven false. In times of low vacancy rates, demand for all kinds of rental units maintains higher rents, even among less desirable units. Therefore, expectations about "trickle-down" vacancies have not materialized.

These developments have not gone unnoticed by the United Nations, which has sharply criticized the Canadian government for failing to take action to address this burgeoning social problem. In 1998, the United Nations Committee on Economic, Social and Cultural Rights queried how the federal government could justify the termination of funding for new social housing units when so many households could not secure appropriate housing in the private market. The Committee also highlighted the growing crisis of homelessness and questioned the government's commitment to working to eliminate homelessness.

Canada takes great pride in its social policy. For many, then, the current situation is an embarrassment, blemishing our reputation for providing strong programs to redress social inequities. Action is required if we are to ensure that one of the most basic needs, decent shelter, is available for Canada's families and children.

Getting to a Housing Strategy that Meets the Needs of Children: The Shape of the Debate

Government inertia on housing issues and the absence of a clear national housing policy, along with specific decisions and initiatives affecting income distribution, have contributed to the housing problems currently experienced by about 15 percent of Canadian families and children. The stock of good quality, reasonably priced housing has declined and many Canadian households, particularly those with children, still do not have the earning capacity to ensure such housing.

Extensive and compelling evidence now reveals the multifaceted connection between adequate and reasonably priced housing and children's well-being. We are not the first to note it. The link between poverty and poor child outcomes in every aspect of life was highlighted at a 1998 national research conference, "Investing in Children: Ideas for Action," sponsored by Human Resources Development Canada. The conference brought together over 350 participants from different community and academic sectors "to showcase the most recent NLSCY research on Canadian children and families, and to engage researchers, practitioners, and policy-makers in discussion on the application of these findings to policy and program development."[23]

Economic security was identified as a fundamental necessity for child well-being and a crucial component of policy relating to children and youth. Housing was shown to be integrally related to adequate family income, effective parenting, and strong and supportive communities. Conference participants and presenters stressed the need to improve stable, reasonably priced housing for children and families within a larger context of social and economic justice.

If the goals of the NCA are to be achieved, then children's housing issues must be at the forefront of the implementation strategy. The problems linked to the absence of adequate and reasonably priced housing will not be completely redressed through measures aimed only at improving child care or enhancing educational opportunities. Unless direct action is taken to improve housing affordability, the situation will continue to deteriorate.

To date, the connection between housing and child outcomes has been overlooked or set aside by most governments, even as they emerge from their years of deficit cutting and restraint. A review of the literature, including provincial reports and websites, found that the Provinces of Saskatchewan and British Columbia and the City of Toronto are the only governments that explicitly identify housing as a children's issue. (Manitoba recently renamed its family services department the Department of Family Services and Housing, but its role in housing has not yet been articulated.)

Saskatchewan specifically includes its Remote Housing Projects program within its Action Plan for Children, noting that addressing housing conditions is essential to improving the quality of life for children and their families in the northern region of the province. British Columbia explicitly recognizes that housing is one of the primary factors influencing the health and well-being of families and children, and includes the numbers of households in core housing need and households on waiting lists for subsidized housing among its indicators of population outcomes for the Ministry of Children and Families. In addition, the British Columbia Ministry of Health categorizes sound housing policy as a form of health promotion. The City of Toronto observes in its Toronto Report Card on Children, 1999, that provincial policy decisions have made housing less affordable for low-income families.

There is, however, a lively debate among national organizations about how to redress the situation. They present a number of options about who is responsible for taking the lead in housing policy and about what forms it should take.

Whose responsibility is housing policy?

Some advocates focus on reinstating a pan-Canadian policy under federal leadership. Many groups, individually and collectively, have been involved in lobbying the federal government to institute a new national housing policy. The Federation of Canadian Municipalities, Canadian Centre for Policy Alternatives, Canadian Public Health Association, Canadian Housing and Renewal Association, Caledon Institute of Social Policy, Campaign 2000, and the Toronto Disaster Relief Committee are but some of the best-known groups.

In general, these groups seek the active involvement of the federal, provincial, and municipal governments, with participation from the community, not-for-profit, and corporate sectors in addressing the issue of housing affordability.

What are the available policy instruments?

There is a wide range of proposals for policy. For example, the Toronto Disaster Relief Committee (representing a broad range of social policy and housing experts, academics, community workers, and social activists both in Toronto and across the country) has called for a national housing strategy entitled the "One Percent Solution." Endorsed by over 400 organizations nationally, the One Percent Solution demands that all levels of government commit an additional 1 percent of their total annual budgets to the creation of new social housing units. At present, all levels of government combined spend about 1 percent of their budgets on housing, so the solution would be for governments to double their current expenditures.

The Caledon Institute, the Canadian Housing and Renewal Association, and the Canadian Centre for Policy Alternatives have urged the federal government to endow a non-profit foundation to provide for, in one form or another, the construction of new social housing.[24]

The Canadian Housing and Renewal Association has recently undertaken a number of initiatives to address housing need. These include:

- a consultation on housing affordability policy;
- an assessment of the effectiveness of social assistance and social housing in meeting housing need;
- a project to develop a range of new or adapted financial mechanisms or products to attract private-sector investment and participation in the development and preservation of reasonably priced housing units;
- the development of a program framework for housing affordability for Canada, which will address operating principles and the roles of all three levels of government and other organizations.

How should the particular needs of Aboriginal families and children be addressed?

Many of the policy documents written by these organizations also recognize the dire housing situation of Aboriginal peoples in Canada, and endorse the recommendations of the Royal Commission on Aboriginal Peoples. The Commission offered extensive and detailed recommendations about improving housing availability, affordability, and conditions for Aboriginal people, starting with the observation that "housing policy must begin with the determination to meet the need for a healthy and suitable environment for all families and households. The removal of acute threats to health and safety is the most urgent requirement."

What about the needs of children?

Most of these organizations also urge governments to pay heed to the critical needs of children in a national housing strategy. In its National Housing Policy Options Paper, for example, the Federation of Canadian Municipalities (FCM) notes that the responsibilities of the federal government include health, social well-being, child poverty and child development, homelessness, immigration, and international commitments – adding that each is directly related to housing. To address the needs of children, the FCM states, "federal actions must extend beyond the National Child Benefit and include housing programs."

The FCM and others call on the federal government to:

- invest capital to help create new reasonably priced housing;
- repair and preserve existing reasonably priced housing units;
- provide housing as part of multiple services for high-needs communities;
- encourage private responses through tax and other policies;
- continue to share the cost of housing subsidies.

In April 2000, the Big City Mayors' Caucus endorsed the FCM strategy. In a news release, the Caucus noted the connection between housing and other family problems: "For the Canadians living the reality behind [housing] statistics, the problem is much more than simply housing. It affects their overall well-being, health, and productivity, as families are increasingly unable to find money in their budgets for food, medical supplies, clothing, and the other necessities of life."

What is the overall approach that should be taken?

Clearly, the work undertaken and policy recommendations offered by all of these organizations and individuals focus on the plight of low-income families and children in core housing need. But is a broader approach needed? As noted by the Standing Committee on Human Resources Development and the Status of Persons with Disabilities:

> Issues that affect the lives of children are not easily compartmentalized within one government department. The lives of children are influenced by policies and programs that are cross-jurisdictional as well as cross-departmental. A successful public policy framework must recognize and respond to the life-course of children. The multidimensional nature of children's lives needs to drive this policy framework; bureaucratic exigencies can no longer take pride of place over children's needs.[25]

The National Children's Agenda provides a unique opportunity for governments to come together to develop a cross-jurisdictional, comprehensive, and long-term strategy to redress family and children's housing problems within the context of encouraging good outcomes for Canada's children. Making substantial investments in the early years of children's lives can reap enormous dividends over the longer term.

While services for children and families are a provincial responsibility, child health, poverty, homelessness, and social well-being have been singled out as national priorities. Such issues cannot be addressed unless and until children's housing needs have been met. The NCA identifies physical and emotional health, safety and security, success at learning, and social engagement and responsibility as its foremost goals for Canada's children. Yet these goals do not exist in a vacuum. Moreover, children do not live by themselves. Strategies must pay heed to the overall economic security and stability of the entire family unit. Further, it is of minimal benefit to provide community programs or enhanced educational interventions to children who are hungry and in a chronic state of dislocation or homelessness. If the NCA goals are to be achieved for all of Canada's children, parents must have the skills and strength to nurture their children and the economic means to provide them with adequate food, clothing, and shelter.

Next Steps

Clearly, there is no panacea for the multiple and interrelated issues that contribute to – and result from – housing affordability problems for families with children. Solutions must include a range of interventions from all levels of government, such as tax incentives, land use regulations, and financing initiatives to encourage private-sector investment in high-quality affordable housing. Such interventions alone will be inadequate to address the growing demand from lower-income families. Significant public investment in new social housing construction will be required if we are to arrest the housing crisis. Policy must address issues of bricks and mortar in conjunction with broader considerations about community development, amenities such as schools and transportation, and programs and supports to ensure that social housing does, in fact, reap the desired benefits for families and children. While community supports are of little value in the absence of housing, the presence of housing alone does not guarantee that all objectives will be realized.

Debates about the role of housing in social policy have traditionally focused on whether affordability problems result from a shortage of household income or a shortage of available housing. The information presented in this paper suggests that, from a children's policy perspective, solutions must reflect both issues; it would be folly to address housing supply in isolation from income problems. Further, housing policy must be integrated with other aspects of children's policy and social policies in general. As just one example, other social programs, such as the highly subsidized day care program in Quebec, could help to ease the financial strain experienced by some lower-income families, thereby reducing the income component of affordability problems.

Although these recommendations have been repeatedly voiced by housing and social policy analysts over the past decade, little progress has been made in bringing together decision-makers from the various sectors. To date, there have been few opportunities for inter-sectoral dialogue and policy development among the upper echelons of all three levels of government and community representatives. Each policy sphere has been making decisions in isolation, without leadership from any sector, such that no coherent approach has evolved.

The Social Union Framework Agreement sets the stage for the integration of the various policy spheres. It outlines three principles to govern the direction of social policy – common purpose, citizen focus, and collaboration. Within this context, arguments for including affordable housing as an NCA priority are all the more compelling. The NCA provides an opportunity for constructive dialogue on child outcomes among government, communities, and experts in both housing and children's policy. Federal, provincial, and territorial reporting requirements and, with them, indicators of success on the NCA have yet to be determined. This chapter establishes the importance of affordable housing for children's wellbeing and provides the information needed by policy makers to include housing among the indicators reflecting progress toward positive child outcomes. Let the discussion begin.

Merrill Cooper is a principal of Guyn Cooper Research Associates, a Calgary-based firm that specializes in social policy and programs research and evaluation. She is the author, with Michelle Clarke, of Homeless Youth: Falling between the Cracks: An Investigation of Youth Homelessness in Calgary, *published by the Youth Alternative Housing Committee in 2000. This article is excerpted from* Canadian Policy Research Networks Discussion Paper No. F|11, *January 2001, available on the CPRN website at www.cprn.org.*

Endnotes

1 Canadian Housing and Renewal Association, *Housing Needs Across Canada: A Snapshot* (Ottawa: CHRA, 2000).

2 Hwang, Stephen, et al., *Housing and Population Health: A Review of the Literature* (Ottawa: CMHC, 2000).

3 Dunn, James R., "Housing and Health Inequalities: Review and Prospects for Research." *Housing Studies* (2000) 15 (3).

4 Fuller-Thomson, E., J.D. Hulchanski, and S. Hwang, "The Housing/Health Relationship: What Do We Know?," *Reviews on Environmental Health* (January 2000).

5 Sandel, Megan, Joshua Sharfstein, and Randy Shaw, *There's No Place Like Home: How America's Housing Crisis Threatens Our Children* (San Francisco: Housing America, 1999).

6 Ross, David P., and Paul Roberts, *Income and Child Well-being: A New Perspective on the Policy Debate* (Ottawa: Canadian Council on Social Development, 1999).

7 Hetherington, E.M. (ed.), *Review of Child Development Research*, Volume 5 (Chicago: University of Chicago Press, 1975); and Zuravin, S.J., "Is There a Connection?," *Children Today* (1985) 14: 9–13; Cohen-Schlanger, M., "Housing as a Factor in Admissions of Children to Temporary Care," *Child Welfare* (1995) 74 (3).

8 Mayor's Action Task Force on Homelessness, Report of the Mayor's Action Task Force on Homelessness. *Taking Responsibility for Homelessness. An Action Plan for Toronto* (Toronto: 1999).

9 Canadian Public Health Association, Position Paper on Homelessness and Health (Ottawa: CPHA, 1997); Klerman, Lorraine V., *Alive and Well? A Research and Policy Review of Health Programs for Poor Young Children* (New York: National Center for Children in Poverty, Columbia University School of Public Health, 1991); and American Academy of Pediatrics, "Health Needs of Homeless Children and Families." *Pediatrics* (1996) 98(1): 351–353.

10 Chaudhuri, N., "Child Health, Poverty and the Environment: The Canadian Context." *Canadian Journal of Public Health* (1998) 89 (Supp. 1): S26–S29, p. S27.

11 Royal Commission on Aboriginal Peoples, *Report of the Royal Commission on Aboriginal Peoples*, Volume 3; and Young, T.K., et al., *The Health Effects of Housing and Community Infrastructure on Canadian Indian Reserves* (Ottawa: Department of Indian Affairs and Northern Development, 1991).

12 Canada Mortgage and Housing Corporation, *Housing Canada's Children* (Ottawa, 2000).

13 Canada Mortgage and Housing Corporation, "Housing Need Among the Inuit in Canada, 1991," *Research and Development Highlights, Socio-economic Series* 35 (Ottawa, 1997),

14 Hwang, et al., *Housing and Population Health*.

15 DeWit, David J., David R. Offord, and Kathy Braun, *The Relationship Between Geographic Relocation and Childhood Problem Behaviour*, Paper W-98-17E (Ottawa: Applied Research Branch, Strategic Policy, Human Resources Development Canada, 1998), p. 41.

16 Boyle, Michael, "Home Ownership and the Emotional and Behavioural Problems of Children and Youth," *Child Development* 73(3) , 2002, 883–892.

17 DeWit, Offord and Braun, *The Relationship Between Geographic Relocation and Childhood Problem Behaviour*.

18 Ross and Roberts, *Income and Child Well-being*.

19 Boyle, Michael H., and Ellen L. Lipman, *Do Places Matter? A Multi-variate Analysis of Geographic Variations in Child Behaviour in Canada*, Paper W-98-16E (Ottawa: Applied Research Branch, Strategic Policy, Human Resources Development Canada, 1998).

20 Kohen, Dafna E., Clyde Hertzman, and Jeanne Brooks-Gunn, "Neighbourhood Influences on Children's School Readiness," Paper W-98-15E (Ottawa: Applied Research Branch, Strategic Policy, Human Resources Development Canada, 1998)

21 Ark Research Associates, *Core Housing Need Among Off-reserve Aboriginal Lone Parents in Canada* (Ottawa: CMHC, 1997); Ark Research Associates, *The Housing Conditions of Aboriginal People in Canada, Summary Report* (Ottawa: CMHC, 1996); Canada Mortgage and Housing Corporation, "Housing Need Among the Inuit in Canada, 1991."

22 Canada Mortgage and Housing Corporation, "Migration and Mobility of Canada's Aboriginal Population." *Research and Development Highlights, Socio-economic Series, Issue 24.* Ottawa, 1996.

23 Human Resources Development Canada, *Investing in Children: Ideas for Action, Report from the National Research Conference*, October 27–29, 1998 (Ottawa, 1998).

24 Battle, Ken, Sherri Torjman, and Michael Mendelson, *The Payback Budget of 2000* (Ottawa: Caledon Institute of Social Policy, 2000); Canadian Housing and Renewal Association, *Housing Works! A Proposal to Establish a National Housing Foundation* (Ottawa: CHRA, 1999); Canadian Centre for Policy Alternatives and CHOICES: A Coalition for Social Justice, *Healthy Families: First Things First*, Alternative Federal Budget 2000 (Ottawa, 2000).

25 Standing Committee on Human Resources Development and the Status of Persons with Disabilities, *Interim Report* (Ottawa: Government of Canada, 1999).

Chapter 6

Like Falling Off a Cliff:
The Incomes of Low-Wage and Social
Assistance Recipients in the 1990s

JOHN STAPLETON

In a wonderful comedy routine from years gone by, an interviewer talks to the manager of a plant where workers hand-fold paper clips. The manager explains that a good man can hand fold 100 paper clips a day for which he receives three cents per clip. The interviewer notes that in a week that this proverbial good man would make only $15.00 and asks how a man could live on this much money. The reply was: "We don't pry into the personal lives of our employees."[1]

Who are the Working and Welfare Poor Adults?

In round numbers, the number of Ontarians (without disabilities) between 18 and 65 now receiving income security through social assistance (Ontario Works) in 2003 is roughly 225,000. When their dependants are counted in, the number of people we are talking about doubles to approximately 400,000.[2] Again, in round numbers, the cost of benefits is a little over $2 billion when municipal costs are taken into account. Ontario's share of this cost puts Ontario Works at between 2 percent and 3 percent of Ontario's budgeted expenditures for 2003–04.[3]

Minimum-wage employees in Ontario also number about 225,000: most are adults. At least 100,000 minimum-wage workers depend on minimum wages as the main source of their family income (that is, they are not part-time workers or summer students).[4]

This group of 325,000 adults in Ontario who either receive social assistance or who work for minimum wages for their family income are the subject of this paper. They make up approximately 5 percent of

Ontario's working age population.[5] If judged by income security measures, we treat their parents (poor Old Age pensioners) and their children reasonably well, just not them.

In the early 1990s, Ontario went through a recession that resulted in a restructuring of the labour market and economy from its industrial base to an information age economy. In some quarters, the subsequent recovery from recession was termed the "jobless recovery."[6]

During the transition, middle-class people started to increase their hours of work and along with that extra work, they started to feel that they no longer had the ability or capacity to meet their life commitments to family and friends. They also weathered massive cutbacks in programs for themselves and the less well-off in return for a promise of an improved economy and a better life.

Low-wage workers and people who from time to time have received social assistance have not been part of the mainstream of the information age economy. Their hours of work have tended to decrease. Their Internet use is below the average.

Somewhere around the middle of 1993, for reasons that we do not really understand, we started to dislike the 5 percent of working-age people in Ontario who are social assistance recipients and low-wage workers.

It may seem odd to lump social assistance recipients with minimum- and low-wage workers. After all, social assistance recipients are a lot less popular than people who work. If we look at the political rhetoric alone, one would think that there is a chasm between those who work and those who do not.

Yet when we look at the programs and social policies that relate to both working and welfare poor adults in Canada, there is an equally odd similarity – the programs and social policy that affect both groups have eroded to an unprecedented extent over the last ten years.[7]

When I talk about the ways we "dislike" low-income, working age adults, I am not talking about the feelings we have for them, the stories we tell about them, or the names we call them. I am talking about the way we treat them in social policy.

Some may feel more respect for the working poor than for people receiving welfare. But the fact is, the social policies we have created over the past ten years have punished them as if we disliked them equally. In any case, almost no non-disabled adults remain on welfare throughout their working years. The line between the working poor and welfare poor is fluid, as poor adults of working age move back and forth across it.

So if we have to look at them as a group, we can ask ourselves why we have treated them as we have over the past ten years.

What is the Evidence that We Dislike Them?

Let's start with social assistance recipients. Between 1967 and 1993, social assistance benefit levels rose 563 percent in 23 increases, more than enough to keep pace with inflation.[8] Since 1993, these benefits have dropped more than 35 percent through a combination of more than 14 percent in inflation and the 21.6 percent reductions of 1995. The longest period since 1967 that Ontario went without a social assistance rate increase (until 1993) was three years. It has now been more than 10 years since the last increase.

Many of us dislike social assistance rate increases, which are implemented largely to help make ends meet, because they do not support work effort. Yet if we look at some of the measures that have been put into place in Ontario to support work effort among social assistance recipients, we note that:
- the so-called "earnback" provision that allows recipients to earn back the difference between the social assistance rates in 1993 and 1995 has not increased in the eight years since it was created, not even with inflation;[9]
- the Employment Start-up benefit that was raised in 1993 to a flat amount of $253 remains at $253;[10]
- the earnings exemptions that allow a person on social assistance to work and retain a portion of his or her assistance now have time limits that reduce their value with the amount of time worked.[11]

So it is not just social assistance rates that have been reduced and that continue to erode with inflation. Work incentives have also eroded. This seem strange to those of us who believe in the importance of getting people back to work. To understand this trend, we have to look at the policies that affect low-wage working people outside the labour force.

But first, let's consider those who work at low wages outside the social assistance system entirely. Since 1995, when minimum wages were last increased, they have lost almost $1.60 an hour in real terms.[12] Minimum wages have gone through a long slow decline over the years since the late 1960s, but a precipitous decline over the past decade.

Employment Insurance has seen a long slow erosion since the 1970s – but nothing like the decline in eligibility for marginal employees over the last decade. Benefits have gone down in real terms and coverage has decreased drastically. At the same time, the federal EI Account began to run a significant surplus.[13]

Because we know that the line between welfare and working poverty is fluid, we should also look at how trends have affected people trying to move from welfare to work. In Ontario, full-time minimum wages were higher in 1977 than social assistance for a family of four, but by 1993, minimum wages were higher than social assistance only for single persons. This relationship has not changed significantly in the last decade.[14]

In the meantime (between 1993 and 2003), almost everyone else in Canada has done fairly well. We have enjoyed growth over the last ten years. Our exports are strong. We have stayed in the UN's top ten countries to live in (despite recent setbacks). We have eliminated ongoing deficits, paid off some of the debt, introduced a raft of provincial and federal tax cuts, and watched real incomes rise and unemployment go down.

But it's one thing to say that it has not been a bad decade in terms of the overall economy, and another to state that everyone is doing well. It is important to consider the income security of other groups in Ontario and Canada.

How Are Other Groups Faring?

Let's start with seniors' incomes. Canada's seniors have enjoyed unprecedented growth in their incomes and net wealth over this same time period. We have almost eradicated poverty for seniors in Canada through the Old Age Security (OAS) system and the Ontario supplement under the Guaranteed Annual Income System (GIS) for the Aged.[15] During the decade in question, OAS/GIS increased 40 times in consecutive quarterly increases. Canada Pension Plan (CPP) benefits increased 10 times in ten yearly increases. Both plans have kept pace with inflation.

Children too have benefited enormously in benefit increases over the ten-year period from 1993 to 2003. Through the introduction of the National Child Benefit initiative in 1998, they have enjoyed a series of extraordinary increases in this benefit (higher than inflation) along with the indexation of rates first announced in 2000.[16]

People with disabilities have fared less well than children or seniors, but they have still done better than those without disabilities. In Ontario, there was no cut to the Ontario Disability Support Program, although it has eroded with inflation. CPP for persons with disabilities has kept up to date with inflation, and a variety of other programs have been put in place to assist persons with disabilities in the last ten years. Although considered insufficient by many of those who advocate for persons with disabilities, people with disabilities who are poor have done better than those who are working age and who do not have disabilities.

One can conclude, therefore, that the erosion in benefits and social policy for low-income, working-age Ontarians is real. This one group (both working and on welfare), more than any other group, has fallen behind.

Is it Just an Ontario Problem?

Ontarians interested in social policy issues may believe that penalizing the welfare and low-income working poor is an Ontario phenomenon. They would be wrong. The National Council of Welfare[17] has provided ample evidence that welfare incomes have gone down almost across the country. Indeed, British Columbia has gone even further. It has not only eliminated earnings exemptions in their entirety for social assistance recipients, B.C. has become the first province in Canada to introduce lifetime time limits on the receipt of social assistance.[18]

The Caledon Institute has noted minimum wage erosion throughout the country.[19] And Employment Insurance, of course, is a national program. Its failure to cover job loss in low-wage sectors of the economy is a cross-Canada phenomenon.

Is the Public Unaware of the Plight of Poor Working-age Canadians?

Low-income working age Canadians seem to have fallen into disfavour. But before reaching the conclusion that this situation reflects societal attitudes, we need to know about public awareness of the problem.

We seem to hear more about child poverty than adult poverty. Anti-poverty activists have had some success in obtaining air time, especially in Ontario, for campaigns such as "Pay the Rent and Feed the Kids"[20] and "Ontario Needs a Raise."[21] It is no secret that there hasn't been either a welfare rate increase or a minimum wage increase in several years. On the other hand, there is hardly a groundswell of support for those who suffer as a result.

Economists and statisticians (Judith Maxwell, Rene Morissette, Jane Jenson, Don Drummond), activists (such as Laurel Rothman of Campaign 2000 and Sue Cox of the Daily Bread Food Bank), and authors

(Michelle Landsberg) have added their voices to a emergent and influential movement to seek new solutions for low-income working-age Canadians and Ontarians.[22] We can therefore conclude that there is public awareness at least to some degree, of this dilemma.

So why the erosion? Why the new asymmetry? Why the lack of societal recognition that one group has seriously lagged? Where else can we look for answers?

Tracing the Sources of Public Attitudes

One of the images that persist is that of the welfare Cadillac, symbolizing the idea that some people who don't work seem to be doing better than the rest of us. The image reflects a public view that is ever suspicious of fraud and of those whom the public believes disdain work.

Yet there is good reason to believe that the public believes that a lot of the problems related to the looseness of the welfare system have been resolved. In the United States, polling results reveal that people would be willing to take savings realized from cuts in the welfare system and reinvest them in helping recipients back into the mainstream of community life.

In addition, minimum-wage workers are generally employed in poorly paid, difficult jobs. The public as a whole respects that fact and usually extols the working lifestyle. Therefore, we cannot look to dislike of their lifestyle to support the lack of program currency and social policy for working-age Canadians.

Perhaps there is a "success ethic" in Canada that causes us to dislike low-income adults. There is no doubt that Canadians believe in and value success in employment. Remaining in minimum-wage or low-wage jobs for a lifetime, or moving on and off welfare may run counter to a Canadian "success ethic." We may believe that with a little more effort, most people can move beyond low-wage jobs. They may believe that other values such as staying in school or hard work ought to result in getting out of a low-wage bind or the need for government assistance.

To the extent that we believe collectively in success, we also believe that poverty reduction is an individual duty. We will look at this belief more closely later in this paper.

Our attitudes may also relate to the "racialization" of poverty. In all discussions of poverty in Canada, especially urban poverty, the issues of race and ethnicity have always been important. The difficulties associated with resettlement and obtaining credentials for foreign-trained professionals, and the Catch-22 of Canadian work experience (you have to get it in order to get work, but you can't get work if you don't have it) are well covered in the media, particularly with the current shortage of health workers.

Poverty is higher among certain racial and ethnic communities. In order to confirm racial discrimination as one of the roots of our dislike for working-age poor adults, we would have to look back to 1993, the start of the period when social policy and programs began to abandon the working-age poor.

What we find is that as part of the NDP Expenditure Control Program, the government brought in new cuts in social assistance that reduced the social assistance payments of sponsored immigrants $100 a month if they lived outside the homes of their sponsors. Sponsored immigrants living in the homes of their sponsors received no shelter allowance.

These changes were implemented to recognize the resources sponsors agreed to provide to immigrants who have turned to social assistance for help. Accordingly, there has never been any intent to discriminate against any group.

The point is that social assistance reductions have affected all communities. These reductions were carried through into 1995 and were added to the 21.6 percent welfare reductions of 1995. They continue to this day.

There is also no doubt that immigrant and racial communities were especially hard hit by changes to EI and minimum-wage policies and that public attitudes towards working-age adults have overtones of racial discrimination.

A large part of the story of immigration and resettlement in the public mind is about overcoming adversity to make the most of opportunity. In many ways, it's what immigrants are supposed to do, not only in the minds of the public, but in the minds of immigrants themselves.

However, it is too easy and too convenient to look to racial or immigrant barriers as an overarching explanation of the our dislike for working-age poor adults. It is certainly part of the policy mix, and an important one, but we must look elsewhere for major reasons for the decade-long malaise.

Some Thoughts on Why We Dislike the Working-age Poor and a Few Possible Solutions

I will provide five possible explanations for our attitudes towards the working-age poor and suggest some measures that concerned Canadians could take to help working-age, low-income Canadians enjoy better levels of income security.

The new importance of work

More and more, our society values paid work outside the home as the answer to poverty. The public believes that social policy change is not required for anyone who is capable of working.

Getting a job and working one's way up towards the top is in some ways a Canadian dream. Many if not most Canadians believe that individual effort, good work habits, and a variety of work-related virtues that translate into work readiness are not society's responsibility.

We no longer think of people requiring benefits because they have remained outside the labour force to conduct other socially useful tasks such as raising children.[23] If one wants to pursue other goals such as raising a family, then one ought to get help through work, not through public assistance programs. If the job doesn't provide the benefit, many people believe, then maybe the family ought to be postponed.

In other words, paid work has become the arbiter of important life decisions. Balancing work and life means to the majority of us that work comes first. We have little sympathy for those who let their lives get in the way of paid work.

Yet good benefits usually come to those who have good jobs. Accordingly, income-security programs administered by governments need to help people balance life and work. Those of us with good jobs tend to think that we did things "on our own" or without help from others, when in fact we had invaluable supports during our upbringing. We often have workplace benefits that we take for granted. But these benefits (such as one year's paid leave for the birth of a child) are not available to everyone, and definitely not to low-income people.

Perhaps if such workplace benefits were offered to low-wage employees, we would be more accepting than we would otherwise be when these programs are offered as income-security programs.

Coffee shops, Business Depot, and work symbolism

As a society we have become aware of a number of striking differences between the work life of the middle class and those working in low wage jobs. For example,
- Hours of work are increasing among higher-wage employees; and falling among those less well paid. This is a fairly new phenomenon.

- Unemployment is rare for anyone with a Grade 12 education who is able-bodied and who does not have any obvious personal deficits such as an addiction.
- Technology is improving the tools available to work off site.
- Many professionals have begun to build up large vacation banks of time that they will never take for these purposes.

But for all of these symbols of a new workplace that is alien to the experience of low-paid worker in service, manufacturing, or hospitality industries, the presence of two urban phenomena may be the most estranging of all: the proliferation of trendy coffee shops and the ubiquity of business stores catering to every aspect of office business technology. Starbucks has replaced the coffee shop of old just as the Business Depot has, in some respects, replaced the corner store.

The new-style coffee shop has a highly mobile get-it-and-go clientele. For example, the newest of the Starbucks experiences boasts a "no-sitting-pour-it-yourself" venue along with experiments in wireless remote.

Meanwhile, to some extent the city corner store has been replaced by business emporia that cater to students, small office owners, and corporate customers while offering the ideal place to hang out to see the latest in office gadgetry. Places like the Business Depot cater to middle-income Canadians who use the Internet and wish to use all forms of business wares to enhance their environments. These are not stores for the working or welfare poor.

Yet in meeting the needs of middle-class working Canadians, these places tend to displace and marginalize the low-end working worlds of low-income workers who cannot afford lattes and laser printers. In this way, the image of the low-income working Canadian is getting more blurred than ever, making it tougher than ever to define them in the imagination of the middle-class public.

With the disappearance of the local hangout, the diner, and the sixties-style coffee shop from the downtown area, middle-income and low-income people no longer encounter each other on common ground. White-collar workers bound for work never cross the path of the low-income, hard-working stiff coming off a tough night shift. He has disappeared from view.

The advent of good luck culture

We should not be surprised by our view of poverty that translates it into a matter of individual failure to succeed. However, many of us also see poverty in terms of "a string of bad luck."

One of the most significant changes in our society over the last 30 years is the growth of legalized gambling. Therefore it is not surprising that people would start to see the element of luck being more woven into the fabric or our views of success and failure. The idea is, of course, that a run of bad luck may be followed by unexplainable good fortune – being in the right place at the right time – maybe winning a few bucks and putting it to good use.

Social policy based on supporting good luck or alleviating bad luck is impossible. The very fact that poverty is seen by some of us as a matter of chance generally means that social policy solutions are held in less regard.

The secular evangelism of overcoming adversity

Overcoming long odds and impossible conditions has long been a staple of our entertainment fare, but all in all, seems to be more pervasive in the new millennium. However good this may be for individual morale, it begins to form part of our collective apology for programs that unnecessarily create adversities to be overcome.

Consider the following examples of adversity culture: severe income and asset tests placed on social assistance recipients, the lack of tax-advantaged savings vehicles for the poor, perverse financial disincentives, absent benefit programs in low-wage work, and high recovery rates on benefits – all represent "adversities" in our social programs. But we tend to view the onerous elements of programs as ennobling aspects of adversity to be overcome rather than simply bad program design. We accept these features as problematic, but secretly, many of us believe that they build character in those who face them.

We start to say things such as "These people need to make the leap," or "It's about time these people started to become self-sufficient." Interestingly, middle-class people never seem to have to make these leaps themselves and they certainly do not become entirely self-sufficient. To paraphrase Ambrose Bierce, these tonics are "admirably suited to the needs of my neighbour."

For every story about how someone rose to success after starting out with three cents in his or her pocket, no education, and a family to feed, there are a hundred stories about those who did not. We implement social policy and programs for the majority, not for the odd success story that didn't need either the policy or the programs to begin with.

The solution here is simple. Bad design is bad design. Designs created to fit with the needs of mythology are still bad designs. Adversity is not ennobling in a social policy context. When we create adversity for adversity's sake, the result is inefficient programs as well as unnecessary social and economic costs.

Time jealousy

Just prior to Canada Day, the *Toronto Star* profiled a quintessentially Ontario family with two children and both parents working. Like many Canadians, the adult family members worried about taxes and education and quality of life.

However, as increased work hours have encroached on family life, middle-income Canadians have begun to worry about their ability to meet commitments to stay in touch with family and friends, and enjoy other aspects of social life.

This is not a new story. It is heard all over Canada among educated workers who are finding a 24/7 work world difficult to navigate. We have no standards from the past to tell us how to make the crucial decisions that will balance our work and family life.

Of course, advertisers have long known about this issue and push an assortment of gadgets to help us meet our commitments. Perhaps the most successful have been cell phone advertisers. "Mommy's having a meeting!" squeaks a gleeful child at the beach showing Mommy meeting her commitments to both job and family, work and recreation, children and boss, through the magic of the cell phone.

Like it or not, our imagery of the poor, which used to be about people who we thought did not have choices, has now become the negative image of people who have "time on their hands," people who can meet their commitments because they do not have a job, or working poor people with few hours of work. These are people who can stay home with their kids and have a limited set of responsibilities.

The lack of ability to meet commitments, more than anything else, has encroached on the sense of empathy that the general public once had for the poor.

Yet the reality is different. A life lived on minimum wage means constantly doing without, constantly failing to meet commitments, filled with endless hours juggling and rejuggling finances and sorting out minor economic crises that middle-income people would solve with a cheque and some minor belt-tightening.

Let's look at what the groundbreaking *Transitions* report said in 1988 about the lives of the poor:

Compared with higher-income groups, low-income Canadians

- Experience a greater prevalence of health problems and are ill more often. Poor families require more hospital care, mainly because of their relatively higher-than-average length of stay in hospital.
- Are more than twice as likely to suffer mental disorders.
- Have fewer years of life that are disability free.
- Are less happy. The tendency to report "happiness" decreases with decreasing socio-economic status. Poor people also perceive their health being worse than that of people with higher income and higher education.
- Die younger. Men can expect to live 6.3 fewer years and women 2.8 fewer years. To a much greater extent than higher-income persons, they die from accidents, poisonings, violence, and respiratory and digestive disorders, some of which are preventable.[24]

Advocates and the media unwittingly feed the opposite image by talking about "Welfare recipients" or the "working poor" as if they were inert beings who defined their daily existence in terms of their immediate source of income, leading a sceptical public to view them as poor problem solvers with time on their hands.

By default, these are folks who don't *want* to get out of their economic circumstances. The fact that their lifestyle is one that they perceive as often failing to meet their commitments to economic self-sufficiency and failing to provide properly for dependants is not a story that middle-income people often hear.

The Failure of Traditional Advocacy in Addressing Adult Poverty

Advocates may be impeding progress in improving the lot of low-income adults by continuing to embrace old ideas of adequacy tied to increased welfare. They confuse the public by being critical of welfare while calling for large increases. In addition, advocates are often silent about the crucial role of work, as they do not wish to be seen as supporting schemes that require work as a precondition of improved income-security measures. Their support for higher welfare may have inadvertently inhibited progress towards improvements for all low-income adults.

The cyclical story of the working and welfare poor

Working poor people cycle on and off welfare. Welfare recipients cycle into and out of work. Each time they go to welfare or fear going to welfare, the normal economic build-up of assets and income taken for granted by so many Canadian families is interrupted.

Middle-income Canadians often think of *themselves* as the working poor, over-taxed or otherwise "hard done by." But their lives, for the most part, continue to improve throughout their adult years. They pay off mortgages and gradually build up wealth.

This is not the case for the working and welfare poor. Everything – from rules governing assets while on welfare to the lack of savings plans that provide tax benefits for the poor – tends to conspire against poor people trying to break out of poverty.

But just as it is hard to get working poor people to describe themselves as such, it is equally hard to get welfare recipients to see themselves as exactly that. They break the mould by constantly claiming to be examples of their vocation, but currently not participating. They are mothers' friends, volunteers, students, and caregivers, never welfare recipients.

What this means is that welfare recipients and working poor tend to be exactly like "us" – people who do not feel they have the time or resources to meet their commitments, people who want to do better, overcome adversity, and make it.

The story of many of the poor as moving constantly from welfare to work and back again is not the story that advocates are telling. The story that is circulating is a story of idleness and time available to do the things that middle-income people see as an impossible dream. All of this conspires to make us unsympathetic to the plight of people who are not like the rest of us. When we ourselves had more time, we wanted to help; now we do not.

The answer is to get the real story out; to focus on the daily struggles poor people make to move away from welfare, not the story of how they don't have enough welfare money. Advocates need to tell about the impediments to work, the impediments to meeting commitments, and the impediments to overcoming adversity.

The importance of the costs of living and working

The public at large has not seriously come to grips with the seeming contradiction posed by enduring welfare caseloads and "Help Wanted" signs in store windows that go unanswered. Advocates have not helped make the connection for the public that the two phenomena are related. More importantly, they have not shown the public that high welfare costs and labour shortages cost the public money and lower the quality of our infrastructure. Each of these deficits adds costs and reduces the quality of our economy and society as a whole.

Although there is much talk about the cost of living in Canadian society, there is little available analysis of the costs of living and working.[25] But work costs are growing, especially in urban environments. The cost of housing, taxes, transportation, prepared meals, work clothing, personal workstations at home, and a variety of mobile devices to stay in touch are all part of the cost of working. So too are child care, drug costs, dental care, and personal grooming.

Most of these items are sunk costs rather than variable costs that fluctuate according to income. However, to the extent that they do vary, the poor pay more and get less advantage from paying these costs.

For example, higher-paid staff will have better pensions, more opportunity to save, medical coverage of various sorts, and other subsidies; the better the job, the more the assistance is the norm.

However, if it is true that the poor pay a greater percentage of the cost of working, it becomes clearer why they cannot afford to take certain jobs. Negative incentives (the difference between wages and welfare) have grown over the years, but the costs to take a job have grown too.

Public discussion on the cost of living is common, but one seldom hears about the parallel cost of working. If the cost of living is the only part of the equation that ordinary Canadians ever see, then they will continue to wonder why the low-end jobs are not taken by the very recipients of social assistance that they think should take them.

Minimum wages multiplied by the average hours of a minimum-wage job totals just over $900 a month. The costs of living and working in Toronto costs more than that. A $520 welfare check just to live may be more economically viable than trying to live *and* work in Toronto.

And for those who think that there is a need to lower welfare rates still further, this type of change would not make it one bit more plausible to take minimum-wage work in downtown Toronto.

The real answers are to make work pay and to provide income supplements to persons in the low-end labour market. Raising welfare rates to levels that approximate adequacy is a notion popular only with advocates. As far as the public is concerned, that message falls on deaf ears, as work must be part of the equation.

Telling the story better – "It's about ends, not means"

Advocates who have the right ideas about reform spend a lot of time talking to other advocates and insufficient time talking to the public that may be interested in the issues that they champion.

Often, advocates have called for increased social assistance or increased EI payments with improved coverage. However, a public that is increasingly concerned with outcomes or ends as opposed to the means of providing the outcome, often finds it difficult to understand why more social assistance, better EI, or improved minimum wages are required in the first instance. Advocates need to show that the purpose of providing better benefits, once an anti-poverty objective, is now urgently required to preserve any possibility that an employable person will be in a position to take a job in the first place.

Simply put, it costs money to get a job and retain a job. Job searches cost money. Work expenses cost money. Advocates need to begin the job of public education to illustrate that the current erosion of benefits and social policy for working-age Canadians is more than another opportunity for low-income people to overcome adversity.

Advocates need to show that there is a point of no return from adversity, when wages become so low and costs so high that the life to which we are sending social assistance recipients is economically impossible.

Conclusion: Fix the Programs, Not the People

Transitions, the Report of the Social Assistance Review Committee in 1988, returned over and again to the need to assist the welfare and working poor by increasing equality of opportunity and improving and assisting self-reliance. Much time was given in *Transitions* to debunking false distinctions in the public mind between the welfare and working poor (often the same people at different times), false stereotypes of who receives social assistance, and the incorrect notion that people on welfare do not want to work.

However, the goal of changing public attitudes in *Transitions* centred on providing information to the public to resolve contradictions in the public mind respecting who receives assistance and why.[26] The goal is now different. It now centres on the new themes of convincing the public that working-age, low-income Canadians:

- are charged with overcoming much more adversity than the public at large and much more adversity than is reasonable;
- do not have "time on their hands";
- have more difficulty meeting commitments than average Canadians;
- cannot depend on good fortune to help them through;
- need programs and social policy improvements like other members of society.

While historians will doubtless debate the reasons for emerging asymmetry in income security and social policies for working-age, low-income Canadians, one point is clear: welfare and minimum-wage solutions no longer work.

In 2003, Ontario faced an election that could have been an acid test for the poor in Ontario. However, all three political parties have invested very little political capital in income security, while some like the NDP have highlighted the minimum wage as a major issue. But small increases and vague bromides appear to be the order of the day while more and more Ontarians are finding it increasingly difficult to make the leap from welfare to work in a reasonably promising economy.

It is now time to take these voices and the voices of others, and create a new and convergent process to provide the framework for public education and program reform.

Welfare deconstruction is a new approach to income security reform that attempts to break down inoperative distinctions between the working poor and welfare poor.[27] They are often one and the same people, spending most of their lives without EI or welfare while spending brief spells on these programs that are designed to help but which often hinder the return to self-sufficiency.

The Ontarian and Canadian public is right to react in a lukewarm way to increases to programs that have not been increased in years. The solutions lie elsewhere, in programs that support work as opposed to non-work, and that provide incentives to work, rather than guaranteeing long periods of intractable poverty. Anti-poverty activists and advocates have for the most part come to the collective conclusion that welfare and traditional EI solutions are as unattainable as they are unsustainable.

So what are the solutions? In design terms, the break-up of welfare into its component parts and the extension of a limited number of crucial benefits to the working poor is a key element of the framework. EI reform to assist people in the last-hired, first-fired and part-time, low-wage economy is the other. However, the detailed design is the objective of the approach, not its beginning.

The process must begin with the education of the critical and yet-to-be-convinced public. They have spoken at least twice with their support of welfare cuts and mandatory workfare in Ontario in 1995 and British Columbia in 2001. But they did not necessarily call for the relentless erosion of the three pillars of income security for the working-age poor. Some themes that may capture public interest and create opportunities for debate are as follows:

- Both left and right agree that the vulnerable poor ought to be in (or be provided the opportunity to be in) the paid labour force.
- The cost of living and working especially in larger Ontario cities is unsustainable on either welfare or a minimum wage income or the combination of the two. Without EI, want ads will remain in windows and welfare caseloads will remain static.
- People are starting to notice the asymmetry in income security. The forty consecutive increases in old age security in the face of a 35-percent erosion in welfare are clearly visible over a ten-year period.
- Debate is beginning to move away from anti-poverty issues to issues related to helping people sustain a working lifestyle.
- The importance of meeting commitments in work and family life is becoming more and more a standard theme among middle-income working Ontario and Canadian families. Welfare imagery in contrast, fosters images of persons who don't work who have easily met commitments to life in the home. These unrealistic images need to be challenged.

Finally, Canadians need to understand that programs that create disincentives to working, asset development, and self-sufficiency create problems for society as a whole. Higher taxes, poor health, and job and skill shortages cost money and squander resources. This can be the second-hand smoke of the move to provide income security in new and innovative ways.

This is the first time in Canada's and especially Ontario's income security history that we have experienced such long-term and relentless erosion of the three pillars of financial well-being for low-income, working-age adults. There is no time like the present to begin to restore it in new ways that will stop us from penalizing low-income people and help us meet the income security and social policy goals of all Canadians.

John Stapleton worked for the Ontario Government in the Ministry of Community and Social Services for 28 years in the areas of social assistance policy and operations. During his career, he was the senior policy advisor to the Social Assistance Review Committee and the Minister's Advisory Group on New Legislation in the 1980s and 1990s. His more recent government work concerned the implementation of the National Child Benefit. After leaving government in late 2002, John has been Community Undertaking Social Policy Fellow at St Christopher House in Toronto in association with Massey College at the University of Toronto. He now freelances as a social policy consultant with governments while continuing to work with such diverse interests as St. Christopher House, the

Caledon Institute of Social Policy, and the Soldiers' Aid Commission of Ontario. John maintains an active interest in the history of social assistance in Ontario. He lives in Toronto.

Endnotes

1 Bob Elliott and Ray Goulding, *Hand Folded Paper Clips*, performed on the Tonight Show hosted by Johnny Carson in the 1970s.
2 Ontario Ministry of Community, Family and Children's Services, Social Assistance Statistics, April–June 2003.
3 The Hon. Janet Ecker, Ontario Budget 2003.
4 See Ken Battle, *Minimum Wages in Canada: A Statistical Portrait with Policy Implications*, www.caledoninst.org/Abstracts/MinWage.htm.
5 Treasury and Economics Ontario, Ontario Statistics.
6 Bruce Little, *Globe and Mail*, July 21, 2003.
7 www.caledoninst.org/pov97b.htm.
8 Andy Mitchell, unpublished manuscript on Ontario social assistance and inflation rates.
9 Ontario Works Regulation, www.e-laws.gov.on.ca/DBLaws/Regs/English/980134_e.htm#P1043_90300.
10 Ontario Works Regulation, www.e-laws.gov.on.ca/DBLaws/Regs/English/980134_e.htm#55.(1).
11 Ontario Works Regulation, www.e-laws.gov.on.ca/DBLaws/Regs/English/980134_e.htm#49.(1).
12 Battle, *Minimum Wages*.
13 Standing Committee comments on Bill C-2 in December 2000 when the EI surplus rose higher than $30 billion, www.oag-bvg.gc.ca/domino/other.nsf/html/01hr01_e.html. Also see CLC comments at: clc-ctc.ca/web/menu/english/en_index.shtml?load=action.web.ca/home/clcadmin/en_alerts.shtml?scrl=1&scr_scr_Go=15&AA_EX_Session=c34dc61d34d370bed47194300758c53d.
14 *Time for Action* (1992) the second report of the Minister's Advisory Group on the implementation of new Social Assistance legislation in Ontario following *Transitions*. The Advisory Group was chaired by Professor Allan Moscovitch.
15 Rene Morrisette, "Families on the Financial Edge," *Perspectives*, Fall 2002, www.statcan.ca/Daily/English/020718/d020718i.htm.
16 The Manley Budget provides details on the growth of child benefits at www.fin.gc.ca/budtnoce/2003/budliste.htm#speech.
17 National Council of Welfare, Welfare Incomes 2002, Spring 2003, www.ncwcnbes.net/htmdocument/reportwelfinc02/WelfareIncomes.pdf.
18 British Columbia introduced time limits for recipients of welfare in 2002. See www.news.gov.bc.ca/default.asp?st=16.
19 Battle, *Minimum Wages*.

20 See http://www.chaseo.org/PTRFTK-campaignposter.html, www.paytherent.ca/pdfs/brochure.pdf, www.paytherent.ca/

21 See www.ocsj.ca/docs/flyer-english.pdf.

22 For example, www.cprn.com/cprn.html, www.cprn.com/docs/corporate/ssp_e.PDF, www.statcan.ca/Daily/English/020718/d020718i.htm, and www.td.com/economics/special/special.html.

23 See Clifford J. Williams, *Decades of Service, A History of the Ministry of Community and Social Services*, Ontario, 1983, for a discussion of changing values and social services.

24 *Transitions*, p. 460.

25 Low Income Cutoffs and Market Basket Measures generally cover issues relating to living frugally and carefully, but do not overtly cover the costs of work.

26 *Transitions*, pp. 510–512.

27 See Marc Lee, *Snakes and Ladders, A Policy Brief on Poverty Dynamics, Canadian Centre for Policy Alternatives*, October 2002.

Chapter 7

Housing Discrimination in Canada: Stakeholder Views and Research Gaps

SYLVIA NOVAC, JOE DARDEN, J. DAVID HULCHANSKI, AND ANNE-MARIE SEGUIN

Housing policy should include consideration of equitable access to housing, but there is little information about housing discrimination in Canada. Research from the United States cannot be directly applied to the Canadian situation, since the U.S. has a different history of social relations and different patterns of segregation among ethno-cultural groups.

This study, part of a larger review of the housing discrimination literature carried out for Canada Mortgage and Housing Corporation, identified what research has been done on housing discrimination in Canada in order to identify gaps that should be filled and suggest a research agenda that could guide future housing policy. The study took the form of a literature survey and interviews with 40 key informants.

What is Housing Discrimination?

Housing discrimination consists of any behaviour, practice, or policy in the public or private sectors that directly, indirectly, or systematically causes harm through inequitable access to, or use and enjoyment of, housing by members of historically disadvantaged social groups.

Discrimination is not the same thing as prejudice. Prejudice may or may not lead to discriminatory behaviour and discriminatory behaviour may be caused by motives other than prejudice.

Canadian law prohibits both direct discrimination and "adverse effect" discrimination. However, most Canadian case law deals with discrimination in relation to employment rather than housing.

Discrimination can take many forms. The most obvious is the denial of housing to an individual or family, but it may also take the form of charging certain people higher prices or rents for housing, applying more stringent or inappropriate screening criteria to some people, or treating certain residents differently from other residents.

As research into social equity continues, the definition of discrimination has expanded, because certain types of behaviour that were once unchallenged are now recognized as discriminatory. New forms of discrimination are coming to light, especially forms of indirect or systemic discrimination. These include statistical discrimination, and discrimination on the basis of social condition.

Statistical discrimination consists of judging people, not on their individual characteristics, but according to their membership in a certain group. For instance, the application of minimum income criteria to screen tenants has been contested as a discriminatory practice. In another example, a landlord may reject a potential tenant because that person comes from a group that the landlord associates with disruptive behaviour.

Discrimination on the basis of poverty, low education, homelessness, or illiteracy is a growing problem, but only Quebec's Charter of Human Rights prohibits discrimination on the basis of "social condition." Attempts to add this provision to the Canadian Charter of Human Rights or to human rights legislation in other provinces have been unsuccessful.

Previous Research Findings

Landlord behaviour

A few studies suggest that resident landlords tend to behave differently from absentee landlords (absentee landlords were more likely to rent to new immigrants, for example) and that resident landlords are over-represented in human rights cases on housing discrimination and harassment.

Some researchers distinguish between informal landlords – those who own one or a small number of properties – and commercial landlords. The informal landlords tend to want to control their properties more closely and are more likely to ignore tenants' rights.

A few Canadian studies have looked at landlords' behaviour towards certain ethno-racial groups and have identified instances of discrimination against certain immigrant groups. Some landlords cited their own experience of communication problems, overcrowding, noise, cleaning problems, and lease violations as reasons for excluding certain groups.

The changing profile of renters may have affected landlords' attitudes. Since the early 1980s, renting has become more strongly associated with low income levels, as those who can afford to do so make the transition to homeownership. Many landlords reject families living on social assistance, and most prefer working couples, which puts single mothers and other types of households at a disadvantage.

Although in several provinces, including Ontario, it is against the law to refuse to rent to a household that depends on social assistance payments, this type of discrimination is routinely practised by some landlords, according to at least one Toronto study. Research also suggests that landlords apply more stringent financial screening criteria when vacancy rates are low and there is competition for housing.

Racial discrimination

Studies conducted since the 1950s have found evidence of racial discrimination in Canada, especially by landlords who were unwilling to rent to racial minorities. Some of the studies involved paired researchers or auditors – one white and one black, or one Aboriginal and one non-Aboriginal – who would approach agents and landlords about available rental housing. The earliest studies found more instances of discrimination than studies conducted in the 1970s and 1980s, but racial discrimination has by no means disappeared.

Although in the 1950s and 1960s, racial discrimination was often blatant, today it may be practised in more subtle ways. For example, landlords may use economic criteria to exclude certain racial groups.

The highest levels of discrimination are experienced by blacks, followed by South Asians. Recent studies have found that certain immigrant groups avoid dealing with the problem of discrimination by using social networks within their own ethno-cultural group to find housing.

Researchers have also noticed a discrepancy between individual and group perceptions of discrimination. People tend to perceive a higher level of discrimination against their group than against themselves as individuals.

There is anecdotal evidence of racial harassment in the Canadian housing system, and some social housing agencies have anti-racist harassment policies. However, no systematic studies have been done in

Canada or the United States, although several have been conducted in the United Kingdom.

Racial discrimination may take the form of "neighbourhoodism" – discrimination against those who live in a particular area, for example, large public housing projects, such as Regent Park in Toronto. Researchers have documented instances of people living in such neighbourhoods being unable to obtain home insurance, get delivery services, or have a taxi driver pick them up from the area. Landlords may also reject applications for rental housing when they see that the applicant lives in one of these stigmatized neighbourhoods.

Sex and gender discrimination

Several feminist analysts of housing have demonstrated a male bias in the design and planning of housing. Examples include underground parking garages or isolated basement laundry rooms, which many women consider unsafe. Other researchers have criticized housing policy that appears to focus on housing traditional families and ignores the needs of non-family households or households headed by women.

Several studies have found that women renters are sometimes harassed or intimidated by housing providers. The problems cited include unannounced visits to the unit when the tenant was absent, prying into the tenant's personal life, insults and verbal abuse, threats of eviction, threats to cut services, and refusal to make needed repairs.

Women with children, younger women, divorced women, single mothers and women on social assistance report difficulties in securing housing that they have attributed to their sex and family or financial status. No systematic studies, such as those using paired auditors, have been done in Canada to confirm these experiences, although one such U.S. study revealed sexist discrimination in the housing market.

Interestingly, although the auditors' results clearly showed that single women and single mothers were offered rental units less often than single men and single fathers, the female auditors themselves were not aware of being discriminated against.

Sexual harassment of women by landlords and superintendents, or by other tenants is reported far less frequently than sexual harassment in the workplace, but researchers have found it to be a fairly common problem that has led to formal human rights complaints. Women may underreport such events for a variety of reasons, including fear of retaliation by the harasser, lack of awareness of their rights, or psychological effects from previous abuse.

Researchers have documented sexual harassment in rental housing and non-profit supportive housing. In rental housing, as many as half of the incidents were perpetrated by landlords and housing agents; in non-profit housing, the perpetrators were nearly always other tenants.

The worst-off group is probably women of colour who are lone parents; these women are discriminated against because of their race, sex, family situation, and low income all at the same time. However, their experiences are not adequately captured either by human rights prosecutions or by research, since most approaches to discrimination deal with one factor at a time (either racial discrimination or sexual discrimination, but not both).

Discrimination against youth, gays and lesbians, and people with disabilities

No systematic research has been conducted on discrimination against youth, gays and lesbians, and people with disabilities, but anecdotal evidence suggests that such groups experience discrimination. Young people may be refused housing by landlords who demand a credit history, and gays and lesbians may be harassed because of their living arrangements. People with disabilities face disadvantages related to housing design and accessibility. One women's advocacy organization has reported that women with disabilities are more likely to be exploited or abused in their homes than non-disabled women.

Discrimination on the basis of social status

People who are homeless, or who live in public housing or emergency shelters, or who receive employment insurance or social assistance may be subject to discrimination in housing. Research suggests that discrimination on the basis of income is growing, through the use of credit checks, rent-to-income ratios, and requests for guarantors.

Discrimination in land use planning

Certain land use planning tools have been criticized as being inherently discriminatory. Zoning bylaws, for example, by restricting housing forms, may create neighbourhoods that exclude renters or certain kinds of households.

Discrimination is also apparent in the public reaction to certain development proposals, including opposition to the creation of emergency shelters, group homes, social housing, apartment buildings, co-operative housing, seniors' homes, or other types of housing geared to particular groups.

The Not In My Back Yard (NIMBY) syndrome is well documented and is often linked to fears that the proposed housing will lower property values, although studies have refuted such outcomes. Mediation and alternative dispute resolution have sometimes been used to deal with such opposition.

Steering and discrimination in housing finance

No Canadian studies focus on discrimination in home buying, but two studies have looked at the role of real estate agents in directing certain buyers to certain areas – a process known as "steering" that may lead to residential segregation. Both studies found little evidence of steering in Canada, but several studies conducted in the United States have found evidence that some agents steer blacks towards predominantly black neighbourhoods and whites towards predominantly white neighbourhoods. More studies are needed to determine the extent of steering in Canada.

There is no recent Canadian research on discrimination in mortgage lending, although that does not mean that it does not occur. U.S. studies suggest that blacks are denied home mortgage loans at a higher rate than whites, even when the black and white applicants have similar qualifications such as income, credit records, and other eligible characteristics.

The gap increases among marginal applicants (for example, those with a less-than-ideal credit record) according to the applicant's race or sex. Other U.S. studies indicate that women and racial minorities may be discouraged from applying for a mortgage in the first place.

Although there is no evidence of residential mortgage discrimination in Canada, community groups have expressed concern over bank closures in certain low-income neighbourhoods. Also, residents of some neighbourhoods served by credit unions or caisses populaires, which do not pool risk, may find it more difficult to obtain mortgages, because these organizations have less ability to absorb financial losses than the national banks.

Anecdotal evidence suggests that people in certain neighbourhoods with large-scale public housing projects may have difficulty obtaining insurance, but no systematic studies have been done to confirm this.

Stakeholder Views on Discrimination

The authors interviewed 40 people from across Canada about selected aspects of housing discrimination. The interviewees were drawn from various stakeholder groups, including landlord and tenant advocates, housing service providers, government planners and housing policy analysts, human rights specialists, lending and real estate agents, and representatives of financial institutions.

Defining housing-related discrimination

Most informants equated housing discrimination with the denial of access to housing by a landlord. Only a few included the treatment of existing tenants. Many were aware of instances of harassment, although some considered harassment more a matter of interpersonal conflict than discrimination.

Nearly all the informants agreed that racial discrimination occurred, but they held differing opinions about its prevalence. For example, people in areas with a large Aboriginal population reported that discrimination against this group was common.

Many informants stated that discrimination by income level is common, because of income-based screening. Others felt that those who were new to the housing market – youth, immigrants, and the formerly homeless – and those with psychiatric or developmental difficulties were at a special disadvantage. Several even felt that the elderly were the target of discrimination by landlords who may believe that they are too old to care for themselves.

Informants stated that people with disabilities are subject to particular forms of discrimination, usually related to access. For example, a blind person who relies on a guide dog may be denied housing if the landlord forbids pets.

Families with children may be excluded from certain kinds of housing, because landlords assume that children mean greater wear and tear on a rental unit. Single mothers may also be denied access to housing because landlords believe that a woman may not adequately supervise her children or attend to property maintenance (other than keeping the place clean).

Screening and risk assessment

Several informants argued that landlords need to screen tenants in order to minimize their financial risk, and that landlords were often treated more unfairly than tenants, because they had to absorb losses caused by damage or rent arrears. One person suggested that the government needed to take more responsibility for housing people with severe mental health problems, rather than expecting the private sector to house people with such disabilities.

Informants suggested that financially irresponsible or exploitive tenants constituted 5 to 10 percent of all tenants, but there is no hard data available, and landlords must do their own assessments of potential risks. It is expensive and often futile to attempt to prosecute tenants who do not pay rent. Landlords may resort to stereotypes to screen out potentially defaulting tenants.

More landlords are demanding formal applications that collect information on the tenant's employment, income, previous rental history, credit status, and character, and require verification from previous landlords or character references. Some landlords also seek information from businesses that check into tenants' backgrounds, in particular their earlier relationships with other landlords.

Institutionalized discrimination

Informants provided many examples of systemic housing discrimination, including:
- the "man-in-the-house" rule, by which women on social assistance may have their benefits revoked if a welfare agent claims that they are living with a man who is contributing to the household finances;
- the criteria for obtaining priority on a housing waiting list;
- lack of physical access to housing for people with disabilities;
- government tax policies that favour homeowners over renters;
- zoning and planning practices that exclude certain kinds of households from certain areas, such as minimum lot frontage rules that ensure that only expensive housing can be created in an area, thereby excluding lower-income households.

Many informants mentioned NIMBYism, which can forestall the creation of special needs housing, or even of regular multi-unit housing. One informant mentioned that public meetings can even lead to violence when hostility to a proposal is particularly high.

Discrimination in housing purchase and finance

An informant in the real estate industry mentioned that discrimination by agents may occur when an agent:
- avoids doing business with a client from a particular social group;
- steers a client towards certain neighbourhoods; or
- gives certain clients a lower level of service.

The real estate industry is self-regulating, and the only mechanism to ensure public accountability is the process of complaining to a business agency or human rights commission.

Little information is available on discrimination in mortgage lending, but no informant was willing to state that it did not occur. In Canada, banks do not provide information about their lending policies, so there is no public accountability in this area. Nor do banks maintain databases that track successful and unsuccessful applicants.

Informants from the financial sector reported that loan officers use a debt-service-to-income ratio to determine whether or not to approve an application, but that most officers have some discretion, and some may refuse loans to certain applicants by making assumptions about future income streams.

Signs of change

Few informants felt that racial discrimination was declining, but most felt that landlords are cautious about overt expressions of racism and that discrimination was exercised in more subtle ways. Several felt that discrimination on the basis of income was increasing.

Human rights legislation is not a guaranteed deterrent to discrimination. Sophisticated commercial landlords who can pay for legal advice are not as worried about human rights challenges as small landlords who cannot absorb as much loss. The commercial landlords also know that human rights cases are time-consuming and that tenants may drop the case before it is heard.

Informants mentioned variables that affect the prevalence of discrimination:
- vacancy rates: in general, the lower the rate, the higher the probability of discrimination;
- ease of tenant evictions: the more difficult it is to evict a tenant, the greater the likelihood that the landlord will try to avoid renting to certain groups perceived as high-risk;

- type of landlord: small-scale landlords who live alongside their tenants may be more likely to practise discrimination.

One informant suggested that negative portrayals of certain groups in the media might lead to discrimination against those groups.

When asked about emerging areas of discrimination, many informants mentioned minimum income screening criteria and the lack of protection against discrimination by social condition in all provinces except Quebec. Others mentioned rules established by non-profit or co-operative housing; the rules are designed to maintain the stability of the housing, but may penalize individuals. For example, some co-operatives require residents to contribute labour to the management of the project, which may be more onerous for single mothers than for couples. A few informants suggested that non-profit housing operated by some ethnic groups or religious groups may exclude those of different ethnicities or religions, although these projects may constitute a form of affirmative action.

(In)Effectiveness of legislation

Many informants felt that the effectiveness of legislation lay in its enforcement as much as in its wording, and that enforcement was lax or ineffective. Litigation is a time-consuming and expensive way to resolve discrimination issues. A few informants felt that higher vacancy rates would do more than legislation to lessen discrimination. Others said that an increased supply of social housing would reduce discrimination, because social housing providers can take on more risk than private landlords.

Landlord advocates wanted to see more education about rights and responsibilities in the housing system. Tenant advocates wanted to see a more efficient and streamlined human rights process, so that tenants would not give up cases because they were dragging on.

Several informants called for more research, particularly housing audits, to document the extent of housing discrimination, so that effective solutions could be developed in response.

Conclusion

The research available confirms that housing discrimination continues to exist in Canada, particularly but not exclusively in the private rental sector. The existing studies are small scale, limited to a few cities, and nearly all have focused on the rental sector and on racial discrimination. Little systematic research is available on the homeownership sector or on other forms of discrimination. Also, most of the studies have focused on *access* to housing, rather than on the treatment of people once they have secured housing.

The interviews found that people vary in their impressions of the extent of discrimination according to their occupation or association. As expected, tenant and human rights advocates were most likely to consider discrimination a serious problem. However, most agreed that the current system for resolving disputes is ineffective and that the existing data on housing discrimination are inadequate for directing policy decisions.

The study shows that systematic research is badly needed, especially:
* housing audit studies (especially paired testing) in major cities, focusing on blacks, Aboriginals, female-headed households, families with children, youth, people with physical disabilities, and low-income households;
* surveys of perceived discrimination and its effects on home-seeking behaviour and outcomes in both large and small urban centres;
* surveys on the housing experiences of specific ethnic groups in specific cities.

Studying mortgage lending practices will be more difficult, because of the confidentiality of transactions. However, exploratory research involving surveys of the general population and of mortgage holders might indicate the nature and extent of discrimination in this area.

The full report, titled Housing Discrimination in Canada: The State of Knowledge, *is available on request from the Canadian Housing Information Centre: Phone: 1-800-245-2642; Fax: 1-800245-9274; Email: chicQ@cmhc-schl.gc.ca*

Sylvia Novac is an independent research consultant specializing in gender and housing issues and a research associate at the Centre for Urban and Community Studies where she is the Research Co-ordinator for the Housing New Canadians Research Working Group, a multi-community investigation of recent immigrants and the Toronto rental housing sector.

Joe Darden is a professor in the Department of Geography and Urban Affairs, Michigan State University. His research interests are urban social geography; residential segregation; and socio-economic neighbourhood inequality in multiracial societies.

J. David Hulchanski is Director of the Centre for Urban and Community Stud-

ies, a professor of social work, and the Dr. Chow Yei Ching Professor of Housing at the University of Toronto.

Anne-Marie Seguin *is a professor at INRS Urbanisation, Culture et Société, Institut national de la recherché scientifique. Her research interests are urban social geography and more specifically social exclusion, urban social policy and housing trajectories.*

Chapter 8

Housing Affordability: Immigrant and Refugee Experiences

ROBERT A. MURDIE

Since Canada's formation in 1867, immigration has been important for Canadian nation-building. Immigration trends, however, have changed dramatically since Clifford Sifton's plea at the turn of the last century for "honest men" who would till the land and make a living for themselves and their families. Instead of moving to the Canadian Prairies, immigrants are now concentrated in Canada's metropolitan centres, especially the three largest cities (Montreal, Toronto, and Vancouver). Of immigrants who arrived in Canada in the 1990s, 94 percent lived in census metropolitan areas in 2001 and almost three-quarters lived in Montreal (12 percent), Toronto (43 percent), and Vancouver (18 percent).[1] These also tend to be the most expensive housing markets in the country, where new immigrants likely face the greatest affordability problems.

For immigrants and refugees, finding a suitable place to live in a supportive community is an important first step towards successful integration. This is especially true for refugees, whose arrival in Canada was not planned and who have often experienced considerable disruption in their move from one country to another. The success of immigrants in achieving suitable housing is determined largely by the nature of the local housing market – the opportunities that are available within the constraints of household resources. For many newcomers, the process of finding appropriate housing is made more difficult by the lack of adequate financial resources, high housing costs, a shortage of rental vacancies, and discriminatory practices in the housing market.

Postwar Immigration Trends

During the period after the Second World War, the immigrant flow to Canada has become much more diverse in terms of source countries, visible minority status, entry class (economic, family, humanitarian), and economic status. These changes have resulted from the introduction of a point system in the 1970s that is applied to all immigrants, regardless of origin and race, and from an increased emphasis on the educational qualifications and skills of potential immigrants. Also, in the 1970s, economic restructuring reduced the demand for manual workers and increased the need for both high- and low-skilled workers in the newly emerging service industries.

The outcome has been a decline in immigration from Britain and other European countries and an increase in newcomers from Asia, Africa, Central and South America, and the Caribbean. Between 1961 and 1971, almost 70 percent of Canada's immigrants came from Britain and continental Europe. Between 1991 and 2001, the share of immigrants from Britain and the rest of Europe declined to about 20 percent, and the proportion from Asian countries increased from 12 to 58 percent.[2] At the same time, Canada's visible minority population increased from 4.7 percent in 1981 to 11.2 percent in 1996 and 13.4 percent in 2001.[3] Chinese, South Asians, and Blacks are the three largest visible minority groups, accounting for two-thirds of the visible minority population. Of these, South Asians are the fastest-growing group.

Canada's recently arrived immigrants also represent a wide spectrum of economic groups, including refugees admitted on humanitarian grounds, people joining family members already in Canada, business people with money to invest, and independent immigrants admitted on the basis of their educational achievement, labour market skills, and language proficiency.

These factors, coupled with recent evidence suggesting a rise in the proportion of low-income households among newly arrived immigrants, especially from Africa and from South, East, and West Asia, directly affect the ability of immigrants to afford good-quality housing.[4] The problem is particularly acute in Montreal, Toronto, and Vancouver. Low incomes, however, are only part of the picture.

Many immigrants, such as business immigrants, are asset-rich but income-poor. As Ley notes for Vancouver,[5] many of these immigrants can afford good-quality ownership dwellings soon after they arrive. The low incomes of most immigrants and refugees, however, mean that they must try to find housing in the private and public rental sectors. Unfortunately, due to high housing costs and a shortage of supply, many new immigrants are not able to afford good-quality accommodation when they arrive in Canada. Furthermore, those who pay a high proportion of their income on shelter may not be able to afford other essentials, such as food and clothing.

Relatively little is known about immigrants and housing affordability in Canada. The evidence that does exist comes from a variety of sources. At the national level, the best evidence comes from special analyses by Canada Mortgage and Housing Corporation (CMHC) of the 1996 census and preliminary results from the first wave of the Longitudinal Survey of Immigrants to Canada. These studies have been supplemented at the local level by more detailed studies, primarily in Toronto. This is not surprising, given Toronto's role as the major gateway centre for immigrant settlement in Canada and the relatively high cost of housing, both rental and homeownership, in Toronto. Other cities for which studies of particular immigrant groups are available include Calgary, Vancouver, and Kitchener-Waterloo.

Immigrants and Housing Affordability: The National Perspective

Canada Mortgage and Housing Corporation identifies three components of appropriate housing in its Core Housing Need model: adequacy, suitability, and affordability. *Adequacy* refers to the physical quality of the dwelling, *suitability* to the appropriateness of the dwelling for accommodating a particular size and type of household, and *affordability* to the maximum proportion of before-tax income that a household should theoretically spend on shelter. When households fall below a minimum standard of housing, as defined by CMHC, and cannot afford to rent housing locally that meets these standards they are said to be in "core need."[6]

Based on detailed analysis of the 1996 census, CMHC found that 21 percent of immigrants were in core need, compared to 17 percent of non-immigrants.[7] There were considerable differences among immigrants, however, depending on their year of arrival in Canada. Not surprisingly, recently arrived immigrants were more likely to be in core need. Almost 40 percent of immigrants and 43 percent of non-permanent residents (including refugee claimants) who arrived between 1991 and 1996 were in core need. For immigrants arriving before 1991, the percentage in core need dropped as their length of residence in Canada increased, ultimately declining to the same level as non-immigrants (28 percent for those arriving between 1986 and 1990; 22 percent for those arriving between 1976 and 1985; and 16 percent for those who arrived before 1976). Immigrants who rented housing were more likely to be in core need than homeowners. This was especially the case for recently arrived immigrants. Of the immigrants who arrived between 1991–96 who were in core need, 80 percent were tenants.

Recently arrived immigrants also had higher average shelter-cost-to-income ratios. For all immigrant households arriving in 1991–96, the ratio was 33 percent compared to 22 percent for non-immigrants. The ratio dropped according to length of residence in Canada, so that the shelter-cost-to-income ratio for immigrants who arrived before 1976 was the same as that of non-immigrants. For both immigrants and non-immigrants in core need, the shelter-cost-to-income ratio was about 50 percent, regardless of time of arrival for the immigrant population. Given the remarkably high proportion of income devoted to shelter, relatively little is left for other essentials such as food, clothing, and transportation.

The figures above are averages for the entire country. For census metropolitan areas (CMAs) that attract a relatively large number of recent immigrants, the proportion of immigrants in core need varied considerably, based largely on the size and location of the CMAs, and the housing costs in each city. For immigrants arriving between 1991 and 1996, the proportions are:

- Ottawa-Hull: 48 percent;
- Montreal: 44 percent;
- Toronto and Quebec City: 42 percent each;
- Vancouver: 38 percent;
- Hamilton, Kitchener-Waterloo, London, and Windsor: about 35 percent each;
- Calgary, Edmonton, and Winnipeg: about 30 percent each.

With low vacancy rates and increased rents in the private rental market, the virtual cessation of new social housing construction, and rapidly escalating house prices in the larger gateway cities, it is hard to know whether immigrants arriving in the 1990s will be able to improve their housing position as rapidly as those who came in the 1960s and 1970s.

The Longitudinal Survey of Immigrants to Canada is designed to study the early settlement of immigrants in Canada and their adjustment over time. The first set of interviews was conducted between October 2000 and September 2001, about six months after the respondents arrived in Canada. Interviews with the same group of approximately 12,000 immigrants will be conducted two years after arrival and four years after arrival. The interviews cover a wide variety of topics, including housing circumstances and residential mobility.

Results from the initial interviews indicate that about one-quarter of the immigrants, primarily those who came to join relatives, did not need to look for housing after arrival.[8] Of those who needed to find housing, about 40 percent experienced one or more difficulties. The most serious problem was cost of housing. Almost one-third mentioned cost and one-quarter mentioned the lack of a guarantor or co-signer or the lack of a credit history. Ontario respondents were most likely to indicate housing costs as a barrier to finding adequate housing (37 percent).

In addition to the problems experienced in searching for housing, the Longitudinal Survey of Immigrants to Canada includes a rich set of data on housing tenure, housing type, size of dwelling, housing costs, and assistance obtained in looking for housing, all of which can be cross-tabulated with other variables such as country of birth, gender, visible minority status, family composition, and economic position. Further analysis of these data, as they become available, promises to deepen our understanding of the immigrant housing experience in Canada and determine the extent and rapidity of immigrant integration in Canada's diverse housing markets.

Immigrants and Housing Affordability: The Local Perspective

Another group of studies concerning immigrant housing experiences has been undertaken at the local level. In some cases, the studies relate to a single immigrant group, in other cases two or more groups are compared. All point to the difficulties that immigrants and refugees with limited financial resources face in accessing affordable housing. The focus here is on Toronto, but examples will also be provided from other Canadian cities.

Canada has attracted a wide diversity of immigrant groups in recent decades. This is particularly true in Toronto, which a recent book on immigrant integration identified as *The World in a City*.[9] Not all of these immigrants are low income and not all have difficulties affording appropriate housing. In a study using 1996 census data, Murdie and Teixeira[10] concluded that on average, immigrant renters from West Central Asia (primarily Afghanistan, Iran, and Iraq), South Asia (primarily Sri Lanka, Pakistan, and Bangladesh), the former U.S.S.R. and East Africa (primarily Ethiopia, Somalia, and Sudan) spend more than 30 percent of their income on rent. Recent immigrant renters from these areas (arrival 1991–96) spent around 40 percent of their income on housing.

Combining variables measuring housing conditions (in need of major repair), crowding (more than five persons per household), and affordability (percentage of income spent on rent), the authors concluded that immigrants from South Asia (excluding India), West Central Asia, Central and South America and the Caribbean, East Africa, and Vietnam exhibit (in that order) the most problematic housing conditions. These groups all include a relatively large number of recent immigrants, and all have comparatively low incomes and large households. They are also visible minority groups with a potential for higher levels of discrimination in the housing market.

A more detailed analysis of affordability by immigrant groups in Toronto has been undertaken by the Housing Experiences of New Canadians in Greater Toronto study.[11] The purpose of this study is to evaluate and compare the housing careers of immigrants and refugees in Toronto's squeezed rental market. Three immigrant groups have been analysed (Jamaican, Polish, and Somali). The three groups were chosen in order to have two visible minority groups represented (Afro-Jamaican and Somali) and one non-visible group (Polish). The study is based on interviews with approximately 60 respondents from each group who arrived in Toronto between 1987 and 1994.[12] For all three groups, success in the rental housing market depends on individual and household characteristics such as income, source of income, household size, and visible minority status.

Income is undoubtedly the most important, in that it determines the amount that can reasonably be spent on rent and the amount that is left for essentials such as food, clothing, and transportation. It can also be a discriminatory factor in that many landlords will not rent to households that have to pay more than certain percentage of their income (typically 30 percent) on rent.

Respondents from all three groups had a relatively high level of education before coming to Canada, but all have had difficulty translating their educational attainment into well-paid jobs in Canada. The Poles came with the highest level of qualifications and have fared the best. As a group, the Somalis had higher educational qualifications than the Jamaicans, but have had more limited success in the labour market. Success in the labour market is reflected in income differentials, with Somalis occupying the most tenuous financial position and Poles the most favourable position. All three groups, however, had a higher proportion of households in the low-income category (less than $20,000) than the overall figure for Toronto households.

Source of income, especially social assistance, is another factor restricting choice in the private rental market. The shelter allowance component of social assistance falls far below average apartment rents in Toronto, and landlords tend to treat apartment seekers on social assistance with mistrust. At the time of interviewing, Somali respondents (40 percent) were much more likely to be on social assistance than Jamaicans (20 percent) and Poles (17 percent). Even so, this was an improvement from the situation at the first permanent residence stage, when 79 percent of Somalis were on social assistance.

Household size is also important, given that there are relatively few large rental apartments in Toronto. Somalis have much larger families (3.6 persons per household on average) than the Poles (2.5 persons per household) and Jamaicans (2.8 persons per household). Upon first arrival in Toronto, household size was even larger for the Somalis (4.4 persons per household on average). Understandably, landlords in both the private and public rental sectors are concerned about potential wear and tear from housing more people than a unit was designed for. The Somalis, however, are often desperate and some resort to hiding their children when searching for an apartment.

Discriminatory practices also play an important role in the successful search for rental housing, especially for visible minority groups in a tight rental market, in which a landlord can choose from a large number of applicants for a vacant apartment. The Housing New Canadians study investigated the respondents' perceived perceptions of discrimination in finding rental housing. As expected, Jamaicans and Somalis, the two visible minority groups, claimed more personal discrimination than the Poles. Interestingly, however, income was the highest scoring indicator of perceived discrimination for the Poles and Somalis and second highest for the Jamaicans. This suggests that affordability is a major problem for these groups in securing rental housing in Toronto's tight market and that landlords may be using income as a predictor of ability to pay the rent.[13]

In the context of these personal and household characteristics, what were the mean monthly rent and the rent-to-income ratio for the three groups? Ironically, the mean monthly rents were lowest for the Polish respondents and highest for the Somalis, the opposite of expectations based on income. Over time, the Poles had increased their rental payments and at the same time increased their housing consumption. Rents for the Somalis increased dramatically from the first permanent residence to the residence immediately before the current residence. Thereafter, rents for this group declined slightly along with housing consumption. By this time, many Somali households in the sample had found accommodation in the public rental sector.

The housing affordability problem for the Somalis is best expressed in rent-to-income ratios. Half the Somalis in the private rental sector were paying 50 percent or more of their income on rent compared to 19 percent for the Jamaicans and 15 percent for the Poles. Seventy-one percent of the Somalis were paying more than 30 percent of their income on rent in contrast to 39 percent of the Poles and 61 percent of the Jamaicans.

When those living in private rental accommodation were asked about the difficulty of paying rent, the Poles expressed the least difficulty. Only 12 to 15 percent acknowledged difficulty over the three moves. In contrast, half of the Somalis expressed difficulty for the first permanent residence and 57 percent for the residence immediately before the current one. This dropped to about 30 percent for the current residence after many Somalis had adjusted their rent cost and consumption patterns. Many Jamaicans also had difficulty paying rent – 39 percent for the first permanent residence, 53 percent for the residence immediately before the current one, and 38 percent for the current residence. For both the Somalis and Jamaicans, high rents were identified as the primary reason for leaving their previous residence and moving to the current one. The Somalis, in particular, were forced to develop strategies to lower their rent burden, such as moving into lower-quality, more crowded housing. Some were also able to find accommodation in subsidized housing. The outcome of both these strategies is a more dispersed pattern of settlement with reduced possibility of forming an institutionally complete neighbourhood catering to the religious, cultural, and consumption needs of the group.

The findings from the Housing New Canadians study have been reinforced by other studies of the experiences of recent immigrants and refugees in Toronto. In a study of 300 Latin American and Muslim immigrants and refugees in west Toronto, Zine[14] found that 62 percent of the respondents found the housing search "very difficult" and 32 percent found it "somewhat difficult." The major reasons for the difficult housing search were lack of income and being on social assistance. In particular, social assistance payments have not kept up with the increased rent costs in Toronto and landlords are reluctant to rent to families on social assistance. Almost 70 percent of the sample felt that they had experienced discrimination in their search for housing, based on factors such as income, ethnicity, and gender. Interestingly, the percentage was higher for Latin Americans (80 percent) than Muslims (57 percent). On average, the respondents were paying a very high proportion (64 percent) of their income on rent. The rent-to-income ratio was highest for those who had been in Canada for one year or less (69 percent), but dropped substantially (to 49 percent) only for those who had been in Canada for 10 years or more.

Alfred found a similar situation for a sample of 156 predominantly Chinese immigrants living in downtown Toronto.[15] Of her sample, 85 percent found that it was "somewhat difficult" or "very difficult" to find a new residence. The most common reason for leaving the previous residence (42 percent) was high cost. Also, 93 percent of the sample spent more than 30 percent of their income on rent; almost half were spending 60 percent or more and almost 20 percent were paying 70 percent or more. There was little difference in rent-to-income ratios between those who had recently arrived and those who had been in Canada for three or more years.

In a more general context, a recent in-depth study by Access Alliance Multicultural Community Health Centre of 30 homeless immigrants and refugees and 27 shelter and drop-in staff found that lack of affordable housing was the most important factor in putting immigrants and refugees at risk of homelessness. Their conclusion was that "The current housing market in Toronto is inadequate for meeting the needs of immigrants and refugees."[16]

Studies from other cities in Canada have also pointed to serious affordability problems for immigrants and refugees in the private rental sector. In Calgary, for example, Danso and Grant[17] found that affordability was probably the most difficult problem facing 103 African immigrants that they interviewed. Over half of the respondents spent more than 30 percent of their income on rent. In Vancouver, drawing on the experiences of a sample of 97 Kurdish, Polish, Somali, and Vietnamese immigrants and refugees, researchers reported that high rent was the most difficult problem in looking for accommodation.[18] The cost of housing was identified by 87 percent of the respondents, ranging from all of the Kurds to three-quarters of the Poles. The Kurds and Somalis, both of whom have larger families on average than the Poles and Vietnamese, particularly felt discrimination because of their children.

Finally, Bezanson, in an in-depth study of housing and resettlement of 15 Afghan refugees in Kitchener-Waterloo, found that a combination of high rents and low incomes was the most important barrier that this group faced in securing affordable housing. All of the 14 households in market housing were paying more than 40 percent of their income on rent and 6 were paying more than 60 percent.[19]

Conclusion

Although there are relatively few studies on immigrants and housing affordability in Canada, all evidence points to a serious affordability problem for most of the groups studied. Furthermore, studies that have examined housing affordability by year of arrival in Canada indicate that although housing costs may be an extreme problem for recent arrivals, many immigrants experience affordability problems for at least a decade after arrival. Many tenants continue to pay at least 50 percent of their income on rent, often for relatively inferior housing stock, and therefore seem to be making little headway in the housing market. Nor is the problem limited to Toronto. Evidence from Calgary, Vancouver, and Kitchener-Waterloo indicates similar problems in these cities.

In the rental market, Poles in Toronto and Vancouver seem to have made much greater progress than Somalis or Jamaicans in Toronto, or Kurds, Somalis, and Vietnamese in Vancouver. Afghans in Kitchener-Waterloo and Latin Americans and Muslims in Toronto are also experiencing problems. Many of these groups include refugees who have come to Canada with few resources and limited prospects for quick access to well-paying jobs. In contrast to immigrants, their arrival was not planned. Most are faced with limited opportunities and increased rents in the private rental market and long waiting lists in the subsidized sector. Many often face various forms of discrimination in Toronto's tight rental market.

It must be pointed out, however, that not all immigrants and refugees experience serious affordability problems. Many make a remarkably quick entry into good-quality and affordable housing. Some immigrants have sufficient resources to afford homeownership upon arrival or soon after. For example, Hong Kong immigrants settling in Toronto who came to Canada between 1991 and 1996 had a homeownership rate by 1996 of 71 percent, compared to only 27 percent for all immigrants arriving during this period and 61 percent for non-immigrants.[20]

Of immigrant groups who arrived in Toronto in the 1950s through to the 1970s, the Italians and Portuguese, among others, have attained a remarkably high level of homeownership, over 90 percent for the Italians and more than 70 percent for the Portuguese in 1996.[21] These groups arrived in Toronto when purchasing a home in the inner city was much more affordable than it is now. By doubling up in crowded accommodation, working long hours in relatively well-paid construction and manufacturing jobs, and obtaining mortgage financing from informal sources, they were able to achieve homeownership relatively quickly. A more limited and more expensive rental housing stock means that recently arrived immigrants and refugees with limited financial resources and fewer job opportunities will face a much more difficult housing career than their predecessors.

Robert A. Murdie is an urban social geographer whose current research interests include ethnic residential segregation and housing analysis. He has taught undergraduate and graduate courses in housing policy and ethnic geography at York University. Until recently, Professor Murdie was the Housing and Neighbourhood domain leader for CERIS, the Joint Centre of Excellence for Research on Immigration and Settlement (Toronto). Professor Murdie obtained his B.A. from Waterloo Lutheran University (now Wilfrid Laurier University) and his master's and Ph.D. degrees from the University of Chicago.

Endnotes

1 Statistics Canada, *Canada's Ethnocultural Portrait: The Changing Mosaic.* Ottawa: 2001; Census: Analysis Series, Statistics Canada, 2003, pp. 7–8.
2 Statistics Canada, 2003, p. 39.
3 Statistics Canada, 2003, p. 44.
4 Garnett Picot and Feng Hou, *The Rise in Low-income Rates among Immigrants in Canada.* Ottawa: Business and Labour Market Analysis Division, Statistics Canada, 2003.
5 David Ley, "Myths and Meanings of Immigration and the Metropolis." *The Canadian Geographer*, vol. 43, no. 1, 1999, pp. 2–19.
6 Canada Mortgage and Housing Corporation, *Special Studies on the 1996 Census Data: Canadian Housing Conditions*, Research Highlights 55-1. Ottawa: Canada Mortgage and Housing Corporation, no date.
7 Canada Mortgage and Housing Corporation, *Special Studies on the 1996 Census Data: Housing Conditions of Immigrants*, Research Highlights 55-3. Ottawa: Canada Mortgage and Housing Corporation, no date.
8 Statistics Canada, *Longitudinal Survey of Immigrants to Canada: Process, Progress and Prospects.* Ottawa: Statistics Canada, 2003.
9 Paul Anisef and Michael Lanphier, eds., *The World in a City*, Toronto: University of Toronto Press, 2003.

10 Robert Murdie and Carlos Teixeira, "Towards a Comfortable Neighbourhood and Affordable Housing: Immigrant Experiences in Toronto." Chapter 3 in Paul Anisef and Michael Lanphier (editors), *The World in a City*. Toronto: University of Toronto Press, 2003, pp. 132–191.

11 See www.hnc.utoronto.ca. The section of this chapter based on evidence from the Housing Experiences of New Canadians in Greater Toronto Study draws from a longer article: "Housing Affordability and Toronto's Rental Market: Perspectives from the Housing Careers of Jamaican, Polish and Somali Newcomers." *Housing, Theory and Society*, forthcoming. A short summary of some of this material was published as "Immigrants, Housing and the Rental Affordability Problem." *Canadian Housing*, vol. 20, no. 2, pp. 23–25.

12 Further details concerning the conceptual framework and research design of the study are available in Murdie, Robert, "The Housing Careers of Polish and Somali Newcomers in Toronto's Rental Market." *Housing Studies*, vol. 17, no. 3, 2002, pp. 423–443.

13 J. David Hulchanski, "The Concept of Housing Affordability: Six Contemporary Uses of the Housing Expenditures-to-Income Ratio." *Housing Studies*, vol. 10, no. 4, 1995, pp. 471–91.

14 Jasmin Zine, *Living on the Ragged Edges: Absolute and Hidden Homelessness among Latin Americans and Muslims in West Central Toronto*. Toronto; Informal Housing Network, 2002.

15 Audrey Alfred, *"It's too expensive and too small": Research Findings on the Housing Conditions of Newcomers*. Toronto: St. Stephen's Community House, 2002.

16 Access Alliance Multicultural Community Health Centre, *Best Practices for Working with Homeless Immigrants and Refugees*, Toronto, 2003, p. 32.

17 Ransford Danso and Miriam Grant, "Access to Housing as an Adaptive Strategy for Immigrant Groups: Africans in Calgary." *Canadian Ethnic Studies*, vol. 32, no. 3, 2000, pp. 19–43.

18 MOSAIC, *Housing Needs of Ethno-Cultural Communities*. Vancouver: MOSAIC Settlement Services, 1996.

19 Rachael Zacharias Bezanson, *Make Yourself at Home: Exploring Housing and Resettlement with Afghan Refugee Households in Kitchener-Waterloo, Ontario*. Unpublished master's thesis, University of Waterloo, 2003.

20 Murdie and Teixeira, 2003, p. 180.

21 Murdie and Teixeira, 2003, p. 175.

Chapter 9

Housing as a Social Determinant of Health

TOBA BRYANT

While there is increasing awareness of a housing crisis in Canada, there is little discussion of how housing issues – especially housing insecurity – are related to the health of Canadians. Can housing insecurity be conceptualized as a social determinant of health? As documented by federal NDP leader Jack Layton in his book *Homelessness: The Making and Unmaking of a Crisis* (2000), according to many indicators – the number of Canadians who sleep in the streets, who use temporary shelters and who spend more than 30 or 50 percent of their income on housing – Canada's housing policy has clearly failed to meet the needs of a significant proportion of Canadians.

In 1986, the World Health Organization's *Ottawa Charter for Health Promotion* recognized adequate housing as a basic prerequisite for health, but it is only recently that researchers have focused on housing as an important determinant of health.

The current housing crisis and associated housing insecurity are the results of radical changes in housing policy over the last two decades. The problem of affordability in the private rental housing market first emerged as a major issue in the early 1980s, and it remained for the most part not addressed through the 1990s. The housing crisis is now seen as a national disaster. The federal government has even appointed a Co-ordinator of Homelessness Initiatives.

Many analysts attribute the growing number of homeless and insecurely housed Canadians to reduced state involvement in housing. Indeed, Canada now has the most private-sector-dominated, market-based housing system and the smallest social housing sector of any

Figure 1: Social Housing Starts in Ontario (mostly co-ops, non-profits), 1970–2000

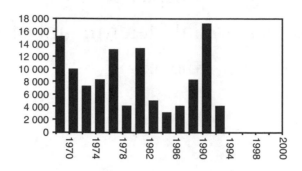

Source: Ontario Ministry of Municipal Affairs and Housing, 2001.

Western nation, with the exception of the United States. Other factors include continuing high levels of unemployment and lack of affordable rental accommodation. The result is increasing numbers of families and individuals who are underhoused, living in motels, dependent on the shelter system, or living on the street.

The 1990s marked the withdrawal of the federal government and many provincial governments from the provision of social housing. Social housing reflects a commitment by the state to support affordable housing for all. One illustration of the process of governments' withdrawal from the provision of housing for Canadians is the Ontario Progressive Conservative government's reversal in 1995 of 25 years of commitment by Ontario to providing housing for its citizens. As Figure 1 shows, there has not been a single social housing start in Ontario since that time, with the not surprising result that the use of shelters has increased significantly.

Shelter use is up across Canada. National data are not available, since not every province collects data on shelter use. In his book on homelessness, Layton reports that on an average night, shelter use is approximately 300 people in Vancouver, 1,200 in Calgary, 460 in Ottawa, and about 4,000 in Toronto. The numbers have increased in Toronto, Calgary, Edmonton, Hamilton, and Mississauga. The Federation of Canadian Municipalities reported that in 1996, 43 percent of households across Canada spent more than 30 percent of their income on rent. That same year, over 21 percent of Canadian households spent more than 50 percent of their income on rent, an increase of 43 percent since 1991.

It hardly seems necessary to argue the case that housing is a health issue, yet surprisingly few Canadian studies have considered it as such. In the U.K., where the housing and health tradition is more established, numerous studies have shown strikingly high incidences of physical and mental health problems among homeless people compared with the general population. Wendy Bines, in *The Health of Single Homeless People* (1994) reported on the health problems of 1,280 homeless people in the U.K. People who used hostels, bed and breakfast accommodation, drop-in centres, and soup kitchens were much more likely to have musculo-skeletal and chronic breathing problems, headaches, skin ulcers, seizures and other complaints. Those sleeping in the streets had the most severe health profiles.

The 1992 *Street Health Report*, a survey of the homeless population in Toronto, found that homeless people were at much greater risk than the general population for a variety of chronic conditions including respiratory diseases, arthritis or rheumatism, high blood pressure, asthma, epilepsy and diabetes. Despite this evidence, housing issues have not been high on the agenda of most health researchers in Canada. One reason may be the difficulties presented by this area of study for those trained in traditional methods.

Epidemiology is defined as the distribution and determinants of diseases and injuries in human populations. Epidemiologists aim to identify the unique causal effects of single variables upon health outcomes through various experimental and correlational procedures. The identification of the health effects of housing does not easily lend itself to such a model. Living in disadvantaged housing circumstances clusters with a variety of other indicators of disadvantage. Indeed, Mary Shaw and her colleagues argue in *The Widening Gap: Health Inequalities and Policy in Britain* (1999) that "Health inequalities are produced by the clustering of disadvantage – in opportunity, material circumstances, and behaviours related to health – across people's lives."

When epidemiological research has considered housing, it has tended to focus on aspects of housing and health that can be isolated for measurement such as the presence of mould and the impact on respiratory infections in children, or overcrowding and its impact on mental health. But it has used models that attempt to identify the effects of these factors independently of the contextual variables associated with disadvantage in general. Figure 2 is an example of a traditional epidemiological model that could be deployed to examine the relationship between housing and health.

**Figure 2: Traditional Epidemiological Model
of the Housing and Health Relationship**

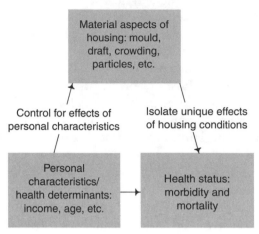

The model identifies the material conditions of housing, such as mould and drafts, as areas of prime interest. Studies attempt to control for the effects of research participants' personal characteristics. They then distil the unique effects of housing conditions from other potential variables that may influence health. The approach searches for the association between the material aspects of housing independent of personal characteristics and other health determinants.

Unless studies are longitudinal and are based on very large numbers, the results produced by these analyses are frequently exercises in ambiguity. They usually say little about how life situations interact with policy environments to create these situations of disadvantaged housing. They also say little about the relationship between housing and other social determinants of health. Research that attempts to isolate the effect of poor housing is unable to measure or capture the complexity of and interaction among the determinants of health.

Nevertheless, when extensive studies are carried out, housing disadvantage is a unique predictor of poor health outcomes. Alex Marsh and colleagues reported on these issues in the 1999 U.K. report *Home Sweet Home: The Impact of Poor Housing on Health*. They drew upon the very large longitudinal database from the National Child Development Study to study the link between housing and health in more than 13,000 citizens. They found housing played a significant and independent role in health outcomes.

Greater housing deprivation during childhood and adulthood each contributed to severe/moderate ill health at age 33 years. Overcrowding was related to respiratory and infectious diseases. For those who experienced overcrowding in childhood to age 11, there was an increased likelihood of experiencing infectious disease. In adulthood, housing deprivation is linked to an increased likelihood of respiratory disease.

Such studies, while identifying potential relationships, focus on individual characteristics rather than the broader factors that influence health and well-being. They oversimplify the relationship between housing and health and other social determinants of health. New ways of thinking about housing and its relationship to health are needed.

Geographer James Dunn of the University of Toronto and colleagues are identifying – with funding from the CIHR Institute of Population and Public Health – gaps in Canadians' understanding of the housing and health relationship. They have developed a thoughtful population health framework of housing as a socioeconomic determinant of health. Since studies have demonstrated a positive association between social status and health status, Dunn states "Housing, as a central locus of everyday life patterns, is likely to be a crucial component in the ways in which socio-economic factors shape health" (see *Housing as a Socio-Economic Determinant of Population Health: A Research Framework*, 2002; www.housingandhealth.ca). The authors outline three aspects of housing that are especially relevant to population health.

- *Material dimensions* of housing are concerned with the physical integrity of the home such as state of repair; physical, biological, and chemical exposure; and housing costs. Dunn notes that housing costs are critical because they are one of the largest monthly expenditures most people face. When housing costs eat up the majority of a person's income, it affects other aspects of their lives.

- *Meaningful dimensions* of housing refer to one's sense of belonging and control in one's own home. Home is also an expression of social status – prestige, status, pride, and identity – all of which are enhanced by homeownership. These dimensions provide a surface for the expression of self-identity, and represent permanence, stability, and continuity in everyday life. One would expect living in crowded or substandard housing to have profound health effects, as one would the worse case of being housed in a shelter or living on the streets.

- *Spatial dimensions* of housing refer to a home and its immediate environment, for example, the proximity of a home to services, schools, public recreation, health services, and employment. While these

Figure 3: Model Incorporating Additional Factors

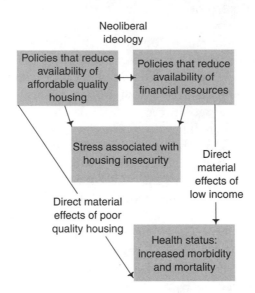

include systematic exposure to health hazards – toxins in the environment and asbestos insulation – they are also about the geographic availability of resources and services in relation to one's abode. This consideration introduces the need for understanding the policy dimensions associated with the availability of resources and services in communities. These concepts should stimulate new ways of Canadian thinking about and studying the role that housing plays in health.

The availability and affordability of housing plays an important role in relationship to other social determinants of health. People can go without many things, but going without housing is potentially catastrophic. If citizens are required to spend increasing proportions of available resources on maintaining a roof over their head, the resources available to support the other determinants of health are diminished.

The Daily Bread Food Bank 2002 fact sheet, "Turning our Backs on Our Children," showed that social assistance rates have not kept up with rents in Toronto. In 2001, a single parent, usually female, with one child, received 59 percent of Statistics Canada's low-income cut-offs. The average monthly welfare income of such a single parent would be $957, while rent for an average one-bedroom apartment was $866 and for a two-bedroom, $1,027.

Figure 4: Housing Affects Other Health Determinants

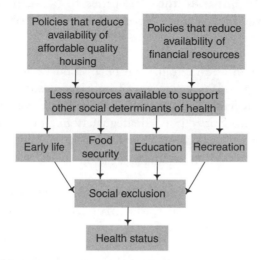

It is difficult to imagine how it would be possible for such a family to cover other important expenses such as food with that after-rent income. Plentiful evidence is available to indicate that lack of material resources contributes to illness and disease, a situation made worse by the stress and uncertainty of living in such conditions. This process is shown in Figure 3.

Unaffordable housing and housing insecurity do not occur in a vacuum. Figure 4 shows how policy decisions create the conditions that influence the availability and affordability of housing and other social determinants of health. The availability and cost of housing has direct material effects on health. Policy decisions can also reduce financial resources, with direct material effects on health. Both types of policy decisions contribute to housing insecurity, increased stress and increased incidence of social exclusion, illness and disease. This model identifies neoliberal ideology as being responsible for the declining availability of affordable housing and financial resources for many citizens.

In spite of the ample evidence regarding the relationship between housing and health, government actions are frequently at odds with a social determinants approach to health. Governments are not seriously addressing social and health inequalities and the role played by housing policy in widening these inequalities. Political strategies are needed to highlight how these health and social inequalities threaten the health of all Canadians. To illustrate the difficulties to be surmounted, in 1991 Paul Martin headed a Liberal Opposition task force on housing, which stated in its report:

> The federal role in housing must not be a residual one. The connection between housing and other aspects of both social and economic policy means that the federal government must take a lead role ... Our market housing system has not responded adequately to all of society's needs ... The Task Force believes that all Canadians have the right to decent housing, in decent surroundings at affordable prices.

After becoming finance minister, where he was well positioned to take action on the housing crisis, Martin chose not to implement the recommendations of his own task force.

Toba Bryant is a postdoctoral fellow at the Centre for Health Studies at York University in Toronto. She studies how the ideological stances of government policy-makers shape state receptivity to the concept of the social determinants of health and other structural aspects of society. Before undertaking doctoral studies, Dr. Bryant was a policy analyst and evaluator in health and social policy in the non-profit sector. She received her B.A., M.S.W. and Ph.D. at the University of Toronto. Dr. Bryant's doctoral studies were supported by a fellowship from the Social Sciences and Humanities Research Council. An extended version of this article appeared in Policy Options/Options Politiques *March 2003 and can be viewed at* www.irpp.org/po/.

Chapter 10
Homelessness and Health

STEPHEN W. HWANG

Homelessness, which is a focus of increasing concern in Canadian cities, has important health implications. Homeless people have high levels of morbidity and mortality and may experience significant barriers to accessing health care. This chapter addresses three key issues. First, who are the homeless? Second, what health problems are common among homeless people? Third, how does the health care system respond to the needs of the homeless?

Who Are the Homeless?

According to the United Nations, "absolute homelessness" describes the condition of people without physical shelter who sleep outdoors, in vehicles, abandoned buildings, or other places not intended for human habitation. "Relative homelessness" describes the condition of those who have a physical shelter, but one that does not meet basic standards of health and safety; these include protection from the elements, access to safe water and sanitation, security of tenure, personal safety, and affordability.[1] In this review, "homeless people" refers to people who are sleeping in shelters for the homeless and those who are "absolutely homeless."[2] This is the definition that is most frequently used in health-related research. Although homelessness is commonplace in many developing countries, this review focuses on homelessness in Canada.

The capacity of shelters for the homeless is a useful starting point for estimating the size of the homeless population (see table below). These data suggest that each night about 8,000 homeless people, that is, about 5 persons per 10,000 population, are sleeping in shelters in the nine largest metropolitan areas of Canada. The number of individuals who use these shelters at least once over the course of a year is about five times this figure.[3] In Toronto, for example, 28,800 people used such shelters in 1998.

Table 1: Homeless shelter capacity in Canada's metropolitan areas with a population over 500,000*

| Metropolitan area | Population (1000s) | No. of beds | | | |
		Adult shelters	Youth shelters	Family shelters	Total
Toronto	4,586	2,074	441	1,650	4,165
Montreal	3,424	1,118	44	25	1,187
Vancouver	1,999	339	25	51	415
Ottawa/Hull	1,056	325	30	201	556
Edmonton	914	395	29	0	424
Calgary	903	798	80	0	878
Quebec City	687	125	8	15	148
Winnipeg	678	144	24	61	229
Hamilton	658	109	30	65	204
Total	14,905	5,427	711	2,068	8,206

*Homeless shelter capacity excludes overflow, beds at detoxification centres, and beds at shelters exclusively for battered women. City populations shown are for census metropolitan areas in 1998, as defined by Statistics Canada.

Shelter counts underestimate the number of homeless people, because they do not include individuals who are sleeping on the street. Although these individuals are particularly difficult to count, they represent a sizable population in some cities. In Vancouver, as many as 600 homeless people, or 3 per 10,000 population, sleep outside every night, exceeding the number of people staying in shelters.[4]

These figures indicate that the total number of homeless people in Canada on any given night is probably of the order of tens of thousands. In many cities, the number of people who are homeless has clearly increased in recent years. Toronto, which has the country's largest homeless population, has seen mean nightly shelter occupancy rise from 1,902 individuals in 1990 to 3,790 in 1998.[5] Between 1992 and 1998, Calgary's homeless population more than doubled from 447 to 988.[6] In

Ottawa, the total number of overnight stays at men's shelters increased by about 8 percent between 1996 and 1998.[7]

The demographic characteristics of the homeless population vary significantly from city to city. Contrary to common stereotypes, homelessness affects a wide range of people, including families with children. Families occupy 42 percent of shelter beds in Toronto and about 35 percent of shelter beds in Ottawa. The average shelter stay for these families lasts 1.5 to 2 months. In contrast, other Canadian cities do not have significant numbers of homeless families. The phenomenon of homeless families in Toronto and Ottawa may reflect the convergence of multiple factors, including poverty, high housing costs, and a shortage of subsidized public housing units.

Single men constitute the largest segment of homeless people in most Canadian cities: about 70 percent of the homeless population in Vancouver,[8] Edmonton,[9] and Calgary, and about 50 percent in Ottawa. In Toronto, single men occupy 35 percent of shelter beds. Although most single men stay in the shelter system for only a few nights, single men also account for 75 percent of chronically homeless individuals (those who stay in shelters for one year or more). Homeless men tend to be relatively young, with the majority between 25 and 44 years old.[10]

Single women account for about one-quarter of homeless people in Vancouver, Edmonton, and Toronto, but as few as 10 percent of homeless people in cities such as Calgary and Ottawa. Studies in the United States suggest that a number of characteristics distinguish homeless single women from homeless women accompanied by children. Single women are more likely to be chronically homeless, older, and to have a history of substance abuse or mental illness.[11]

The terms "homeless youth" and "street youth" are used interchangeably to refer to teenagers and young people below the age of 20–25 years. These young people first leave home at a mean age of 15 years, and many of them come from families where they experienced physical or sexual abuse.[12] Toronto, Montreal, and Vancouver have the largest numbers of street youth in Canada. Because most of these young people do not sleep in homeless shelters, shelter-based counts greatly underestimate the size of these populations. In Toronto, for example, about 75 percent of homeless youth do not use shelters.[13]

Aboriginal people are overrepresented in Canada's homeless population by a factor of about 10. Individuals of Aboriginal origin account for 35 percent of the homeless population in Edmonton, 18 percent in Calgary, 11 percent in Vancouver, and 5 percent in Toronto, but only 3.8

percent, 1.9 percent, 1.7 percent, and 0.4 percent of the general population of these cities respectively. A disproportionate number of homeless people who sleep on the street rather than in shelters are of Aboriginal origin.

Health Problems Among Homeless People

Homeless people have a greatly increased risk of death. Compared with the general youth population of Quebec, mortality rates among street youth in Montreal are 9 times higher for males and 31 times higher for females.[14] Among men using shelters for the homeless in Toronto, mortality rates are 8.3 times higher than the mean for 18–24 year olds, 3.7 times higher than the mean for 25–44 year olds, and 2.3 times higher than the mean for 45–64 year olds. However, death rates among homeless men in Toronto are about one-half those of homeless men in U.S. cities.[15] Mortality rates are lower in Canada because of a number of factors, including lower rates of homicide and HIV infection and, possibly, Canada's system of universal health insurance.

Homeless people suffer from a wide range of medical problems. Disease severity can be remarkably high because of factors such as extreme poverty, delays in seeking care, non-adherence to therapy, cognitive impairment, and the adverse health effects of homelessness itself.[16] Homeless people in their forties and fifties often develop health disabilities that are more commonly seen only in people who are decades older. Individuals living on the street tend to have a worse health status than shelter residents.[17]

Medical problems that are particularly prevalent among homeless adults include seizures, chronic obstructive pulmonary disease, arthritis, and other musculoskeletal disorders. Conditions such as hypertension, diabetes, and anemia are often inadequately controlled and may go undetected for long periods.[18] Respiratory tract infections are common. Oral and dental health is often poor.[19]

Skin and foot problems are frequently seen among the homeless. People living on the street are particularly prone to develop skin diseases such as cellulitis, impetigo, scabies, and body lice.[20] Foot disorders such as corns, callouses, and immersion foot are usually the result of inadequate footwear, prolonged exposure to moisture, long periods of walking and standing, and repetitive minor trauma.[21] Proper foot care requires early detection of problems, education regarding foot hygiene, and the provision of adequate shoes and socks.

Homeless people are at increased risk of contracting tuberculosis (TB). Conditions favouring TB outbreaks in shelters include crowding, large transient populations, and inadequate ventilation.[22] More than half of all TB cases among homeless people represent clusters of primary tuberculosis rather than reactivation of old disease. Published data on TB in Canada's homeless population are limited. The incidence of active TB among homeless people in Toronto is 71 per 100,000 (about 10 times the average Ontario rate).[23] Treatment of active TB in homeless people can be complicated by non-adherence to therapy, prolonged exposure to infection, and the development of drug resistance.[24]

Common risk factors for HIV infection in homeless youth in Canada include prostitution, multiple sexual partners, inconsistent use of condoms, and injection drug use.[25] Infection rates were 2.2 percent and 11.3 percent among homeless youth seeking HIV testing at 2 clinics in Vancouver in 1988.[26] The higher rate was seen at a clinic that served street youth involved in prostitution. In contrast, the prevalence of HIV infection was only 0.6 percent in a sample of homeless youth surveyed in Toronto in 1990.[27]

The pattern of HIV risk factors in homeless adults is distinct from that of youth. In a 1997 study of a representative sample of adults using shelters for the homeless in Toronto, 25 percent had a history of using injection drugs and 41 percent had a history of using crack cocaine. These drug use behaviours, rather than sexual behaviours, were associated with an increased likelihood of HIV infection. The overall HIV infection rate in this study was 1.8 percent.[28]

Sexual and reproductive health is a major issue for street youth. In Montreal, 25 percent of homeless youth have engaged in prostitution. Sexually transmitted diseases are widespread, even among street youth who do not work as prostitutes; gonorrhea and chlamydia are the most prevalent infections. Anecdotal reports suggest that teenaged pregnancy is common among street youth in Canada; in a recent study in the United States, 10 percent of homeless females aged 14–17 years were found to be pregnant.[29]

Violence is a constant threat to the health of homeless people. A survey in Toronto found that 40 percent of homeless individuals had been assaulted and 21 percent of homeless women had been raped in the previous year. Homeless men are about 9 times more likely to be murdered than their counterparts in the general population.[30]

Unintentional injuries are a leading cause of morbidity and mortality, especially among homeless men. Injuries are often the result of falls or being struck by a motor vehicle. Deaths due to an unintentional overdose of drugs or alcohol, or both, are also common. Exposure to the elements is a major hazard. In cold weather, the risk of frostbite and hypothermia is substantial, and deaths due to freezing are not uncommon.[31] In hot weather, severe sunburn and heatstroke can occur.

The prevalence of mental illness and substance abuse among homeless people is difficult to determine precisely, but consistent patterns have emerged from methodologically rigorous studies conducted in the United States and Canada. Contrary to popular misconceptions, only a small proportion of the homeless population has schizophrenia. The lifetime prevalence of schizophrenia is only 6 percent among Toronto's homeless population, and U.S. studies have found prevalence rates of 10 to 13 percent. Affective disorders are much more common, with lifetime prevalence rates in the range of 20 to 40 percent.[32]

Alcohol use disorders are widespread, with lifetime prevalence rates of about 60 percent among homeless men. Problems with alcohol are six to seven times more prevalent among homeless people than in the general population. Not as much data is available on the abuse of substances other than alcohol; in U.S. studies, the median prevalence of drug use disorders is 30 percent. Cocaine (especially crack) and marijuana are the illicit drugs most often used by homeless people in Canada. Dual diagnosis with both mental illness and substance abuse is not uncommon.[33]

Patterns of substance abuse and mental illness vary across demographic subgroups. Homeless single women are more likely to have mental illness alone, without any substance use disorder. The prevalence of substance use disorders in men is about twice that in single women. Compared with all other subgroups of homeless people, female heads of homeless families have far lower rates of both substance abuse and mental illness.

Homelessness and the Health Care System

Homeless adults have high levels of health care use and often obtain their care in emergency departments.[34] Homeless people are admitted to hospital up to five times more often than the general population and stay in hospital longer than other low-income patients.[35] These prolonged stays in hospital result in significant excess health care costs. Unfortunately, homeless patients are sometimes discharged to shelters, even when their ability to cope in such a setting is marginal at best. One solution to this problem is the development of respite facilities to provide homeless people with a protected environment for recuperation after a stay in hospital.[36]

Homeless people face many barriers that impair their access to health care. Lack of health insurance is a problem for most homeless people in the U.S.[37] Although Canada has a system of universal health insurance, many homeless people do not possess proof of coverage because their identification has been lost or stolen. In Toronto, 7 percent of homeless individuals report having been refused health care at least once because they lacked a health insurance card.[38] In addition, many homeless people do not fill prescriptions they have received because they do not have insurance benefits and cannot afford the cost of the medication.[39]

Homeless people face other barriers to health care that are unrelated to insurance status. Homelessness entails a daily struggle for the essentials of life. These competing priorities may impede homeless adults from using health care services, particularly those perceived as discretionary. In addition, many health recommendations regarding rest or dietary changes may be unattainable. In Toronto, 72 percent of homeless people with diabetes report difficulties managing their condition that are usually related to their diet and the logistic challenges of coordinating meals with medications.[40]

The health care system often fails to provide adequate treatment for homeless people with mental illness or substance abuse.[41] The assertive community treatment (ACT) model is an effort to address this problem. An ACT team of psychiatrists, nurses, and social workers follows a small caseload of homeless mentally ill clients, seeking them out in the community to provide high-intensity mental health treatment and case management. Compared with usual care, patients receiving ACT have fewer psychiatric inpatient days, more days in community housing and greater improvements in their symptoms.[42]

Conclusion

Homelessness affects a significant number of Canadians of all ages and is associated with a high burden of illness, yet the health care system may not adequately meet the needs of homeless people. More research is needed to identify better ways to deliver care to this population. Health interventions alone, however, are unlikely to overcome the adverse effects of homelessness and related social ills. The search for long-term solutions to the problem of homelessness itself must remain a priority.

Stephen Hwang is one of the leading researchers on homelessness and health in Canada. He is a clinician-scientist in the Inner City Health Research Unit at St. Michael's Hospital, and holds a prestigious Career Scientist Award from the Ontario Ministry of Health. In his work, Dr. Hwang has examined death rates among homeless people in Canada and the United States, risk factors for death among homeless people, barriers to access to health care for the homeless, and chronic disease management in the homeless. Recent studies have examined mortality among homeless men in Toronto, the effect of homeless shelter use on risk of death, access to prescription medications among the homeless, and barriers to appropriate care among homeless persons with diabetes. Dr. Hwang completed his undergraduate training at Harvard University, his medical degree at the Johns Hopkins School of Medicine, and his master of public health degree at Harvard. Dr. Hwang practises general internal medicine at St. Michael's Hospital in Toronto, and acts as staff physician at Seaton House, the largest homeless shelter in Canada.

The original article appeared in the Canadian Medical Association Journal *164(2), 2001, and can be viewed at* www.cmaj.ca/cgi/content/full/164/2/229.

Endnotes

1 P. Begin, L. Casavant, N.M. Chenier, *Homelessness*, Ottawa: Library of Parliament, Parliamentary Research Branch, Document PRB 99-1E, 1999. www.parl.gc.ca/information/library/prbpubs/prb991-e.htm.

2 C. Jencks, *The Homeless*, Cambridge: Harvard University Press, 1994.

3 J.D. Wright, J.A. Devine, "Housing dynamics of the homeless: implications for a count." *American Journal of Orthopsychiatry* 65, 1995, pp. 320–9.

4 City of Vancouver, *Prevention of homelessness*, Vancouver, 1998. www.city.vancouver.bc.ca/commsvcs/housing/sochouse/1council/1998/98-12-17.htm.

5 A. Golden, W.H. Currie, E. Greaves, E.J. Latimer, *Taking Responsibility for Homelessness: An Action Plan for Toronto*. Report of the Mayor's Homelessness Action Task Force. Toronto: City of Toronto, 1999; City of Toronto, *Toronto Report Card on Homelessness 2000*, Toronto, 2000.

6 City of Calgary, *Count of Homeless Persons in Downtown Calgary, May 21, 1998*, Calgary: Community and Social Development Department, Social Research Unit, 1998.

7 Region of Ottawa-Carleton, *Homelessness in Ottawa-Carleton*, Ottawa: Policy, Planning and Performance Management Services Branch, April 1999.

8 S. Acorn, "Mental and physical health of homeless persons who use emergency shelters in Vancouver," *Hospital and Community Psychiatry* 44, 1993, pp. 854–7.

9 Edmonton Homelessness Count Committee, *A Count of Homeless Persons in Edmonton*, Edmonton, 1999.

10 S.W. Hwang, "Mortality among men using homeless shelters in Toronto, Ontario," *Journal of the American Medical Association*, 283, 2000, pp. 2152–57.

11 M.R. Burt, B.E. Cohen, "Differences among homeless single women, women with children, and single men," *Social Problems* 36, 1989, pp. 508–24.

12 M.D. Janus, F.X. Archambault, S.W. Brown, L.A. Welsh, "Physical abuse in Canadian runaway adolescents," *Child Abuse and Neglect* 19, 1995, pp. 433–47; J.L. Radford, A.J.C. King, W.K. Warren, *Street Youth and AIDS*, Ottawa: Health and Welfare Canada, 1989.

13 Community Social Planning Council of Toronto. *Surviving the street: street youth and squeegeeing in Toronto*. Toronto, 1998.

14 E. Roy, J.F. Boivin, N. Haley, N. Lemire. "Mortality among street youth," *Lancet* 352, 1998, p. 32.

15 Hwang, op. cit.

16 D. Wood, ed., *Delivering Health Care to Homeless Persons: The Diagnosis and Management of Medical and Mental Health Conditions*, New York: Springer Publishing, 1992; C. Crowe, K. Hardill, "Nursing research and political change: The street health report," *Canadian Nurse* 89, 1993, pp. 21–4.

17 L. Gelberg, L.S. Linn, S.A. Mayer-Oakes, "Differences in health status between older and younger homeless adults." *Journal of the American Geriatrics Society* 38, 1990, pp. 1220–29; L. Gelberg, L.S. Linn, "Assessing the physical health of homeless adults," *Journal of the American Medical Association* 262, 1989, pp. 1973–79.

18 S.W. Hwang, A.L. Bugeja, "Barriers to appropriate diabetes management among homeless people in Toronto," *Canadian Medical Association Journal* 163(2), 2000, pp.161–65.

19 J. Lee, S. Gaetz, F. Goettler. "The oral health of Toronto's street youth," *Journal of the Canadian Dental Association* 60, 1994, pp. 545–48; P. Pizem, P. Massicotte, J.R. Vincent, R.Y. Barolet, "The state of oral and dental health of the homeless and vagrant population of Montreal." *Journal of the Canadian Dental Association* 60, 1994, pp. 1061–65.

20 J.A. Moy, M.R. Sanchez, "The cutaneous manifestations of violence and poverty," *Archives of Dermatology* 128, 1992, pp. 829–39.

21 K. Wrenn, "Foot problems in homeless persons," *Annals of Internal Medicine* 113, 1990, pp. 567–9; K. Wrenn, "Immersion foot: A problem of the homeless in the 1990s," *Archives of Internal Medicine* 151, 1991, pp. 785–8.

22 Prevention and control of tuberculosis among homeless persons. Recommendations of the Advisory Council for the Elimination of Tuberculosis. *Morbidity and Mortality Weekly Report* 41, 1992, pp. 13–23; C.M. Nolan, A.M. Elarth, H. Barr, A.M. Saeed, D.R. Risser, "An outbreak of tuberculosis in a shelter for homeless men: A description of its evolution and control," *American Review of Respiratory Disorders* 143, 1991, pp. 257–61.

23 P.F. Barnes, H. el-Hajj, S. Preston-Martin, M.D. Cave, B.E. Jones, M. Otaya, et al., "Transmission of tuberculosis among the urban homeless," *Journal of the American Medical Association* 275, 1996, pp. 305–7; L. Yuan, A.E. Simor, L. Louie, S. Pollock,

R. Gould, F. Jamieson, "Tuberculosis clusters among the homeless in Toronto, Canada," 37th Interscience Conference on Antimicrobial Agents and Chemotherapy, Sept 28–October 1, 1997, Toronto.

24 A. Pablos-Mendez, C.A. Knirsch, R.G. Barr, B.H. Lerner, T.R. Frieden, "Nonadherence in tuberculosis treatment: Predictors and consequences in New York City." *American Journal of Medicine* 102, 1997, pp.164–70.

25 N.E. MacDonald, W.A. Fisher, G.A. Wells, J.A. Doherty, W.R. Bowie, "Canadian street youth: Correlates of sexual risk-taking activity," *Pediatric Infectious Disease Journal* 13, 1994, pp. 690–97.

26 L. Manzon, M. Rosario, M.L. Rekart, "HIV seroprevalence among street involved Canadians in Vancouver," *AIDS Education and Prevention* Fall 1992 (suppl.), pp. 86–89.

27 E.E. Wang, S. King, E. Goldberg, B. Bock, R. Milner, S. Read, "Hepatitis B and human immunodeficiency virus infection in street youths in Toronto," *Canadian Pediatric Infectious Disease Journal* 10, 1991, pp. 130–33.

28 Mental Health Policy Research Group, *Mental Illness and Pathways into Homelessness: Proceedings and Recommendations.* Toronto: Canadian Mental Health Association, 1998.

29 J.M. Greene, C.L. Ringwalt, "Pregnancy among three national samples of runaway and homeless youth," *Journal of Adolescent Health* 23, 1998, pp. 370–77.

30 Crowe and Hardill, op. cit; Hwang, "Mortality among men."

31 M. Tanaka, S. Tokudome. "Accidental hypothermia and death from cold in urban areas," *International Journal of Biometeorology* 34, 1991, pp. 242–6.

32 P.J. Fischer, W.R. Breakey, "The epidemiology of alcohol, drug, and mental disorders among homeless persons," *American Psychology* 46, 1991, pp. 1115–28.

33 Ibid; A.F. Lehman, D.S. Cordray, "Prevalence of alcohol, drug, and mental disorders among the homeless," *Contemporary Drug Problems* 20, 1993, pp. 355–83; R.G. Smart, E.M. Adlaf, "Substance use and problems among Toronto street youth," *British Journal of Addiction* 86, 1991, pp. 999–1010.

34 D.K. Padgett, E.L. Struening, H. Andrews, "Factors affecting the use of medical, mental health, alcohol, and drug treatment services by homeless adults," *Medical Care* 28, 1990, pp. 805–21; D.K. Padgett, E.L. Struening, H. Andrews, J. Pittman, "Predictors of emergency room use by homeless adults in New York City: The influence of predisposing, enabling and need factors," *Society Science and Medicine* 41, 1995, pp. 547–56.

35 J.V. Martell, R.S. Seitz, J.K. Harada, J. Kobayashi, V.K. Sasaki, C. Wong, "Hospitalization in an urban homeless population: the Honolulu Urban Homeless Project," *Annals of Internal Medicine* 116, 1992, pp. 299–303; S.A. Salit, E.M. Kuhn, A.J. Hartz, J.M. Vu, A.L. Mosso, "Hospitalization costs associated with homelessness in New York City," *New England Journal of Medicine* 338, 1998, pp. 1734–40.

36 J. Goetcheus, M.A. Gleason, D. Sarson, T. Bennett, P.B. Wolfe, "Convalescence: for those without a home — developing respite services in protected environments," in P.W. Brickner, L.K. Scharer, B.A. Conanan, M. Savarese, B.C. Scanlan, editors,

Under the Safety Net: The Health and Social Welfare of the Homeless in the United States, New York: WW Norton & Co., 1990, pp. 169–83.

37 L.R. Stark, "Barriers to health care for homeless people," in R.I. Jahiel, ed., *Homelessness: A Prevention-Oriented Approach*, Baltimore: Johns Hopkins U. Press, 1992, pp. 151–64.

38 Crowe and Hardill, op. cit.

39 S.W. Hwang, P.M. Windrim, T.J. Svoboda, W.F. Sullivan, "Physician payment for the care of homeless perople," *Canadian Medical Association Journal* 163(2), 2000, pp. 170–71; S.W. Hwang, J.L. Gottlieb, "Drug access among homeless men in Toronto," *Canadian Medical Association Journal* 160(7), 1999, p. 1021.

40 Hwang and Bugeja, "Barriers to appropriate diabetes management."

41 H.R. Lamb, L.L. Bachrach, F.I. Kass, *Treating the Homeless Mentally Ill: A Report of the Task Force on the Homeless Mentally Ill*. Washington: American Psychiatric Association, 1992; D. Bhugra, *Homelessness and Mental Health*. New York: Cambridge University Press, 1996.

42 A.F. Lehman, L.B. Dixon, E. Kernan, B.R. DeForge, L.T. Postrado, "A randomized trial of assertive community treatment for homeless persons with severe mental illness," *Archives of General Psychiatry* 54, 1997, pp. 1038–43; D.A. Wasylenki, P.N. Goering, D. Lemire, S. Lindsey, W. Lancee, "The hostel outreach program: assertive case management for homeless mentally ill persons," *Hospital and Community Psychiatry* 44, 1993, pp. 848–53.

Chapter 11

How Did We Get Here? The Evolution of Canada's "Exclusionary" Housing System

J. DAVID HULCHANSKI

Governments have many choices when it comes to providing housing assistance for low-income households. These fall into two general categories: (1) cash assistance to individual households to help them pay for housing; and (2) construction subsidies that bring down the monthly cost of housing. Many Western nations offer both: they provide cash transfers to help low-income households pay their rent and fund a large non-market social housing sector.

Over the past five decades, the Canadian government has succeeded in creating a sustainable homeownership sector, using a combination of regulations, a mortgage insurance system, and tax benefits. Very little private-sector rental housing is being built and, since 1993, very little new social housing (non-market housing that is owned and managed by government, non-profits, or non-equity cooperatives) has been created. About 5 percent of Canada's households live in non-market social housing. This compares with 40 percent in the Netherlands, 22 percent in the United Kingdom, 15 percent in France and Germany, and about 2 percent in the United States.[1]

The Canadian government's role in helping lower-income Canadians obtain adequate and appropriate housing by providing social housing can be divided into four distinct periods.

1. The first is the period up to 1964 in which the government avoided any significant involvement.
2. The second was a two-decade-long commitment to building a non-market social housing sector as part of a broader social safety net, which ended in 1984.

3. The third was a decade-long decline in the allocation of new federal money for housing assistance, ending with a full withdrawal in 1993.
4. The fourth period, from 1994 to the present, is much like the first – no significant federal involvement. This period also saw a devolution to the provinces of most federally assisted housing built during the previous periods, and, like the first period, a small "affordable housing" program that seems to produce more press releases than housing units.

Period 1, 1949–63: Leave it to the Market and Hope for the Best

Canada was one of the last major Western nations to introduce a social housing supply program.[2] The United States began building public housing in the 1930s. Canadian legislation enabling federal subsidies for public housing was adopted in 1938 but never implemented. Only in 1949 was the *National Housing Act* (NHA) amended and a public housing supply program launched. However, between 1949 and 1963, only 12,000 public housing units were built (an average of 850 units a year).

Why so few units? Why did the government even bother to administer such a small program? John Bacher's history of Canadian housing policy provides the answer: "The low levels of social housing built under the 1949 NHA amendments were not the product of incompetence but of the intentions of the civil servants and ministers who had drafted the legislation."[3]

The 1949 NHA amendments were, in large part, a taxpayer-funded public relations campaign aimed at addressing criticism of the federal government's inaction on meeting severe rental housing needs among low-income households. "CMHC [Canada Mortgage and Housing Corporation] took the attitude that the passage of [the legislation] had achieved the intended purpose of reducing the political vulnerabilities of the federal government with regard to low-income housing."[4]

Thus, during the period leading up to 1964, there was no significant federal role in social housing.

Period 2, 1964–84: Build an Inclusive Housing System by Addressing the Social Need for Housing

The 1964 amendments to the NHA finally implemented the recommendations of the housing studies of the 1930s and 1940s by creating a federally funded, municipally administered public housing program. The amendments allowed for a direct relationship between the federal government and provinces or municipalities. Most of the approximately 200,000 public (government-owned) housing units were built between 1964 and the mid-1970s.[5]

In 1973, the federal government introduced sweeping amendments to the NHA, including the establishment of an assisted homeownership program, a neighbourhood improvement program, a housing rehabilitation program, a municipal land assembly program, a native housing program, and a new non-profit and co-op housing program.

These programs were based on direct federal government relationships with non-profit and co-op housing groups and municipalities in the case of social housing supply, individual owners in the case of the housing rehabilitation program, and individual municipalities in the cases of the Neighbourhood Rehabilitation Program and the land assembly program. This funding approach sidestepped the provincial governments and their housing corporations, thereby increasing the visibility of the federal government in housing and urban affairs. (The minister responsible for the Ministry of State for Urban Affairs was also responsible for the Canada Mortgage and Housing Corporation and housing policy and programs.)

When the 1973 amendments to the NHA were announced, Ron Basford, the minister responsible for urban affairs, told the House of Commons: "When we talk ... about the subject of housing, we are talking about an elemental human need – the need for shelter, for physical and emotional comfort in that shelter." He went on to describe the rationale for the government's role in supplying low-cost housing:

> When we talk about people's basic needs – the requirements for survival – society and the government obviously have an obligation to ensure that these basic needs of shelter are met.
>
> I have already acknowledged this obligation in stating that good housing at reasonable cost is a social right of every citizen of this country. ... [This] must be our objective, our obligation, and our goal. The legislation which I am proposing to the House today is an expression of the government's policy, part of a broad plan, to try to make this right and this objective a reality.[6]

This inclusionary philosophy informed policy and program debates until the 1984 election of the Mulroney Conservative government.

Period 3, 1984–93: From a Small Federal Role in Housing, to No Role At All

The November 1984 "mini-budget" made a number of cuts in housing programs. Housing was identified as one of several expenditure areas that would receive further review.[7] A consultation paper on housing was released two months later.[8] It announced that new spending commitments on housing were not feasible due to "the budgetary constraint." Rather, "any new initiatives in housing can be taken only by redirecting funds allocated to existing expenditures or by making existing programs more effective and less costly."[9]

By the end of the year, the government announced its new housing policy in a 33-page booklet titled *A National Direction for Housing Solutions*. This policy document was based on a June 1985 report of a task force that had reviewed all spending areas. That report, called *Housing Programs in Search of Balance* was not publicly released until a year later. In that report,[10] the government stated that it considered the status quo inefficient and expensive:

> The record of current programs in meeting social housing needs is dismal. Because expensive, long-term supply programs have been used and programs have not been directed solely to those in need, there has been a minimal impact on resolving the housing problems of low income Canadians.

In order to save money and be more efficient, the report focused on better targeting of housing subsidies and a cheaper method of delivering subsidies. "Housing programs have benefited Canadians at all income levels," the report argued; it "is time to redress this imbalance, to favour those with the greatest need for assistance." A policy principle was asserted: social housing programs should "not be designed to benefit the general populace."[11]

This assertion was more ideological than factual. Social housing programs benefited a very small segment of low- and moderate-income renter households, mainly the elderly and families. Access to most social housing was means-tested. The 1973 NHA had permitted a slightly greater social mix in non-profit housing in order to produce more balanced and socially sustainable communities, rather than "projects" that housed only the most destitute. Targeting criteria were not raised, as they rarely are, in the analysis of subsidy programs for homeownership or private-sector rental housing.

The other concern was the long-term commitment involved in providing housing assistance for low-income households: "Supplying new social housing units is a costly form of assistance and results in long term subsidy commitments with little flexibility for new initiatives."[12]

Housing is indeed expensive and there is no magic formula for building adequate housing at below-market costs. The long-term commitment refers to the policy choice of financing the construction of social housing over a long period, rather than making a larger down payment at the beginning. The lack of flexibility refers to the fact that the only way out of these long-term commitments is politically difficult: evict the tenants and sell the housing.

The housing subsidy method that allows complete flexibility is a cash transfer to help households pay their rent. These transfers are called "shelter allowances" or "housing vouchers." They can be cut off at any time, the amount can be decreased or increased with ease, and they can be adjusted to keep up with actual housing costs, or not. They also have the political and ideological advantage of being "market conforming."

A policy of cash transfers means that government could avoid subsidizing non-market housing. Instead, the consumer in the private housing sector is subsidized, and he or she passes on the subsidy to the landlord. The private-sector housing lobby was a strong proponent of this approach and the Mulroney government was sensitive to their claim that non-market social housing was "unfair competition." The 1985 policy statement notes that:

> Non-profit and co-operative housing has made a significant contribution to the stock of rental housing. ... At the same time, this feature of the program has been criticized by private sector representatives who perceive the provision of subsidized market rent units as creating unfair competition. It has even been suggested that the program restricts private sector activity by reducing demands for market accommodation.[13]

No evidence was ever produced to support the claim that social housing supply restricts the market provision of housing. The report recommended a "shift in the balance" towards shelter allowances as "a more cost-effective social housing strategy."[14]

In the end, however, the Mulroney government agreed with the critics of shelter allowances. "It is not my intention to proceed with a shelter allowance program," announced Bill McKnight, the minister responsible for housing, in October 1985. He said the finance ministry's advisors had found that it would be yet another expensive entitlement program that would do little to diminish the nation's housing problems. "My reasons for not favouring a shelter allowance," McKnight explained to the 1985 meeting of the Canadian Real Estate Association, "include the considerable uncertainty about its cost, the fact that it would not add to the stock of housing available to low-income households in some market areas and that it would not deal with the housing problems faced by special need groups such as the elderly and the handicapped."

Instead, McKnight announced that his government was "committed to the continuation of non-profit and co-operative housing as a way of assisting those who cannot afford accommodation in the private market" and that he wanted to use the co-op housing sector "to foster security of tenure for moderate-income households who cannot afford access to homeownership." Even this commitment, however, could not withstand efforts to cut the budget deficit. With ever-diminishing financial support over the 10-year life of the government, Finance Minister Don Mazankowski finally ended all funding for new social housing in his 1993 budget. Though the Liberal Party won the national election later that year, the new Finance Minister, Paul Martin, implemented the termination of the social housing supply program. The supply of social housing fell from an annual level of about 25,000 new units in 1983 to zero following the 1993 termination of the federal program.

Period 4, 1993–Present: Leave It to the Market and Hope for the Best

There is an interesting parallel between the federal housing program in 1949 and the housing program announced in the 2001 federal budget. After many years during which the government had been subject to increasing criticism for not providing any new housing assistance for low-income households and homeless people, the 2001 federal budget included money for housing. However, the $680 million allocation for an affordable housing program is spread over five years – that is $136 million a year, distributed over a country with 11 million households, of which 10 percent to 15 percent face housing problems, in which tens of thousands of people are homeless.

The federal government hoped that the provinces would contribute an equal amount, allowing the new housing to assist lower-income households. Most provinces, with the exception of Quebec, refused to match fully the federal contributions. At least the federal government has something to talk about when it is challenged on what it is doing about the urban housing crisis, now and for the next five years. Bacher's assessment of the impact of the 1949–63 public housing program will likely apply to the program announced in 2001: "The legislation stabilized the basic thrust of federal policy simply to stimulate residential construction by disturbing the existing private market as little as possible."[15]

Given the failure of the private sector to supply new rental housing and the extent of homelessness across Canada, the only reasonable assessment is to view the initiative as damage control for the government. It is enough money to subsidize a steady stream of press releases, but not enough to make a difference. In other words, there has been no change in federal housing policy. We may see, a few years from now, the same effect that Bacher noticed in relation to the 1949 legislation: "that the passage of [the legislation] had achieved the intended purpose of reducing the political vulnerabilities of the federal government with regard to low-income housing."[16]

Along with the loss of a social housing supply program that once built 20,000 to 25,000 units per year, the change in federal funding for social assistance has had an equally devastating impact on the lives of poor and destitute households. The turning point for income assistance policy in Canada came in the 1995 federal budget. Until then, federal funding for social assistance was provided to the provinces through a designated transfer program called the Canada Assistance Plan (CAP). The CAP *Act* specified five clearly defined rights:

- the right to an adequate income;
- the right to income assistance when in need;
- the right to appeal welfare decisions;
- the right to claim welfare whatever one's province of origin;
- the right to welfare without forced participation in work or training programs.

The 1995 federal budget cut transfers to the provinces, eliminated the CAP, and rolled federal funding for social assistance, postsecondary education, and health into the new Canada Health and Social Transfer (CHST). With this action, the federal government understood that it was releasing provinces from the requirement to provide adequate assistance based on the defined rights in the CAP legislation, with the exception of the ban on discrimination on the basis of province of origin. Since 1995, most provinces have made significant changes to the nature and delivery of social assistance programs. In part as a result of these changes, the pool of households at risk of homelessness has increased, along with the number of people actually experiencing homelessness.

The value of welfare support also began to decline in the 1990s, as provinces did not adjust rates to reflect inflation or changes in housing costs. In addition, a number of provinces reduced the amount provided (for example, Ontario cut social assistance rates in October 1995 by 21 percent). The purchasing power of social assistance benefits is lower in 2001 than in 1986 and substantially lower than the peak amounts over the 15-year period. Table 1 provides a summary for the four largest provinces. The 2001 rates are 20 to 40 percent lower than the peak rates in these four provinces. Even if families on social assistance spend 50 percent of their benefits on rent (about $7,000 per year), this amounts to only $580 per month for rent. There are very few one-bedroom apartments – let alone larger apartments adequate for a family with children – available in the larger cities for that amount of money.

Table 1: Welfare Benefits in Four of the Largest Provinces, 1986 to 2001*

	1986	Peak (year)	2001	2001 as % of peak
Ontario	$17,060	$22,596 (1992)	$13,452	60%
Quebec	$15,573	$15,650 (1993)	$12,041	77%
Alberta	$19,690	$19,690 (1986)	$13,425	68%
British Columbia	$15,891	$17,368 (1994)	$13,534	78%

* For a couple with two children (in constant 2001 dollars).
Source: National Council of Welfare (2002), Welfare Incomes, 2000 and 2001, Ottawa, Table 5A.

What about the provincial and territorial role in social housing and related urban and social programs in the period since 1993? Most of their policies and program changes have not been helpful. It is important, however, to place provincial and territorial budget cuts in housing, social spending, and urban affairs in the context of the federal government's downloading of the deficit onto provincial taxpayers. Provinces can either raise taxes to make up for the cuts in federal transfer payments (creating the conditions for a taxpayer revolt and boosting the popularity of politicians who promise tax cuts) or they can pass on the cuts to groups that have no electoral clout.

Federal cash transfers to the provinces and territories have been falling since the early 1980s. The share of federal expenditures transferred to the provinces and territories ranged from 4 to 4.6 percent of GDP in the early and mid-1980s. Since 1996 it has ranged from 2.7 to 2.9 percent of GDP.[17] In short, huge amounts of money that were once transferred to provinces and territories were unilaterally withdrawn. The money had previously been used for health, education, and welfare programs. Some federal funding, particular for health care, has since been restored.

Another way of looking at these federal budget cuts is to examine the share of total budget revenues that federal cash transfers represent. In Ontario, for example, during the first period (1980–86), an average of 17 percent of provincial revenues came in the form of federal cash transfers. During the second period (1987–95), this had fallen to an annual average of 13.4 percent. By the third period (1996–2001), only 9.3 percent of Ontario's budget revenues came from federal cash transfers.[18]

In addition to the cuts to transfer payments, housing budget cuts (direct federal spending on housing, not transfer payments) now save the federal treasury about $1.5 billion a year. The approximately $2 billion of federal money now spent on housing (1 percent of total federal spending) pays for subsidies on about 550,000 social housing units built before the termination of the federal role in housing supply in 1993. Dismantling the social housing supply program meant that provinces and municipalities had to bear the indirect costs of inadequate housing and homelessness. These include the costs of physical and mental health care, emergency shelters and services, and policing.

Towards an Inclusionary Housing System

The policy and program changes over the past 20 years (periods 3 and 4) mean that the right to adequate housing, the right to an adequate standard of living, and even the right to live depend upon having enough money. For most of this century the Canadian government did not even try to have a coordinated urban strategy. The death in early February 1999 of "Al," a homeless man who was sleeping on a heating grate directly under the window of the office of Ontario Premier Mike Harris, along with the death later the same month of Lynn Bluecloud, a homeless woman who was five months pregnant, within sight of the Prime Minister's office window in Ottawa, dramatically underline the consequences of an exclusionary housing system.

During the 1970s, market conditions changed, making it unprofitable for the private sector to build unsubsidized rental apartments. Given that any long-term investment was risky because of dramatic fluctuations in inflation and interest rates, why would anyone invest in rental apartment buildings? Given that condominiums were now possible, and a developer could get an immediate return on investment once the units were sold, why would anyone build rental apartment buildings? Given that rental apartment developers had to compete for zoned building sites with condominium developers who were building for a higher-income group of consumers and therefore could always afford to pay more for the land, why would anyone build rental apartment buildings? Given that the gap between rich and poor, between homeowners and renters, continued to widen, why would anyone build for a group of consumers (renters) who could not afford the rent levels in new apartment buildings?

Given all these factors, there was indeed no good reason to build or invest in rental apartments; therefore, very few developers built rental housing. A market with a great deal of demand but very little supply is a market that has failed.

Since the mid-1970s, most new private-sector rental housing has been subsidized by a string of expensive subsidy programs. None of these programs helped create any low-rent housing. The only way to produce low-rent housing for people in serious need, and to keep the rents on those units low, is to subsidize construction and to protect this public investment by keeping the housing off the market (that is, in non-profit and non-equity co-op forms of ownership). There is nothing new in this observation. Humphrey Carver wrote in 1948 that there "is not much value debating the fact that, to date, there is no known method of providing low-rental housing except through public agencies supported by some kind of contribution from public revenue."[19]

The housing recommendations of the Prime Minister's Caucus Task Force on Urban Issues (Table 2) call for a return to the policies of Period 2: a national housing program that recognizes the nature of the "ultimate housing problem" – the supply of low-rent housing. The minister responsible for the Canada Mortgage and Housing Corporation when the Task Force report was issued, David Collenette, went on record in support of both an active federal role in urban issues and the direct provision of social housing. In an August 2002 speech he suggested it might be time for the federal government to get back into the social housing field. According to the minister, "the private sector is not going to voluntarily build low-cost housing – which is what we need in communities in this country."[20]

A week later, A. Charles Baillie, the Chairman and CEO of TD Bank Financial Group, called for a return to the provision of social housing at a major conference on Canada's future:

Our cities – once a source of national pride – are deteriorating from a lack of infrastructure investment and an increase in poverty and homelessness. The construction of rent-assisted housing units has dropped from about 6,000 per year in Ontario to almost zero. ... No one disputes, for example, that there is a dire lack of social housing in our cities, but the problem will not be solved while each level of government views it as another's responsibility.[21]

Table 2: Housing Recommendations of the Task Force on Urban Issues, 2002

The Task Force recommends that the Government of Canada:
14. Establish a National Affordable Housing Program that could include:
Strengthening the mandate of Canada Mortgage and Housing Corporation to develop a National Affordable Housing Program in collaboration with all orders of government, and housing providers;
Building on existing federal housing programs;
Changes to CMHC mortgage underwriting criteria to allow a more customized and flexible system;
Providing additional resources and flexibility in the RRAP [Rental Rehabilitation Assistance Program] to rehabilitate existing properties;
Examining the federal tax environment related to rental housing and creating appropriate incentives;
Establishing grants against the cost of CMHC mortgage insurance;
Providing targeted mortgage insurance for brownfield redevelopment in areas where there is a shortage of affordable housing;
Facilitating agreements with municipalities to transfer small tracts of surplus land, owned by the Canada Lands Company, to community groups; and
Offering grants to community housing groups to support the restoration and conversion of heritage properties for affordable housing.
15. Extend the Supporting Communities Partnership Initiative (SCPI) beyond three years in order to meet its objectives to eliminate homelessness.

Source: Sgro, 2002: 20.

The cost of completing Canada's housing system – creating one that is inclusive rather than exclusive – is not all that expensive, given Canada's wealth and the federal budget surpluses over the recent five years. The core of such an initiative is the provision of more social housing. The Prime Minister's Task Force, the Federation of Canadian Municipalities,

the National Housing and Homelessness Network, and other organizations all recognize that non-market social housing must be built as it
was before. The track record of subsidized private rental construction is
not a good one. Few of the subsidies helped low-income tenants and,
when they did, it was only for a short period or in poor-quality buildings. Such programs are not socially or fiscally sustainable. They are not
long-term investments that directly help those most in need.

Canada spends about 1 percent of its budget, close to $2 billion, on
programs and subsidies for all social housing (about half a million units).
This non-market housing, most of it built with direct federal subsidies,
accommodates 5 percent of all Canadian households. Phasing in a social
housing supply program of about 20,000 to 25,000 units a year – the
level provided during the early 1980s – together with related housing
programs, would mean phasing in over the coming decade another 1
percent of the federal budget for housing.

What about the provincial role in housing? Provinces should cost-share
some of these programs. In the area of social assistance, provinces can help
with housing affordability by maintaining social assistance and disability
rates, including their housing component, at realistic levels (i.e., with periodic cost of living adjustments). This would help reduce the number of
people at risk of homelessness. One possible sharing of costs between the
federal government and the provincial and territorial governments relates
to the distinction between the "bricks and mortar" subsidies for the construction and rehabilitation of housing, and the subsidies to people – the
income-tested rent supplements. The federal government could supply
the former, the provinces and territories the latter.

Both levels of government, however, receive their revenue from the
same taxpayers. Government actions and inaction have contributed to
the rental housing crisis and homelessness-making processes that
emerged in the 1980s. Over the next decade a coordinated and properly
funded effort can address the most severe failures of Canada's housing
system. The federal government should lead the way and should do so
as part of a comprehensive urban strategy. The solution today is the
same as it was when Carver wrote *Houses for Canadians* in 1948.

> It will be necessary to supplement the supply of housing. Under the social
> and economic conditions characteristic of a society such as ours, the
> recourse to public housing and the operation of rental subsidies seems to
> be an expedient which cannot be avoided if the national housing program
> is to be maintained.[22]

In the end, the debate over whether and how to address housing need and homelessness comes down to a set of ethical questions. Will those in a position to make the necessary decisions do so? This is a political problem. There is no scientific or objective way to arrive at an answer about a political problem. That said, the nature of the problem is now well understood. Moreover, the package of solutions are not complicated or even very expensive for a country with Canada's wealth.

A focus on the human right to adequate housing for all Canadians, which was the basis of housing policy from the mid-1960s to the mid-1980s, is essential for the promotion of sustainable urban development, human development and social cohesion. As Article 22 of the Universal Declaration of Human Rights asserts, everyone is entitled to "the economic, social and cultural rights indispensable for his dignity and the free development of his personality." Human poverty is a denial of basic human rights. Human development, the process of enlarging people's choices, requires respect for and leads to the further realization of all human rights – economic, social, cultural, civil, and political. Individual and community well-being are intertwined, and human development requires strong social cohesion and equitable distribution of the benefits of progress to avoid tension between the two.

In a highly urbanized country such as Canada, the quality of city life, and the efficiency of cities as places to live and work, depend on the degree to which Canada has fair and inclusive societal institutions and polices. This has always been the core issue: the degree to which public policy addresses the needs of *all* Canadians. A *sustainable* housing policy must be one that attempts to move in the direction of creating a socially just housing system.[23]

Of course, this is easy to say. Implementation is hampered by the various interests that come into conflict in a society in which housing and urban land are market commodities. Changes to policies and programs, even minor adjustments to regulations, can provide dramatically different financial benefits to different groups. This is why there are homeless-making processes at work in Canada's housing system. Policies, programs, regulations, and the tax system have been allowed to evolve in a fashion that produces hardship for many in the rental housing sector of the housing system. There is no conflict-free consensus in the area of urban housing policy. The history of the last fifty years proves this point beyond a shadow of a doubt.

This chapter is drawn from a longer paper published by the Canadian Policy Research Networks (CPRN), Housing Policy for Tomorrow's Cities, December 2002 (www.cprn.com).

J. David Hulchanski *is director of the Centre for Urban and Community Studies. His research and teaching focuses on housing policy, social welfare, community development, and human rights. In the 1980s he was a professor in the School of Community and Regional Planning at the University of British Columbia and Director of the UBC Centre for Human Settlements. He has a M.Sc. and Ph.D. in urban planning and is a member of the Canadian Institute of Planners. In 1997 he was appointed to the only endowed chair in housing studies in North America, the Dr. Chow Yei Ching Chair in Housing.*

Endnotes

1 A.J.M. Freeman, A.E. Holmans, and C.M.E. Whitehead. 1996. "Is the UK Different? International Comparisons of Tenure Patterns." London: Council of Mortgage Lenders, a study carried out by the Property Research Unit of Cambridge University.

2 John C. Bacher, *Keeping to the Marketplace: The Evolution of Canadian Housing Policy.* Montreal: McGill-Queen's University Press, 1993.

3 Bacher, *Keeping to the Marketplace*, p. 183.

4 Bacher, *Keeping to the Marketplace*, p. 185.

5 Albert Rose, *Canadian Housing Policies, 1935–1980.* Toronto: Butterworths, 1980.

6 Canada, *House of Commons Debates*, March 15, 1973, p. 2257.

7 Canada, Department of Finance, *A New Direction for Canada: An Agenda for Economic Renewal.* Ottawa, November 1984.

8 Canada Mortgage and Housing Corporation, *Consultation Paper on Housing.* Ottawa, 1985, p. 4.

9 Ibid.

10 Canada, Task Force on Program Review, *Housing Programs in Search of Balance.* Ottawa, June 1985, p. 39.

11 Canada, Task Force on Program Review, *Housing Programs*, pp. 9–11.

12 Canada, Task Force on Program Review, *Housing Programs*, p. 9.

13 Canada Mortgage and Housing Corporation, 1985, *A National Direction for Housing Solutions.* Ottawa, p. 46.

14 Canada, Task Force on Program Review, *Housing Programs*, p. 9.

15 Bacher, *Keeping to the Marketplace*, p. 210.

16 Bacher, *Keeping to the Marketplace*, p. 185.

17 Canada, Department of Finance, Fiscal Reference Tables, September 2001.

18 Ibid.

19 Humphrey Carver, *Houses for Canadians.* Toronto: University of Toronto Press, 1948, p. 125.
20 Quoted in Chase, Steven, "Collenette waxes 'radical' on city funding." *Globe and Mail*, August 12, 2002.
21 A. Charles Baillie, "Seizing the Moment: Creating Canada's Future." Toronto Dominion Bank. CAN>WIN 2002 Conference, Toronto, Aug. 20, 2002 (www.td.com/communicate/speeches/20aug02.html).
22 Carver, *Houses for Canadians*, p. 124.
23 Peter Marcuse, "Sustainability is Not Enough." *Environment and Urbanization*, vol. 10, no. 2 (1998), pp. 103–111.

Chapter 12

Where Are We Going? Recent Federal and Provincial Housing Policy

MICHAEL SHAPCOTT

The 1990s was a lost decade for affordable housing funding, policies, and programs in Canada. The federal government, which started major cuts to housing programs in 1984, cancelled all funding for new social housing in 1993. Most provinces followed suit. As well, many senior governments cut social spending – including cuts to income assistance programs – and held down the minimum wage, depressing the household incomes of low-, moderate-, and even middle-income Canadians.

These policies helped to generate the nationwide supply and affordability housing crisis and homelessness disaster that grew worse in the late 1990s and into the early 21st century.

Meanwhile, since the early 1970s the private sector had, for the most part, shifted its investment away from the construction of new affordable rental housing. By the 1990s, there were few new private rental units being built. In many parts of the country, the number of private units lost to demolition and conversion outpaced new construction.

The not-for-profit sector (co-op and community-based non-profit housing providers) was unable to build new units after the mid-1990s in most parts of the country, because government support had evaporated. Private funders were unwilling to lend to non-market housing developers. The number of new social housing units being built dropped to almost zero by the end of the 1990s.

The era from 1990 to 2003 also coincided with the rise of Paul Martin. In 1990, as Liberal housing critic, he had been a strong champion for increased government investment in social housing. From 1993 to 2000, as federal finance minister, Martin not only failed to fulfil his promise to renew spending, but presided over huge cuts in social spending. In 2003, as prime minister, Martin dropped the junior housing minister post from his first cabinet – sending an ominous signal to housing advocates.

That same period also saw a rise in housing advocacy. Community-based groups formed or were strengthened throughout the country. In 1999, they came together to create the National Housing and Homelessness Network. By 2000, housing advocates were creating new partnerships with municipalities, faith groups, unions, community organizations, and even business groups.

Some local and national private-sector groups, such as the Toronto Board of Trade and the TD Bank Financial Group, began to speak out about the housing crisis, calling for renewed government investment.

In 1998, the Toronto Disaster Relief Committee (TDRC), a community-based housing and homeless advocacy group, launched its Disaster Declaration and One Percent Solution campaigns. The work of the TDRC, along with partners at the local and national level, started the political momentum towards a patchwork of funding and programs.

Public opinion began to focus on the nationwide housing crisis and homelessness disaster in the late 1990s. National and regional opinion polls showed that a significant majority of Canadians wanted their governments to take action, even if it meant raising taxes. Effective political pressure convinced the federal government in 1999, 2001, and 2003 to make the first, tentative steps towards a new national housing strategy.

But those hard-won gains were not able to ease the crisis, partly because federal, provincial, and territorial governments generally failed to meet even the limited promises they made, and mostly because those commitments fell far short of the growing need.

The Growing Crisis

The election of the Mulroney Conservatives in 1984 heralded the first in a decade-long series of cuts to federal housing programs. Total spending was cut by $1.8 billion up to 1993, when all new spending on social housing programs was eliminated.[1]

While in opposition, the Liberals promised to restore funding for housing – most famously in a national Liberal housing task force report co-authored by Paul Martin.[2] But they promptly forgot those commitments when they were elected to government in fall 1993. In fact, the Liberals continued to cut housing and other social spending. Despite

Housing Spending by Canada, Provinces, Territories, 1993–2000

	1993–1994 ($ millions)	1999–2000 ($ millions)	Dollar change	Percent change
Newfoundland	18.1	8.0	−10.1	−55.8
Prince Edward Island	2.3	3.2	+0.9	+39.1
Nova Scotia	24.2	14.3	−9.9	−40.9
New Brunswick	32.7	31.8	−0.9	−2.8
Quebec	286.3	288.3	+2	+0.7
Ontario	1,140.9	837.1	−303.8	−26.6
Manitoba	46.6	43.2	−3.4	−7.3
Saskatchewan	43.1	40.5	−2.6	−6.0
Alberta	287.3	93.2	−194.1	−67.6
British Columbia	83.4	90.9	+7.5	+9.0
NWT / Nunavut	69.7	114.4	+44.7	+64.1
Yukon	4.9	11.1	+6.2	+126.5
Total: provinces, territories	2,039.5	1,576.0	−463.5	−22.7
Canada (CMHC)	1,944.9	1,927.9	−17	−0.9
Total – all Canada	3,984.4	3,503.9	−480.5	−12.1

Source: Canada Mortgage and Housing Corporation, 2001

Canada's growing population, starting in 1995, the Organisation for Economic Co-operation and Development reported a net decrease in social spending in Canada.[3]

The federal government's own Finance Department has confirmed the big spending cuts of the 1990s, boasting in its November 2003 economic and fiscal update that "federal program expenses-to-GDP ratio has declined significantly, from 15.7 per cent in 1993–94 to 11.5 per cent in 2002–03. This decline is largely attributable to the expenditure reduction initiatives, announced in the 1995 and 1996 budgets, aimed at eliminating the deficit."[4]

Seven of Canada's ten provinces also cut housing spending during the 1990s. In dollar terms, the biggest cuts came under Conservative governments in the two richest provinces – Ontario and Alberta – which together cut $497.9 million in the seven years before 2000. The provincial spending cuts continued into the new millennium, not just in Ontario (which downloaded its provincial housing programs to municipalities in 1998) and Alberta (which cancelled funding for seniors' supportive housing in 2002). The recent election of Liberal governments in Quebec and British Columbia also led to erosion of provincial social housing programs. In 1996, Finance Minister Paul Martin announced plans to transfer federal social housing programs to provinces and territories. The scheme not only meant that the federal government was abandoning a national role in affordable housing, but the transfer deals signed with provinces and territories locked in an annual cut to housing spending.

A study by the Canadian Housing and Renewal Association in 2003 shows the dramatic impact of the Martin decision over the next few decades. The federal government will drop from supporting about 600,000 social housing units in 1998 at a cost of about $1.7 billion to zero dollars and zero units by 2040.

Federal social housing spending, 1998 to 2040

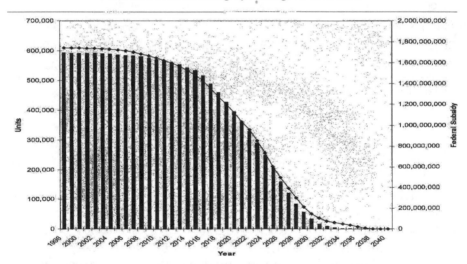

Source: Canadian Housing and Renewal Association, 2003

Martin's 1996 decision to abandon a federal role in social housing is unprecedented among developed countries. Even the United States, with its fierce commitment to private-sector solutions, maintains a national housing program (though it is under constant attack by the Bush administration, which is anxious to make additional cuts to pay for its agenda of increased military spending and tax cuts).

In 1998, the *National Housing Act* was amended as part of a government-wide initiative launched by Martin to "commercialize" many government functions. Canada Mortgage and Housing Corporation (CMHC), the national housing agency created at the end of the Second World War to help low- and moderate-income Canadians secure a good home, faced a new, commercial mandate. Its mortgage insurance fund (a key tool used by social housing providers to secure private financing) was turned into a revenue-generator.

CMHC has been spectacularly successful in making money for the government. In 2002, the agency reported a net income after taxes of $544 million, a sizable increase from the $160 million reported in 1998.[5] The cost has been higher mortgage insurance premiums, which have raised a big financial hurdle for community-based non-profit housing providers.

Government cuts to housing funding and programs created only half of the pain suffered by renter households in Canada. Until 1996, the federal government provided provinces and territories with three main pools of social funds: the Canada Assistance Plan, education support, and health insurance and medical care.

In 1992–93, the federal government gave the provinces and territories $17.9 billion in social spending. By 1995, after three full years with Paul Martin as finance minister, the federal payment to provinces had been cut by $1.2 billion to $16.6 billion. Then Martin introduced the Canada Health and Social Transfer (which combined health, education, and social payments to the provinces and territories) in 1995. In 1996–97, the CHST was $14.9 billion – a further cut of $1.8 billion. And other financial adjustments that year cost the provinces and territories another social spending cut of $153 million.[6]

Martin's spending cuts were so successful that, by the end of the 1990s, the federal government was facing record surpluses. In his last budget as finance minister, Martin decided to turn those surpluses into a multi-year tax cut.

Meanwhile, the cuts to social spending gave the green light to provincial governments, such as the Conservatives under Mike Harris in Ontario, to make their own cuts to welfare and other social spending.

By 2003, federal finance minister John Manley asked the rhetorical question: "Who thought we would have been able to implement a five-year $100-billion tax cut plan, amounting to the largest cuts in Canada's history?"[7]

The $100 billion in tax cuts from 2000 was on top of an accumulated $150 billion in tax cuts already made by Martin and by the Mulroney government before him. A study by the Canadian Centre for Policy Alternatives in 2002 estimated that 64% of the benefits of those $250 billion in tax cuts went to the highest-income earners.[8]

Plenty of money for tax cuts for the wealthy, but no money for desperately needed affordable housing for low- and moderate-income households.

The Affordability Crisis

Even without the supply crisis caused by the withdrawal of the government and private sectors from new affordable rental construction, stagnant and declining renter household incomes ensured that the affordability crisis would get worse each year. Average rents increased in most parts of Canada at or above the rate of inflation in the 1990s and into 2004, which meant that the existing rental housing stock was getting less affordable every year. Rising rents led to economic evictions in Ontario and elsewhere.

Low-, moderate-, and middle-income tenants have literally been priced out of the private rental market. In 2002, rents in Toronto "eclipsed price-sensitive thresholds," according to an official analysis by the national housing agency.[9] Growing rental vacancies in a handful of areas in 2003 came at the same time that a record number of households were desperate for affordable housing. Tenants simply could not afford the rents set by the market and were forced to double or triple up in substandard units, or – in increasing numbers – to take refuge in shelters for the homeless.

In 2003, Canada Mortgage and Housing Corporation reported 11,484 vacant rental units in the Toronto Census Metropolitan Area (which includes the city and the surrounding suburban regions). At the same time, there were more than 100,000 households on the social housing waiting lists in the greater Toronto area.

The housing supply and affordability crisis triggered a huge increase in homelessness across Canada in the 1990s and early 21st century. A cross-Canada homelessness survey by the National Housing and Homelessness Network in 2001 reported: "Most experts agree that at least 250,000 people will experience homelessness during the course of a year. A comparison of hostels in just seven Canadian cities shows the number of bed nights occupied by homeless people over the course of the year doubled from 1.4 million in 1987 to 2.4 million in 1999."[10]

The survey revealed overcrowded shelters across the country, people forced to sleep on mats on the floors, a growing number of people turned away because there was no room, deteriorating health conditions in hostels, and significantly higher-than-normal death rates among homeless people. The biggest increase in homelessness in most parts of the country was among families and children, and the chief culprit was the affordable housing crisis.

Private-sector Salvation?

As federal and provincial governments cut housing and social programs, they hoped that the private sector would step in. The strongest proponent of private-sector salvation was Ontario's Mike Harris, whose Conservative Party governed the province from 1995 until 2003.

Harris's first housing minister, Al Leach, confidently predicted that his government's pro-private market housing policies would generate tens of thousands of new units. The province cancelled 17,000 units of co-op and non-profit housing, gutted rent regulation laws, and offered a package of tax and grant subsidies to private developers.

Private investment in rental housing dropped from more than 20,000 new units annually in the early 1970s to less than 2,000 units annually in the late 1990s.[11] Private-sector lobbyists and right-wing think-tanks blamed the drop on rent regulation, but the province's first rent control laws had been introduced in 1975 – well after investors had already shifted their development dollars to shopping malls and condominiums.

Stagnant and declining renter household income meant that tenants couldn't afford the rents that private landlords needed to charge to cover the cost of new development, plus earn a reasonable return on investment. Even the limited amount of new private construction in the late 1990s and early part of the 2000s was almost entirely at the upper end of the rent scale.

In the mid to late 1990s, private investors did find a profitable niche in the rental market. Real estate investment trusts bought up older rental buildings with moderate rents, then, taking advantage of lax rent regulation laws in most provinces, forced up rents to ensure a big return to their investors. One such trust, called ResREIT, boasted that it was able to drive up rents 22% and 37% over a couple of years on properties that it had bought.[12]

The Ontario government tried to sell its private-sector mantra by dressing up the old "trickle-down" theory in new clothing. According to the province's rental housing supply advisory group, "even rental development at the high end increases affordability, because it adds to the overall stock, putting downward pressure on rents and freeing up more affordable units as higher income tenants move into the new supply."[13]

This process, called "filtering," didn't work in Ontario. Instead of the confident promise of thousands of new private rental units, the province experienced a loss of at least 45,000 private rental units from 1995 to 2002, along with a further loss of 23,300 social housing units,[14] at a time when the province's growing population was increasing the need for new affordable rental units.

Jeanne M. Wolfe, professor of planning at McGill University, wrote in 1998:

> Responsibility for social housing has been devoluted from the federal government to the provincial and territorial governments, who in turn shift administration and management to regional and municipal agencies. And while the proportion of needy families is increasing, the deficit-minded Federal government only maintains its financial commitments to existing projects with no new funds presently available. Market solutions are being promoted by both the public and private sectors through a wide range of activities. The result is no single housing policy, but a patchwork of provincial and local initiatives ... However, it is only in Canada that the national government has, except for CMHC loans, withdrawn from the social housing field. The rush to get out of the responsibility for managing existing projects and building new, low-income housing has taken advocates by surprise. It was never imagined that a system that had taken 50 years to build up could be dismantled so rapidly. Social housing policy in Canada now consists of a checker-board of 12 provincial and territorial policies, and innumerable local policies. It is truly post-modern.[15]

The Community Mobilizes

As the nationwide affordable housing crisis and homelessness disaster grew worse in the 1990s, community-based groups began to mobilize in various parts of the country.

The Toronto Disaster Relief Committee (TDRC) was created by a group of homeless people and advocates in the summer of 1998. Their goal was to expose the homelessness disaster and call for a comprehensive solution. In October 1998, TDRC launched its Disaster Declaration campaign, which called on governments across the country to declare homelessness a "national disaster." Advocates argued that homelessness qualified as a disaster in the same way that ice storms, floods, forest fires, and other natural events triggered disaster relief legislation and funding. The TDRC's State of Emergency Declaration read:

> We call on all levels of government to declare homelessness a national disaster requiring emergency humanitarian relief. We urge that they immediately develop and implement a National Homelessness Relief and Prevention Strategy using disaster relief funds both to provide the homeless with immediate health protection and housing and to prevent further homelessness.[16]

The Disaster Declaration was almost immediately adopted by Toronto's City Council, and the campaign quickly went national. By late November, the Big City Mayors' Caucus of the Federation of Canadian Municipalities (FCM) adopted the declaration. The FCM, which represents thousands of local governments, set up a National Housing Policy Options Team at its April 1999 annual meeting.

The TDRC coupled the Disaster Declaration with its call for the One Percent Solution. In the early 1990s, federal, provincial, territorial, and municipal governments spent about 1% of their overall budgets on housing and related services. The TDRC called for governments to double that amount – spend another one percent.

The One Percent Solution would require the federal government to spend an additional $2 billion annually. Provinces and territories would be required to match that amount. The new money would create a funding envelope to build new affordable housing, to provide improved income assistance to address housing affordability, and to provide housing-related support services where required.[17]

Homelessness became part of the Toronto political agenda during the 1997 municipal election campaign when Mel Lastman, a candidate for mayor of the newly amalgamated "mega-city" of Toronto, confidently pronounced that there were no homeless people in the suburban municipality where he had been mayor for many years. That same night, a homeless woman was found dead in Lastman's North York.

Newly elected Mayor Lastman created the Mayor's Homelessness Action Task Force in January 1998, and appointed the head of the Toronto United Way, Anne Golden, as chair. Over the next year, the Mayor's Task Force prepared a detailed report that was released in January 1999.

Called *Taking Responsibility for Homelessness: An Action Plan for Toronto*, the report set out 105 detailed recommendations for action.[18]

Many task force reports tend to fade quickly, so Anne Golden proposed that her report be the centrepiece of a national symposium on housing and homelessness co-sponsored by the City of Toronto and the Federation of Canadian Municipalities. Municipal delegations were invited from across the country. Conference planners accepted the suggestion from housing advocates that half of the delegates be homeless people, tenants, and community advocates.

The homeless symposium in March 1999 brought together hundreds of politicians, housing officials, and advocates. Two days before the event, the federal government appointed Labour Minister Claudette Bradshaw, a former social agency director, as federal coordinator for homelessness. Her first public appearance was at the Toronto symposium, but she had no new funding and no new programs to announce.

Community advocates organized during the forum and agreed to create the National Housing and Homelessness Network. They convinced the symposium to adopt both the Disaster Declaration and the One Percent Solution. The 1999 event marked the start of a new national partnership between advocates and municipalities.

Minister Bradshaw went on a national tour during the summer of 1999. Everywhere she went, she heard about growing homelessness and the need for a new national housing strategy. In fall 1999, the federal government announced a modest increase in funding for its Residential Rehabilitation Assistance Program that would allow substandard and abandoned buildings to be converted to affordable housing.

The National Homelessness Strategy

But the breakthrough came in December 1999, when Minister Bradshaw announced the federal homelessness strategy, including the Supporting Community Partnerships Initiative. The original plan was that $753 million over three years would be sent to 10 major cities across the country to pay for additional homeless shelters and transitional housing, along with services for the homeless. Included were special funds for Aboriginal and youth homeless programs. The National Housing and Homelessness Network greeted the federal announcement by saying:

> The good news: Powerful community-based work right across Canada has forced the federal government to take action on homelessness. The

bad news: We're got to push much harder before we get a national housing program that will truly help to end homelessness ... This is not a national strategy, but a patchwork response to Canada's national homelessness disaster and housing crisis. Successful projects will have to put together elaborate funding packages from various sources. Therefore, groups will have to spend months or years fundraising instead of building housing and providing services. This is the downside of the trend towards "partnerships." Multiple funding sources place the barrier much higher even for the best projects. Instead of a single program that delivers the funding, project sponsors will have to approach of variety of government, private sector and community sources. Putting additional new money into helping homeless people is welcome, and will likely lead to a handful of new one-off projects in various parts of the country. It is a step, but unless there is a massive federal reinvestment in a national housing program, it cannot be called a step in the right direction. It is simply a step leading to nowhere in particular.[19]

In other words, the homeless would probably be a little more comfortable after federal funding started to flow, but they wouldn't be any less homeless.

Another concern with the homelessness announcement was the focus on 10 cities to the exclusion of the rest of the country. Several provinces and all three territories were shut out, along with small towns and rural areas throughout Canada – because the government had decided that homelessness is a big-city issue. Advocates succeeded in convincing the federal government to open up the program to the rest of the country, but no extra dollars were added. The $753 million pie was simply divided up into smaller slices: 80% of the money was directed to the 10 large cities; the remaining 20% went to the rest of the country.

In September 2000, provincial and territorial housing ministers met for their annual summit in Fredericton, New Brunswick. For the first time in six years, the federal government sent its housing minister. The National Housing and Homelessness Network (NHHN), the Federation of Canadian Municipalities, and the Canadian Housing and Renewal Association all sent representatives to lobby ministers.

The NHHN, along with its Quebec partner, the Front d'Action Populaire en Réaménagement Urbain, built a symbolic house in front of the hotel where the ministers were meeting. The network released its first national report card on housing and homelessness in Fredericton. Advocates dominated the media agenda for the meeting, but ministers finished their three days of talks with a bland communiqué that offered further study without any commitment to action.

Housing and homelessness crept onto the political agenda of the federal election in fall 2000, as a growing number of opinion polls showed that a majority of Canadians were deeply concerned about the housing crisis and wanted governments to take action. Four of the five major political parties promised increased funding for housing, including the governing Liberals, which promised $680 million over four years for new housing.

Federal, provincial, and territorial housing ministers held their next annual meeting in London, Ontario, in August 2001. The pressure was building on the federal government to honour its promise for more funding for housing. NHHN convinced ministers to listen to the national groups. The ministers were reluctant to bring advocates into the formal meeting, so they allowed four national organizations 15 minutes each to address the ministers.

It was a small, but important victory. Non-governmental groups rarely have a voice at federal-provincial-territorial meetings. NHHN had managed to open a small window at the housing summit.

The National Housing and Homelessness Network, the Federation of Canadian Municipalities, the Canadian Housing and Renewal Association, and the Co-operative Housing Federation of Canada collaborated on key messages in their separate presentations.

The network released a new report card and staged a demonstration in front of the hotel. Advocates and homeless people from Quebec and Ontario came to London to deliver a noisy and energetic call to the ministers to adopt a fully-funded national housing strategy.

The ministers didn't quite reach a deal, but they did set a deadline. They agreed that the federal, provincial, and territorial governments would sign off on a new national housing strategy within three months. Their next housing summit was set for November 2001 in Quebec City.

Once again, the four national groups gathered at the national housing meeting. They privately lobbied the ministers, made formal presentations, and released reports on key features of a proposed new national housing strategy. And, in the face of one of the worst blizzards in years, as the winds howled up the St. Lawrence River, hundreds of homeless people, low-income tenants, and advocates held a demonstration in front of the hotel where the ministers were meeting. The combined actions had a powerful effect.

Affordable Housing Framework Agreement

The ministers emerged from their talks with the announcement that they had signed an Affordable Housing Framework Agreement. Under the terms of this deal, the federal government would invest $680 million over five years (the same amount the Liberals promised during the 2000 election, but spread out over an additional year) and the provinces and territories were supposed to match that with an additional $680 million. It wasn't the full One Percent Solution, but it was an important step forward.

Each of the provinces and territories were required to sign a bilateral housing deal with the federal government that set out the details of the new housing. All 13 did over the next 18 months. But two concerns quickly emerged:

- A major loophole in the original agreement allowed provinces and territories to pass on the costs to municipalities or third parties, such as social housing providers. Ontario, which was supposed to match the federal government's contribution of $245 million, offered only $20 million in new provincial funds. The rest was supposed to come from cash-strapped municipalities and housing developers. Other provinces were also unable or unwilling to match the federal dollars.
- The loose definition of "affordable housing" in the bilateral deals meant that the provinces and territories could fund new units with high rents, and even ownership units that were not affordable to the target group of low- and moderate-income households. Under the program, the maximum per-unit capital grant was set at $50,000, which meant that truly affordable housing would likely not be built under the program.

Advocates and national organizations continued their national campaign. Their goal was to press federal, provincial, and territorial governments to honour the commitments that they had made in Quebec City, and to convince them to increase spending to meet the goal of the One Percent Solution.

In August 2002, Prime Minister Jean Chrétien gave one of his senior ministers, David Collenette, responsibility for housing. The newly appointed senior federal housing minister mused in his first speech:

> Perhaps it is time for the federal government to get back into social housing ... In the '60s and '70s, CMHC was remarkably developmental and progressive. Whether it was low-cost housing, not-for-profits, limited-

dividend buildings or co-ops, all was done by CMHC. And then governments said, "No, we think the private sector should take over." The fact is, the private sector is not going to voluntarily build low-cost housing, which is what we need in communities in this country.[20]

In the September 2002 Speech from the Throne, which set out the legislative agenda for the federal government in the new session, the government promised:

[The government] will extend its investments in affordable housing for those whose needs are greatest, particularly in Canadian cities where problem is most acute. It will extend Supporting Communities Partnership Initiative to provide communities with the tools to plan and implement local strategies to help reduce homelessness. In a number of cities, poverty is disproportionately concentrated among Aboriginal people. The government will work with interested provinces to expand on existing pilot programs to meet the needs of Aboriginal people living in cities.

Political pressure, including a growing call for a "new deal for cities," prompted the federal government to add an additional $320 million to its affordable housing program in the February 2003 federal budget – for a total of $1 billion over five years, or an average of $200 million annually (10% of the One Percent Solution).

In the same budget, the federal government extended its homelessness strategy by adding $305 million over three years, plus an additional $128 million to its housing rehabilitation program.

Positive momentum was continuing in the political sphere, but few new units were actually being built. The National Housing and Homelessness Network, in an attempt to keep political pressure on the senior levels of government, released a series of national housing report cards every six months after the framework deal was signed in November 2001.

A depressing picture emerged: few new units in most parts of the country. And about half the provinces continued to cut provincial housing spending after signing the housing framework deal, even though they had agreed to increase provincial spending to match the federal dollars.

The NHHN report cards drew criticism from some provincial officials, who complained that the network's information was wrong. The 13 bilateral housing deals signed between the federal government and the provinces and territories required an annual public report listing spending, number of new units created, and a full performance audit. But the governments never released a public accounting, so the network based its reports on the best available data.

By 2003, the important advance that came with the signing of the affordable housing framework agreement in November 2001 had stalled. In April 2003, federal, provincial, and territorial housing ministers gathered for a national summit in Winnipeg. The national network upped the ante by calling on the federal government to use its powers under the bilateral housing deals to bypass provinces and territories that were unable or unwilling to meet the commitments they had made in Quebec City 18 months earlier.

Prime Minister Chrétien appointed Steve Mahoney as a "junior" housing minister just before the Winnipeg meeting. It was a clear signal that the federal government was adding some muscle to the housing file. Mahoney, taking his lead from the network and other housing advocates, told the media that he was prepared to get tough with the provinces and territories.

In October 2003, Ontario voters tossed out the Conservatives and elected a Liberal government under Dalton McGuinty. McGuinty's election platform included significant housing commitments, including a promise of 20,000 new affordable housing units and other measures. Advocates hoped that new housing would finally be built in Ontario two years after the housing framework deal had been signed. That deal had earmarked $245 million from the federal government for new affordable housing in Ontario which, combined with the $245 million matching share from the province, would fund at least 10,000 new units (based on an average capital grant of $50,000 per unit). However, that hope was dampened by the announcement by McGuinty, soon after his election, that his "discovery" of a significant provincial deficit meant that all election promises were now on hold.

On December 5, 2003, Minister Mahoney sent a letter to the National Housing and Homelessness Network with the first new numbers. The minister reported that only $88 million had been committed by the federal government as of October 2003. That is less than 9% of the $1 billion that the federal government had promised to spend. The bleak assessment by the NHHN was confirmed by the federal government.

One week after sending that letter, Mahoney was dropped from the federal cabinet. Paul Martin was sworn in as prime minister, capping his personal political campaign over the previous decade to rise to the

Federal affordable housing recorded spending to 2003

Province	Allocation ($m)	Recorded spending ($m)
Newfoundland and Labrador	$15.14	0
Prince Edward Island	$2.75	0
Nova Scotia	$18.63	$0.07
New Brunswick	$14.98	0
Quebec	$161.65	$43.72
Ontario	$244.71	$1.20
Manitoba	$25.39	$0.48
Saskatchewan	$22.93	$0.94
Alberta	$67.12	$8.50
British Columbia	$88.70	$26.70
Northwest Territories	$7.54	$1.89
Yukon Territory	$5.50	0
Nunavut	$4.96	$4.96
Total	$680.00	$88.48

nation's top political post. In Martin's first cabinet, housing was handed to David Anderson, the environment minister. Advocates and the media criticized Martin for downgrading housing.

Soon after, Martin quietly named Andy Scott as the junior housing minister. But Martin's finance minister, Ralph Goodale, launched a national budget consultation saying that all federal spending – except for new military helicopters and the massive tax cuts – would be under review.

Housing advocates started the year 2004 worried that the hard-won gains of the previous five years could come unravelled.

The Challenge Today

Federal, provincial, and territorial housing and social spending cuts of the 1980s and 1990s fuelled the growing homelessness disaster and housing crisis. Effective advocacy managed to win some important gains, but senior levels of government failed to meet even the minimal commitments that they made to fund new homes and services.

The fiscal capacity of governments to respond to the housing crisis by meeting the goal of the One Percent Solution ($2 billion annually) was eroded by massive tax cuts at the federal level, and in many provinces.

By the end of the 1990s, advocates had managed to convince the public, the media, and most politicians that the housing crisis was real, and that strong action was required by senior levels of government.

And while there has been grudging acceptance of the need for action and a limited commitment in the form of a growing patchwork of funding and programs, federal and provincial politicians have failed to enact the fully-funded and comprehensive national housing strategy set out by the National Housing and Homelessness Network and other national groups.

One enduring symbol of the depths of the crisis came in January 2004, when the federal government agreed (after considerable political pressure from advocates) to open an emergency shelter for the homeless in downtown Toronto after two extreme cold weather alerts. Two days after it was opened, about 75 homeless people were sleeping on the cots and more were expected.

The federal government has been mostly unwilling to invest in housing solutions, so it has been forced to open empty military spaces where the homeless can huddle with some measure of warmth and comfort.

Michael Shapcott is co-chair and a founding member of the National Housing and Homelessness Network and a founding member of the Toronto Disaster Relief Committee, the Toronto Coalition Against Homelessness, and the Bread Not Circuses Coalition. He is the coordinator of the Community/University Research Partnerships (CURP) program at the Centre for Urban and Community Studies, University of Toronto (see: www.urbancentre.utoronto.ca/curp. html).

Endnotes

1 Carter, Tom, *Canadian Housing Policy: Is the Glass Half Empty or Half Full?*, April 2000, Canadian Housing and Renewal Association, pp. 3–4.
2 For a text of the Martin report, go to www.housingagain.web.net.
3 Organisation for Economic Co-operation and Development, *Social Expenditure Database, 1980 to 1997, Social Expenditures for Canada*, 2000.
4 Finance Canada, *Economic and Fiscal Update*, November 3, 2003, p. 27.
5 Canada Mortgage and Housing Corporation, *Opening Doors*, Annual Report, 2002, p. 8.

6 Finance Canada, *Fiscal Reference Tables*, October 2003, p. 19.
7 Finance Canada, *Economic and Fiscal Update*, November 3, 2003, p. 16.
8 Finn, Ed, *Where's the Money Coming From*, Canadian Centre for Policy Alternatives, 2002, p. 1.
9 Canada Mortgage and Housing Corporation, *Rental Market Report 2002*, Toronto CMA, October 2002, p. 1.
10 National Housing and Homelessness Network, *State of the Crisis*, 2001, p. 10.
11 Ontario Rental Housing Supply Working Group, *Affordable Rental Housing Supply: The Dynamics of the Market and Recommendations for New Supply*, Interim Report, May 2001.
12 Shapcott, Michael, *Profiting From a Manufactured Housing Crisis*, Canadian Centre for Policy Alternatives, June 2002, p. 2.
13 Ontario Rental Housing Supply Working Group, *Affordable Rental Housing Supply: The Dynamics of the Market and Recommendations for New Supply*, Interim Report, May 2001, p. 4.
14 Shapcott, Michael, *State of the Crisis, 2003: Ontario Housing Policies Are De-housing Ontarians*, Canadian Centre for Policy Alternatives, March 2003.
15 Wolfe, Jeanne M., *Canadian Housing Policy in the Nineties*, McGill University, January 1998.
16 Toronto Disaster Relief Committee, *State of Emergency Declaration*, October 1998, p. 4.
17 For more on the One Percent Solution, see the TDRC website: www.tdrc.net.
18 The report is on the web at www.city.toronto.on.ca/mayor/homelessnesstf.htm.
19 National Housing and Homelessness Network, *Where's the Housing: To End Homelessness, Canada Needs More Homes*, December 17, 1999.
20 Collenette, David, Speech to the Couchiching Conference, August 2002.

Part II
Perspectives on the Current Situation

Chapter 13

A New Paradigm for Affordable Housing: An Economist's Perspective

DON DRUMMOND, TD BANK FINANCIAL GROUP

I feel we're a little bit like pretenders in this field. When we did the Toronto Report and the report on the cities across Canada, we did venture a little bit into the housing area, but not very much. We've only been working at this for a couple of weeks, while many of you have been working at this for a long time – some of you for your careers. So we're a little bit new. That should make me feel a little bit uncomfortable. But there's a bit of a context, that makes me feel not too uncomfortable.

For some reason economists are asked to give a lot of presentations and media interviews and so forth. I've noticed in the three years I've been at the bank that people are really skeptical of us talking about economic forecasts, which you'd presume would be our natural domain. On the other hand, everyone seems to expect me to be an expert on terrorism, then war strategy, then public health, and now veterinary science. I don't remember studying any of that stuff in the university. So actually talking about housing is getting a little bit closer to our domain.

I'd like to begin by reviewing the available statistics, with which many of you will be familiar. The good news is the majority – about two-thirds – of Canadians are housed adequately, suitably and affordably as in CMHC's definition. About 14 percent failed at least one of those tests, but could rectify the problem without having to go over the 30 percent golden rule on their budgets. The group of primary concern is the 17 percent who are in core housing need. In other words, they're spending more than 30 percent on housing or they have some inadequacy in their housing and would need to spend more than 30 percent to make their housing adequate.

Now there's some debate about whether the 30 percent is the appropriate number. So let's look at those who are spending more than 50 percent of their income on housing. Obviously anybody spending more than 50 percent on shelter has got very little money left over for anything else. It's still a substantial group – 7 percent – and it has gone up 2 percentage points since 1991. If we break this number down between owners and renters, we can see that the housing affordability problem is not nearly as severe for homeowners as for renters, a result that won't come as a surprise. But the numbers are pretty high and they've gone up since 1991, as you can see in the table below.

Table 1: Proportion of Households with an Affordability Problem (by census year)

	1991	1996	2001
Owners and renters			
30% or more	22.7	26.6	24.1
50% or more	9.4	12.0	10.6
Owners			
30% or more	15.4	16.9	16.0
50% or more	5.4	6.5	6.2
Renters			
30% or more	34.8	43.2	39.6
50% or more	16.0	21.6	19.0

Shelter costs refer to gross rent for renters and owner's major payments for owners.
Source: Statistics Canada (1991, 1996, and 2001 census), TD Economics

Just who are these people that are in core need? The thing that really stands out is it tends to be dominated by people living alone. Females living alone make up 27 percent of households in core housing need, males living alone make up 17 percent. A large number of these in turn are seniors, particularly females living alone. Female lone parents make up 17 percent and one-family households with children make up another 17 percent. Families without children are having less of a problem.

Of the households spending at least half of their income on housing, certain groups are overrepresented. You can see that 15–29 year olds are 11 percent of Canadian households but overrepresented in this group at 21 percent. Lone parents with children and people earning less than $20,000 are also overrepresented, as you'd expect. And then by defini-

Table 2: Canadian Households in Core Housing Need in 1996 (%)

Females living alone	27%
Males living alone	17%
Female lone parent	17%
One-family households with children	17%
One-family households without children	13%
Living with others	6%
Male lone parent	2%
Multiple family household	1%

Source: CMHC, TD Economics

tion, most but not all of the people earning less than $20,000 depend on government transfers, and this group is also overrepresented.

Interestingly, seniors are in the middle of the affordability problem. Seniors are 21 percent of all households; 26 percent are spending more than 30 percent of their incomes on housing, but they are underrepresented among those who spend more than 50 percent. I think that would be a sign of the modest success that has been achieved by OAS, GIS, and CPP. It's moved the seniors away from the bottom end of the poverty list and put a lot of the households into that $15,000 to $25,000 category. Seniors are not the poorest of the poor anymore, but they still have some difficulties, particularly women living alone.

Table 3: Those in Need and Spending at least Half their Income on Housing in 1996

	% spending 50%	% of all households
15 to 29 years of age	21	11
Lone parent with child under 18	16	6
Earning less than $20,000	86	20
Relying on government transfers	58	22

A good part of the problem has to do with income levels.

If you look at a median family income, you can see that Canada had a very rough ride from the late 1980s right through the mid 1990s – in fact, median income came down in real terms quite sharply over that period. The lowest quintile, that is, the lowest 20 percent, were perform-

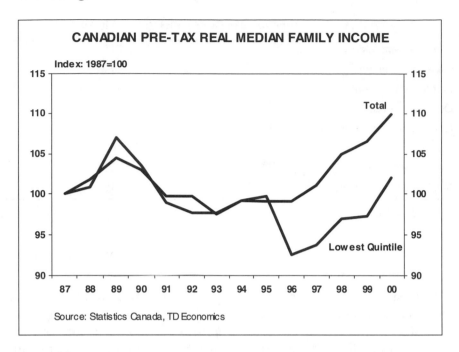

CANADIAN PRE-TAX REAL MEDIAN FAMILY INCOME

Index: 1987=100

Total

Lowest Quintile

Source: Statistics Canada, TD Economics

ing pretty much the same as the national average up to the mid 1990s. Starting from the second half of the 1990s, we had a very strong recovery in the median or close to the average, but we can't say the same thing for the bottom quintile – in fact it dropped very sharply in the second half of the 1990s, back to the income levels they were at back in 1987, which represents a widening of the income distribution.

If you look at the shelter cost divided up by income quintiles, as you would expect, the affordability problem is concentrated at the lower end with 39 percent of the people in the lowest quintile of the income distribution having an affordability problem.

These figures represent the demand side – incomes have fallen in absolute terms at the bottom end of the distribution. You get a fairly similar picture on the supply side.

The stock of rental supply available to those with the lowest incomes has come down quite sharply between 1998 and 2002; we've had modest increases elsewhere. But that hasn't prevented the rental rates from going up. These are somewhat higher than the rate of inflation since 1998 and 2002 and of course at the upper end the increases are sharper.

Is this just an urban problem? I think that the common perception has been that the problem is concentrated in large urban centres. But the

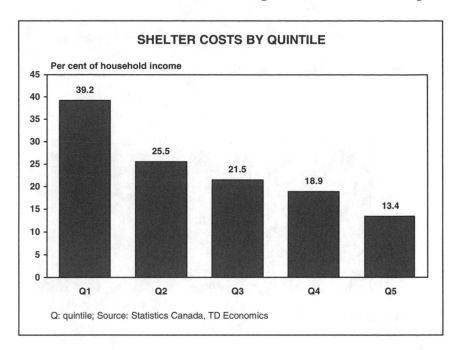

SHELTER COSTS BY QUINTILE

Per cent of household income

Q: quintile; Source: Statistics Canada, TD Economics

Table 4: Percent of Households Experiencing Affordability Problems

	30% or more spent on shelter	50% or more spent on shelter
All households		
Canada	24.1	10.6
CMA	25.9	11.3
Non-CMA	20.9	9.2
Renters		
Canada	39.6	19.0
CMA	39.7	19.2
Non-CMA	39.3	18.5

Source: Statistics Canada, TD Economics

table above shows that affordability problems are only slightly less severe outside the Census Metropolitan areas than inside.

So the problem is not really just an urban problem, it is spread right across the large cities, small cities, rural areas – if you're a renter.

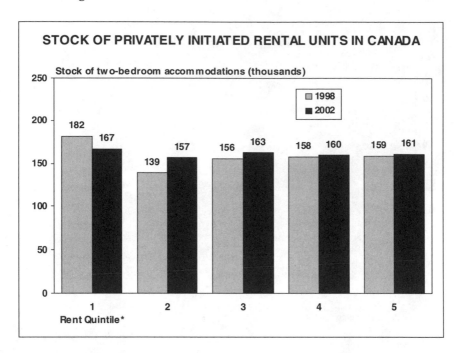

STOCK OF PRIVATELY INITIATED RENTAL UNITS IN CANADA

Stock of two-bedroom accommodations (thousands)

Rent Quintile*

Table 5: Percent of Renter Households Experiencing Affordability Problems

	30% or more spent on shelter	50% or more spent on shelter
Vancouver	43.2	22.3
Calgary	36.5	16.0
Edmonton	37.3	16.9
Regina	42.6	21.1
Winnipeg	37.9	16.1
Toronto	42.2	20.0
Ottawa	36.4	17.1
Montreal	36.4	18.1
Halifax	43.7	22.0

Source: Statistics Canada, TD Economics

We can also look at the results for each of the major cities. The problem is most severe – as you'd expect – in some of the bigger cities, such as Vancouver and Toronto. But they're not alone in these difficulties. Some of the smaller ones, such as Regina and Halifax, have problems at the level of Vancouver and Toronto. The problem is generally equally severe in all of the nine Census Metropolitan areas that we picked.

In the last year, there has been considerable attention paid to the fact that vacancy rates are finally rising after a long period of declining or remaining very low. But if you actually look at the rental stock at the bottom 40 percent of the rent rates, you don't see the same increase. Where the increase in the vacancy rates is occurring is at the higher end. In fact, if you take a market like Toronto, the vacancies are at the really high end – units that rent for $1,500 to $2,000 a month. So it's not very interesting to the constituency we're speaking about here.

The vacancy rate is extraordinarily high at the moment, but that has not filtered into a pick-up at the bottom end. The same thing is true for two-bedroom units. You can see that the supply is not increasing at that bottom end and the vacancy rate has not picked up.

So we have stagnation and even decline on the income or demand side and declining supply at the lower end. What are the factors contributing to this situation?

We've seen a number of changes in tax provisions that have lowered the rates of return in rental housing. We've also seen a shifting of responsibilities for social housing down to the municipalities and the lesser involvement of the provinces. We've seen a changed mandate at the CMHC, which is trying to move to a more commercial basis, and that has had an impact. And there are arguments on both sides on the question of rent controls. Some would argue that they've kept the rents down. I would argue that over the long term they have contributed to the diminishing supply of housing and have kept certain investors out of the markets who might have otherwise been interested.

There has been quite a change in the last couple of years, in part, I think, because of the increasing awareness of the problem. The government is easing up a little bit on the purse strings after largely solving their deficit problems. Many of them are still in debt, but they are increasing the rate of spending somewhat. We've also had a number of important increases in the National Child Tax Benefit. And I would argue the Child Tax Benefit is beginning to do for low-income families with children what the OAS and GIS did in a previous generation for older people. It is taking them out of the most extreme depths of poverty. We have a number of further increases coming over the next couple of years, and that affects the demand side of the equation.

On the supply side we have the federal initiative of the affordable housing framework (which has evoked something of a patchwork of responses from the provinces), the homelessness strategy, a number of separate provincial and municipal measures, and very recently some changes in increased flexibility on the part of CMHC.

The usual take on the problem is that there's too little supply for low-income families to afford. One approach to the solution is to recommend a vast array of subsidies and encourage the supply of multiple units. (I'm exaggerating a little bit for the purposes of creating a straw man.) I have three problems with that kind of common paradigm.

First, it treats income levels as a given. I don't think there is any need to treat them as a given. Second, most of the recommendations tend to work on the total supply of rental housing, and are not particularly targeted at the lower end. You can argue that obviously there's some trickle-down effect, but I think that it would be somewhat limited in the short term. Third, I think many of the recommendations are inefficient in the sense that they have a high public cost relative to the actual increase in the number of affordable units that would be delivered.

I think we need a broader paradigm. It's not so much that there's not enough supply at the low end. The problem is basically that there's too many poor people in Canada. Obviously there will always be a bottom 20 percent. But the income levels of the bottom 20 percent are just too low at present and have been stagnant since the mid 1980s. The transfer system has been partly successful, but is certainly inadequate in some circumstances.

It's no accident that a large number of the people with affordability problems are single women living on OAS and GIS. Your payments are lowered to 50 percent if your spouse dies. Your costs don't go down to 50 percent, they are probably about 70 to 75 percent for a single relative to a couple. So there are some inadequacies there. Also, we've had widespread cutbacks in the welfare rates in almost all provinces over the last 10 years. Governments, in their attempts to be frugal, have created very high taxback rates, so the marginal tax rates that many people on the social assistance face can easily be 80, 90, or even 100 percent of income, which has created something of a welfare poverty wall.

There are many examples of unfair, unequal treatment of households in similar income situations. Certain support programs are available for people who are not working, but as soon as they start to work, they lose their eligibility for those programs. The child tax benefit in a certain sense is trying to deal with that. But if you increase the income support for people who are not working, that increases the demand for housing and therefore the price at the bottom end of the housing market, and of course makes housing less affordable for people who are not getting some kind of income transfer.

If you accept the broader paradigm, the first place to start is on a macroeconomic level. Of course, when you have a favourable economic environment, a lot of the problems that you're trying to target specifically do improve on their own accord. They aren't fully resolved, but they move in the right direction. So I think we need to step back for a moment and realize the tremendous value of having a strong macroeconomic environment, strong growth, low inflation, and low interest rates. The rising tide doesn't lift all boats, but it's a lot better than when the tide's going out. Nobody gets lifted then.

As we have seen, low interest rates have worked exactly the way they're supposed to work in the housing market. They've moved many people into homeownership, and those people have vacated a lot of the rental supply. There is some filtering down occurring.

But if the problem is too many low-income people, we need to ask, why are there too many low-income people? Well, part of the reason is that Canada does not have a strong lifelong education system. It always astonishes me that a highly industrialized country like Canada has such a high high-school drop-out rate. The biggest payoff on the education front is actually not from higher education, but from getting most people through high school and we have a lot of people who aren't doing that.

Also, we've built up a system with very high marginal effective tax rates. I don't mean the tax rates paid by the highest-income individuals. On average in Canada they pay 45 percent relative to the marginal effective tax rates that lower income Canadians pay. Most families in Canada with family incomes between $20,000 and $40,000 pay at least 60 to 70 percent as a marginal tax rate. And you can discover many examples where people are paying 80 to 90 percent marginal tax rates. It really does dull any incentive people have to try to increase their income on their own, because they're going to lose it either through taxes or through in-kind benefits.

We know that in the long run, people are better off if they can save. But if you are going to earn only $20,000 to $30,000 in a working career in Canada, it's actually unproductive to save any money. You will lose all of it. You will get back a small tax deduction at the time you save it, and you will lose more than all of that money when you go into retirement and face the clawback rates that we have in Canada. So that's not very helpful.

We also need to look at immigration. We all say in Canada that immigration is our key to economic growth, but it's only the key to economic growth if immigrants are integrated successfully into the Canadian economy. We've had a lot of problems with that recently. We are not advertising the type of jobs that are available here, we are not helping people integrate into the job market, we are not recognizing degrees – if an individual is short one course, the system requires them to redo a whole program. So we really have to do a better job on that, recognizing that in five years' time, immigration is going to be 100 percent of the Canadian growth rate of population and that by 2010 it will be about 140 percent. Our Canadian-born population is just about at its peak right now and is about to start decreasing.

We're always going to need an income support system. Even the best macroeconomic environment is not going to be enough. And there are things that we need to work on, such as the splitting of pension benefits, which I have already mentioned. My father died and my mother all of a sudden gets 50 percent of the pension; we worked out that her costs are about 75 percent of what they were before.

I would argue that if there's one area that's due for to a complete overhaul, it would be the whole income support system. We must work to get rid of those welfare and poverty trap rules and stop treating people who are in different circumstances but fairly similar incomes so unequally.

On the shelter side, we have rent supplements and shelter allowances. I would argue that shelter allowances would probably be the better way to go to give people freedom of choice. Shelter allowances don't lock people into certain locations, if they have to be mobile for their jobs. There are still some difficulties, however. For example, in Ontario you get the same shelter allowance from the provincial government whether you have a lower-cost apartment in Kingston or a high-rent apartment in Toronto.

Now there's been a great debate in the literature between demand-side measures and supply-side measures. People seem to feel that they have to pick one or the other. I think you need both. In the short term at least, if you increase incomes on the demand side, you will largely be increasing rents and that will flow to the landlords. Ultimately, that will increase the supply. At the same time, however, you need to do something on the supply side. You need not only long-run macroeconomic solutions, but also demand and supply solutions for the short term to both create new supply and to preserve the existing supply.

Finally, we need to remove market distortions. Many existing taxes are as unambiguously distortionary as the much higher multiple property tax rates relative to single units in Toronto.

In particular, capital taxes have no place whatsoever in the tax arsenal. They're the worst taxes we've got. Some other provinces have already eliminated them and the federal government is eliminating them over a five-year time period. As the municipalities get squeezed on their tax sources, they've been raising the development charges to very high levels. Meanwhile, some of the zoning restrictions on the size of the units are strangling supply.

We've tried two calculations to shed some light on this issue. When I was on the working group on affordable housing for the Toronto City Summit Alliance, we tried to calculate the shelter gap, that is, the difference between incomes at the low end and average rents. We found a huge disparity. But I think it's somewhat unrealistic to take someone in the bottom 20 percent of income and say the objective is to get them into an average apartment at an average cost. So as an alternative, we took the average income at the bottom 20 percent of the income distribution and we compared that to two-thirds of the median rent. Even then, the gap on an annual basis is still very big: $2,500 on average, and in big cities like Vancouver and then Toronto, it was $4,000. So even for that relatively modest objective in which we're not housing these people at anywhere near the average quality, there still is a big gap.

So we tried an alternative. We took the average income for the bottom 40 percent and compared that amount to three-quarters of the average rent. The gap is smaller, on average $800 but it's still too wide for Vancouver and Toronto, at $2,400, and $2,005, respectively. Although some might dispute these figures, I still think it shows unambiguously that there is a huge affordability problem.

There has been a lot of discussion of taxes in the context of affordable housing. To me, the proper approach on a tax measure is to ask: Would changing this tax correct a market distortion? I would argue that whether it improved the affordable housing directly or not, if it corrects a market distortion, it should be reformed. Because if it's not correcting a market distortion, it is really just another name for a subsidy.

I chaired the committee of the Canadian Chamber of Commerce on Economic Policy. We went through all the resolutions of the various different chambers across the country and of course, one of the key principles of the Canadian Chamber of Commerce is that we want to end business subsidies. But the list was full of requests for tax breaks. That's just a subsidy by another name and I think a lot of people don't understand that. What everybody forgets in Canada is that tax reductions aren't free. They have a cost to them, for governments and for society, since governments could do something else with that money. But people talk as if somehow this money just grows on a tree. And if the government changes something in the tax provisions and it costs several hundreds of millions of dollars, it's several hundreds of millions of dollars that they could have used for another purpose. So I'd argue that if the tax change is not efficient in terms of changing affordable housing, then none of those measures are particularly efficient in dealing with affordable housing.

Here are some of the common tax issues that appear in most of the reports on housing.

1. You cannot have access to small business income tax rates unless you have more than five employees.
2. Capital Cost Allowance (CCA) losses cannot be deducted against income.
3. You cannot pool a CCA, so if you sell one rental unit to buy another one, you have to pay a capital gains tax on the first before you can buy the second one.
4. The CCA is too high.
5. There's been some tightening on what you can deduct in soft costs and many of them have to be capitalized.
6. Capital taxes should be eliminated.
7. The GST on rental housing construction should be lowered or eliminated. As of 2000 there has been a rebate in the federal government's terms. The goal is to try to get back the GST on rental to about what the old manufacturer's sales tax burden would have been. There's some dispute about whether that's successful or not, but that's the logic.
8. And of course, property taxes on multi-unit properties are much higher than taxes on single-unit properties. (In terms of multiple tax rates, at least in Ontario, you can get an exemption for a limited period for new development. Initially it was for eight years. Now municipalities have the right to extend that to 35 years, but I would still argue that as the existing stock is obviously far more important than the new housing stock, that that's still a very important impediment to the market.)

There are also arguments for raising the depreciation rate of 4 percent to 5 percent. I would actually argue that the 4 percent depreciation rate is already above the rate of economic depreciation and I would suggest that the economic depreciation rate is probably about 2½ percent.

To me, numbers 6 and 8 are unambiguously distortionary. Some of the others, whether they're distortionary or not is largely in the eye of the beholder. If you accept that rental income is passive income, you can maybe justify some of these measures, but if you don't accept that, then some of them are distortionary.

I think one thing that's very clear from this – all of those tax measures are not specifically targeted at the affordable end, they're targeted to the entire rental supply. So in terms of the number of units that they would generate at the affordable end, they're going to involve a fairly large public expense to generate a small number of units.

According to a lot of the literature, the Ontario government is saying that if you do these things, it will generate such a rental supply that the governments will actually end up with more money. Almost by definition if that was the case, then you don't need to do them, because the market will do them on their own, so that's a little bit dubious.

There are also suggestions for new tax-related measures. There's a lot of interest in the U.S. low-income housing tax credit. Some of the studies suggest that some benefits are diluted by syndicate fees – the premiums that are charged. Apparently, the credits are not working very well. So it seems to be a bit of an open question. It hasn't solved the problem in the U.S. Typically there are five or six layers of subsidies on top of this before you get the whole benefit.

One argument put forward for introducing these credits in the Canadian context is that the federal government can change the tax base without going through painful discussions with the provinces. That's only partially true. The federal government can change the tax base and affect any province in a tax collection agreement, but Quebec is exempt on the personal income tax and Alberta, Ontario, and Quebec are exempt on the corporate income tax side. So you're missing about 50 percent of the country on the corporate tax side and as a former Assistant Deputy Minister for tax policy, I can tell you that the days in which the federal government manipulated the federal tax base without consulting the provinces are long gone.

Labour Sponsored Venture Capital Corporations (LSVCC) tax credits have been put forward as another possibility, along with tax-free bonds. Ontario is experimenting with tax-free bonds at the moment. I would argue that that it is a very inefficient approach. You get a lower cost of funding for building housing, but the lower cost of funding is exactly equal to – or at best is equal to – the forgone federal and provincial taxes. So it's another form of subsidy. And in fact with the Canadian market, with the huge participation of foreign buyers who would not get tax-free bonds, you would actually get less of the savings from the cost of funding than the forgone taxes.

I think we should not forget about the renovation and rehabilitation of existing stock. In many cases that is a less expensive way of preventing the loss of housing and it could be tailored towards community needs. In the short term we're not going to get a lot of new supply, so this may be a more appropriate way to go.

Finally, I'd like to come back to the idea of removing market imperfections. I've talked about the capital taxes and the property tax distortion. We also need to look at zoning issues, the supply of land, and restrictions on unit size. Although we should be rightly concerned about having such a different quality of housing for people at different levels of income, often the objective is to provide the average type of apartment dwelling for everyone. Perhaps we could be a bit more modest in our expectations, particularly in terms of the size of the unit. We could use rooming-house-style units, which may be in 200 to 300 square feet, as opposed to a typical apartment that may be 300 to 400 square feet. Obviously we'd get a lot more into the same area and you could lower the costs. This kind of housing might not be an individual's permanent destination and abode, but it would provide adequate housing in the short term. So that might be a lower-cost solution.

Of course, many of the numbers I've mentioned will change when we finally get the 2001 census results. We expect to see a fairly important increase in the incomes of seniors towards the latter part of the 1990s and early 2000. The aggregate numbers may offset some of the patterns I've described.

Don Drummond is Senior Vice President and Chief Economist of the TD Bank Financial Group. Mr. Drummond joined the federal Department of Finance upon completing his studies at Queen's (M.A. in Economics). During almost 23 years at Finance, Mr. Drummond held a series of progressively more senior positions in the areas of economic analysis and forecasting, fiscal policy and tax policy. His last three positions were respectively, Assistant Deputy Minister of Fiscal Policy & Economic Analysis, Assistant Deputy Minister of Tax Policy & Legisla-

tion and most recently, Associate Deputy Minister. In this latter position Mr. Drummond was responsible for economic analysis, fiscal policy, tax policy, social policy and federal-provincial relations. In particular, Mr. Drummond coordinated the planning of the annual federal budgets. Mr. Drummond, who joined the TD Bank in June 2000, leads TD Economics' work in analysing and forecasting economic performance in Canada and abroad. For Canada, this work is conducted at the city, provincial, industrial, and national levels. TD Economics also analyses the key policies which influence economic performance, including monetary and fiscal policies.

Chapter 14

The Business Case for Affordable Housing

ELYSE ALLAN, TORONTO BOARD OF TRADE

It is healthy to have debate and discussion about the best incentives and approaches for building affordable housing. It's clear that we all share the same goal, so the question is therefore what are the best strategies and tactics by which we can achieve that goal.

Affordable housing is a social issue affecting quality of life. However, it's also a critical business issue.

In April 2003, our Task Force on Affordable Housing released a report entitled *Affordable, Available, Achievable: Practical Solutions to Affordable Housing Challenges*. You can find the report in its entirety on our website, www.bot.com. Our message to governments was clear. We believe that the shortage of affordable housing is a problem that can be solved.

Today I'll explain why the Toronto Board of Trade is concerned about affordable housing. I'll bring you up to date on the Board's involvement in the issue over the last few years, and give you five reasons why the issue affects the business community. I'll conclude by explaining what governments must do to increase the supply of affordable housing in urban centres.

The Toronto Board of Trade is committed to a competitive and vibrant Toronto. Currently, Toronto is the most significant generator of prosperity for the region, province, and country, but signs of stress on the city are everywhere. In fact we believe that without enhanced investment in the city's infrastructure, Toronto will be unable to maintain its competitive edge. If that happens, the city will end up playing a diminished role in the economic life of the province and the nation.

In recent submissions to government we have tabled solutions to the problems of Toronto's crumbling infrastructure. In particular, we believe that the shortage of affordable housing is one of the major infrastructure issues facing our city. Our CEO Forum on Urban Competitiveness confirmed this. In response, the Board has developed a five-year proposal to secure priority short-term funding to stem the decline in our key city assets.

Our five-year plan, which would be the first step towards a new deal for Toronto, calls for targeted, short-term capital funding to be invested in our existing housing stock. Our objective is to strike a partnership of investment, to protect what we already have. I know a number of you have spoken about the importance of protecting and preserving the housing stock that we have in place now. From a financial and fiscal standpoint, this would secure the best return for initial investment and therefore we fully agree.

Yet what we have isn't much. City-owned housing stock is crumbling. Close to half the units were built prior to 1974 and have no capital reserves to support ongoing maintenance and upgrade needs. Nevertheless, this housing stock is an asset we cannot afford to lose. The reason: approximately 70,000 households are on the waiting list for housing in Toronto.

The Toronto Board of Trade has been involved for several years in the issue of affordable housing. The supply of affordable housing affects the success of all businesses in the Toronto area and, along with other infrastructure components, helps to determine whether or not companies and employees locate in the city.

A lack of affordable housing can lead to a host of serious social and economic problems including homelessness and crime, as well as a general deterioration in the quality of city life. It has important consequences for the desirability of Toronto as a tourist destination and major convention centre.

Three years ago this month, the Board released *Building Solutions to Homelessness: A Business Perspective on Homelessness and Toronto's Housing Crisis*. That report contained recommendations directed at the federal, provincial, and municipal governments on solving the crisis of homelessness and the shortage of affordable housing.

Later that year we put forward a policy resolution at the Canadian Chamber of Commerce annual meeting, which was passed unanimously by local chambers of commerce right across Canada. We took an update of that resolution back to the Canadian Chamber of Commerce last

September. Once again, local chambers of commerce and boards of trade across the country passed it unanimously.

Briefly, our resolution called for the development of a national housing policy and the creation of a tax and regulatory environment that promotes the building of new affordable housing. We also called for the review of best practices in other jurisdictions, and innovative financing and liability arrangements to encourage the redevelopment of brownfields for affordable housing.

I began my remarks with a promise to give you five reasons why the supply of affordable housing is important to Toronto's business community. Here they are.

First, affordable housing is a strong selling point for attracting and retaining employees. Toronto competes with some 300 international city-regions and many smaller centres for investment, new business, and employees. People prefer cities that offer a good supply and mix of housing that people of varying occupations and income levels can afford.

Second, Toronto must be able to house people who provide essential services. The people most affected by Toronto's affordable housing crisis are often lower-income earners who work in important industries to the city such as tourism, hospitality, and retail.

Third, businesses in Toronto must remain competitive with respect to labour costs. As housing costs rise, so must wages. To stay competitive with other global companies, firms in Toronto must be able to keep their wage bills reasonable.

Fourth, businesses need healthy and productive employees. Companies pay a high cost in terms of lost productivity, absenteeism, and illness when employees are forced to commute long distances to work or are constantly worried about living costs and accommodations.

And finally, affordable housing represents a partial solution to Toronto's growing traffic problems. More than 70 percent of major highways in the GTA are now congested in peak periods, resulting in serious delays in business deliveries and significantly increasing businesses' transportation costs. More affordable housing in the city represents a partial solution to this growing problem.

I'm reviewing these five areas for you because many times people ask me why business is suddenly interested in the issue of affordable housing. It's true that up until 1995 the Toronto Board of Trade never addressed this topic. That year, though, we started taking a look at what I would call more social issues. Many of you have been talking about these issues for 25 years. I wish I could say that about the Toronto Board of Trade, but that's not been the case.

I think it's important to explain what motivated the business community to start thinking about affordable housing, and how business looks at and understands the issues. We need to reflect these ideas back to others in the business community who maybe aren't as involved. It's terrific that our members now see the linkage between the quality of life, including homelessness and many other social issues, and the success of business. And to the extent business understands that linkage, I think people who are more engaged on the social service side can also understand the importance of a healthy business community to a healthy social services action plan and agenda. While we may have different approaches for tackling the problems, understanding one another's motivations is very important. And so that's why we've spent a lot of time articulating how affordable housing makes a very valuable and important contribution to a competitive and vibrant Toronto.

The affordable housing crunch will only become worse as the region grows. A recent study by the city suggests that population and employment across the GTA will grow by about 2 million residents and 1.5 million jobs between 1996 and 2021. This influx of new residents will put an immense strain on all facets of the city's infrastructure, including affordable housing.

As Toronto has grown, the supply of affordable housing has shrunk. Many people who work in Toronto can no longer afford to live here. Those who find a place often struggle with the high costs of shelter, while others who choose to live outside Toronto become unwitting contributors to urban sprawl and traffic congestion.

As I mentioned earlier, the Toronto Board of Trade believes that the affordable housing problem can be solved. The solutions do not always require more government funding, but they often rely on changes to government policy. For example, we would like to see the following recommendations from our report implemented by the end of the year:

- The federal government should take a leadership position on affordable housing by developing and implementing a comprehensive and coordinated national housing strategy.
- The CMHC needs an enhanced mandate to allow it to expand its research activities and communication functions and improve its coordination of non-profit housing initiatives.

- Some simple changes to the federal tax system would encourage the building of new multi-residential rental units and provide a payback to the government after the construction of just 6,000 units.
- Better protection must be provided to those who remediate brownfields sites for the construction of affordable housing.
- Surplus crown lands should be offered first to developers building affordable housing.

Our report includes a number of other recommendations which would entail higher costs or be undertaken over a longer term. These include:

- The provincial and the federal governments should jointly create a fund or tax incentive to help developers of affordable housing defray the costs of cleaning up brownfield sites.
- A tax credit should be introduced to finance affordable housing, somewhat like the labour-sponsored venture capital funds.
- Provincial opportunity bonds should be exempt from federal taxation.

The citizens of Toronto need affordable housing. It is the responsibility of governments to ensure a policy framework is in place that will encourage the private sector to become active in the creation of affordable housing.

We encourage governments to work with the private sector to increase the supply of affordable housing. The time has come to make the policy and tax changes required to ensure an adequate supply of affordable housing.

The recommendations in the report focus on surplus land, brownfields (particularly in a mature city like Toronto, where access to land is a challenge), and the role of CMHC. We also discuss taxation changes, some of which are mentioned in Don Drummond's report.

We absolutely believe that the government has to be a direct investor in affordable housing. The purpose of the report was to get the private sector engaged. Part of that was driven by the success that we see or perceive the United States to have with respect to private-sector activity in affordable housing, the strength of the non-profit intermediaries that have been created, and the role of the banks and the financial institutions. So the report was intended to focus on the private-sector role.

However, the Board is a member of the Toronto City Summit Alliance, which has called for direct investment by government, including the continuation of programs such as SCPI. We don't believe government has enough money to do it alone. There's probably merit in going back to a model of partnerships where you have a strong government role, coupled with a very active and vigorous private-sector market. It's not one to the exclusion of the other. It requires both sectors cooperating to address the needs across the country.

In terms of income and demand-side issues, given what I have heard over the past several years and in the discussions at the City Summit last year, it's hard not to address the issues of income and wages. A debate on those issues among the business community, labour economists, and others would probably be a very healthy way to broaden people's understanding. Whether my membership would support that position at this point, I don't know. But, we'll certainly be raising the issue for their consideration.

We acknowledge that the tax changes we recommend are a form of federal investment. Whether revenue is forgone through tax incentives or money is spent through grants, there's still a cost to the public sector. We need to continue debating the situation in which you have a private-sector developer with a dollar that can be leveraged with some capital investment from the government – what's the best way to do it? Our members envisioned investment working through a tax model, because that is the model that they know. If you have grant models that still allow you to leverage private-sector capital, then we're still accomplishing the same thing.

So the question is, can you create vehicles that will somehow attract more of that private-sector money? Perhaps both grant and tax mechanisms will be necessary in order for us to reach the ultimate goal.

Elyse Allan is President and CEO of the Toronto Board of Trade, Canada's largest local chamber of commerce. The Board's first female CEO in its 150-year history, Elyse previously held senior management positions in the private sector. She spent most of her career with GE in the United States and Canada. In 2001 she was named Executive of the Year by the Canadian Chamber of Commerce. She is active in public policy making, having co-chaired the Toronto City Summit, the Ontario Business Tax Panel, and the federal government's GTA Innovation Summit. She has extensive board experience, including vice-chair and board member of Providence Centre Hospital, Power Smart Inc., chair of the Humber College advisory board, and director of the Arthritis Society.

Chapter 15

Should We Build Housing for Low-Income People?

STEVE POMEROY, FOCUS CONSULTING

I'm not going to try to lay out all the elements of a comprehensive strategy. Indeed that has been done by other speakers and has also been documented in a number of studies including the FCM strategy and also the Caledon Institute paper that I did last year. What I'm going to do is focus on a few elements you might want to consider if we're talking about a more comprehensive approach.

First off, if one is talking about a developing a comprehensive strategy, one of the key elements is having comprehensive support and building a constituency of support for the idea and helping to bring it forward politically. I think that's where we've dramatically failed in the past. We've always been a very divided and fragmented camp. The housing industry has always argued, "We just need shelter allowances because people have housing, they just pay too much, so let's do that." The non-profit sector comes back and says, "That's just going to line the landlords' pockets, so that's a dumb idea. Let's build more non-profit housing." The industry comes back and says, "That's really inefficient, let's not do that." Government stands on the sidelines and watches.

And I think we have to get over that kind of arguing and start to build a better coalition of support across the housing sector, including the developers and the financiers. I'm very pleased to see TD here today bringing a perspective from the business and finance sector to this important issue. They're obviously key players, given that housing is very capital-intensive and needs a lot of financing. So that's the first point.

My second point is more controversial. I would like to pose the question: Does it make sense to build new housing for low-income households? Michael Shapcott has framed this discussion with the challenge of keeping rents to $523 or less a month. That's an average across the country and it's a useful number to start with. If you do the math, at least half of that amount is going to be going into operating expenses, utility taxes, municipal property taxes, and administrative costs. Now with today's very low interest rates – maybe 5½ percent – you can leverage maybe $50,000 of debt on the residual income. New housing at the lowest end of the spectrum runs from bachelor- or studio-type units in the lower-cost communities, up to a family-type unit in a high-cost community – you're probably looking at a range of $70,000 to $140,000 in development costs and a capital subsidy of between $20,000 for tiny bachelor units to $90,000 for family units.

It's a question I put on the table – is that politically sustainable? Are we going to get that level of capital grants or the equivalent ongoing subsidy to sustain such a program? We've seen in the past that because it's such a capital-intensive industry and the numbers are so big, it's an extremely vulnerable target in times of government fiscal constraints. And not just Canada, but every single Western democracy has gone through huge cuts in supply-side housing programs because it's such a huge budget target. So we've got to find a way to camouflage it and think in terms of a whole bunch of little targets that can fly under the radar of national budgets.

There's another problem with providing new housing. As much as it's a very big benefit and significant improvement for the quality of life of the individuals who get it, it can be hard to get the necessary political and public support for providing housing. I think the idea of public housing has alienated much of the public in the past. People who are living in a 20- or 30-year-old house that's a little bit rundown and in need of repair, and working a couple of jobs to pay the rent, see a household on social assistance get a nice new property down the street that they could never get themselves. And then we ask them to vote in favour of this program so more of those people can get housing that they can't get. So there's a perception that this is unfair – even though it is based on stereotypes of social assistance recipients. But it's an issue we have to deal with.

And the other key issue is that for every single new non-profit affordable unit we build, we're probably losing two or three. We have to deal with the erosion of the existing housing stock. I was recently doing some research on British Columbia. B.C. is one of the two provinces that maintained a non-profit program between 1994 and 2002. They've created 7,000 new units of affordable housing. But between the 1996 census and the 2001 census, they lost 9,000 units in the relatively affordable existing market rental housing. The net loss is 2,000 units, despite spending about $40 million dollars a year.

So I think we have to ask ourselves how we can preserve that existing stock. Could we have saved some of those 9,000 units? Is the market inefficient? I would say the market is very efficient. Basically when a unit gets older, the market knocks it down and rebuilds just at the point at which it was becoming affordable. Actually, this is beneficial in the sense we care about. Private industry is not building new housing, it's buying the existing housing that makes more economic sense. Maybe we can learn from their model and actually step into the market, intervene, and buy some of these units that are renting at $500 to $800 a month. Even though the affordability gap is still significant, it's less than the new stock and we don't have to pay the supply premium on the income side and then try to do the other things that others have talked about for stimulating the market and pushing a little bit to get the supply going – admittedly at the top end.

I think tax credits are something we should take a look at. I don't think they're the best thing since sliced bread, but I think as part of this system and as one of the elements of a strategy, they can make a useful contribution if they're well designed. We had very good examples of very poorly designed direct-spending programs in the past, and I would argue they're just as inefficient as a poorly designed tax program. I think it's not tax expenditures versus direct spending, it's well-designed programs versus poorly designed programs.

In terms of relative efficiency – people have pointed the finger at the Low-Income Housing Tax Credit in the United States, and the transaction cost involved. And certainly in the mid-1980s it was extremely high – people were paying 44 or 45 cents on the dollar for a dollar of tax expenditure. The market has worked extremely well and those things have been bid up in the last couple of years. Investors are now bidding 77 or 78 cents on the dollar for a stream of credits available up to 10 years into the future. The present value of that stream of credit is worth 82 cents. So the transaction cost is about 5 or 6 cents.

When governments deliver programs, there's an administrative cost to that as well, hidden overhead cost we don't see. Look at CMHC's financial statements and consider how much is recorded in the minister's account – the cost of overhead and staff for programs. It's not insignificant. CMHC delivered a program on behalf of the federal government on family violence up in the early 1990s, a $22-million program. $3.5 million went off the top to cover CMHC's administrative overhead. That's a 15 percent cost of administration compared to the 6 percent that I just cited for the low-income tax credit. So if we're going to have an argument on efficiency, let's look at the numbers and compare apples with apples and see which is more efficient.

I think the other benefit of a tax-based program is that unlike direct spending programs, they change investor behaviour. The government of Canada has used tax expenditures and things like film tax credits because they're concerned about the Canadian cultural industry and the Canadian film-making industry. They've used them to encourage people like me to invest in retirement programs and to get people to invest in capital markets for high-risk investment in labour-supported investment funds. If we need to change behaviour, it is in the area of trying to encourage investments in more affordable housing.

I would argue that direct spending doesn't actually do that. And indeed the federal-provincial program is another example of a very poorly designed program. It's basically a result of a lot of political compromise. At the end of the day, we have a program that's trying to be all things to all people and is largely ineffective. On the one hand, it's missed the mark on the market side by putting in constraints that basically deter the industry from building any units, given the criteria of an average market rent. You're taking on de facto rent control and you're building for 20 years for a grant of $20,000 to $50,000. If you actually do the math and charge the rent you could have charged without pushing the rent artificially lower, you'd be better off without the grant.

The non-profit sector is more interested in providing units at the very low end of the market. They'll play the game, they'll put in the units, but they're not very happy about it. They want to be building units for folks who can only afford $400 or $500 a month, not for those who can afford $800 or $900 a month. In the past we've seen programs that have evolved over time. The assisted rental program in the mid 1970s went through four iterations in three years. I hope that they do the same with this program and take a sober second look at it and say "What do we really want to achieve? We have all those dollars, and we haven't spent any of them yet. Can we actually rejig some of the criteria in cooperation with the provinces to try to make it work better?"

Under the old non-profit programs it was very difficult to do acquisition rehab. I was involved in a few of these myself in my early years. We'd find the absolute worst building in town, buy it and rehab the hell out of it. It was extremely inefficient. We also had policies that said that if you were going to do an acquisition rehab all the people in the building had to be eligible for social housing, but then you had to turf them all out, and so it would create more problems.

The silver lining about the current program is that you can do pretty well what you want. But you now have to cobble together your resource funding. People have done that, through various small municipal and provincial grant programs and that kind of thing to buy buildings. But don't go and buy the worst building in town. Buy a 20- or 30-year old building that's reasonably sound. The pension funds, the institutional investors – that's what they're doing. For the most part, they're buying buildings up to 100 years old and they want a large portfolio. There's a whole chunk of buildings between probably 10 or 12 years up to about 80 years old that are in reasonably sound condition. They certainly could use an improvement, but you don't need to actually knock the thing down and start again yet.

I'm not saying that you should not do any supply, I just think that you have to constantly think about the best-buy kind of decisions. Perhaps buying a building today, running it as an existing rental, having some tenants and maybe five or ten years from now, when the building does actually need to be replaced, you have paid off the land and the building earlier and you can consider any supply downstream with those efficiencies built in.

On the operating side, I'm not a big fan of using high-tech stuff. I think we've probably gone the other way to reduce capital costs. We've put in very inefficient utilities like electric baseboard heaters, because it's cheaper on the capital side, but you pay in the long run on the operating side or through the rent and utility costs.

Steve **Pomeroy** *is the President of Focus Consulting Inc, based in Ottawa, and specializes in affordable housing policy and research. After a short time working as a municipal planner and a project development consultant, he spent 10 years with Canada Mortgage and Housing Corporation, where he held a number of positions in social housing, market analysis, and housing policy. From 1990 to 1994 he was manager of the CMHC Centre for Future Studies in Housing and Living Environments. In addition, he served on two major policy task forces: the 1990 Expenditure Review Committee of Cabinet, and the 1993–94 Social Housing Policy Review Team. Since becoming a consultant in 1994, Mr. Pomeroy has written more than 60 research reports and housing strategies for provinces and municipalities. These assignments cover housing affordability and rental housing, alternative financing, homelessness, the interface between hous-*

ing policy and social policy, affordability indicators, and socio-economic analysis. He has a graduate degree from the University of British Columbia in Urban Planning with a specialization in Housing and Urban Land Economics (1984).

Chapter 16

The Municipal Role in a National Housing Policy

ELISABETH ARNOLD

The Federation of Canadian Municipalities has just concluded its annual meeting and the general consensus at that meeting was that we have to continue and work harder with our partners in the housing community, because although we've made some progress in terms of having some commitments for affordable housing, we have very few of those long-term affordable housing units delivered in our communities. The challenge right now for us is to find ways to produce results with the resources available – they are not the resources that we've asked for, but they are more resources than we had in the recent past. Even so, many of those units are not being delivered in our communities.

One of the committees that the Federation of Canadian Municipalities has formed is called the National Housing Policy Option Team (NHPOT) and it is our advocacy arm on affordable housing for the Federation. We work with organizations like the National Alliance to End Homelessness, the Canadian Housing and Renewal Association, and others to put together strategies and we will continue to do that.

I would like to talk about some specifics of the FCM agenda and also speak a little bit as a municipal councillor about the difficulties of implementing housing strategies at the local level.

The FCM strategy has been built into our budget submissions for this year's budget cycle. We have a three-pronged policy that has been developed to meet the needs of the diversity of municipalities large and small across the country.

1. A capital grants program to provide new and renovated housing for those who cannot afford market rents in markets where vacancy rates are low.
2. Canada-wide shelter allowances, rent supplements, or improved shelter components of welfare for those who have shelter but cannot afford it.
3. Changes in tax regulation and CMHC mortgage underwriting policies to make it easier for both the private and the not-for-profit housing sectors to provide affordable housing.

We have had some movement on the first part, with the capital grants, although we have received in the last budgets about a tenth of what FCM believes is required to meet the housing need. We do not have a Canada-wide system of shelter allowances, although we obviously have different responses in different provinces across the country. And we have not made much headway on tax regulations and mortgage underwriting.

From the perspective of FCM, without substantial reinvestment in housing from the federal government and without changes in the other policy areas that I've outlined, a worse crunch is coming. Looking at the 1996 Statistics Canada analysis, our sense is that given the growing income gap, the demand for affordable housing (when I say affordable housing, I mean housing that is affordable to the lowest-income Canadians) is going to grow and it's going to become more and more difficult to meet those needs.

One of the challenges facing FCM is that we represent a great diversity of cities and towns across the country. As the statistics from the TD Bank confirm, housing and issues of homelessness are no longer big-city problems only. We have heard, for example, from municipalities like Peterborough, Ontario, that have severe affordable housing problems and problems with homelessness. We have heard from municipalities like Canmore, Alberta, that are facing incredible demands for affordable housing in a high-growth economy.

Each city and region has its own problems, and they manifest themselves in different ways. Cities and towns have different resources and capacities to respond to those problems and they work under very different funding and legislative arrangements. So we need a national housing policy, but we need one that is flexible and diverse enough to respond to individual municipalities' situations.

I wanted to read to you the motion that was passed in my own city council, Ottawa, with respect to this matter a few months ago. I think it reflects the position of municipalities across the country. And that is: "We urge the federal government to ensure that any new funding for affordable housing be made available in a manner that supports local housing policies and programs and be directed to build the most housing for those most in need as identified by local communities."

We in Ottawa and municipalities across the country have worked very hard to develop local housing plans. They take different forms, but they all reflect the fact that it's in municipalities that the results of housing problems manifest themselves. People who have a housing affordability problem have a whole host of other problems as well. Their incomes are not sufficient to meet the broad range of basic necessities in their life. We need a comprehensive response to that issue that not only involves an affordable housing component, but also recognizes that municipalities are being called on to deal with issues of food security, health issues, and childcare as well as housing. When someone is paying 50 percent or more of income for housing, he or she is not going to be able to meet those other needs as well. So as municipalities are grappling with how to respond to this issue, they have a whole host of other demands that are coming at them at the same time.

In 2001, the government of Canada committed $680 million to an affordable rental housing program for five years. And in the recent budget the government added another $320 million over the next five years. So we're at about a billion dollars over the next five years. We also had an extension of RRAP, the Residential Rehabilitation Assistance Program, at roughly its past yearly funding level. However, that is not sufficient to meet our goal of addressing the affordable housing program.

The bigger problem is that only a few provinces and territories have seriously implemented the affordable rental program to date. And even in those provinces and territories, we hear concerns from our colleagues about issues such as long-term affordability, access to that money, and the kind of housing that is being produced.

Our friends in Alberta were very enthusiastic about the delivery of the program there. Quebec was very fast off the mark, although we now have some concerns about what will happen with a changed government. But in British Columbia, although the agreement was signed, we have been told that the housing dollars are being used to replace health care dollars by funding long-term care units for seniors. We have a problem in this patchwork delivery mechanism for producing housing across the country.

We're talking about designing a comprehensive federal national housing program, and it needs to be flexible, but it also has to meet our national goals. And that is the crux of the problem. And so I think one of the challenges that we need to address in a forum like this is, "How do we design a national housing strategy or national housing program that remains flexible but also meets some basic requirements?" FCM would like to work with you to help identify what the criteria should be.

Also, how do we design a program that could be delivered directly with municipalities, without letting the provinces, for example provinces like Ontario, "off the hook" if they're not prepared to come to the table?

FCM's position is that if municipalities are given responsibility with the appropriate resources, they are very efficient delivery mechanisms. I believe that that is true. However, when you're looking at redistribution programs, it becomes difficult to ensure equity when municipalities have very different capacities and different political priorities. It is hard to administer a national program without very clear criteria for the delivery of those programs. The goal is to have national criteria for long-term, affordable housing, with cost-shared programs that involve a partnership with the municipalities.

The problems that have been identified for municipalities relate to many of the suggestions made by the TD Bank. First of all, municipalities have a very limited capacity in terms of financing. Our existing tax base, the property tax base, is not very flexible. There's no great desire in any municipality across the country to raise property taxes, so funding housing from the property tax base is not a sustainable way of operating.

Municipalities vary widely. Some municipalities have a large land supply that could be used and others don't. Some municipalities have the ability to find other ways of financing because of different provincial legislation, and others don't. Municipalities have a very difficult time looking at a long-term sustainable investment in affordable housing.

We also have had a lot of success in developing official plans that have very progressive affordable housing components in them, but we have a much more difficult time actually implementing those plans. For example, we tried to include in the new Ottawa official plan a requirement that there be 25 percent affordable housing in new developments. Council decided to take that out, because the development industry threatened to take the whole official plan to the Ontario Municipal Board over that one clause. So it is no longer in our official plan, although we continue to work to find new mechanisms to ensure an adequate supply of affordable housing.

I also want to touch on property tax equalization. The experience in my own municipality reflects that of other municipalities across the country. I think people would agree that because most people get elected where homeowners are the majority and tenants are the minority, the Council decisions reflect the interests of homeowners over renters. Thus it is very difficult, if not impossible, to move towards equalization of the property tax base, because it would mean increasing the tax burden on homeowners. We need to talk about political realities as well.

Question: Does FCM have a mechanism to share experiences among municipalities?

Yes. One of the programs that we've been using to try to share best practices is the Affordability and Choice Today program (ACT) through CMHC. For example, we have been able to see in some cases that a relaxation on zoning regulations has been successful in providing opportunities for more affordable housing in many municipalities across the country.

Question: What do you suggest to combat NIMBYism (the Not In My Back Yard syndrome)?

It's a long public education process. One of the ways we've been successful in Ottawa has been to allow secondary suites. That's something that is more palatable to people, because they see it as a way to include an elderly person in their household. We have not been successful, however, in moving the permission for rooming houses beyond the inner core of Ottawa. How can we do that?

I think it's partly a general public education process, but also, more importantly, we need to do more aggressive political lobbying. The fact of the matter is that property taxes will go up if we are not able to find adequate accommodation for people across the whole city. We have to link the cost of not having affordable housing to the interests of property taxpayers, for example through increased social service and health care requirements, or through emergency services requirements – the whole gamut of services that municipalities are responsible for. I think that that's probably the best way to go, because the equity argument doesn't really work very well. Often, the downtown councillor speaking to someone in a suburban part of the city knows that they're not interested in the equity argument, they're interested in the cost argument.

Elisabeth Arnold was elected to Ottawa City Council in 1994 and served three terms as councillor. In 2001, she was elected to the Board of Directors of the Federation of Canadian Municipalities and in 2002, she was appointed co-chair of FCM's National Housing Policy Options Team. Elisabeth had worked previously as the Coordinator of Housing Help, a storefront program that provides information and assistance on housing-related issues and as Coordinator of the Community Development Program at the Sandy Hill Community Health Centre in Ottawa. She was also a founding member of the Ottawa Vietnamese Non-Profit Residence Corporation, served as Vice-Chair of the founding board of the Women's Action Centre Against Violence, and was a member of the Board of Directors of Centretown Citizens Ottawa Corporation, Ottawa's largest private non-profit housing provider, prior to election to City Council. After deciding not to run for re-election in 2003, she launched her own community planning practice in Ottawa. Elisabeth has a bachelor's degree in geography from Simon Fraser University and a master's in urban planning from Queen's University.

Chapter 17

The Unique Needs of Aboriginal People

JIM LANIGAN,
NATIONAL ABORIGINAL HOUSING ASSOCIATION

It's important for Aboriginal people to be a part of forums such as this. I believe that if we can solve the Aboriginal problem, we should be able to solve any problem in affordable housing.

I'd like to offer some background on the National Aboriginal Housing Association. We've been in existence since 1994. A member-based organization on a national level, we link Aboriginal housing corporations from the Grey Mountain Housing Society in Whitehorse, Yukon, to the Melville Native Housing Association in Happy Valley, Labrador.

We receive very limited federal funding and generally we count on the goodwill of our members and private-sector organizations to support the kinds of things that we do. The Association advocates on behalf of and represents the concerns of Aboriginal people in the development of federal housing policy and in the delivery and management of housing services for Aboriginal people. On an Aboriginal political level, the Association links with the Assembly of First Nations, the Métis National Council, the Congress of Aboriginal Peoples, and the Native Women's Association of Canada.

I don't know if we're going to be able to provide answers to the questions that are raised today or just create additional questions. I do know that answers to the questions quite often don't get you the solutions. And the one sure thing is some land and some money would go a long way to solving problems in the Aboriginal community. That is one reason why we're here.

The title of the forum was a drawing card: $523 a month or less for affordable housing in the country. We completed a study in Ottawa, called the *Feasibility Study to Overcome Barriers to Aboriginal Home Ownership*. Among our tenant population and a 900 Aboriginal family waiting list, it was determined that 99 percent of both the tenants and waiting-list families had incomes under $35,000 and of that percentage, 73 percent of household incomes were under $15,000. We found that 79.6 percent of our tenants pay less than $350 a month and only 6 percent pay $500 a month or more. So you can see what $523 a month means to us. We're far below that level. If we're going to be able to address affordable housing, there must be special initiatives undertaken to do that.

This situation really brings new meaning to the word *affordable*. With incomes of 33 percent below the national average, Aboriginal people have long held the bottom rung of housing affordability, not only on First Nations lands, but also in Canada's metropolitan centres. In spite of federal initiatives such as the Urban Aboriginal Strategy, Supporting Communities Partnership Initiative, and the Affordable Housing Framework, the shortage of adequate and affordable housing continues to be prevalent. Little progress is being made as our people continue to be over represented in the ranks of the homeless.

To understand why we're in the position that we're in, we have to go back a little bit in history and look at where we've been, so that we can determine where we need to go. If we look back we find that in 1972, Ron Basford, the Minister Responsible for Housing, declared that access to adequate housing was a right of all Canadians, including Aboriginal people. He committed his government to ensuring the building or acquisition of 50,000 housing units for Aboriginal people residing off reserve. To deliver on this commitment, the rural and remote housing program and the Urban Native Housing Program were established in 1973.

Various parties have different interpretations of whether these programs were successful or not. But we believe that they were extremely successful. What was important in the introduction and development of these two programs was that Aboriginal people themselves were involved in the design of the program. Aboriginal housing corporations emerged and accepted responsibility for delivery. The resulting units became home to Aboriginal families.

These programs recognized the affordability barrier and responded to the needs of the constituency they were designed to serve. Over the years, the two programs produced 20,000 units of housing across Canada – 9,000 in rural communities and 11,000 in cities. It should be noted, however, that only the urban program was specifically targeted to those of native ancestry. A large percentage of the rural program serves non-Aboriginal households.

In 1993, both programs were capped, some 30,000 units short of Mr. Basford's desired goals back in 1970. With a no-growth policy in social housing and a rapidly increasing movement of Aboriginal peoples to urban centres, it didn't take long for the shortage of affordable housing to grow into a homeless crisis of significant proportions.

To compound matters, the federal government relinquished its responsibility for social housing, shuffling a very hot potato to the provinces for them to deal with. And in the case of Ontario, social housing programs were further devolved to municipalities. Today, these programs remain capped. There does not seem to be any desire by most provinces to increase funding in this area. The question, particularly in Ontario, is how are municipalities going to meet this demand? Where will they get the money to address it? Are the city taxpayers going to pay? I think not.

The National Aboriginal Housing Association has been doing considerable work trying to determine what the solutions are. In terms of strategy, we believe that all federal housing initiatives must have an urban Aboriginal component. National Aboriginal organizations representative of Aboriginal peoples and the members of the National Aboriginal Housing Association must be involved in the design of such initiatives.

Further, programs such as the Homelessness Initiative (SCPI) and the Affordable Housing Framework have not considered Aboriginal needs. They are ill-designed for our purposes and are difficult if not impossible to access for most Aboriginal service providers.

Experience tells us that programs are best designed by the people who experience the problem. The Aboriginal community particularly must solve its own problems. We have waited for a long time to come to the conclusion that nobody else can solve our problems for us.

In terms of the strategy, we require 20,000 housing units over the next five years just to address the backlog on our waiting lists. Mr. Basford's promise of adequate housing fell short by 30,000 units. Thirty years later we are requesting a doubling of the existing Aboriginal housing portfolio. Based on our preliminary analysis, we have a current backlog requirement of well over this number. Meeting this figure will satisfy current priority waiting lists, but will not necessarily address the continuing growth of the urban Aboriginal population. The federal government must take steps to ensure that the existing Aboriginal portfolio is protected under the current federal-provincial social housing agreement.

There is some concern that the shift in responsibilities for social housing will bring about the integration of mainstream and Aboriginal housing in the name of efficiency. The unique problems of Aboriginal peoples, which includes cultural sensitivity of services, must continue to be a consideration.

In terms of the principles that we espouse, self-determination of Aboriginal peoples must be respected. The Aboriginal community must be consulted and must deliver on any future programs. This is consistent with international covenants on the self-determination of indigenous peoples, to which Canada is a signatory. It is also consistent with domestic court decisions and federal Aboriginal policies, such as the inherent right of self-government and the response to the Royal Commission on Aboriginal Peoples, *Gathering Strength: Canada's Aboriginal Action Plan*.

Housing is considered the cornerstone of urban Aboriginal governance. By ensuring Aboriginal peoples' access to adequate and affordable housing, the issues of health, education, and employment can be improved.

The Board of Directors of the National Aboriginal Housing Association recognizes that the needs and demands are significant. However, that is to be expected, given a decade of inaction and the unfulfilled housing targets of yesteryear. The signs are optimistic and the public is aware of the poverty and social issues of the Aboriginal peoples residing in Canada's metropolises. Government appears more prepared to take action on the housing front and the National Aboriginal Housing Association and its members have the capacity to act on this strategy. What we need now is the financial commitment from government.

Today, government recognizes the unique housing needs of Aboriginal peoples. It now must go a step farther and take action to develop responsive and accessible Aboriginal housing programs in cooperation with Aboriginal peoples. The National Aboriginal Housing Association and its members have the capacity to act on the strategies we have developed. What we need now is movement and financial commitment on the part of governments.

Jim Lanigan is Metis and originates from Big River, a village in northern Saskatchewan. Throughout his career he has accumulated a wealth of management experience that spans the corporate sector, Aboriginal organizations, and the public service. He has worked in British Columbia, Saskatchewan, and Ontario. His involvement in community development led to his election as Vice President of the B.C. Association of Non Status Indians and he served in several executive positions in its successor organization, the United Native Nations Society in Vancouver. After completing a three-year Executive Interchange as a senior programs and policy advisor with the Metis National Council, he has returned to the Department of Canadian Heritage, Aboriginal Affairs Branch. He is President of Gignul Non Profit Housing Corporation. The Corporation administers 162 units of rent-geared-to-income housing for Aboriginal families and owns and operates the Madawan Aboriginal Seniors Lodge.

Chapter 18

A Municipal Perspective on a National Housing Strategy

GREG SUTTOR, CITY OF TORONTO

Municipalities, in recent years, have become more prominent in affordable housing. They are the sphere in which the consequences of the expanding housing problem are most direct, where the fallout falls out. They are a major funding partner in today's new programs, especially in Ontario and Quebec. And in the past four years they have proved to be an effective advocate, through the Federation of Canadian Municipalities. I'm going to speak from a municipal perspective about national strategy, although I am not speaking on behalf of the City I work for.

I'll make a few comments on where we've come from in the past five years, where we are now, and where we might go in a broader or future national strategy. Our principal need is to have the federal and provincial governments to engage with us on a multi-year basis. The biggest challenge, really, is not on the housing supply side, but on the rent supplement and rental assistance side.

In the past five years, there have been four significant milestones, in terms of frameworks of thinking about national strategies, and two big program announcements which are also movements in that direction.

The first milestone was Toronto's Homelessness Action Task Force in 1999, which got wide attention across the country. It outlined an approach to new affordable supply which was feasible without a new omnibus social housing program – relying principally on federal dollars but with other contributors and local coordination. It's a model that's now being rolled out in "Let's Build" in Toronto and more broadly in the federal affordable housing initiative. The Task Force also talked about rental assistance programs, and about reinvesting surplus federal housing money into rent supplements.

The second milestone was the Rental Housing Action Plan, *Unlocking the Opportunity*, a City of Toronto report prepared jointly with development industry representatives in 2001, which dealt with private-sector rental investment. That segued fairly directly into Ontario's Housing Supply Working Group and into related processes now reporting to the federal-provincial-territorial ministers of housing, albeit with outcome unclear. It also led to activity by the Toronto Board of Trade and others in the private sector.

Third was the paper prepared by Steve Pomeroy for the Caledon Institute in 2001, *Toward a Comprehensive Affordable Housing Strategy for Canada*. That was a major piece of framework thinking around a national strategy, well worth revisiting.

The fourth milestone – not the most recent, but the subject of brief reflections here – was the Federation of Canadian Municipalities' National Strategy in 2000. It proposed three groupings of activity: first, capital grants for new housing but also for rehabilitation; second, federal tax measures to attract investment plus changes to the CMHC role in mortgage insurance; and third, rental assistance. The latter was named as a provincial responsibility, whether in the form of shelter allowances or rent supplement.

Worth recapping is the cost of the FCM proposals. The capital grant was essentially $1.5 billion a year. That's what FCM proposed at the time, hoping to create about 35,000 units a year at a $45,000 average grant. On the rental assistance side, they proposed ramping up by $60 million a year to $600 million or so after a decade. For $60 million the number of extra households you might help each year could range from 40,000 (the FCM estimate) to 10,000 households (which I think more realistic). This is not a lot if you look at the scale of need.

Three brief reflections on the FCM strategy. First, why do we want to create new supply? This will not address the affordability problem in general. There are several reasons, which are worth repeating as we look at rising vacancies, at least in Ontario. You need to deal with incremental growth in rental demand as our urban population expands; this is a long-term need regardless of cyclical ups and downs in vacancy rates. This growth includes the suburban expansion of cities, and the need to build some rental housing there to avoid "monocultural" middle-class suburbs and income-polarized central cities, which is certainly the direction we're heading. You need to provide special-needs housing – supportive housing. You need to reinvest in older neighbourhoods and older stock, in ways other than gentrification and up-market redevelopment. And there are two political rather than social policy reasons to build housing. You get an enduring product that can't just be swept away when the next Mike Harris comes to power. And building has political appeal: it captures people's imagination in a way no income transfer program ever will.

A second reflection on the FCM strategy is triggered by the remarkable and very welcome new TD Economics paper. One of the emphases in the latter is that it may not be cost-efficient or market-neutral to support housing by way of investment incentives and taxation-related measures. But while I agree about the need for direct spending, what we are also dealing with is how public policy structures the market. There's no such thing as a neutral market, a market that arises from spontaneous forces. Markets are created by institutions and laws, and we can choose to structure markets toward certain social ends. Certainly, questions of cost-efficiency of spending are important. But we should not understate the importance of measures that will retain multi-sectoral political support, or of the need to achieve housing ends through the private sector as well as through public programs. We need to consider what is important to the private sector as well as to those in the affordable housing sector and the public sector. It's great that we've reached a point where there's a lot of engagement from the private sector and we'd like to keep that engagement. I, for one, am afraid that with slack rental markets and a potentially vulnerable property sector, we may lose that that momentum.

The TD Bank paper also stresses income policy as a fundamental dimension of the housing problem, which it is. The question is, how much can we address income policy in a discussion about housing policy? Arguably the biggest thing the federal government has done recently, or the feds and the provinces, is the National Child Benefit Supplement and its enhancements. In many ways this achieves the same thing as rental assistance: more disposable income and more choice for lower-income families.

In the past five years, along with these framework-for-thinking milestones, we've had two big federal program announcements: the SCPI (Supporting Communities Partnership Initiative) program and the federal affordable housing initiative – federal/provincial in some degree. There was also the extension of RRAP (Residential Rehabilitation Assistance Program), first in 1999 and now in 2003 onward. They, too, are milestones, because real strategies are made of actions, not of words.

What will these programs do for our communities? In the next three to five years, we will be delivering the new affordable housing program of 10,000 units in Ontario, 30,000 or more across Canada. The funding is close to $200 million a year if it rolls out over five years. RRAP is a bit more than $100 million a year nationwide. SCPI is also about $100 million a year nationwide. SCPI isn't just about housing, of course, but a significant part of it is. In total we're talking about $300 to $400 million a year of federal capital nationwide.

In the case of Toronto, we could well see commitments of capital funding to about 1,000 units a year over the next three years, under the new affordable housing program. The emerging direction in the SCPI plan for 2003–2007 suggests a housing emphasis – perhaps up to 500 units over the period. And RRAP will fund close to 500 units a year, mostly rental and rooming houses. And in the new affordable housing program we are on track to get private-sector investment and involvement in a way we've not had before. We hope that can lead to some efficiencies in development, but it will also require close monitoring of the public spending. Other larger Ontario municipalities have or will have versions of the same thing.

So, with these major announcements we have pieces of a national housing strategy, yet they do not constitute a strategy. What are some of the issues we face in moving forward with these pieces? As a first approach and as a lead-in to broader comments, let me name the five biggest challenges we appear to face from a municipal viewpoint.

The first three challenges are essentially practical matters. How can we ramp up the delivery and commit all those dollars in three years? If we want to spend the funds in five years we must commit them to projects in three, so that there is time for land use approvals and construction. Second, how do we deal with increasing NIMBY issues in local delivery? The ramping up will take a lot of work, and NIMBY needs a more proactive response, but these are essentially practical problems for which we can find local solutions. Then there is the Ontario problem of the framework for delivering the Community Rental Housing Program, but on that score we can hope that things will continue to improve politically, as they have in recent months.

The next challenges that appear are broader. How do we make sure that this is not a one-off, three-year spike in activity, but instead enhance and extend it? How do we ensure real provincial matching funding, so that cities aren't on the hook to cost-share? And is there a way of making a major dent in the housing waiting list, which 1,000 units a year really won't achieve?

These larger challenges lead us to the question of what we need in a national strategy, or how we get there from here. For general frameworks of thinking, one should go back to the Caledon paper and the FCM paper. Here, let me offer a few themes and ingredients to keep in mind.

First, we need a multi-year federal-provincial agreement. We need a framework that goes well beyond a single three- to five-year initiative. Moreover, such an agreement needs to have the flexibility that this odd federation of ours requires and yet the clout to lever real provincial engagement.

Second, we need assured funding levels. Under the current funding arrangements, we can commit funding to 1,000 or more units a year in Toronto – 3,000 a year across Ontario – over the next three years. Certainly 1,000 a year is good, although 2,000 would be better. But if offered a choice, I'd take 1,000 a year for a longer period, not a higher spike.

Third, we need to reinforce multi-sectoral support. This involves mortgage insurance measures and taxation measures which the private sector has supported and from which they will benefit as housing investors. It includes tax credit vehicles which have proved to be so robust in the U.S. as a means of supporting affordable housing.

Fourth, we need real provincial cost-sharing, and fifth, we need rental assistance. These two are related, in that the federal government has been willing to come in with capital, but rent supplement or rental assistance is seen as a provincial responsibility. This is the most difficult area in a national strategy, and it needs more thought than advocates or the municipal sector have given it to date.

Ask most municipal councillors why they want new rental housing: it's to house people who are currently on the waiting list. Toronto's current waiting list is 50,000 households. Nationwide, the number of tenant households paying over 50 percent of income on shelter indeed fell between 1996 and 2001, but still stands at about 735,000. We do need affordable new supply. But the bulk of the problem doesn't require new units. Those 735,000 people don't need to vacate their homes and move into costly new ones. They need help to stay where they are now.

The key point about rental assistance is that it is expensive. For example, take one Toronto City Summit Alliance recommendation. In effect it was for 2,500 added rent supplement units in new housing each year, for 10 years. So, 2,500 times $6,000 annual cost (a low-cost estimate for Toronto, about right for Ontario) yields $15 million cost per year. Ramping up over a decade, the average, at the five-year mark, is already $75 million a year. This is equal to the federal contribution in Toronto under the full $1 billion new affordable program. Over a lifetime of, say, 25 years of subsidy, the capitalized value of that $6,000 for 2,500 units approaches $300 million – five times what the federal government contributes in capital to those units. To cover assistance for tenants in existing units is at least as expensive per unit, and requires much larger amounts globally.

The point here is that ongoing expenditures required under the current framework of thinking well exceed capital expenditures being put in on the federal side. No wonder most provinces aren't keen to ante up.

So we've got a big challenge there. It's wonderful that the federal government is coming up with these capital grants, but to really serve low-income households and the $524 a month which is the stated target of today's forum, we need other forms of assistance too.

It's instructive to take that $524 figure and translate it to an affordable housing project being built. Under today's model in Toronto, market rents average $975 and rent payments by those on rent supplement average $375. If you do the math, you will find that $524 is almost exactly a building that is three-quarters rent supplement and one-quarter average market rent. That's who we need to house and it will take a lot of rent supplement to do it. We could deepen the capital subsidy – that would be useful thing to do with the extra $320 million announced in the 2003 federal budget. But you still need a lot of rent supplement.

So this balance between capital and ongoing operating expenditures, which have been deemed to be federal and provincial responsibilities, respectively, is tough to achieve. We need to think more about that if we are to get to multi-year federal provincial frameworks, as well as thinking about other dimensions of those frameworks. And we need to do it within the next three years, if the current programs are to be the start of something ongoing rather than just a spike.

Greg Suttor has worked at the municipal level in housing policy for several years, and is currently Policy Development Officer for the City of Toronto. He was the lead staff on housing issues for Toronto's Homelessness Action Task Force, lead writer of the 1999 Federation of Canadian Municipalities National Housing Policy Options paper, and author of the 1996 Metro Toronto housing needs study. He contributed to shaping the housing role of the new City of Toronto, including the start of the "Let's Build" program and the SCPI 2000–2003 Community Plan. Mr. Suttor is active in the Canadian Housing and Renewal Association through its Research and Policy Committee and its editorial committee. Before municipal amalgamation in Toronto, he worked in housing policy for Metro Toronto, the Metro Toronto Housing Company Limited, and the former City of Toronto, as well as in non-profit housing development. He has an M.A. in Urban and Regional Planning from the University of Waterloo.

Chapter 19

A Wake-Up Call for
Non-Profit Housing Providers

JON HARSTONE,
GANESH COMMUNITY DEVELOPMENT CO-OP

It's self-evident that the only way that decent affordable housing can be built is to use some kind of government subsidy or grant program. This isn't new information. Ontario's first social housing legislation, the *Hanna Act*, was passed in 1913 and was used to finance the development several projects, including Riverdale Courts, now Bain Housing Co-op. Many of the problems we are seeing go back even farther – to the Great Fire of 1901. The city put in place a new fire code that made it nearly impossible to build affordable housing in the city.

Most of the solutions being suggested are technical in nature. I want to discuss the attitude of the non-profit housing sector. If we are going to develop permanent affordable housing, we have to involve the non-profit sector. The private sector has a different agenda. I'd like to figure out how we can get the non-profits to do more.

Although lack of money is the biggest obstacle, there is also a problem with the expectations of the non-profit housing providers. And unless this changes, non-profits are not going to be part of the solution. This paper addresses some of the changes in the non-profit housing provider's mindset that are needed to develop housing at $523.67 a month.

Non-profit groups have been spoiled by 30 years of 100 percent government funding. They were spoon-fed money. And it fostered a certain mindset. "We don't need to talk to the community. We don't need to talk to the unions or the churches. All the money is coming from the government. Problems with NIMBYism? We'll just hire a big a big-name OMB lawyer from McCarthy Tétrault. We've got a whole slew of them. We can wipe out anybody, because we've got all this money."

Today, these groups can't imagine developing housing unless they have 100 percent financing. They see the housing crisis as the government's problem and responsibility. They think the government should give them the money to fix it, just as they did in the good old days. This is rear-view mirror vision. Too many non-profit groups are talking about how things were so much better in the past that they have no idea where things are now or where non-profit housing is going. As a consultant to non-profits, I find it difficult to work with some of these groups.

One quick example to prove the point. Most non-profit groups I've met with consider getting an appraisal to be a waste of time and money. No wonder their projects never get off the ground. Well, I'm sorry. Under the new realities, if you don't have an appraisal, you're not even at the starting gate. Yet they don't understand that. The task of educating the non-profits is vast.

In retrospect, the wonderful government programs that provided 100 percent financing may have done more harm than good when it comes to developing an infrastructure that enables the ongoing development of affordable housing. Although the programs created lots of units, there was no lasting legacy in the capacity of the sector. Everything was focused on the government.

The government programs also stripped away all the equity. When a 35-year mortgage reached the end of 35 years, the attitude was, "Hey, let's refinance the whole building." You never got a stream of payments that you could use to do more asset development.

Here's a story that highlights the problem: A colleague recently attended a board meeting for a project funded by the City. The board recognized that the project's expenses would be higher than they had originally budgeted. The project wasn't viable. Instead of trying to find a solution, the board decided that it they ran into trouble they would give the building back to the City. It was City's project after all! The group seems to believe that they were doing the City a favour when they sponsored the project.

What blows me away is that the group didn't think the project was worth fighting for. The board members didn't feel any ownership about this money. It wasn't an investment.

Our communities need to realize that they're investing in the housing. The city now asks for about $5,000 per unit as a contribution. This particular group raised over $200,000, but they were willing to walk away from the project because they didn't think about it as an investment. They didn't own the project; the city did. We've got to change this attitude. We have to change things so that the group gets a benefit. We can't let the government strip away the assets; we've got to ensure that the groups get some benefits. There's a completely different attitude in the United States. Non-profit boards in Canada don't think about growing assets. They don't think of what they're doing as accumulating assets, because they're not supposed to think that way.

When I work with groups, I try to get them to think differently. I talk about the organization having to invest in the project and tell them that they should expect a return on their investment. Thinking about equity as an investment changes the way the board thinks about who owns the project and who ultimately benefits from the project.

I try to get boards to think about asset growth, and how to use their own assets to grow the organization. I think we need to look at intensifying existing social housing projects to get more housing built.

One group in Toronto developed a social housing project but the provincial government took them down because they used their reserve fund. You weren't allowed to use your reserve fund for development, so the province put them into receivership because they were in violation of their agreement and then handed over the new building and the old building to the Toronto Housing Company. So much for trying to be creative about how we do housing. I mean if the response for being creative is you get taken down, no one's going to do it.

Many of the groups I work with complain about the amount of government oversight. They've never dealt with a private lender; they have no idea what oversight is. They don't understand that it's a matter of balancing risks. When the government provided 100 percent of the money, they also bailed out projects that ran into difficulty. The government has the right to interfere with a project's operations if it minimizes the government's risk. I am concerned that the City is going to continue to bail projects out. Doing so will encourage groups not to take responsibility for their projects.

I went to a meeting recently at which the group worked with a development consultant. The consultant advised them to lowball their bid to the city for a new program. The reasoning was: get the city on the hook, then we can increase the funding just as in the old days when we got loan increases. There's no responsibility for coming in with a financially appropriate business plan and making a proper project proposal. This is a legacy of 30 years of government spoon-feeding.

In order to be meaningful players, non-profit boards have to take more responsibility, more ownership of the projects. I am not suggesting that boards should be more entrepreneurial or business-like. These are often code words for bad business decisions. Rather, I think nonprofits have an obligation and responsibility to do value-driven development. I'm not sure how to accomplish this; part of me thinks that doing something like getting directors to sign personal guarantees is needed. However, the government has to do its part and stop being so paternalistic. Both parties need to change the way the partnership is structured.

Many of you know about the project that St. Clare's Multifaith Housing Society developed at 25 Leonard Avenue, across the street from Toronto Western Hospital. It's a four-storey concrete building which we converted into 50 units of transitional housing using $2.25 million of SCPI funding. The building has been occupied for 18 months. We located that building before SCPI was even announced. Most other nonprofit groups wait for the government to put a proposal call before they start looking for projects.

We are planning to add two floors, with 27 single room occupancy units, to the building. The units will be small; only 210 ft^2, and we are planning to use a manufactured housing system to save money and time. We will be submitting an application to City's Let's Build proposal call on June 16. The Committee of Adjustment is considering our application for minor variances on July 9. We decided to submit this proposal. If there is no Ontario Municipal Board appeal, the units will be occupied within nine months.

The capital costs of the project are about $65,000 per unit. If the City grants our request to waive the municipal taxes and provides a capital grant/loan of $40,000 per unit, we will be able to rent all the units for the shelter component of Ontario Works ($325 a month). This means that people currently living in shelters can move into the building without needing a rent supplement.

Some of you will see that there is a problem with my math – $325 a month is enough to cover the operating expenses, but it won't cover the payments of a $25,000 per unit mortgage. We intend to refinance the entire building. Originally we had five years of rent supplements. In the last budget, the provincial government agreed to extend the rent supplements until 2023. We can add $600,000 to the mortgage, and maintain the current payment by lengthening the amortization.

What I'm trying to do is intensify the use of the building, by using our own assets to grow the organization and accomplish socially responsible development – value-driven development. This isn't rocket science, but it is affordable housing and it does meet Michael Shapcott's number criteria. Yes we're using a government grant, but not too much. Not as much as some organizations. St. Clare's is intensifying the use of its own properties, and will bootstrap the project using the equity it has in the building.

The question we should ask is "Why aren't there more projects like this one on the drawing boards that are going into the government for approval under this latest proposal call?"

Jon Harstone is the president of Ganesh Community Development Co-operative, a non-profit consulting firm that assists community groups develop and manage affordable and supportive housing. Over the past 30 years Mr. Harstone has worked for several non-profit housing organizations, including Homestarts, Colandco Land Trust, and the Co-operative Housing Federation of Toronto. Among his recent projects is the conversion of 25 Leonard Ave. into 50 units of transitional housing for St. Clare's Multifaith Housing Society, and the conversion of two unused elevator shafts into 16 apartments at 81 Dalhousie St. for Margaret Laurence Housing Co-op. Mr. Harstone is an honorary Lifetime Associate of the Co-operative Housing Federation of Canada, and he chaired the Development Committee of the Co-operative Housing Federation of Toronto for more than 10 years. Mr. Harstone is an architectural historian who served for nine years on the board of Heritage Toronto, and is the former chair of the Toronto Local Architectural Conservancy Advisory Committee (LACAC).

Part III
Options for an Affordable
Housing Strategy

Chapter 20

Toward a Comprehensive Affordable Housing Strategy for Canada

STEVE POMEROY

This paper presents an overview of the issues underlying the affordable housing problem and sets out a series of options that should be considered as part of a comprehensive national housing strategy.

Defining the Problem – The Nature of Housing Need

The primary basis for social housing policy is the presence of circumstances (housing need) in which individuals or families are not able to meet their shelter needs through their own resources. The appropriate choice of policy instruments depends on the nature of the housing problem being addressed.

Housing need in Canada has been defined in terms of adequacy, suitability, and affordability. These problems are the basis for the definition of housing need established by Canada Mortgage and Housing Corporation, and are used in defining and measuring need by all provinces and territories. This measure is called *core housing need*.

"Core housing need" means (a) that a household is experiencing at least one of the following three housing problems, based on established housing standards and (b) that the household has insufficient income to resolve this problem without assistance.

- *Suitability*: This standard uses national occupancy standards to determine if households have a sufficient number of bedrooms based on the family composition (effectively a measure of crowding).
- *Adequacy*: A standard that measures housing condition to determine if the dwelling is safe, has basic plumbing, and is in a reasonable habitable state of repair.

- *Affordability*: A standard based on a ratio of housing expenditures to total household income; a household paying more than 30 percent of its income for housing is considered in need.

Table 1: Core Housing Need, 1996

Total	1,725,655	
Renters	1,172,270	68%
Owners	553,385	32
Unattached individuals	878,415	51%
Single female	245,950	28
Single male	149,330	17
Living with others	52,705	6
Families	847,235	49%
Two parents with children	144,030	17
Couples, no children	110,140	13
Female lone parent	144,030	17
Male lone parent	16,945	2
Multiple family	8,475	1

Source: CMHC; 1996 Census

If a household is below one or more of these standards, a second test is applied to determine if a suitable and adequate dwelling is available in its community for rent within 30 percent of the household's income. This measure uses the median rent of an appropriately sized private rental unit and converts the rent to an annual income required to afford this unit based on spending 30 percent of income for rent.[1] A household with gross income below this level, and living below any of the three housing standards, is defined as being in core housing need.

This formal housing need measure is based on data collected by Statistics Canada. Before 1996, the Household Income, Facilities and Equipment database was used; since 1996, the Survey of Household Spending has been used to collect data, but CMHC has not published updated housing need data since the 1996 census. Thus 1996 census data remain the most recent official basis for housing need statistics, and are used in Table 1 to indicate housing need.

CMHC reports that 1.7 million households or 7.6 percent of the total were in core housing need in 1996. This figure compares to 1.2 million households or 12.2 percent of the total in 1991.

These core need problems are divided almost evenly between unattached individuals (51 percent) and families (49 percent). Single females make up more than one-quarter (28 percent) of all households in need. Seniors make up just over one-fifth of households in need, distributed between unattached individuals and family couples. Among families, lone parents are the largest category in need.

More than two-thirds of households in need are renters (68 percent), even though renters represent only 35 percent of the population. Renters usually experience an affordability problem; owners in need tend more often to have adequacy problems (e.g., poor condition of dwelling).

Affordability is, by far, the most serious problem: 95 percent of core need among renters relates to affordability. Not surprisingly, low income is a key determinant of core need: 85 percent of households with incomes below $10,000 and 61 percent of those with incomes below $20,000 are in core need.

In the 1990s, heightened awareness about homelessness added a new dimension to these housing need categories – absolute homelessness and households "at risk." Absolute homelessness means living without four walls and a roof, and perhaps more important, without a door that one can lock to create private living space and security. "At risk" is the term for families and individuals who have formal shelter, but whose circumstances are precarious. They are deemed at risk of homelessness for one of several reasons – the cost of shelter consumes such a large part of their income that they are vulnerable to rent arrears and eviction; they are temporarily living with a friend or relative but have no permanent place of residence; they are personally at risk of physical or mental abuse; or they have disabilities that may cause them to lose their shelter.

One measure used to help determine the number of households at risk is a very high shelter cost burden – paying more than 50 percent of income for shelter. In the United States, the 50 percent benchmark is used to indicate "worst case need" or "severely burdened households." These terms have not been used in Canada, but the 1996 census identified 830,000 renters above this benchmark – 22 percent of all renters.

Understanding the affordability problem

Affordability problems are created by a combination of low incomes and relatively high rents. The 1990s were characterized by stagnant incomes, especially among renters. Between 1991 and 1996, the average real income of renters declined by 12.4 percent.[2] Although incomes grew after 1996, most renters did not share in the gains. As higher-income renters exercised the option of moving into ownership, the renter profile came to be dominated by the remaining lower-income households.

Table 2: Social Assistance Families as Percentage of
All Families in Core Housing Need

	Family %	Lone Parent %	Non-family %	Total Non-senior %
Atlantic	65	87	55	68
Quebec	64	80	68	70
Ontario	46	75	42	52
Prairie	40	54	39	44
B.C.	37	65	27	38
Canada	49	74	49	56

Source: Statistics Canada, HIFE 1996 data file.

Estimates suggest that more than half of core need households are recipients of social assistance. The percentage varies by household type and region, reflecting variations in the level of welfare benefits. Analysts now use a shelter-cost-to-income ratio of 50 percent as an indicator of severe affordability problems. As the shelter component of social assistance often makes up as much as 50 percent of the total welfare payments, social assistance caseloads affect the number of households with serious affordability problems.

Between 1990 and 1995, the number of households in core housing need increased by 47 percent and the number of households paying more than 50 percent of income for rent grew by 43 percent. During the same period, there was a marked increase in welfare caseloads, associated in part with the 1990 recession and slow recovery. Since 1995, welfare cases have followed a steady decline, in part due to reduced benefits in some provinces, more restrictive eligibility (especially for single people and youth), and the improving economy.

Data from the Statistics Canada 1998 Survey of Household Spending indicate that the number of renter households paying more than 50 percent of income for rent fell from 830,000 in 1995 to 464,000 households in 1998. At the same time, the number of renters paying between 30 and 50 percent of income on shelter increased by 250,000 households – suggesting that while incomes may have improved marginally, many households are still paying well over 30 percent for shelter and continue to experience affordability problems.[3]

Shifting factors underlying affordability problems

Between 1991 and 1995 real rents declined, although marginally (-2.5 percent), so the primary cause of increased affordability problems was weak income. Since 1996, increasing rents have become the more important factor – rising by as much as 25 percent between 1996 and 2000 in some centres. This percentage varies across the country, with the largest increases evident in Alberta, Saskatchewan, and Ontario. Rents in Alberta jumped more than 20 percent in only three years, while those in Ontario grew by more than 10 percent.

While rising rents in Ontario have been identified as a consequence of removing rent controls, the more important factor in all provinces has been the persisting low levels of new supply and the consequent decline in rental vacancy rates. As the supply of available units fails to keep pace with population and household growth, rents rise. This problem is especially acute in the lower end of the rental sector, where low-income households seek accommodation.

Low levels of new construction

Most housing in Canada is produced and operated in the private market. The social housing stock – units built and operated by public agencies, non-profit corporations, and cooperatives under various social housing programs – accounts for roughly 700,000 dwelling units in a total stock of just over 10 million dwelling units. Rental housing accounts for just under 4 million units, so social housing constitutes less than one-fifth (18 percent) of the rental housing stock.

Some social housing units are in mixed-income projects and provided at market rent, although most have subsidized rents. The 1996 census reported 1.6 million units renting below $500 a month (affordable at 30 percent of income for households with income of $20,000). So social housing makes up about one-third of the existing affordable stock. By comparison, two-thirds of affordable units are in the private rental sector and include older apartments and apartment suites in homes.

These statistics reveal the important role played by the private sector in contributing to a stock of housing that, over time, has remained or become affordable. But the stock in this sector is also susceptible to erosion. As rents rise with inflation, the number of private units renting below affordable benchmarks declines. In other cases, units may be demolished or the property is converted to condominium ownership.

Between 1991 and 1996, the number of renter households in Canada increased by 180,000. This growth was not matched by new production. In the same period, only 111,000 new rental units were constructed, just over half of them (54 percent) built as social housing. The rest, produced for the private sector, were typically at higher rents, well above affordable levels. The shortfall in new production (roughly 70,000 units) was taken up by vacancies in the existing stock.

Following a building boom in the late 1980s, the level of private rental development slowed in the early 1990s, and privately initiated development has continued to fall. New private rental housing construction fell from an average of well over 30,000 units a year in the 1980s to only 13,000 between 1990 and 1995 and subsequently to only 6,000 annually from 1995 to 1999.

In the mid 1990s, new social housing programs were almost entirely eliminated.[4] As a result, the decline in private rental construction was exacerbated by the cessation of social housing construction (except a little in B.C. and Quebec).

Lack of new rental construction worsens problem of affordability

This decline in new supply – both private and social – has largely driven the affordable housing crisis. Although low rental vacancy rates and increasing rents are a prerequisite to new rental investment, developers and investors have shown limited interest in new construction. Risks to investors and developers remain high while the rate of return on investment is poor and uncompetitive.[5]

Low supply and continuing demand have inevitably applied pressure to rents, exacerbating the affordability problem. At the lower end of the market, there are far more households seeking lower priced units than there are units.

Constrained access to affordable units

The problem is not solely an issue of absolute shortage of modest rent units. A related concern is limited access for lower-income renters.

As a rational entrepreneur, a landlord seeking to rent out a vacant unit typically will try to minimize risk – he or she will prefer tenants perceived to have greater capability of paying the rent. Inevitably, lower-income households will face a greater challenge in securing housing – especially if due to their inability to pay high rents, they previously have been evicted or are in arrears and do not have a sound reference.

In a tight rental market, tenants with good jobs will be preferred. While there is a fine line between prudent landlord behaviour and discrimination, the result is constrained access for low-income tenants, especially social assistance recipients and lone parents with children.

Erosion of the existing affordable housing stock

This situation is worsened by a process of ongoing erosion of the existing privately owned affordable stock. Between 1991 and 1996, the number of rental units renting below $500 declined by 310,000 (roughly 10 percent of the total rental stock). At a time when new rental construction was falling toward an all-time low level, the erosion of lower-priced stock is perhaps the most serious issue facing the affordable housing sector.

Responding to the Need – Possible Policy Options

The goal of social housing policy is to help low- and moderate-income households obtain adequate and suitable housing at a price they can reasonably afford. Three general approaches are possible:

1. Reducing the construction cost of housing so that the rent charged can be lower ("supply measures"), including direct public or non-profit production, measures to lower the costs of production, and incentives for private production with conditions on the level of rents.
2. Increasing a household's ability to pay by increasing or supplementing its income. These "demand-side measures" affect the household's effective demand. Such measures include rent supplements or allowances and income assistance.
3. Influencing the price of existing rental housing, including controlling rent levels to protect affordability, diverting demand (e.g., by helping households buy a home), and encouraging transfers in ownership from private for-profit owners to not-for-profit owners. These approaches are not discussed in detail, except where they relate to the two main categories.[6]

In the next two sections, the following measures are explained and the advantages and disadvantages of each are reviewed. The final section looks at integrating these measures into a comprehensive strategy.

1. Supply measures:
    • Direct support for public/non-profit production;
    • Incentives for private rental unit development;
    • Creating a level playing field for rental development;
    • Reducing development costs;
    • Encouraging lower-cost forms of development – single-room occupancy, secondary suites;
    • Shifting patterns of ownership (toward non-profit ownership).
2. Demand measures:
    • Rent supplement;
    • Shelter allowance;
    • Reform of social assistance shelter benefits.

The measures in each set are not mutually exclusive. In many cases, supply and demand measures complement each other.

Supply Measures

Supporting public/non-profit production

Direct public supply of housing has been the predominant program response in Canada through the postwar period. Although various program designs have been employed, the essential elements of this approach include:

• A public or not-for-profit owner/operator with a specific mandate to operate housing for low-income households.[7]
• Some form of subsidy, either as a capital grant, favourable mortgage rate, or ongoing subsidy, so that the rents charged to tenants are affordable. Generally, the project is governed by an operating agreement specifying the obligations of the operator and requiring the provider to continue serving lower-income eligible households.
• Typically, operating agreements and any ongoing subsidy that match the amortization period of the mortgage. Once the mortgage is paid off, the project rents are required only to cover operating costs and it is assumed that even at low rents, the operator will be able to continue serving lower-income households (in very poor, 100-percent-targeted projects, this may not be feasible without some renewal of subsidy).

- In most non-profit approaches, "affordable rents" established on a rent-geared-to-income ("RGI") basis. Although earlier programs used a 25 percent ratio, most currently employ a ratio of 30 percent of gross income.
- Assisted projects that are fully targeted – meaning that 100 percent of tenants have lower incomes and pay rent on a RGI basis – or mixed income (some units are rented at market rent levels). A mixed-income approach is generally preferable, as it avoids the concentration of very poor households characteristic of earlier public housing.

ADVANTAGES

Non-profit production helps create a permanent stock of units specifically to serve lower-income households – a long-term investment in a permanent asset. This form of ownership also provides some assurance that rents will remain affordable over the long term.

Even after operating agreements and subsidies cease, the public investment remains in place, as the non-profit charter restricts ongoing use to providing affordable housing and most non-profit providers retain this initial motive.

Non-profit programs address both supply and affordability issues, which is why they appear to be quite costly compared to alternatives that address either supply or affordability only. It is possible, however, to separate supply and affordability objectives. One such approach involves using a non-profit organization to develop housing at market rent level, then using rent supplement assistance as a separate mechanism to address affordability. Another variant is to help non-profit housing corporations buy existing privately owned rental properties. This approach does not add to new supply, but does preserve long-term affordability and helps check the ongoing erosion of more affordable existing private rental stock.

Supply programs respond directly to low levels of production and, in so doing, moderate the inflationary impact of low supply.

Through the development process, units can be designed specifically to meet particular needs. New supply funding can be geographically targeted to markets with acute supply problems.

WEAKNESSES

New construction costs and the associated subsidy costs tend to be quite high per unit. Most recent versions of non-profit housing involve long-term (35-year) subsidy commitments. As new commitments are added in each year, the subsidy cost mounts exponentially. This problem raises the concerns of finance officials and makes these programs a vulnerable target in times of fiscal restraint.

The alternative is to "front-end" the cost with a capital grant. However, this option tends to be expensive because of the high cost of new development compared with relatively low revenues at RGI rents (the latter limit capacity to cover operating and mortgage payments).

Income mixing improves the viability of the projects and lowers the average capital grant requirement, but increases the grant cost per RGI household assisted.

Relative to the volume of housing need, new supply programs can help only a very small number of households in need (at their peak, non-profit programs produced only 25,000 to 30,000 units annually).

Incentives for private rental development

In building new rental housing, a developer is faced with a range of costs and, in return, creates an asset that generates a cash flow in the form of rents. The value of the property to a potential investor is determined not by its cost, but by the level of revenue it can generate. The market value of the new property is based on the value of future income flows.

In the same way that an investor in government bonds is prepared to pay a price for a bond based on an expected rate of return, the rental investor converts future income to a current price based on a similar expectation of an annual return on equity. The main difference is that a government bond is a secure investment, easily traded for cash and the annual interest payments are guaranteed. For the rental investor, the asset is more difficult to trade for cash; it must be listed for sale and await a willing buyer. In addition, the annual cash flow is not guaranteed. The property may have vacancies so no revenues are produced, or be subject to regulations (such as rent controls) that constrain the owner's ability to increase rental income and achieve anticipated cash flows.

Compared to alternatives, rental investment is relatively high risk and thus demands a higher expected rate of return. Currently, rates of return remain far below those expected by potential investors. Costs are too high relative to potential rent revenue, mainly because the costs of production are set outside the rental sector. Ownership housing and condominiums establish land values while construction labour costs and materials are established in the wider market that includes commercial development.

In the past, stimulus programs have been used to encourage private development. These include programs that provide a grant or interest-free loan to a developer in return for modestly designed units (which should command lower rents than luxury development) and temporary tax measures that provide favourable tax treatment to investors (namely, creating eligible costs that can be used to reduce taxable income).

Effectively, these programs replace some portion of the investor's own equity with government funds without affecting the rental revenue. The investor's rate of return increases to a level that can make development more attractive.

Currently, potential rates of return on modest rental housing have been estimated at less than 5 percent. Increasing a private investor's rate of return to 12 or 15 percent requires capital grants or interest-free deferred loans of at least $15,000 to $20,000 per unit; this amount varies among cities and depends on the type of unit being developed.

ADVANTAGES

Any type of new supply can alleviate the pressure of low supply. Even new development at the higher end of the rental market will draw some households out of lower priced stock (a so-called "filtering" or "trickle-down" effect).

Household growth and new demand cover a spectrum of incomes, including higher-income households. Without new development, these households occupy lower-priced units and crowd out lower-income households.

Depending on the development economics in a particular city, stimulus measures leverage private investment and cost less than assisting non-profit development (since, unlike private developers, non-profits typically have little, if any, equity to invest).

WEAKNESSES

Stimulus measures are controversial. Even the housing industry has argued that this type of intervention disrupts market equilibrium.

The expenditure does not create permanent affordable housing, although it can do so if certain conditions are imposed in exchange for assistance. But when operating agreements enforcing the conditions and targeting expire, the units are no longer available as affordable housing (the so-called "expiring use problem").

No long-term public asset is created in return for the government investment.

Creating a level playing field for rental development

The poor economics of rental investment are attributable, in part, to the tax treatment of rental housing, which is seen as unfair compared with other investments. Current inequities in the tax system include:

- GST on rental housing. Rental landlords cannot charge GST on rents, yet unlike other goods, rental housing is not zero-rated. So landlords pay GST on supplies and services, but cannot claim input tax credits as they do not collect GST and have no GST remittance against which to claim credits.
- Small rental investors are not considered as "small businesses" and therefore are not eligible for the lower small business tax rate on the first $200,000 of income.
- "Pooling" provisions that once encouraged reinvestment in new rental projects have been eliminated.

Explanation of pooling provisions

When a rental project is sold, investors must pay tax on the difference between the sale price and the depreciated value of the project – i.e., the original cost of the project less the Capital Cost Allowance (CCA) deductions. "Recaptured depreciation" (the difference between the depreciated value of the building – not the land – and the original cost) is taxed at full income tax rates. Capital gains taxes apply to the increase in value above the original cost.

Before 1972, rental investors could defer paying income taxes on recaptured depreciation on buildings sold by "pooling" the recaptured amount with CCA from other buildings. For example, if they acquired another rental project in the same year, they could avoid recaptured depreciation by transferring the excess CCA to reduce the depreciable value of the newly acquired project.

The restoration of pooling (or "roll-over") does not eliminate tax liability. It simply postpones the tax penalty on recaptured depreciation and capital gains for owners of rental properties who invest the proceeds in another rental property. Restoring this provision would create opportunities for existing investors/owners of fully depreciated properties to leverage their existing assets without facing large tax impacts.

It may be more beneficial from a tax perspective to demolish the property and thereby eliminate the recapture of depreciation. When this happens, existing units, which may be relatively affordable, are lost.

ADVANTAGES

These three measures could correct inefficiencies in tax treatment and, while imposing an expenditure on government, do not constitute a temporary disruptive measure – unlike short-term stimulus measures.

The measures might improve after-tax feasibility of new production (at least for higher-rent properties) and could stimulate new construction with a positive moderating impact on the market, easing rent pressures.

Most tax measures apply only to private developers. However, any reduction in GST also would benefit non-profit providers.

WEAKNESSES

Federal finance officials strongly resist increasing tax expenditures and are reluctant to implement tax changes unless a clear case can be made on equity grounds.

These measures have a direct impact upon the production of affordable housing, but may also stimulate market rent development at higher rent ranges.

Reducing development costs

One of the most critical issues confronting both private and not-for-profit development is the relatively high cost of producing new housing, which is a function of land costs, labour, and material costs. Total development costs also have been increasing as a result of layers of taxes and fees on development.

While costs vary across the country and depend on the type of development, new rental housing in a typical urban centre costs $65,000 to $105,000 for one-bedroom apartments and $90,000 to $160,000 for three-bedroom family units.

Land costs generally account for 15 to 30 percent of the cost. In most markets, land values are established by the condominium market and rental developers are usually unable to compete against condominium development for land. Land is zoned based on use (e.g., residential) and density (units per hectare or a ratio of the total site area); land cannot be zoned for tenure. Provincial enabling legislation to empower municipalities to offer bonus densities for rental development could help address this situation. Such a provision could increase density for rental (compared to condominium) use so that the net residual value of the land, per unit, would equate to the values created by lower-density condominium development.

Labour and material costs are established in a competitive market place. Currently, a booming construction industry in many parts of the country has resulted in shortages of both labour and materials with an inevitable upward pressure on prices. An affordable housing strategy with a long-term vision might seek to direct assistance on a counter-cyclical basis, supporting development in markets that are in a downturn to take advantage of lower input costs and help offset the costs of an underused labour force (e.g., lower income tax revenues and higher Employment Insurance payments).

Finally, the trend over the past two decades has been toward a pay-as-you-go approach to funding municipal infrastructure related to new development, rather than covering this expense from general property tax revenues spread across all existing development. This practice has resulted in the imposition by municipalities of development cost levies on new construction. The GST added another new cost to development and has carried provincial sales taxes with it in the Atlantic region where federal and provincial consumption taxes are harmonized.

ADVANTAGES

Measures to lower land costs for rental housing and development charges can reduce the cost of new development. Several municipalities have waived development fees for certain housing types or in certain areas to encourage residential development in the central core and minimize suburban sprawl.

Reduced fees and charges help to encourage private development and new supply while marginally narrowing the development cost gap faced by non-profit organizations seeking to build.

WEAKNESSES

Without other complementary measures, these cost-reducing approaches will not lower costs sufficiently to make development feasible at affordable rents without some subsidy. Even with free municipal land, non-profit development for lower-income households is not feasible without additional subsidy.

Requiring municipalities to lower or remove development costs eliminates municipal revenue and requires the municipalities to shoulder the burden of new development, while the province and federal governments gain income tax revenues from the construction labour and on-going operations (of for-profit housing).

Encouraging lower-cost forms of development

Another way to address the relatively high cost of new development is to encourage alternative, lower-cost building forms.

Two such options are secondary suites in single detached homes (which are often in contravention of local building regulations) and small unit or "single room occupancy" (SRO) accommodation.

The formal approval and explicit encouragement of secondary suites is a controversial option in many municipalities. Such suites have been created in basements or by subdividing the upper floors of existing homes. Unlike rooming house units, secondary units are typically created in a home in which an owner occupant is also resident, so there is close management of tenants (unlike an absentee landlord). The most bothersome issue from neighbours' perspectives is the lack of on-site parking and the resulting use of limited street parking space. The concern from municipalities is one of health and safety. Often suites are self-built and have not benefited from a permit process that requires inspections to ensure that the units are safe (especially the electrical wiring).

Some municipalities have sought to legalize secondary suites, but few have explicitly promoted this use either through encouraging statements in official plan policies or through small grants to existing owners. A demonstration project under Homegrown Solutions (a federally funded seed grant program administered by the Canadian Housing and Renewal Association) provided funding to the town of Sidney, B.C., for a small homeowner grant of $5,000 to help offset installation costs of an adaptable suite for a person with physical disabilities.

The SRO approach involves the development of very small bed-sitting rooms, usually 150 to 300 square feet (a typical bachelor/studio suite is 350 to 400 square feet). Well-designed small suites can provide cost-effective options for urban singles and have become popular in some U.S. cities. Given that almost half of core need households are low-income single individuals, this building form could respond to demand.

SRO-type development can be cost-effective, since the total floor area per suite is much less than that required for a bachelor or one-bedroom apartment. Few residents can afford to own a car, so parking requirements and costs can be reduced in areas served by public transit – if municipalities agree to this regulatory relaxation. A 1999 study for the Ontario Ministry of Municipal Affairs and Housing found that suites could be developed in large urban centres at a cost of 40 to 50 percent of a typical new one-bedroom unit.

Advantages

Alternative building forms such as secondary suites (apartments within homes) and SRO units have significant cost advantages and can supplement more traditional building forms.

These approaches could stretch any limited subsidy funds further since per-unit costs are lower.

Weaknesses

Regulatory barriers and neighbourhood resistance (the "Not In My Backyard" or NIMBY syndrome) may limit opportunities.

Few proponents are pushing this approach. It is a new concept and therefore even more risky than conventional rental, for which there remains limited investor appetite.

Shifting patterns of ownership and facilitating not-for-profit ownership

Much of the effort of the non-profit housing sector is focused on building new housing. Without subsidies, the costs are prohibitive and, even with subsidies, the subsidy requirements per unit remain significant.

In other sectors, where poverty similarly limits access to necessities, the solution is to seek lower-cost options. Food banks provide food at no cost, and used clothing stores offer clothing at affordable prices. If lower-income households can afford a vehicle, or must have one for transport to work, most lower-income households also drive older used cars. While many households seek housing in the older existing rental stock, the practice of drawing upon older depreciated assets is not frequently used by non-profit providers, even though a large housing stock already exists and properties often are provided for sale – typically at values far below the cost of building new.

This dismissal of property acquisition as an option is, in part, a legacy of former non-profit programs. A number of non-profit housing providers did pursue acquisition and rehabilitation, and typically expended more than the cost of building new, because the properties were in serious disrepair. Few providers tried to find reasonably sound 20- to 30-year-old apartment buildings that needed only minor repairs. Moreover, social housing programs required that all tenants be in core housing need, with incomes below specified thresholds. It was problematic to acquire buildings that were already occupied by some tenants who were not in core need, as this would require evictions. So providers avoided this option.

Many more multiple unit rental properties are sold each year than the number of non-profit units constructed by the programs of the early 1990s. Although not all properties would be appropriate, due to poor condition or high price, many existing properties are regularly transacted (and the number could be increased if rollover provisions of the tax system were revised as discussed under a separate option above). Tax reform would encourage existing owners to sell to non-profit buyers without incurring significant income tax impacts and would provide a source for selective acquisition by non-profits.

Currently, as these properties are offered for sale, new private investors (including institutional investors and Real Estate Investment Trusts) are the purchasers. Typically, new investors upgrade the property to increase the rental cash flow. The alternative – purchase by non-profit organizations – could preserve and potentially expand the remaining stock of housing affordable to lower-income households. With non-profit providers, access by lower-income households would be improved as they would no longer be competing against "better" higher-income tenants.

Any such non-profit acquisition will require some subsidy, ideally a capital grant to facilitate a down payment. But because the total cost per unit typically is much lower than building new (40 percent to 50 percent lower), the grants can be more effectively used and stretched to secure more units.

In lower-cost markets – such as Prairie cities – existing detached homes can be acquired for as little as $20,000 to $30,000. Some communities are exploring options for assembling a portfolio of existing homes as rental properties instead of constructing new buildings.[8]

This acquisition approach can also provide opportunities for lower-income households to become homeowners in time. A critical element of an assisted ownership program is counselling and ongoing mentoring as well as linkage to employment and human resource training. Despite low house costs, many lower-income households would be unable to qualify for a mortgage, even though the ongoing ownership carrying costs may be less than paying rent on an apartment. With modest assistance – such as non-profit mentoring, a loan guarantee, and a modest down payment grant of up to $7,500 – low-income households could be assisted in obtaining a home of their own with no ongoing subsidies.

Advantages

The primary advantage of an acquisition approach is the relative cost-effectiveness of the properties, compared with new construction.

Because the properties already exist, purchasers do not have to contend with NIMBY-type challenges.

Acquisition permits the retention of an existing mix of market tenants while slowly introducing lower-income tenants as units become available. Acquisition with existing tenants remaining can effectively facilitate a mixing of income without added cost (since market rents cover break-even rent).

Homeownership and scattered rental portfolios offer options to access existing rehabilitation programs to upgrade dwellings.

Weaknesses

Many providers in the non-profit sector appear to be reluctant to pursue acquisition. Most prefer new construction, as they are concerned with adding to the supply.

The acquisition option is limited by the availability of properties offered for sale on the market and requires careful selection and assessment of potential properties.

The option is better suited for market downturns. The window for an acquisition approach in many cities may already have passed, as the current rental market is under high pressure from low vacancies and rising rents (which tend to raise the value of existing properties for sale).

Demand Measures

While supply approaches can play an important role in moderating the market pressures that exacerbate affordability problems, supply initiatives cannot be implemented on a sufficient scale to tackle the large backlog of these problems. Some form of rental assistance is necessary to address the affordability gap.

Rent supplements

A rent supplement involves an agreement between a public funding agency and a landlord, in which the landlord agrees to enter into a contract to provide rental units for low-income tenants on specified terms. Usually, the tenant's out-of-pocket rent will be based on a rent-geared-to-income basis. The contract will make up the difference between the tenant-paid RGI rent and the actual market rent on the units. During the term of the agreement, there may be an inflationary index to allow the market rent to increase annually, increasing the landlord's rental income but leaving the tenant protected at the RGI rent. As assisted tenants leave, during the term of the agreement, the funding agency has the right to place a new low-income tenant in the unit.

Rent supplements depend on securing the interest of private landlords. However, there is a poor history of rent supplement success in most provinces, despite efforts to advertise for landlords who will participate. Even for properties for which rent supplements have been negotiated, many landlords have elected not to renew these contracts when they expire. Initial terms for agreements in the 1970s were generally for 15 years with renewals now usually on a 3- to 5-year term.

In cities with low vacancy levels, landlords generally can fill their buildings with private market tenants, without the difficulties related to having their tenants selected by a third party. In addition, administrative requirements associated with this approach generally are seen by landlords as a deterrent.

Thus there may not be significant opportunities to use rent supplements to help low-income tenants living in privately operated rental housing. However, there has been a long tradition of stacking rent supplements on non-profit projects.

A number of existing older non-profit projects are not RGI-based, but include units with rents slightly below market levels. This approach is facilitated either by a capital grant or a favourable mortgage rate that helps to lower the break-even rent below market levels. Allocating rent supplements to these units to allow RGI assistance to tenants with very low incomes could provide a low-cost rent supplement option; over time, break-even rents will not rise as quickly as market rents.[9]

A further option is to use a rent supplement program in conjunction with non-profit acquisition of existing properties.

ADVANTAGES

This option addresses affordability problems.

A rent supplement agreement is specific to contracted units, so their condition and quality can be verified.

It can be used with non-profit supply but focuses only on the affordability issue (separate from supply).

Over the long run, it is more cost-effective to stack rent supplements on non-profit housing, as the annual rate of increase in non-profit breakeven costs has been found to inflate more slowly than market rents.

WEAKNESSES

A rent supplement does not address the lack of supply.

The option depends on a willing landlord and available units – but few landlords are interested.

Lack of renewal at term can result in difficulty for existing tenants.

Historically, there has been low landlord take-up of rent supplements due to administrative burden and to restricting use and rent on the contracted units.

Shelter allowance

Unlike a rent supplement in which the landlord is implicated in a formal agreement, shelter allowances are direct payments to the tenant and therefore overcome the necessity of negotiating agreements with landlords.

A feature of shelter allowances, as opposed to rent supplements and social housing supply programs (in which the number of units is limited by the size of the existing stock and any new production), is that all tenants who are in need and eligible for assistance potentially can receive it. There are no waiting lists (and unmet need) with shelter allowances. This option also implies a potential expansion of beneficiaries and higher levels of total expenditure.

With a shelter allowance, the assistance takes into account both income and market rent for the unit.[10] Maximum levels of assistance (i.e., a maximum rent level) can limit overconsumption (i.e., the risk that a household will choose a unit that is larger and more costly than necessary) and also are used to constrain program benefits and manage the overall budget.

The structure of the assistance formula is the primary means of public cost control. By encouraging tenants to select units with low market rents, costs are minimized for both the government and the tenant. By contrast, rent supplements and social housing reduce the tenant's rent to 30 percent of income, regardless of the quality of the unit occupied or the associated market rent. One very low-income household may live in a 40-year-old apartment while a similar household may receive a new townhouse.

An immediate concern is the scope and cost of the program. As many as 1.5 million households might be eligible for supplements. A number of approaches are available to manage this problem.

Since social assistance already includes a shelter allowance, it is practical to separate welfare recipients in this analysis. The options for welfare households are either to reform the existing shelter benefits within welfare (which are already conditionally linked to actual shelter costs up to a maximum) or to limit social assistance to income support and address shelter needs under a separate but linked shelter assistance program.

A costing analysis of a shelter allowance initiative undertaken for the Federation of Canadian Municipalities' National Affordable Housing Strategy estimated the cost of an incremental shelter allowance program, assisting 40,000 households annually. The first-year cost for 40,000 households was determined to be between $30 and $60 million. To address the needs of 400,000 working poor households would therefore cost in the region of $300 to $600 million annually. Adding the 240,000 seniors to this estimate would raise costs to between $500 and $950 million annually.

The wide range of the estimate reflects two different benefit formulas. The lower-cost estimate reflects a program targeted only to households paying more than 50 percent of income on shelter with benefits geared to lower this rent burden to roughly 37 percent of income. The more expensive option reflects a benefit formula that lowers household shelter costs to 30 percent of income, equivalent to the assistance levels in social housing.

The actual costs of a shelter allowance program could be reduced by restricting potential client groups (e.g., welfare recipients), phasing in the benefits, or setting lower benefit levels. Initially, eligibility criteria could be relatively restrictive and benefits could be established at minimum levels to address very high shelter cost. Gradually, the criteria could be relaxed and benefits enhanced to levels that allow tenants to obtain adequate accommodation at a maximum of 30 percent of income, while still ensuring that public program costs are managed and contained.

Although shelter allowances typically are seen as entitlement programs, it is possible to limit enrolment. For example, the approach used in the United States involves using certificates or vouchers, which are limited in number. Like non-profit housing, there would be a waiting list. Households must reapply annually to confirm their continued eligibility. When households served by vouchers are no longer eligible (due to improvements in income or success in finding lower cost housing), the voucher can be reallocated to a household on the waiting list.

ADVANTAGES

The option directly addresses the affordability issue and helps to ease very high shelter burdens.

The allowance can be broad-based or rationed.

The benefit formula allows the mechanism to be targeted and to provide varying levels of assistance to differing target groups and households facing more severe affordability problems.

Used in combination with non-profit supply, a shelter allowance reduces the challenge for new non-profit supply, as it is necessary only to get break-even rents down to market levels.

WEAKNESSES

The option does not address low levels of supply, and subsidy costs are affected by rising rents (caused by low supply relative to demand).

It does not create a long-term asset.

The allowance may be perceived by poverty advocates as a benefit to landlords by subsidizing private sector rents, with no long-term retention of units.

Reform of welfare shelter benefits – A transitional shelter allowance

Almost half of core need households and those facing high shelter-income ratios are social assistance recipients. The shelter component of welfare is not objectively related to actual rental costs and is not indexed to the cost of living. During the first half of the 1990s, this fact was not a problem. But with steep rent increases in a number of centres in the later

1990s, the calculation of the shelter component became an increasingly serious issue.

There is a need to realign intended shelter assistance benefit levels with true shelter costs, and to index benefits to actual market rents (e.g., the median or 40th percentile).

In addition to addressing the inadequacy of current welfare rental assistance levels, it would be effective to link revised benefit levels to ongoing welfare policies that seek to encourage and facilitate the transition from welfare to work.

A shelter allowance for the working poor could be adapted to create a transitional benefit for welfare households. While most provinces and territories have implemented reforms to help social assistance recipients acquire employment skills and work experience, these approaches have not recognized the critical role that stable and affordable housing can play in this process. Other than existing social housing (with a finite stock and long waiting lists), no transitional mechanisms enable households to move off social assistance, accept low-wage work, and still be able to pay the rent.

Welfare households considering work are discouraged, because as soon as they leave welfare, they lose their shelter benefit. Since shelter costs account for such a large part of the household budget, welfare reforms without ongoing housing assistance are ineffective. A shelter allowance, separate from welfare, can be a valuable complement to other initiatives to enable households to move back into the labour force.

Providing ongoing support to assist with the rent provides greater stability for low-income parents with children, helping avoid the arrears and evictions that often cause families to move frequently and disrupt children's development and schooling.

In the case of families with children, a modest shelter allowance in combination with minimum wage work and the new Canada Child Tax Benefit can leave a household with more income than it would receive on welfare, at a cost to government significantly lower than the cost of full welfare benefits.

Typically, shelter allowances are designed to provide relief from excessive rental costs while offering an incentive for the household to economize, limiting program costs. This is achieved by a formula that covers part of the gap between a specified percentage of income and actual rent, up to a rent maximum.

The precise formula can be adjusted to ensure that the recipient does not pay more than a specified percentage of income for rent. The formula can be varied by household size and composition, since larger households have higher food budgets and pay higher rent for larger units. A shelter subsidy of roughly $150 to $250 a month, depending on the market, effectively can reduce a rent burden of 55 percent to a more reasonable proportion of income (30 to 35 percent).

When a person leaves welfare to return to work, such an allowance, costing government less than $3,000 a year, would leave households in a better financial position than welfare benefits that may cost government more than $12,000 to $15,000 a year. The shelter assistance would be phased out as earned income improves. The phase-out can be gradual to avoid the tax-back disincentives that often undermine assistance programs when participants seek to earn an income.

ADVANTAGES

A transitional and separate shelter allowance for social assistance recipients could ensure that they are less at risk of losing their housing when moving off welfare into work.

Such a mechanism would support other work incentive policies.

The costs of this transitional initiative would be significantly lower than ongoing full welfare benefits.

The shelter allowance formula is based on actual rent and earned income and benefits reduce as income increases. The slope of the reduction can be controlled through the formula design.

WEAKNESSES

Over time, more households may remain on assistance and costs could expand – unlike welfare, which tends to be intermittent and transitional.

Implementing this approach requires a significant commitment to welfare reform.

Toward a Comprehensive Housing Strategy

None of the identified options is sufficient on its own to address the full array of housing issues. The nature and magnitude of housing problems vary geographically and depend on local market conditions.

That said, most problems relate to affordability – households spending too large a proportion of an already inadequate income for shelter, leaving little for other necessities.[11] Even households not experiencing an affordability problem face the indirect consequences of an insufficient number of lower-rent units, since some make a trade-off between price and quality, sharing a dwelling with another family (overcrowding) or accepting poor conditions (inadequate housing). Lowering the cost of producing housing is not a realistic option; much effort has been expended on this approach and most feasible options have been tried – except for reducing the various taxes fees and levies imposed by all levels of government. The greatest potential lies in approaches aimed at increasing ability to pay.

Improving households' ability to cover shelter costs would be the fastest and most desirable way to reduce their shelter cost burden. This can be addressed through a conditional income transfer, linked to actual housing costs – such as a rent supplement or a shelter allowance or simply through additional income. Increasing household income, either through supplements or through increased earning capacity (e.g., higher minimum wages, employment training) would also reduce high shelter-to-income ratios and leave more income for other necessities.

This conclusion suggests that income-based options outside the traditional housing policy toolbox merit serious examination. Tax credits or other means of improving income with some conditional link to housing consumption must be explored. The best option is likely the reform of the shelter component of welfare, since this subpopulation is highly overrepresented among households in core housing need.

Although affordability problems predominate, tackling the demand side of the equation alone would not address the lack of new supply that is the cause of rising rents and worsening affordability and that lead to cost inflation in a demand-side subsidy. Nor would demand measures alone curb the ongoing erosion of the existing limited affordable housing stock outside social housing or improve access for those stereotyped as "less desirable tenants."

To control for inflating rents in an undersupplied market, some form of supply response to support new construction is a necessary complement to any demand-side initiative. Any form of new construction will help ease upward pressure on rents, so measures to stimulate private rental development can play an important role.

By the same token, an exclusive non-profit supply option would be equally inadequate, mainly as it costs more to address two problems (supply and affordability) within the same solution and because a very large-scale production program would be required to meet current need.

It would be impractical to tackle the level of outstanding housing need (more than 1 million households) entirely through a new supply program. However, as population and the number of households grows, new supply is required to meet new need – much of which derives from lower-income households with limited effective demand.

If new supply were to be subsidized, non-profit supply would probably generate better public investment in creating a lasting asset and addressing issues of access than subsidies directed to private development. At the same time, impediments to private rental development, particularly the tax treatment of rental investment income, need to be identified and remedied if the necessary volume of new rental production is to be achieved.

The issue of relative cost-effectiveness is a highly contentious one and is not examined in detail here. However, any assessment of policy options should consider this aspect.[12]

The gradual disappearance of lower-priced, relatively affordable existing rental stock is perhaps the most serious issue contributing to affordability problems. Measures to mitigate this phenomenon are critical. Combining the longer-term benefits of non-profit ownership (less inflationary pressure on rents and long-term preservation of affordable units) with the inherent lower cost of buying existing rental properties through an active program to support non-profit acquisition of existing rental properties may be the more effective way to expand the affordable stock. The advantage of the non-profit sector is not its ability to build new affordable housing, but its ongoing ownership and management of assets. The long-term objective is to maximize affordability rather than return on investment.

While an acquisition strategy can help preserve the existing stock of affordable housing, other measures are required to enhance the ability of renters to meet their rental costs and to broadly stimulate new supply.

The key point is that demand and supply measures are not substitutes for each other – although each is preferred and promoted by particular interest groups for differing reasons. They are complementary measures that, when combined in a well considered comprehensive strategy, can help tackle the persisting affordable housing problem.

In responding to the current crisis of low rental vacancy rates, the federal and provincial/territorial housing ministers and their officials must look beyond short-term, small-scale construction programs. In particular, the prevailing nature of the affordability problem – inadequate income and ineffective income assistance benefits – must be addressed as part of the solution. This implies the need for a broader dialogue including ministries responsible for income assistance.

The complete paper by Steve Pomeroy, "Toward a Comprehensive Affordable Housing Strategy for Canada," was published by the Caledon Institute in October 2001. See www.caledoninst.org/Abstracts/894598946.htm.

Steve Pomeroy is the President of Focus Consulting Inc, based in Ottawa, and specializes in affordable housing policy and research. After a short time working as a municipal planner and a project development consultant, he spent 10 years with Canada Mortgage and Housing Corporation, where he held a number of positions in social housing, market analysis, and housing policy. From 1990 to 1994 he was manager of the CMHC Centre for Future Studies in Housing and Living Environments. In addition, he served on two major policy task forces: the 1990 Review for Expenditure Review Committee of Cabinet, and the 1993-94 Social Housing Policy Review Team. Since becoming a consultant in 1994, Mr. Pomeroy has written more than 60 research reports and housing strategies for provinces and municipalities. These assignments cover housing affordability and rental housing, alternative financing, homelessness, the interface between housing policy and social policy, affordability indicators, and socio-economic analysis. He has a graduate degree from the University of British Columbia in Urban Planning with a specialization in Housing and Urban Land Economics (1984).

Endnotes

1 For example, a lone parent with two children of the same gender aged 5 and 8 would require a two-bedroom unit. If the median monthly rent of a two-bedroom apartment is $640, the income required to afford this unit is $25,600 ($640 × 12 months/ .30). Similar households with an income above this level would not be in core need.

2 Statistics Canada, *The Daily*, Cat. No. 11-001E, Ottawa.

3 Another reason for the apparent decline is a shift in Statistics Canada survey methodology. Both the census and former HIFE datafiles used current year rent compared to previous year income. The SHS collects data on income and rent for the same period. So comparison across the two data sources may be inappropriate.

4 Federal funding for new non-profit housing ended effective December 31, 1993, and since programs were cost-shared with provinces and territories, almost all new social housing development ceased. Ontario maintained a unilateral program until 1995. Only B.C. and Quebec still have modest social housing programs (the Quebec programs are more focused on acquisition and rehabilitation than on new construction).

5 One of the critical risks for potential investors is the regulation of the rental sector. While rent regulation has been relaxed in a number of provinces, investors still fear

reintroduction. It is not rent controls themselves that scare investors away, but the uncertainty about future regulatory regimes that increases risk.

6 Rent regulation/control has been omitted from this discussion. Rent controls impose specific limits on the level and frequency with which rents can be increased. Proponents of the former controls point to their impact in preserving affordability; opponents (largely landlords) counter that controls are discriminatory and place undue burden of public policy on one specific sector (rental landlords). Rent controls also have been identified as a deterrent to new rental investment – although, arguably, it is the uncertainty associated with a regulatory regime rather than the controls themselves that constitute the deterrent. Overall, opponents argue that rent controls are a blunt policy instrument with undesirable outcomes – the benefits may not reach the intended beneficiaries. In fact, controls benefit many households that do not require assistance. A substantial portion of the low-rent housing stock is occupied by households with incomes that would allow them to pay higher rent, while those most in need continue to face severe affordability problems.

7 The generic term "non-profit housing" is used in this report. This term can also include cooperative housing – a variant that seeks to assist lower-income households and operates on a not-for-profit basis – although the management structure and philosophy are different (encouraging active resident participation).

8 Such options are not necessarily restricted to lower-cost markets, although the viability is obviously greater. An analysis of real estate listings for one month in 1999 in B.C. found more than 1,000 dwellings (including duplex and townhome units) for sale outside the two major cities for less than $90,000 – affordable to working poor households at a payment of less than $600 a month.

9 Previous research has examined the cost trends of private rent supplements over a 20-year period compared with the comparable cost of stacked rent supplements in non-profits and found that, over time, non-profit break-even rents increase at a slower rate than market rents – suggesting a cost benefit to stacking rent supplements on properties under non-profit ownership.

10 For example, a shelter allowance may provide assistance equal to 85 percent of the difference between actual rent and 35 percent of income. So if income is $1,500 and rent is $600/month (40 percent of income), a shelter allowance may provide relief of [$600 – ($1500 × 35 percent)] × .85 percent = ($600 – $525) × .85 = $64. This lowers net rent to $536 or 36 percent of income. This formula can be adjusted so the net effect lowers the shelter to income ratio to 30 percent, equivalent to social housing rents. A maximum rent, say $600, might be imposed to prevent households selecting expensive units – although there is already an incentive to seek a reasonably priced unit, as the household pays a share of the higher rent.

11 "Food insecurity" is defined as a situation in which household members are forced to compromise on the quality of their diet because they have insufficient income to cover necessities. High housing costs may contribute to this phenomenon. See Statistics Canada, "Food Insecurity in Canadian Households." *The Daily*, August 15, 2001.

12 The key tradeoff is between paying a premium for new supply with the benefit of non-profit ownership, a lower rate of subsidy inflation, and long-term availability of the affordable unit, versus low initial costs but inflating subsidy costs in a shelter allowance as market rents inflate into the future. The comparable present value is sensitive to the initial cost gap and assumptions of rent inflation and discount rates.

Chapter 21

Unlocking the Opportunity for New Rental Housing: A Call to Action

CITY OF TORONTO URBAN DEVELOPMENT ROUNDTABLE,
RENTAL WORKING GROUP

A New Beginning for Rental Housing

NO VACANCY – It's an all too common sight in communities across Canada. It wasn't always this way. Thirty years ago, there was a plentiful supply of new, conventional rental housing in Canadian cities. Today, we have almost no rental production. Last year, for example, only 38 private rental units were completed in the entire Greater Toronto Area.

Rental housing is important for the liveability and vitality of our urban centres. Canada is a growing country seeking newcomers and a young, skilled, and mobile work force. Healthy rental markets are needed to give us the critical edge in the global competition for jobs, investment, and new immigrants. Yet almost two-thirds of Canada's 26 major urban centres have tight rental market conditions with vacancy rates below 2 percent.

As people struggle to find accommodation for their aging parents or for their children starting out in the job market, there is an increasing awareness that the current state of affairs is simply not sustainable. Public demand is intensifying for solutions and action – for a new beginning for rental housing.

"Salting the Earth" for Rental Housing

The present conditions are the unintended outcome of thirty years of actions taken by government – actions designed to address other problems – which have essentially "salted the earth" for new rental housing production.

No single factor is entirely responsible for the serious decline in new rental production over the past thirty years. A complex series of changes, over many years, in taxation, legislation, the business environment, and program responses, has brought us to where we are today.

Equally, no single group or sector working in isolation – not government, not the non-profit sector, not the private sector – can address the problem effectively. Concrete solutions can only be found by taking action to level the playing field for rental housing. This will involve determination to act jointly, to commit, and, most importantly, to ensure that the right tools are in place.

The Urban Development Roundtable – Rental Working Group

The Urban Development Roundtable is a forum for Toronto's development community to exchange ideas with staff of the City's Urban Development Services Department. In early 2000, the Roundtable established a Rental Working Group to address the lack of new conventional rental production in Toronto as a high priority issue.

Working closely with City Planning and Housing Staff, the Rental Working Group is made up of a cross-section of Toronto's rental developers and investors – representing large and small companies, corporate and entrepreneurial – who brought their wealth of business experience and knowledge to the assignment.

The Need to Ensure the Full Range of Rental Housing

In trying to build new rental housing, many of the issues of concern to private developers are of equal concern to the non-profit housing sector (e.g., the amount of equity required as a result of restrictive mortgage underwriting criteria). The call to action outlined here is supported by the Ontario Non-Profit Housing Association (ONPHA).

As well, this plan of action recognizes that programs are necessary to address housing affordability for families and individuals with lower incomes and that program dollars can lever more affordable housing if the obstacles hindering new rental housing production are addressed.

Moving From Knowledge to Action

The reason why there is virtually no new rental investment in Canada has been exhaustively studied. The bibliography at the end of this chapter includes 23 detailed studies related to the economics of rental investment, completed since 1995 alone. Many of these studies have made recommendations for action and many have recommended the same actions.

The purpose of this call for joint action is to move forward an agenda to unlock the opportunity for new rental housing for Canadians. The basic messages are:
• The lack of rental housing has been extensively studied.
• The solutions have been identified.
• The time has come to move from knowledge to action.

A Call to Action

The following list summarizes the sixteen key actions that need to be taken by all three levels of government, which are discussed in more detail in a background technical report. The developer participants on the Rental Working Group, together with others in the development community, have indicated their commitment to build new rental housing if the right conditions can be created.

Building sites are "ready and waiting" and could be developed if these actions are implemented. The initial commitment expressed by the development community would result in the production of 3,500 rental units, equivalent to the amount of private rental housing produced in the City of Toronto in the last 10 years.

Recommendations

ACTIONS FOR THE FEDERAL GOVERNMENT:

1. Change CMHC's restrictive mortgage insurance criteria
2. Amend income tax legislation to encourage new rental production
3. Treat rental properties fairly under GST legislation
4. Stimulate private investment in affordable rental housing
5. Make suitable surplus federal land available

ACTIONS FOR THE PROVINCIAL GOVERNMENT:

6. Allow municipalities to lower property taxes for new rental buildings over the long-term
7. Eliminate barriers to municipal/private partnerships
8. Allow municipalities to reduce or waive fees, charges and requirements for new rental housing
9. Amend PST policy to encourage the full range of new rental housing
10. Encourage more municipalities in Ontario to promote rental housing
11. Address NIMBYism and get the public on side
12. Step up the training of construction tradespeople

ACTIONS FOR THE CITY OF TORONTO:

13. Allow more housing, including more rental housing
14. Reduce or waive fees, charges and requirements for new rental housing
15. Review the parking requirements that apply to rental housing
16. Continue efforts to streamline the development approval process

Important note: During the production of this report, the Province addressed Recommendations 6 and 7 by:
• Extending the new multi-residential property tax rate to 35 years, effective January 1, 2002;
• Amending the Municipal Act to allow for housing to be deemed a "capital facility" thereby allowing the City to partner with the private sector, as well as the non-profit sector, in producing affordable rental housing.

The Consequences of Not Taking Action

Many of Canada's major urban centres have experienced tight rental conditions, for such a long time, that a sense of complacency and acceptance has set in. But now we are truly at a crossroads. There are serious risks if the current situation continues. The following discussion focuses on three key factors:

Significant Future Growth Expected for Groups that Rely on Rental Housing

The sense of urgency is informed by anticipated population growth among people who rely on rental housing: newcomers, seniors, and young people.

Newcomers

Toronto is a major destination for newcomers to Canada, who are attracted to cities like Toronto for their economic opportunity and quality of life. While the GTA has roughly 16 percent of Canada's population, it has 43 percent of Canada's recent immigrants. These newcomers, at least initially, rely on the rental housing market. Eighty percent of Toronto's newcomers are renters. The federal government recently announced its intention to increase the immigration target from 225,000 to 300,000. Many of the immigrants coming to Canada, as a result of the higher federal target, will move to Toronto.

Seniors

Seniors are a group that has traditionally been more reliant on the rental housing market. In the City of Toronto, it is expected that by 2021 there will be 92,000 more people over the age of 65 than today – 52,000 of them will be aged 75 years and over.

Young People

Major cities like Toronto also attract young people for higher education or to start out in the job market. As with the newcomers, these young people make an important contribution to our economy and society. However, they too, rely on a healthy rental market.

A Healthy Rental Housing Market – An Important Economic Tool

Business leaders, including the Toronto Board of Trade, have commented on the negative impact that Toronto's tight rental market conditions are having on the region's ability to compete on a continental and global scale. The high-tech and bio-medical sectors, which rely on a young, skilled, and highly mobile work force, have had difficulty in attracting people to come to Toronto owing to the lack of available rental accommodation and the high cost of housing.

A healthy rental sector is a vital component in the economic life of any major city. Toronto's renters include many of the people who make Toronto a liveable and lively city: artists, office workers, restaurant staff, store clerks, and students. For this reason, we need to ensure that the full range of rental housing is available.

If action is not taken there will be increasing pressure on the existing rental stock with more overcrowding and doubling-up. This will have serious repercussions for the ability of Canada's urban areas to compete for jobs and newcomers, for the liveability of our communities, and for the well-being of families and individuals who rely on the rental housing market for accommodation.

There's No "Smart Growth" Without Rental Housing

The ability to offer a full range of housing options is important for an urban region's competitiveness. The creation of a full range of housing, including rental housing, has become part of many Smart Growth initiatives in the United States. The term "Smart Growth" includes a range of strategies designed to stimulate reinvestment in cities and curb suburban sprawl. The Province of Ontario has endorsed the idea of "Smart Growth" in principle.

Smart growth initiatives are being actively implemented by major U.S. cities that are competing with Canada's urban regions on a global and continental scale for jobs, investment, and newcomers. These U.S. cities, supported by their State and Federal governments, have recognised that there cannot be true "Smart Growth" unless housing, including rental housing and affordable rental housing, is part of the package.

This further underscores the need for joint action to address the rental housing problem and for the need to work harder to ensure the liveability and well-being of our communities.

In the Toronto context, without rental housing, it will not be possible for the outer regions of the GTA to achieve even the residential densities of the former community of North York. The population of the GTA is forecast to grow by 2.6 million people over the next thirty years. If we continue the development trends of the 1990s, an additional area almost twice the size of the City of Toronto will be needed to accommodate this growth. In the past, rental housing ensured more efficient land use and delivery of municipal services. In the future, rental housing will help to ensure that urban growth is more sustainable.

Toronto is a Growing City with a Growing Rental Demand

In 1999, based on CMHC information, the Mayor's Action Task Force on Homelessness estimated that there is new demand in the order of 4,300 rental units in the City of Toronto each year. The City is expected to have about half of the new regional demand for rental accommodation.

In the past, cities have looked to the secondary rental market (rented condominiums, rented houses, apartments above stores, and second suites) to make up some of the shortfall in new conventional rental production. This is not the solution, as it is a less reliable source of rental housing owing to the fact that it can more readily revert to ownership.

For example, between 1996 and 2000, the City of Toronto's condominium apartment stock increased by 17,200 units but its owner-occupied condo apartments increased by 19,400. This meant that, in addition to virtually no new conventional rental production, there was a net loss of 2,200 rented condo units, or an average loss of 46 units/month.

If the City grows as expected, Toronto will need to increase its purpose-built rental housing stock by at least 1,500 to 2,500 new units a year. This level of new conventional supply assumes that some of the supply will be met in the secondary market.

Creating a Level Playing Field for Rental Housing

As noted previously, thirty years of actions – intended to address other issues – eroded the ability of rental housing to compete with other housing opportunities. No single factor was responsible, although some actions did have a more significant impact than others.

The following sections summarize the key changes in taxation, legislation, the business environment, and program responses that have resulted in the shift from the significant production levels in the early 1970s to the "lost decade" for rental housing in the 1990s, when private rental production virtually disappeared.

Changes in Federal Income Tax Treatment

Canada has an income tax system that actively discourages new rental investment. Prior to 1972, Canadian developers had tax treatment similar to that benefiting U.S. developers today. Developers could defer income taxes on profits when a building was sold by investing the money in a new building that cost the same or more.

Today, there is no incentive to sell fully depreciated buildings and invest in new rental housing. However, if deferment was re-introduced, the tax base would be expanded and "frozen and unproductive" capital would be unleashed. There would be no tax loss to government.

Restrictions on the deductibility of soft costs and further reductions in the capital cost allowance (1979, 1981, 1986, 1988, and 1990) as well as the imposition of capital taxes (i.e., a tax on debt), have continued to frustrate attempts to generate new rental housing. The application of the full GST to rental housing in 1991 (in distinct contrast to condominium housing) represented another blow to the rental housing industry.

In other countries, notably the United States, the tax system is used to promote the development of rental housing, including affordable rental housing. In Canada, developers are essentially penalized for investing in rental housing. The loss of tax deferment and restrictions over the past thirty years have essentially thrown the baby out with the bath water.

Legislative Impacts

Analysts often point to the introduction of provincial rent controls in 1975, and again in 1992, as being responsible for the decline in rental production. In fact, the precipitous decline in private rental starts started in 1972, three years before the introduction of rent controls in 1975 in Ontario. Because rent controls were a symptom and not the cause of the decline in new rental supply, the elimination of rent controls in 1998 did not spur new rental production.

However, the imposition of rent controls twice in the past 25 years has had a lasting impact on the perception of the investment climate for new rental housing in Ontario.

Changes in the Business Environment

External factors affecting the business environment can also help to account for the downward trend in private rental starts in Ontario. Even though Ontario adopted a *Condominium Act* in 1967, it was not until the early 1970s that condominium housing became established in the market. For developers of multi-residential housing, the changes in federal tax treatment combined with the imposition of rent controls were push factors that encouraged a shift away from building new rental housing.

The early 1970s also saw changes to the *National Housing Act* which saw the introduction of social housing. With the cancellation of non-profit programs by Ontario in 1995, following the gradual withdrawal of the federal government beginning in the late 1980s, there has been no rent-geared-to-income housing produced since 1997.

Building rental housing is an inherently more risky proposition than building condominiums. Rental housing requires long-term management and maintenance, whereas condos are sold to the owners, who take collective responsibility for management and maintenance.

The additional risk assumed by rental developers translates into higher financing costs. This risk has not been recognized by governments in implementing tax policy and other policies. Restrictive mortgage underwriting criteria imposed by CMHC in the 1990s further contributed to the decline in private rental construction.

Program Responses

In response to the severe decline in private rental production following the 1972 income tax changes, a number of programs were introduced (e.g., ARP, MURBs, CRSP, CORSP) to stimulate private rental production. Some of these (e.g., MURBs) brought back some of the tax treatment which had been available prior to 1972. There was an immediate response to these programs in the late 1970s and early 1980s, resulting in an increase in private rental starts. When the programs ended, the number of new rental starts dropped off once again.

The pattern of industry response to a positive environment has continued. In 2000, there was a small increase in private rental starts as a result of policy changes such as the provincial PST rebate program, reduction of the GST for rental, and changes in the capital gains tax provisions. As well, the provincial government established a new multi-residential tax class which has been adopted by the cities of Ottawa and Toronto.

In addition, some municipalities, including the City of Toronto, have adopted policies to encourage more rental development, such as a "housing first" policy for surplus municipal lands, the establishment of a capital leverage fund, and fee and charge exemptions for non-profit housing. However, the recent changes represent only a very modest start and much more remains to be done to return to the supply situation of the early 1970s.

Unlocking the Opportunity – Sites are "Ready and Waiting"

There is no shortage of development sites to accommodate the full range of housing in the City of Toronto. Some sites are particularly appropriate for rental buildings. These are sites with good access to transit, close to shops, parks, and community services. Some have already been zoned for residential development that would permit rental housing.

They include:

- Areas in Scarborough around the Scarborough Civic Centre and along Eglinton Avenue East
- Areas in Etobicoke on the Queensway, Lake Shore Boulevard, and Eglinton Avenue West
- "Main Streets" in the former City of Toronto

There are also many sites that are not currently zoned for multi-residential housing, but that could be made available and designated.

These include:

- The downtown and the Central Waterfront
- "Brownfield" sites (former industrial lands)
- Sites along major arterial roads that are currently zoned for commercial use
- Subway sites
- Older shopping plazas and malls, often located in the suburbs, that are largely vacant and have been proposed for redevelopment
- Intensification of "tower-in-the-park" apartment sites

Shortage of land is not an impediment. However, until a level playing field is created for rental housing, both private and non-profit, these opportunities cannot be realized.

From Knowledge to Action – What Needs to Be Done

The current situation for rental housing markets in communities across Canada is the outcome of a series of actions over a long period of time. It will take time to re-establish a rental housing industry to produce the amount of new housing to meet future demand and to address the current backlog of demand.

However, we will not be able to ensure the provision of a full range of housing in our communities, ensure smart growth and minimize urban sprawl, and remain competitive on a continental and global scale, if we delay taking action. We have studied the problem and the time has now come to move from knowledge to action.

What the Federal Government Can Do

The federal government is a critical partner in implementing effective solutions through its role in the areas of tax policy, setting policy directions for CMHC, promoting growth, and setting immigration targets. The following are the key actions for the federal government.

Change CMHC's restrictive mortgage insurance requirements

Canada's only source of mortgage insurance for rental buildings is CMHC. This insurance acts as a government guarantee on the mortgage. During the 1990s, CMHC increased its insurance premiums and introduced underwriting criteria that made it harder for developers, private and non-profit, to get mortgage insurance and, therefore, to get adequate financing for new rental construction.

The restrictive changes mean that private and non-profit developers must cover roughly 40 percent of the development costs themselves up-front. This is an onerous burden.

It is essential that the federal government direct CMHC to revise its underwriting criteria. Many of the other actions to create new rental housing will be rendered ineffective if developers cannot have access to reasonable mortgage insurance.

Recommendation #1

The federal government should ensure that there is a level playing field for new rental housing investment by directing CMHC to:
- revise the underwriting criteria it uses to approve mortgage insurance for rental developments;
- lower the requirements for equity demanded of rental investors;
- ensure that its application process is efficient, fair, and transparent;
- allow for an appeal process when an application is rejected.

Amend income tax legislation

Before 1972, owners of rental buildings could defer paying income tax on the profits they made when they sold one of their buildings, by investing the money in a new building that cost the same or more as the building that had been sold. This was known as "pooling" or "rolling over" the Capital Cost Allowance. Developers and investors therefore could take the money earned on the sale of one apartment building and put it towards new development.

Today, rental building owners must pay full income tax on the difference between the sale price of a building and the depreciated value of the project, and capital gains tax if the building sells for more than its original cost. There is no incentive for rental building owners to sell older, fully depreciated buildings and invest in new rental properties. Restoring this income tax deferral plan would help to stimulate new rental development by unlocking a huge pool of capital. The taxes would not be lost to the government, only deferred, and the creation of new rental housing would, in turn, expand the tax base.

Current income tax legislation also treats developers' "soft costs" (such as architects' fees, marketing costs, and the expenses of coordinating new development) in the same way as bricks and mortar costs in developing a building, that is, as depreciable assets rather than deductible expenses. Allowing developers to deduct these "soft costs" from the first year of operation of a new building would also encourage new rental development.

Recommendation #2

The federal government should actively encourage new rental investment by amending income tax legislation to:
- re-introduce Capital Cost Allowance pooling provisions to permit developers to defer income tax on the sale of rental buildings if they reinvest in new rental buildings;
- expand the allowable "soft costs" that can be deducted from the first year of operation for new rental buildings.

Treat rental properties fairly under GST legislation

GST adds to the costs of new rental construction. One of the reasons why rental construction happens in the United States is that there is no federal sales tax on development costs. Eliminating or lowering the GST on the costs of new rental construction would encourage more rental investment.

Once a building is constructed and being occupied, there are further special GST burdens. The full amount of GST payable on the construction of a new rental building is due when the first unit is rented. Developers are not permitted to pay GST on a pro-rated basis as the units are rented. This adds to the cash flow problems for a new building, especially in the first year, and is a further disincentive to new rental investment.

As well, because rents are classified as "GST-exempt," the owner of a rental building cannot claim input tax credits for their expenses in running the building. Owners could only claim these credits if rents were classed as "zero-rated goods." For example, this is applied to groceries and prescription drugs. An amendment would mean that, even though GST would not be applied to rents, investors could claim input tax credits on their expenses which would improve the financial performance of new rental buildings.

Recommendation #3

The federal government should ensure fair treatment for rental housing by amending GST legislation to:
- eliminate or lower the GST on the costs of new rental construction;
- allow developers to pay GST gradually on rental construction as the units are occupied, rather than as a lump sum payment when the first unit is rented;
- re-classify rents as "zero-rated" for GST so that GST credits can be claimed against expenses.

Stimulate private investment in affordable rental housing

The federal government can stimulate the creation of affordable rental housing by offering tax credits to developers who create low cost housing. This strategy has worked well in a number of countries:
- In the United States, the Low Income Housing Tax Credit Program resulted in construction of 600,000 rental units for low income tenants between 1986 and 1996.
- In France, investment pools for affordable housing have been created through tax-exempt savings accounts. Investors in these pools earn 0.25 percent interest tax free. The money in the pool is used for long-term loans to the developers of affordable housing.

The Federation of Canadian Municipalities has also recommended that an existing Canadian investment vehicle, labour-sponsored investment funds (LSIFs), be used to promote investment in rental housing. Individual investors who contribute $5,000 a year to an LSIF would earn a one-time federal/provincial tax credit of 30 percent on their contribution. A fund could be created to provide a pool of money for construction and mortgage financing for affordable housing projects, while offering investors a similar tax credit on their contributions.

Recommendation #4

To encourage the development of affordable rental housing, the federal government should:

- establish a tax credit program;
- allow the creation of tax-exempt savings accounts that act as investment pools;
- allow the use of labour-sponsored investment funds for affordable housing.

Make suitable surplus federal government land available

The City of Toronto has adopted a "Housing First" policy for surplus municipal lands and the Province of Ontario has given the City surplus lands to be developed with affordable housing. The federal government too could support affordable housing by instituting a similar policy for land suitable for rental housing.

Recommendation #5

The federal government should make suitable surplus federal land available, on preferential terms, to encourage the creation of new rental housing.

What the Provincial Government Can Do

The province controls a number of key pieces of legislation that impact on housing matters such as the *Municipal Act*, the *Planning Act* and Provincial Policy Statement, the *Building Code Act*, the *Fair Municipal Finance Act*, and the *Development Charges Act*.

The ability of municipalities to ensure that the full range of housing is provided relies on the tools which the provincial government makes available.

The following are the key actions for the provincial government.

Allow municipalities to reduce or waive fees, charges, and requirements for rental housing

The City of Toronto encourages the creation of non-profit housing by waiving development charges, building permit fees, planning application fees, and parkland dedication requirements. It also has an alternative parking requirement for non-profit housing (former City of Toronto only) which helps keep down the construction costs of non-profit housing.

At present, however, municipalities like the City of Toronto do not have the flexibility to waive or reduce fees and charges as an inducement to new private rental production. Nor do they have the ability, for example, to reduce the parking requirements for rental buildings. This is because municipalities in Ontario do not have the legal authority to distinguish by tenure as an incentive tool. As a result, private rental developers are subject to the same fees and requirements as developers of condominium housing.

To provide this flexibility, the Province of Ontario will have to amend the *Planning Act*, the *Building Code Act*, and the *Development Charges Act*. This is another recommendation which would be revenue-neutral to the Province.

Recommendation #8

The Province of Ontario should amend the *Planning Act*, the *Building Code Act* and the *Development Charges Act* to allow municipalities to reduce or waive fees, charges, or requirements (e.g., parking) for rental housing.

Amend PST policy to encourage the full range of rental housing

Ontario's PST rebate program on construction materials ($2,000/unit) for new purpose-built rental housing includes a unit size limit. The unit types described in the program materials effectively limit the rebate to apartment units. However, many rental developers are seeking to build low-rise and townhouses, often because the costs of stick-build construction is lower than high-rise construction. These low-rise units are also attractive for families with children, who often prefer to rent these larger units. The Province should extend the program to explicitly include low-rise and townhouse buildings by setting appropriate maximum sizes for these units.

A more effective approach would be for the Province to remove or significantly reduce the 8 percent provincial sales tax on materials used in the construction of purpose-built rental housing. Waiving the tax would also be a clear signal that the Province is serious about addressing the costs of constructing new rental housing.

Recommendation #9

The Province of Ontario should continue to provide PST incentives for rental housing by:

- explicitly including low-rise and townhouse rental housing in its PST rebate program;
- eliminating or reducing the PST on construction materials used in building new rental housing.

Encourage more municipalities in Ontario to promote rental housing

Rental housing markets are tight in many Ontario cities. However, responses to this problem vary from city to city: a few cities, including Toronto and Ottawa, have adopted the new multi-residential tax class for rental buildings and Toronto has adopted a bylaw permitting second suites. Development charges vary widely across the province and, in some places, are so high that they discourage the creation of new rental housing.

Since one of the Province's stated policies is to ensure that there is a full range of housing in Ontario communities, the Province should be proactive in encouraging all municipalities to promote new rental housing. As well, this should be a major focus in the review of the Provincial Policy Statement.

Recommendation #10

The Province of Ontario should introduce policies to ensure a greater level of consistency in responding to the need for rental and affordable rental housing in municipalities across Ontario.

Address NIMBYism and get the public on-side

NIMBYism (not in my backyard) is a barrier to rental housing. Unfortunately, there are many negative stereotypes of families and individuals who rent their homes. These stereotypes rarely stand up to closer scrutiny. The fact is that there are very few adults living in Ontario who have not been renters at one time or another. Often this fact is forgotten in the opposition to new rental developments. As well, the cost of addressing NIMBYism only adds to the cost of rental development whether private or non-profit.

A public awareness campaign on the broad spectrum of people who rent and on the value of rental housing would create a greater acceptance of new rental housing. While some tenants are mobile, many tenants live in their housing for a long time and make important contributions to their communities. Rental housing is also an important economic tool.

Recommendation #11

The Province of Ontario should mount a public awareness campaign, in consultation with municipalities, on the need for and benefits of rental housing.

Step up the training of construction tradespeople

Ontario is facing a looming shortage of skilled tradespeople. The trades-people who entered the workforce in the 1950s and 1960s are nearing retirement. Many qualified people left the industry during the recession of the 1990s. Not enough young people are entering the trades to replace those who have left the field. Fewer and fewer high schools offer "shop" programs that lead to careers in the trades, and the number of apprenticeship programs has decreased in recent years. At the same time, the trend among construction companies is to hire people with skills who can work in a variety of areas (electrical work, plumbing, carpentry, etc.).

The Ministry of Training, Colleges and Universities can help to address this shortage by stepping up programs that offer appropriate training, including ESL for skilled tradespeople who immigrate to Canada.

Recommendation #12

The Province of Ontario should take steps to increase the number of people trained in construction-related trades every year, to prevent a shortage of skilled tradespeople.

What the City of Toronto Can Do

In order to meet the current and projected demand for housing, there must be an increase in the supply of conventional rental housing. The following are the actions which should be taken by the City:

Allow more housing, including more rental housing

One barrier to rental housing is the cumbersome process of rezoning and amending the Official Plan when a new multi-residential building is proposed, which may lead to expensive and time-consuming hearings at the Ontario Municipal Board. In the past, some proposals that were approved by the Board were never built because the delay had consumed too much time and the window of opportunity had closed.

The Official Plan and the zoning bylaw can allow for more housing, including new rental housing, by increasing the opportunities for multi-unit residential buildings through intensification and infill. This initiative is important for the quality of life of the City and the liveability of its communities and will ensure that the projected demand for new housing can be achieved.

The City and the Greater Toronto Area cannot achieve their growth objectives in a sustainable way if rental housing is not a fundamental part of smart growth.

Recommendation #13

The City of Toronto should ensure that the Official Plan and the zoning bylaw allow for the production of more housing, including rental housing, to meet the anticipated demand over the next 30 years.

Reduce fees and requirements for rental housing developments

If the Province makes the necessary changes to the *Planning Act*, the *Building Code Act*, and the *Development Charges Act*, the City should act immediately to enact bylaws that would allow it to treat rental housing as a special category, eligible for the kinds of incentives that are now offered to non-profit developers.

Recommendation #14

The City of Toronto should, if allowed to do so by the Province, enact bylaws that will allow it to waive or reduce fees, charges, and requirements to encourage the production of private rental housing.

Review the parking requirements that apply to rental housing

Underground parking can cost in the range of $25,000 to $30,000 per space – sometimes a cost equivalent to the land cost per unit. Car ownership is lower among renters, as many rely on public transit (e.g., seniors, students) and rental managers have reported parking occupancy rates as low as 50 percent. Requiring expensive underground parking that may not be used is inefficient and an impediment to rental development.

To ensure the appropriate parking requirements for rental developments, the City should undertake a parking survey, in consultation with the rental industry, to estimate the typical rate of automobile ownership among tenants.

Recommendation #15

The City of Toronto should conduct a parking survey, in consultation with the rental industry, to determine rates of automobile ownership among tenants to assist in setting appropriate parking requirements for new rental housing.

Continue efforts to streamline the development approval process

The City has worked to ensure that the development approval process is as smooth and efficient as possible. A case-management approach has been instituted, in which one planner is assigned responsibility for a particular application, and is responsible for seeing it through the review process from start to finish. This and other efforts are designed to ensure that developers are not faced with additional expenditures as the result of a long, drawn-out approval process.

Recommendation #16

The City of Toronto should monitor its development approval process to ensure that applications to build rental developments are handled as expeditiously as possible, and that developers of rental buildings are not put to unnecessary expense because of delays.

Next Steps

Business leaders, city officials, housing analysts, and developers agree that Canada needs to re-establish its rental industry in order to remain economically competitive and to meet housing demand.

The rental industry gradually dwindled in Canada because of regulations and restrictions that disadvantaged new rental housing. Removing these regulations and restrictions is a necessary first step. Creating additional incentives will help Canada make up for more than a decade during which little new rental housing was created.

The actions outlined here are intended to support and complement the use of programs for affordable rental housing and to lever additional housing through the more efficient use of program dollars. The actions address issues of concern for both the private rental industry and the non-profit sector. The actions are do-able and the development community has signalled its commitment to get back into making rental housing happen when the roadblocks and obstacles are removed.

An important window of opportunity exists for all levels of government, the private sector, and the non-profit sector to come together and implement actions which will yield concrete results and begin the process of re-establishing a rental industry, thereby ensuring the production of new rental housing on a long-term and sustainable basis.

The members of the **Rental Working Group** *represent a broad cross-section of the rental industry, including builders and developers of rental housing; institutional investors in rental properties; and organizations representing the development, construction, and property management industries. This report is available online at: www.city.toronto.on.ca/torontoplan/pdf/rhintro.pdf*

Bibliography

1995

Lampert, G. The *Challenge of Encouraging Investment in New Rental Housing in Ontario*. Toronto: Ministry of Municipal Affairs and Housing.

Miron, J.R. "Private Rental Housing – The Canadian Experience," *Urban Studies*, vol. 33, pp. 579–604.

1996

Metropolitan Toronto. *Changing Government Role and Public Costs for Housing: Backgrounder*. Toronto: Metro Planning Department and Metro Community Services Department.

Metropolitan Toronto. *Housing Patterns and Prospects in Metro*. Toronto: Metro Planning Department.

1997

Lampert, G., et al. *Prospects for Rental Housing Production in Metro and Rental Housing Financing Mechanisms*. Toronto: Municipality of Metropolitan Toronto.

Metro Toronto Stakeholder Panel on Housing. *Final Report to Metro Toronto Council*. Toronto: Municipality of Metropolitan Toronto.

Miron, J.R. *Renters and Housing Conditions: From the 1980s into the 1990s*. Ottawa: CMHC Background Technical Report.

R. Drdla Associates. *Case Studies of the Municipal Role in Housing*. Toronto Municipality of Metropolitan Toronto, Stakeholder Panel on Housing.

1998

Clayton Research Associates. *Economic Impact of Federal Tax Legislation on the Rental Housing Market*. Toronto: Canadian Federation of Apartment Associations.

Suttor, G. *Proposed Housing Supply Strategy. A Background Paper prepared for the Mayor's Action Task Force on Homelessness*. Toronto: City of Toronto.

1999

Clayton Research Associates. *Understanding Private Rental Housing Investment in Canada*. Ottawa: CMHC Research Report.

Crawford Paterson Campbell, Chartered Accountants. *Fiscal Impact of Federal Tax Legislation on Residential Rental Rates in Canada*. Toronto: Canadian Federation of Apartment Associations.

Enemark, T. "Bad Public Policy Underlies Rental Construction Vacuum." *Multi-Unit Report*, vol. 5, no. 3.

Federation of Canadian Municipalities. *National Housing Policy Options Paper: A Call for Action*. Ottawa.

Lampert, G. *Responding to the Challenge, The Economics of Investment in New Rental Housing in 1999*. Toronto: Ministry of Municipal Affairs and Housing.

Lampert, G. *Review of Potential Changes in Federal Taxes on Housing*. Toronto: Greater Toronto Homebuilders' Association.

Lampert, G. *Update on the Economics of Investment in Rental Housing in Toronto*. Toronto: Rental Housing Supply Alliance.

Mayor's Action Task Force on Homelessness. *Taking Responsibility for Homelessness: An Action Plan for Toronto*. Toronto: City of Toronto.

Ontario Non Profit Housing Association. *Where's Home: A Picture of Housing Needs in Ontario*. Toronto.

2000

Clayton Research Associates, *The Rental Housing Problem in Ontario and What to Do About It*. Toronto: Fair Rental Policy Organization.

Federation of Canadian Municipalities. *National Affordable Housing Strategy*. Ottawa.

Pomeroy, S. *Exploring New Financing Opportunities for Affordable Housing in Canada*. Toronto: Canadian Housing Renewal Association and Ontario Non-Profit Housing Association with the Public Policy Forum.

Toronto Board of Trade. *Policy Statement – Competitive Cities: An Agenda for Urban and National Renewal*. Toronto.

Chapter 22

Affordable, Available, Achievable: Practical Solutions to Affordable Housing Challenges

THE TORONTO BOARD OF TRADE

A Board of Trade Perspective on the Housing Problem

By any measure, Toronto is a vibrant and growing city. Home to over two million people comprising some 90 ethnic groups, the city is a dynamic centre of culture, media, and entertainment, and the business powerhouse that drives the economic engine of Canada.

Yet signs of a decline in the quality of city life are everywhere – from the growing number of the homeless on downtown streets to the rush-hour gridlock that paralyses the main arteries of the city. The *New York Times* has described Toronto as "fraying" under the strain and no longer able to keep up with the demand for housing and other services created by an ever-growing population.

As Toronto has grown, the supply of affordable housing has shrunk. Many people who work in Toronto can no longer afford to live here. Those who find a place often struggle with the high costs of shelter, while others who choose to live outside Toronto become unwitting contributors to urban sprawl and traffic congestion.

How big is the problem of affordable housing in Toronto? According to the Canada Mortgage and Housing Corporation (CMHC),[1] families who pay more than 30 percent of their income on housing are considered cost burdened and may have difficulty affording other necessities such as food and clothing. In 1996 there were approximately 375,000 families (or 33 percent of all families) in the Toronto CMA who paid over 30 percent of their income on housing.[2]

The severe shortage of affordable housing is one of the major issues facing the city. It is a longstanding concern of the Toronto Board of Trade and a key component of the Board's call for a new deal for Toronto. In June 2000, the Board released *Building Solutions to Homelessness: A Business Perspective on Homelessness and Toronto's Housing Crisis*, a report containing recommendations directed at the federal, provincial, and municipal governments.

Our June 2002 report, *Strong City, Strong Nation*, recommended immediate action to address Toronto's crumbling infrastructure and called on government to develop a five-year agreement to support transportation, affordable housing, and Toronto's waterfront. The Toronto Board of Trade has made similar recommendations in a series of federal, provincial, and municipal budget submissions.

We are concerned that, without enhanced investment in the city's infrastructure, Toronto will be unable to maintain its competitive edge, resulting in the city playing a much diminished role in the economic life of the province and the nation.

In recent years, all levels of government have announced initiatives to deal with this pressing issue. However, much more needs to be done. This report contains several recommendations for improving Toronto's stock of adequate, affordable housing.

One way of understanding "affordable housing" is to view it as a continuum. At one end is the shelter system and emergency housing for those in direst need. Transitional and supportive housing is near the centre and permanent stable housing lies at the other end of the spectrum. While emergency and transitional housing represent important needs, this report focuses on permanent affordable rental and affordable ownership housing.

Why Affordable Housing Matters to the Business Community

Affordable housing is one of the major factors in creating an attractive, liveable and competitive city. Along with other infrastructure components, it determines whether or not businesses locate or expand their operations here and influences the willingness of employees and their families to move to or remain in the city. A lack of affordable housing often leads to other social problems, including homelessness and crime, as well as a general deterioration in the quality of city life. Among many other problems, it has important consequences for the desirability of Toronto as a tourist destination and major convention centre. Ultimately, it affects the success of all businesses in the Toronto area and our collective opportunities as employees and citizens.

There are many practical reasons why the supply of affordable housing is important to Toronto's business community.

Affordable housing is a strong selling point for attracting and retaining employees. Toronto competes with some 300 international city regions and many smaller centres for investment, new business, and employees. The cities that attract the best and the brightest people are those that successfully leverage their competitive advantages – housing being one of them. People will flock to a city that offers a good supply and mix of housing that people of varying occupations and income levels can afford.

Toronto must be able to house people who provide essential services. The people most affected by Toronto's affordable housing crisis are lower-income earners who provide important services. These include employees from a broad range of business sectors. Toronto cannot afford to provide such valuable employees and their families with anything less than adequate and affordable housing.

Businesses in Toronto must remain competitive with respect to labour costs. As housing costs rise, so must wages. To stay competitive with other global companies, firms in Toronto must be able to keep their wage bills reasonable.

Businesses need healthy and productive employees. Businesses pay a high cost in terms of lost productivity, absenteeism, and illness when employees are forced to commute long distances to work or are constantly worried about living costs and living accommodations.

Affordable housing represents a partial solution to Toronto's growing traffic problems. More than 70 percent of major highways in the GTA are now congested in peak periods, resulting in serious delays in business deliveries and significantly increasing businesses' transportation costs. Moreover, congestion is forecast to increase dramatically throughout the region over the next twenty years. The Board estimates that the cost of congestion to businesses could reach $3 billion annually, or 1.3 percent of regional GDP by 2021.[3] More affordable housing in the city represents a partial solution to this growing problem.

The affordable housing crunch will only become worse as the city grows. Census data show that 100,000 new arrivals are added every year to the population of the Greater Toronto Area. A recent study by the city suggests that population and employment across the GTA will grow by 2.19 million residents and 1.45 million jobs respectively between 1996 and 2021. This influx of new residents will put an immense strain on all facets of the city's infrastructure, including affordable housing.

Availability and Affordability of Rental Housing

The struggle to find decent, affordable housing in Toronto – a struggle that often pits young working professionals against families and seniors – has become part of the lore of city living. Here is one account:

> They rise at six a.m., grab a coffee and start scanning the classifieds, the alternative weeklies, the on-line listings, the ethnic papers. No time for a shower. They approach the search like a military campaign, the kitchen table strewn with maps, flow charts and highlighters. At seven a.m., they start to place the calls. ... By nine a.m., it's too late: the best places will be gone. Welcome to the world of apartment hunting in Toronto. (Wendy Dennis, "Renter's Hell," *Toronto Life*, March 2002)

For anyone who has chased down apartment space in Toronto in recent years this description might sound all too familiar.

Why has Toronto's rental market become so tight? There are several contributing factors, among them a long-term decline in construction in new rental housing. In Ontario, such construction has fallen from an annual average of 37,000 (private and government assisted) units in the early 1970s to less than 2,000 (private sector constructed) units annually for the four-year period 1997–2001.[4]

Unfortunately, it is no longer economical for private developers to construct affordable rental units. According to a recent report completed for the Ministry of Municipal Affairs and Housing, the spread between the cost of developing new projects and the return required by investors is insufficient to motivate the construction of units with rental rates below $1,000 per month. Developers would require a subsidy of $75,000 per unit to justify construction of units with a targeted monthly rent of $900.[5]

Without action to stimulate new rental construction, the problem will only become worse. According to a recent Ontario government report, the shortfall of new rental units projected over the next fifteen years, based on current rates of production, will be 14,000 new rental units per year.

The loss of rental housing stock due to demolition and condominium conversion is further contributing to a tight rental market. From 1991 to 2001, 8,300 apartment units were demolished across the country.[6] In addition, over 13,000 rental units were lost to condo conversions over a five-year period in the 1990s.[7]

Cities require an estimated rental vacancy rate of at least 2 to 3 percent to ensure an adequate supply of affordable housing. However, in Toronto, the imbalance in the supply and demand of rental space has created a situation characterized by excessively low vacancy rates – at or below 1 percent for much of the recent past – and very high rents, making it difficult for many to make ends meet.

Table 1: Average Rents in the Toronto CMA (dollars)

Average Rents	2000	2001	2002
1-Bedroom	$830	$866	$891
2-Bedroom	$979	$1,027	$1,047

Source: CMHC, Rental Statistics, November 2002.

To afford a one-bedroom apartment costing $891 per month, while paying less than 30 percent of one's income on rent, as recommended by CMHC, a single person in Toronto would have to earn at least $35,640 per year. Many in Toronto, including workers in the hospitality, service, retail, or food and beverage industries, earn less than this figure and would have difficulty affording that one-bedroom unit.

Fortunately, there has recently been an improvement in the rental market. According to CMHC's latest annual report on rental markets, the average apartment vacancy rate in Canada's metropolitan centres rose to 1.7 percent in October 2002 from 1.1 percent in October 2001. This is the first increase in vacancy rates since 1992, and appears to be due mainly to the recent decline in mortgage interest rates, which has encouraged many renters to buy homes. Table 2 shows the improvements in vacancy rates in cities across Canada.

Table 2: Vacancy Rates across Canada (%)

City	1999	2000	2001	2002
Vancouver	2.7	1.4	1.0	1.4
Calgary	2.8	1.3	1.2	2.9
Winnipeg	3.0	2.0	1.4	1.2
Toronto	0.9	0.6	0.9	2.5
Montreal	3.0	1.5	0.6	0.7

Source: CMHC, Rental Statistics, November 2002.

Table 3 shows a similar pattern for other cities in Ontario.

Table 3: Vacancy Rates in Cities across Ontario (%)

City	1999	2000	2001	2002
Hamilton	1.9	1.7	1.3	1.6
Kitchener	1.0	0.7	0.9	2.3
London	3.5	2.2	1.6	2.0
Oshawa	1.7	1.7	1.3	2.3
Ottawa	0.7	0.2	0.8	1.9

Source: CMHC, Rental Statistics November 2002.

While it is encouraging to see vacancy rates improving, this is unlikely to become a long-term trend, particularly for Toronto, with its rapidly expanding population base.

Funding Affordable Housing in Canada and the U.S.

Canadians often assume that our approach to social issues is more comprehensive and compassionate than that in the U.S. But when it comes to affordable housing, we can learn a lot from the Americans.

Affordable housing is funded in dramatically different ways in the United States compared with Canada. For example, the U.S. uses a variety of tax and other incentives to leverage development dollars out of the private sector. Few such programs exist in Canada, and this accounts for the noticeable difference in the total number of rental units completed in each jurisdiction. In the U.S., total rental completions (including both market rate and affordable rental) have accounted for more than 16 percent of total new housing production over the past 10 years. The comparable figure in Canada is 9 percent.[8]

Private enterprise in the U.S. is generally much more active in the affordable housing sector than is the case in Canada. For that reason, the U.S. private sector also tends to be more aware of needs and has formed a much closer relationship with the not-for-profit sector in advocating for more affordable housing.

So-called "third parties" are also more involved in U.S. rental construction. The tax credit system in the U.S. necessitates a third party to bring together those who receive the tax credits (housing financing agencies) and those who wish to purchase them (developers) and to assist with the technical aspects of making the tax credits work. This role is played by an array of institutions in the U.S., including the community development subsidiaries of major financial institutions and non-profit corporations. This broad institutional framework also ensures that communities have the information and the access to programs that are required to tackle their affordable housing needs. A similar network of institutions has not evolved in Canada, largely because of the way we have financed affordable housing.

Charts 1 and 2 outline the primary programs designed to stimulate rental construction in Ontario and the United States.

Practical Solutions

A developer's decision to construct affordable housing, whether for rental or ownership, is affected by government policies at the federal, provincial, and municipal levels.

Taxes are a major consideration. Income taxes, and the GST in particular, have a significant impact on investor decisions. In fact, federal tax policy in the early 1970s was largely responsible for a subsequent decrease in the number of new, purpose-built multi-residential rental units. Property taxes also have a major impact: higher property taxes on purpose-built multi-residential units in Toronto, as compared to taxes on either condominium or other ownership housing, have tended to discourage new rental construction.

Other factors affecting investment include interest rates, access to low-cost mortgage insurance, and the availability of serviced land. Rent-control laws, as well as landlord tenant legislation, also affect the long-term profitability of rental investments.

The Board of Trade believes that changes to government policy represent an important first step in solving the affordable housing crisis. We recognize that governments have taken action in recent years to address the challenge of affordable housing. The province of Ontario has made several legislative and regulatory changes to give municipalities more flexibility in dealing with the issue of affordable housing. The federal government and provinces have also signed a framework agreement on affordable housing. In Ontario's case, a bilateral agreement with Ottawa will result in approximately $360 million in federal funds being invested in affordable housing over a five-year period. Matching grants are to be provided by the province and municipalities.

Chart 1: Major Affordable Housing Programs in Ontario

Measure	Explanation	Estimated Cost
Federal-Provincial-Territorial Housing Agreement	The federal government and each of the provinces and territories will sign bilateral agreements which match federal contributions to provincial/territorial contributions up to $25,000 per unit	$1 billion over 5 years from the federal government. Matching funds can be cash or in-kind contributions. (Ontario's portion is approximately $360 million)
Federal Residential Rehabilitation Assistance Program (RRAP)	A federal program used to upgrade the homes of low-income renters, rooming house residents, and homeowners	$7.5 million to the city in 2000
Canada Mortgage and Housing Corporation	Provides mortgage insurance for commercial and individual residences	
Province of Ontario PST grants	The province provides grants of $2,000 per unit for a new purpose-built rental unit	Total investment of $20 million
City of Toronto "Let's Build" Program	The program has many components that encourage new affordable housing. These include: loans from a Capital Revolving Fund; exemptions from municipal development charges; property tax exemptions	Total amount of the CRF is $10.8 million

Toronto has also been active on this issue through its Let's Build program. This offers prospective builders the services of experienced development and housing professionals, who can assist in the planning and development process, plus a toolkit of incentives to increase the economic viability of affordable housing projects. These incentives may include the use of city-owned land, the waiving of development fees, tax incentives, and one-time financial assistance from the city's $11 million Capital Revolving Fund for Affordable Housing.[9]

But the Board of Trade believes much more can be done. The recommendations that follow are divided into those that could be carried out

Chart 2: Major Affordable Housing Programs in the United States

Measure	Explanation	Estimated Cost (U.S. $)
Community Reinvestment Act (1977)	Encourages financial institutions to reinvest in their communities. Each lender's performance is publicly disclosed. Helps prevent "red-lining" of poor neighbourhoods	NA.
Low Income Housing Tax Credit	A subsidy program created within the U.S. Tax Code for rental housing. States receive a per capita allocation	Over $3.4 billion annually
Tax Exempt Bonds	Bonds which are exempt from federal and state taxes, generally with terms of 10 to 30 years	Proceeds of bonds undertaken in support of rental housing totalled just over $3 billion in 2000
Community Development Block Grants	Provides formula-based federal block grants to communities for redevelopment and revitalization activities	CDBG annual appropriation is over $4 billion; approximately $200 million annually is used for affordable housing
HOME Investment Partnership Program	Provides federal grants to state and local levels to assist in housing strategies tailored to low income needs	The program was funded at $1.8 billion in 2001
Fannie Mae	Purchases mortgages in the secondary mortgage market in the U.S. Develops community lending mortgage products for low-income purchasers	Fannie Mae has committed $2 trillion by 2010 to the "American Dream Commitment" which will increase affordable ownership and affordable rental

within the next year, with little cost to government, and those which could be implemented over the next five years and have higher costs associated with them.

We also believe that the private sector can play a leadership role in expanding the city's stock of affordable housing, providing it is allowed to generate reasonable returns in doing so.

Solutions for the Short Term

Many of our recommendations can be fully implemented within one year. They include: the development of a national housing strategy; changes to the mandate and focus of the Canada Mortgage and Housing Corporation (CMHC); federal tax changes; and the sale of surplus lands.

Canada needs a national housing strategy

The federal government has a leadership role to play in developing a national housing strategy. Affordable housing is a national problem. We believe that Canada needs a national coordinated housing strategy, involving all levels of government, which would focus on increasing the availability of affordable housing.

Such a strategy would recognize the need to foster an investment climate that encourages the construction of affordable rental and ownership housing, promotes housing and support services, and provides financial assistance to low-income tenants who are most at risk in cities like Toronto.

The Board of Trade recommends:
- that the federal government develop and implement a comprehensive and coordinated national housing strategy to address the shortage of affordable housing;
- that the federal government enhance CMHC's mandate to allow it to expand its research activities and communication function and improve its coordination of nonprofit housing initiatives;
- that the federal government direct the CMHC to use a portion of its mortgage insurance fund surplus to lower mortgage insurance terms and premiums for multi-residential projects.

Canada's national housing agency needs to focus on affordable housing

The Canada Mortgage and Housing Corporation (CMHC) is Canada's national housing agency. It provides mortgage insurance and financial assistance for low-income Canadians, conducts research, and administers the federal government's housing agreements and programs. But the agency has few tools to promote affordable housing, and little flexibility to implement new ideas.

CMHC's effectiveness would be enhanced if it had the authority and used its resources to research solutions to the affordable housing crisis, coordinate affordable housing funding, and disseminate information about affordable housing across Canada. CMHC should also be given the tools to support construction of affordable rental and ownership housing, if this direction becomes part of a future housing policy.

CMHC's surplus is projected to grow from $1 billion in 2001 to $3 billion in 2006. We believe that CMHC should use a portion of its growing surplus to ease underwriting criteria for multi-residential projects.

Federal tax changes will spur the development of more rental housing

Efforts by the federal government over the past 30 years to close loopholes in the federal tax system have discouraged private investment in rental housing. Changes in several areas – the tax treatment of losses due to Capital Cost Allowance (CCA), the amount of CCA deductible, allowable soft cost expenses,[10] and the application of tax on capital gains – have substantially reduced the attractiveness of rental construction. The application of the GST to the full cost of new rental housing is also a serious deterrent to investment.

The 2000 federal budget extended a residential rental property rebate of 2.5 percent to newly constructed, substantially renovated, and converted rental accommodation. However, we believe that substantial changes in the tax system are still needed to encourage investment in rental housing and must be part of any national housing policy.

Recent cost-benefit analyses suggest that just three measures will yield revenues to the federal government that more than offset revenue loss due to tax changes: a full GST rebate, an increase of the CCA rate to 5 percent, and immediate deductibility of soft costs. Construction of just 6,000 or more incremental units will fully cover the costs incurred by making these changes.[11]

The Board of Trade recommends:
- that the federal government allow a full rebate of GST on new rental housing projects;
- that the federal government increase CCA to 5 percent for new rental housing;
- that the federal government expand the "soft costs" which can be deducted in the first year of operation of new rental properties.

The cost of building affordable rental and ownership housing can be lowered

Various government agencies and departments – including Canada Lands, Public Works and Government Services Canada, the Ontario Realty Corporation, and municipal Chief Administratorss Offices – are charged with the disposal of government lands as part of their mandate.

A big challenge in developing affordable housing is procuring land. This could be addressed, in part, by giving priority in purchasing government lands at market value to investors who intend to build affordable housing.

Such investors also face problems in gaining access to financing and meeting onerous zoning requirements. We suggest that institutions responsible for selling government surplus land show greater flexibility by accepting conditional offers with a term of one year instead of six months, and by requiring only a nominal deposit on the land (less than the current 10 percent).

The Board of Trade recommends:
- that governments at the federal, provincial, and municipal levels give priority to developers planning to build affordable housing by making land available at market rates;
- that governments at the federal, provincial, and municipal levels give their agencies in charge of selling surplus land the flexibility to accept one-year conditional offers from developers of affordable housing;
- that conditions for the above be based on such criteria as receiving zoning for the property and arranging financing;
- that greater flexibility be allowed in the amount of deposit required from those building affordable housing.

Solutions for the long term

In the United States, over $8.5 billion annually is spent by governments on affordable housing. These programs in turn encourage the private sector to invest in construction, with spin-off benefits throughout the economy. Programs available to the province of Ontario (including the federal-provincial housing agreement) equal approximately $85 million per year for affordable housing – a meagre amount by any measure.

Our longer-term recommendations would require a significantly larger financial commitment from governments and be implemented over a five-year period.

The tax system can be used to prevent the demolition of older affordable housing

Federal tax laws require an investor who sells an investment in rental property to pay taxes if the sale price exceeds the depreciated value of the project. The taxes payable are based on a combination of recaptured depreciation and capital gains, and act as a deterrent to selling the project. In some cases, the investor demolishes the existing property to avoid the tax consequences of recapture.[12] Since 2000, the city of Toronto has lost 431 rental units to demolition.[13]

There are two ways that the federal government could amend tax policy to discourage investors from demolishing affordable rental buildings. It could allow individuals to defer capital gains tax if the proceeds of the sale of one rental property are invested in another rental property. It could also allow individuals to receive a reduction on the amount of taxes on capital gains owing on the disposition of a rental property if the property is given to a public foundation that would continue to manage the building as an affordable housing project.

Both of these tax policy changes would discourage investors from demolishing older affordable housing investments.

The Board of Trade recommends:
• that federal taxation laws be changed to allow the deferral of capital gains tax and recaptured depreciation on the sale of a rental building – provided the proceeds are invested in another rental building of greater or equal value;
• that Section 38 of the *Income Tax Act* (Canada) be amended to encourage gifts of land or land and buildings to public foundations established for the purpose of providing affordable housing.

Property taxes should be fair and equitable

Another way to increase the supply of rental housing is to provide property tax equity across the property tax system. Multi-residential and business property owners are taxed at a much higher rate than the residential tax class. In our report of June 2000, the Board of Trade called on the city to remove the eight-year time limit that allowed new multi-residential developments to be taxed at the rate equal to the residential class. A provincial *Assessment Act* amendment now permits municipalities to increase the time limit from 8 to 35 years for new rental units.

While we continue to support fair multi-residential tax treatment, we are concerned that this reduction may be carried out, as suggested in a recent provincial report,[14] by distributing the costs of the reduction among all property classes.

The Board of Trade recommends:
• that the province ensure that over time, the property tax burden is fairly balanced across property tax classes.

Tax changes will encourage businesses to invest in rental housing

Since 1972, income tax rules affecting rental housing have become increasingly punitive. Individual investors who may own one or two rental properties are not entitled to deduct CCA losses against other income.

Small businesses that invest solely in rental properties are excluded from the favourable tax treatment afforded other small businesses by the small business deduction. Specifically, small businesses, which do nothing but rent real estate and have fewer than five employees, are excluded from this beneficial tax rate.[15]

Both the federal and provincial governments assess capital taxes against large corporations, including those that invest in real estate. Assessing capital taxes on businesses that invest in new rental housing decreases the expected return to these companies from their investment and serves to discourage investment.

We were pleased with the announcements in the 2003 provincial and federal budgets to eliminate the capital tax by 2008.

The Board of Trade recommends:
• that the federal government allow all investors in new rental housing projects, and not just principal business corporations, to deduct CCA losses against other income;
• that the federal government allow the small business deduction to be extended to all small businesses that invest in new rental housing.

Brownfields can provide a new pool of land for affordable housing

Brownfields are idle or underused properties that may be contaminated but also have potential for remediation. They are located mainly in established urban areas, where existing municipal services are readily available, or along transportation corridors. It has been estimated that there may be as many as 30,000 brownfield sites in Canada.[16]

In Ontario, brownfield sites are located in almost all established communities with an industrial past. Greater Toronto and Hamilton have the largest number of old industrial sites in this province, and an estimated 10 to 15 percent of these sites are brownfields.[17]

Those interested in redeveloping brownfields are often faced with several challenges, including financing, environmental liability, and cleanup costs. The Board of Trade participated in the Brownfields Policy Review and subsequently made comments on Bill 56, the *Brownfields Statute Law Amendment Act*. Despite the good work of the province in removing barriers to remediation and redevelopment of brownfields, much more progress can be achieved.

We urge the provincial and federal governments to make a larger, longer-term financial commitment to brownfield remediation by providing financial incentives in line with the level of commitment provided in the U.S. In addition to municipal tax relief and a brownfield fund, potential incentives could include tax abatement, tax credits, waiving of fees, and provincial sales tax rebates.

There are many approaches to remediation and re-using brownfields safely. One method that could be used for developing sites for affordable housing is the risk-based remediation approach. This method restores brownfields to a state as safe as they would have been had a dig-and-dump approach been used, but at much reduced cost. This allows developers to recapture property for affordable housing at a relatively low cost.

The federal, provincial, and municipal governments should develop procedures to encourage the use of such approaches where properties are to be used for affordable housing. Streamlined and supportive approval regimes are needed to support these efforts. Governments should also permit former owners and polluters of such property, who properly contribute to the remediation and development of affordable housing, to be exempted from potential future liability, both civilly and under the regulatory regime. Such methods should include review and approval under the *Brownfields Statute Law Amendment Act* procedures, together with indemnities from the Province and the municipality, to provide protection from potential liability. Using such an approach would safeguard people's rights, while ensuring that any risks associated with such development would be borne by the public, which would benefit most from more affordable housing.

While the province allows the city to provide municipal tax incentives to owners of brownfields, both the federal and provincial governments have failed to put in place funding or incentives to encourage clean-up and redevelopment.

The Toronto Board of Trade is encouraged by the recent report by the National Round Table on the Environment and the Economy, which recommends a national strategy for the cleanup of brownfields. We welcome the attention paid to harmonizing federal and provincial regulations to promote a favourable environment for private sector participation in brownfields cleanup.

The Board of Trade recommends:
• that municipal governments offer tax relief to developers of affordable housing who purchase and remediate brownfields sites;
• that the provincial government and the federal government create a fund or tax incentive that would help defray the costs of cleaning up brownfields sites for developers of affordable housing;
• that the provincial government take further steps to protect those remediating brownfields by clarifying that those innocent parties (developers, bankers, owners, occupiers) who are involved in the remediation and subsequent use of contaminated sites are not liable, either civilly or under the regulatory regime, for contamination that has migrated from the property to another property;
• that the provincial government develop a streamlined approvals procedure for the redevelopment of brownfield sites for affordable housing based on risk-based remediation approaches;
• that the provincial government and the municipalities develop a process to indemnify those involved in the brownfield redevelopment process for affordable housing from any future liabilities (both civilly and under the regulatory regime) that may arise with respect to the property (this would include former owners and polluters of the property who properly contribute to the redevelopment process);
• that the federal government examine innovative financing and liability arrangements that would encourage the cleanup and redevelopment of brownfields for affordable housing.

New sources of financing for affordable housing should be created

In the U.S., the Low Income Housing Tax Credit (LIHTC) has been highly successful in attracting private-sector funding for affordable housing. The LIHTC is a tax credit worth 100 percent of the investment and costs the U.S. treasury approximately $3.4 billion annually. One component of a multi-layered financing system, the tax credit is structured to pay a part of the cost of an affordable housing project. The tax credit does a successful job of levering money out of private-sector investors and encouraging them to invest in affordable housing.

Canada has never had a program resembling the LIHTC, but we have had funds created to assist small businesses (Labour Sponsored Venture Capital Corporations or LSVCCs) since the early 80s. The LSVCC, one of the few tax credit vehicles available to passive investors in Canada offers a 30 percent tax credit that is split equally between the federal and provincial governments.[18] The purpose of the LSVCC is to encourage investment in Canadian companies with less than $50 million in assets and fewer than 500 employees.

A new tax vehicle modelled on the LSVCC – an Affordable Housing Venture Capital Corporations (AHVCC) – could be created to allow ordinary Canadians to invest in affordable housing and receive a sizable tax credit.

The Board of Trade recommends:
• that the federal government consider creating a new tax credit modelled after the tax credit available through labour sponsored venture capital corporations. This new tax credit would encourage ordinary Canadians to invest in affordable housing venture capital corporations, which would in turn invest in affordable housing projects;
• that the federal government exempt interest earned on Opportunity Bonds from federal taxation.

Tax-exempt bonds

Tax-exempt bonds have been used successfully in the United States to raise financing for affordable housing. Proceeds can be used to fund below-market mortgages for both first time homebuyers and for multi-family rental development.[19]

The Ontario government has created tax-free Opportunity Bonds to assist municipalities with important infrastructure projects. The new program is designed to provide a provincial tax exemption to investors in opportunity bonds. Unfortunately, interest earned by investors will still be taxable by the federal government. If this program is to be effective, the federal government must exempt holders of Opportunity Bonds from taxation.

Conclusion

Affordable housing is critical to our competitiveness. The supply of affordable housing affects the success of all businesses in Toronto and our opportunities as citizens. Government must ensure that the policy framework is in place to encourage the private sector to build more affordable housing.

We believe that our recommendations to address affordable housing challenges in Toronto and other cities are achievable.

Resolving affordable housing in Toronto will ensure that we remain a world-class city. It will help the business community remain competitive and keep Toronto a vibrant urban centre.

We encourage government to work with the private sector to increase the supply of affordable housing. The time has come to make the policy and tax changes required to ensure an adequate supply of affordable housing.

This report is available online at:
www.ofcmhap.on.ca/non-profit/FINALBOTAffordableHouseReport03.pdf

Endnotes

1 CMHC website, Frequently Asked Questions, Affordable Housing, October 2002.
2 Statistics Canada, "Census families in private households by selected household and dwelling characteristics, Census Metropolitan Areas," 1996 Census.
3 Toronto Board of Trade, *A Strategy for Rail-Based Transit in the GTA*, July 2001.
4 Ministry of Municipal Affairs and Housing, Housing Supply Working Group Interim Report, *Affordable Rental Housing Supply: The Dynamics of the Market and Recommendations for Encouraging New Supply*, May 2001.
5 Ministry of Municipal Affairs and Housing, Housing Supply Working Group, *Comparative Real Estate Finance Analysis*, prepared by Ernst & Young, 2000.
6 Canadian Housing and Renewal Association, *Municipal Initiatives: Stemming the Loss of Rental Stock*, October 2002.
7 Federation of Canadian Municipalities, *Towards a National Housing Strategy*, A Working Paper Prepared for the FCM Big City Mayors Conference, April 2000.
8 CMHC, extract from *The Role of Public Private Partnerships in Producing Affordable Housing: Assessment of the U.S. Experience and Lessons for Canada*, prepared by Steve Pomeroy and Greg Lampert, in association with James Wallace and Robert Sheehan, July 1998.
9 City of Toronto website, Let's Build Outlook, October 2002.

10 Soft costs are costs which are necessary to prepare and complete the non-construction needs of projects such as architecture, design, engineering, permits, consultants, inspections, etc.

11 Ministry of Municipal Affairs and Housing, Housing Supply Working Group, Second Report, *Creating a Positive Climate for Rental Housing Development Through Tax and Mortgage Insurance Reforms*, November 2002.

12 Ministry of Municipal Affairs and Housing, Housing Supply Working Group, *Options for Changes in Federal Taxes to Encourage New Rental Construction*, report prepared by Greg Lampert and Steve Pomeroy, March 2002.

13 The Toronto Board of Trade, *Strong City, Strong Nation*, 2002.

14 Marcel Beaubien, MPP, Special Advisor to the Minister of Finance, *Property Assessment and Classification Review*, Final Report, Fall 2002.

15 Ministry of Municipal Affairs and Housing, *Housing Supply Working Group, Options for Changes in Federal Taxes to Encourage New Rental Construction*, report prepared by Greg Lampert and Steve Pomeroy, March 2002.

16 National Round Table on the Environment and the Economy, *National Brownfields Redevelopment Strategy*, February 2003.

17 Ministry of Municipal Affairs and Housing website, Brownfields Showcase, February 2003.

18 VanCity Enterprises, *Exploring Tax Based Measures to Attract Private Investment for Affordable Housing: Discussion Paper*, prepared by Steve Pomeroy, December 2001.

19 CMHC, extract from *The Role of Public Private Partnerships in Producing Affordable Housing: Assessment of the U.S. Experience and Lessons for Canada*, prepared by Steve Pomeroy and Greg Lampert, in association with James Wallace and Robert Sheehan, July 1998.

Chapter 23
Aboriginal Housing in Canada

GEORGE DEVINE

No study of housing in Canada can overlook the particular question of housing for Aboriginal people, both on and off reserves. In a country where the average Canadian lives in safe, affordable housing, the contrast with the Aboriginal population is shocking. Among Aboriginal communities, both on and off reserve, a very large proportion of Aboriginal people live in overcrowded conditions and in housing that is in need of major repair. Aboriginal people are 25 percent more likely to be homeless than other Canadians.

Indian and Northern Affairs Canada (INAC) estimates that of the more than 90,000 houses on reserves across Canada in 2001, 44 percent were in need of renovation. Canada Mortgage and Housing Corporation (CMHC) estimated in 1998 that between 50 and 54 percent of off-reserve Aboriginal households occupy dwellings that fall below one or more core housing need standards.[1]

Over 70 percent of Aboriginal people,[2] or just under 700,000, now live off-reserve in urban and rural areas, forming just under 158,000 households,[3] yet there are fewer than 19,000 housing units[4] across Canada specifically funded and targeted for them. A recent study[5] by the National Aboriginal Housing Association (NAHA) found that off-reserve Aboriginal renter households are at a serious disadvantage compared to non-Aboriginal renter households. Some 16.5 percent of Aboriginal household live in units in need of major repair compared to only 9 percent for non-Aboriginal. Aboriginal households have a higher incidence of affordability problems than do non-Aboriginals, with 37 percent spending more than the norm of 30 percent for rent; while 15 percent (one in every six) experience a severe rent burden, paying greater than 50 percent of income for shelter. The off-reserve Aboriginal population has a lower income than non-Aboriginals; 87 percent that of non-Aboriginal households.

In central and western Canadian cities, Aboriginal men, women, and youth are disproportionately represented within the homeless population and the most identifiable segment of street homeless and shelter users.

How do we explain this situation after over 30 years of public involvement and financial investment in Aboriginal housing?

This chapter outlines federal Aboriginal housing policy initiatives and some of the issues those policies have failed to address, and summarizes recent recommendations made by both the Assembly of First Nations (AFN) and NAHA to improve the housing situation of Canada's Aboriginal peoples.

On-reserve Housing

INAC developed the first on-reserve housing subsidy program in the 1960s, providing funding for building and renovating housing. Assistance was in the form of capital grants for construction. Band councils were responsible for establishing housing management regimes which mostly consisted of allocating units to band households. There was no funding for ongoing maintenance, nor were band councils encouraged or supported in developing a property management capability. In most instances, occupants were not required to pay rent and had security of tenure only as long as they continued to live on the reserve and did not abandon the unit.

Many of the conventional Canadian approaches to housing, such as homeownership, do not apply to on-reserve housing. Because most of the land is owned by the Crown, band households are precluded from outright ownership and land title, and from obtaining mortgage financing to repair or upgrade their housing unit. As well, since about 65 percent of the housing is in rural, remote, or special-access areas,[6] there is little or no "market" for on-reserve housing. The consequences of this inability to own the housing unit, the exclusion of securing financing, and the lack of a re-sale market have acted as major disincentives for band households to invest their own scarce financial resources in maintaining band housing.

Given the lack of financial resources on the part of the band council to maintain the housing, and the disincentive for the household to invest in the unit, it was only a matter of time before the housing stock would deteriorate seriously.

A second major policy initiative was launched in the late 1970s, when CMHC became involved in on-reserve housing, mainly through the Non-Profit Rental Housing Program.

Under this program, which was originally designed to be delivered and managed by private non-profit groups in Canada's cities and towns, band councils received a combination of loan financing and operating subsidies to build and operate housing units. The operating subsidies, however, were insufficient to maintain the unit and also repay the federal loan financing. The program required a secure rental revenue stream to ensure housing project viability.

In addition, band councils were required to adhere to a series of operating policies that were culturally insensitive and hard to implement. The most significant of these was the requirement to adopt a national rental scale and definition of income.

Given the fact that the majority of other band households were not required to pay rent for their housing, many bands objected to charging rents under the CMHC program. The disparity in the treatment of band council housing was a legitimate concern, especially in small communities, where most people are related, or know their neighbours well. As a result, the band council either fell into arrears on their federal housing loans, or used other revenue streams to keep the loans current, which meant other band services were neglected.

Where band councils were willing to implement a rental payment system, they were further thwarted by the requirement to use the national definition of income as the bases for determining household income. The definition was designed to reflect the average low-income urban household, in which, for instance, the "head of household" was generally accepted as the major financial breadwinner. In most Aboriginal households, the "head" is the oldest member of the extended family and may not be the principal wage earner. The definition also did not take into account extended family households (which should be included in determining gross household income), or the seasonal and migratory income patterns of many Aboriginal households. As a result, it was virtually impossible for band councils, even if they were willing to do so, to use the definition as a guide for determining household income and setting the percentage of income for monthly rent.

As with the INAC housing, there was no incentive for the household to invest any of its scarce resources in maintaining the unit. Consequently, the program was unpopular among band councils and the housing, like the INAC-funded housing, suffered from deferred maintenance.

Although no serious comparisons have ever been done between Canada's approach to housing its low-income urban populations using the federal-provincial public housing programs of the 1970s and 1980s, and housing its low-income Aboriginal populations during the same period, some serious disparities are obvious. Technically, the rent scale was the same. The low-income household was required to pay a percentage of its income for rent. But the most significant difference was that under the public housing schemes, there was massive public financial investment in the ongoing administration and maintenance of the housing. This was never the situation for on-reserve housing.

Despite the shortcomings in the on-reserve housing programs, there were successes, such as that of the Cree in northern Quebec, where the bands were financially stable, primarily due to the James Bay land settlement, and created meaningful and culturally sensitive housing management regimes. They were able to build up operating reserves, which allowed the local councils to keep the housing in good repair.

These programs remained largely unaltered until 1996, when the federal government approved $140 million in new funding and a new policy for on-reserve housing, intended to give reserve communities more flexibility and control in managing housing funds. The Assembly of First Nations estimated, however, a need for $750 million a year to deal with the ongoing needs of the on-reserve population, and another $2.5 billion to deal with the shortage backlog of adequate housing.

The new policy requires band councils to prepare and implement multi-year, community-based housing programs. As of March 2001, about 400 communities had done so. The remaining communities continued to operate under the pre-1996 policies.

The new policy was the subject of a review carried out for INAC in 2000 and one by the Auditor General of Canada in 2003.

The first review[7] stated that the new program was working and had increased the amount of adequate housing by 7 percent over two years. However, the report also noted the backlog of substandard housing stock. It highlighted the problem of overcrowding caused by the high growth rate on reserves and to an extent, the number of people who had returned to the reserves after regaining their status rights under Bill C-31. The report recommended additional funding for the program, clarification of the policies on shelter allowances, the dedication of additional staff resources, and the dissemination of successful case studies among Aboriginal communities.[8]

Significantly, it recognized the same patterns which have existed in on-reserve housing policies since the 1960s and recommended the use of incentives to help households adjust to a different approach to creating and managing housing:

> Money alone will not help First Nations to complete the turn. For many, the concepts of debt financing or having individuals pay for their own housing through rents or mortgages remains outside the community norms. Incentives are required to help them introduce these concepts to their communities: incentives for implementing home-ownership initiatives; incentives for implementing community-wide shelter charge regimes; incentives that will lead to the development of local housing sub-trade businesses; and incentives that will directly address overcrowding.[9]

The Auditor General's report focused on the roles of INAC and CMHC. In addition to reporting on the financial management of the program, and recommending additional financial controls, the report noted that the roles and responsibilities of the two bodies were unclear, and recommended streamlining the program, which was considered unnecessarily complex. It highlighted the problem of contamination of housing by mould, and recommended a comprehensive strategy, involving Health Canada, to remedy this situation.

Both reports emphasized that much more needed to be done to ensure adequate housing for on-reserve communities and that decent housing was a prerequisite for healthy and productive communities.

In late 2003, the AFN, which represents Canada's reserves, asked the federal government to transfer all responsibility for housing into a new First Nations–run entity that would handle mortgages on reserves and buy housing in urban centres. The AFN recognized that housing on reserves would be in better shape if band members could own their own homes. Under the $300-million proposal, on-reserve housing responsibilities at INAC and CMHC would be folded into the new entity. The AFN calls for housing markets to be set up on reserves so that homeowners would have a larger stake in home maintenance.

The AFN's national chief, Phil Fontaine, acknowledged that creating housing markets from scratch will not be easy. "We're dealing with a pretty complex matter here," he said. "It's clear that the way our people are able to access capital for their housing needs is not doing the job. We need to be more innovative."[10]

INAC has estimated a need for an additional 8,500 houses to accommodate the growing on-reserve population. The need is especially acute, since the Aboriginal growth rate is twice the Canadian average.[11] While current federal policies support the creation of 2,600 houses a year and the renovation of an additional 3,300 houses, new on-reserve households are being formed at the rate of about 4,500 a year. Combined with the massive backlog in deferred maintenance in the existing housing stock, and flawed federal programs, new solutions, which build on self-determination and self-governance, are needed. Increased homeownership is one important component. Another is to invest financial resources to put band councils on the same footing as municipal housing management entities. Most of all, it is important that housing policy makers listen to First Nations band councils and political organizations.

Urban Aboriginal Housing

Public policy intervention in urban Aboriginal housing goes back over 30 years. In 1970, the federal government launched a $200-million demonstration housing program, primarily to find better solutions to housing Canada's inner-city low-income households. One project that managed to get demonstration funds was sponsored by the Native Friendship Centre in Winnipeg. This project consisted of acquiring and renovating 10 existing units for Aboriginal housing.

Although Aboriginal communities were not part of the original targets under the demonstration funding, it was not surprising that other requests to support urban Aboriginal housing projects were received. Friendship Centres were one of the first Aboriginal services created to respond to the early migration of Aboriginal people from rural and remote reserves into cities. They were also the front line for newly arrived Aboriginal families trying to find suitable and affordable housing. With the support of Friendship Centres, Metis, and non-status Aboriginal groups across Canada, five additional non-profit housing corporations were created between 1972 and 1975.

The federal response through CMHC was to make loans available under the new Non-Profit Housing Program established in 1973. Intended primarily for private, charitable non-profits, it provided 100 percent capital financing, and a fixed long-term mortgage interest rate.

There were no operating subsidies and the rental project had to generate at least an economic rent to repay the loan and maintain the units. All of the sponsors used the Winnipeg model of acquiring older existing housing and doing only modest renovations.

In addition, the federal government in 1972, through CMHC, created the Rural and Native Housing Program (RNH) to serve the housing needs of both Aboriginal and non-Aboriginal households in communities of less than 2,000 population. Because the RNH program was not limited to households of Aboriginal ancestry, a large percentage of the units in some provinces are occupied by non-Aboriginals. In the early 1990s, CMHC took steps to transfer management of the RNH portfolio to Aboriginal management groups. When this program was transferred to the provinces and territories after 1996, there was no requirement on the part of the provinces or territories to continue this arrangement.

Because the urban non-profit program still relied on rental revenue, and because, as now, urban Aboriginal household incomes were substantially below the Canadian average, sustainability could not be achieved, since most of the households paid only a minimum monthly rent. As a result, the housing providers had to rely upon additional federal "research" funds to operate. In 1974, CMHC urged provinces to use cost-shared funding under the former *National Housing Act* Section 44, to provide deeper shelter subsidies, thus ensuring a modest degree of financial stability. But provincial take-up was spotty.

In 1977, under pressure from national Aboriginal organizations, CMHC agreed to set aside a specific target: 400 units a year, or 10 percent of the 1978 social housing allocation, for urban Aboriginal housing. Once again, the federal government adopted the new non-profit housing program to deliver the units. Under the new program, the federal government provided mortgage interest assistance in the form of nonrepayable subsidies over the life of the mortgage, usually set at 35 years.

The shortcomings in this program were similar to those of the previous program: given the substantially lower household income, it was difficult to achieve sustainability with a capped subsidy and low rental revenue potential. Housing providers continued to acquire older existing units and undertake only modest repairs. Nevertheless, the Aboriginal portfolio continued to increase in response to demand, as more and more Aboriginal people migrated to cities and towns. But the portfolio was plagued with operating deficits.

In 1983, the federal government approved increased funding for 1,000 existing units, guaranteeing that tenants of native ancestry would pay no more than 25 percent of their income on shelter. This new assistance bridged the gap between operating costs and operating income. This was the first housing response that recognized the reality of the urban Aboriginal community.

Two years later, the federal government formalized this approach with a distinct Urban Native Housing Program. In addition to the deeper subsidies, the new program addressed many of the lingering grievances with the older programs. CMHC agreed to the need for tenant counselling, additional administration expenses, and consideration of non-traditional households in the treatment of household income.

But the agreement to allocate 10 percent of the annual units to urban Aboriginals never materialized, and between 1970 and 1993, when the federal government terminated delivery of new housing, less than 11,000 units were produced.[12]

Overall, urban Aboriginal leaders consider the program a success, especially as it emerged after 1985. Today's portfolio is managed, at the community level, by 110 non-profit Aboriginal corporations and provides housing for about 35,000 individuals of status, non-status, Metis, and Inuit ancestry.

Given the program constraints and a public policy bias that urban Aboriginals should be "integrated" into lower-income communities, a very high percentage of the stock (especially compared to the non-Aboriginal non-profit and co-operative housing) consists of older units, in lower-income, inner-city neighbourhoods. Because of the age of the stock, maintenance costs are higher than those of other forms of publicly assisted housing. CMHC data indicates that in 1995, just over 3 percent of the projects in the portfolio failed to meet the NHA Minimum Property Standards. NAHA believes that this estimate is low, and that in terms of individual units, a much higher percentage would fall below the standards. The average cost of deferred repairs was estimated by CMHC to be approximately $2,200 per unit.

When, in 1993, the federal government, as part of its fiscal restraint policy, halted all new spending for housing, the Aboriginal community fully expected a return to normalcy once the government got its fiscal house in order. Instead of a return to normalcy, with new unit allocations, the federal government announced in its 1996 federal budget that future responsibility for urban Aboriginal housing was being transferred to the provinces and territories. It meant that in the future, provinces and territories would assume the responsibility for the existing portfolio, as well as any new housing for Aboriginal people who lived off reserve, regardless of their status. The federal government would continue to transfer the annual subsidy to the provinces, but this was capped at the 1996 level.

Particularly upsetting to the community leaders who had worked with the federal government to build a success story, the transfer was executed without any consultation.[13] Federal officials and politicians steadfastly refused to invite Aboriginal representatives to its bilateral discussions with provinces and territories. Nor were they ready to enter into any bilateral discussions with Aboriginal organizations on the future management of the programs.

The transfer, which has now occurred in most provinces, has created uncertainty and a serious policy vacuum. Seven years later, no province has yet accepted the new responsibility. There are no urban Aboriginal set-asides in the current federal Affordable Housing Framework, and no requirement on the part of provinces participating in the initiative to target any new housing to the Aboriginal community.

In addition to the lack of new housing, Aboriginal housing providers fear that the existing portfolio and the successes it has achieved will be eroded over time under provincial jurisdiction. There is a lack of protection in the bilateral transfer agreements for maintaining the "Aboriginal character" of housing, including funding for tenant counsellors, a key management tool, and culturally sensitive management regimes. As well, they fear that as provinces set up portfolio-wide benchmarks for operating expenses, including maintenance, that the historically higher maintenance costs in the Aboriginal portfolio will be squeezed.

NAHA, which represents urban Aboriginal housing and shelter providers across Canada, has called for *a national non-reserve Aboriginal housing strategy* that sets out a framework for future federal housing initiatives. NAHA believes that individual Aboriginal communities in Canada, such as the Metis, the Inuit, and First Nations must be able to achieve specific goals under any existing and future program. Working with its national Aboriginal political organizations and its members, NAHA launched the new strategy at its national conference in Vancouver, March 29, 2004.

In addition to setting out housing production targets and the level of capital construction assistance required in major market areas, the strategy sets out guiding principles that all levels of government will be asked to endorse in any future housing initiatives. These guiding principles address issues of federal fiduciary responsibility, self-determination, and the need for consultation. They also address the need for program policies and procedures to foster culturally sensitive management regimes and provide adequate resources to maintain the housing once it is built.

NAHA recognizes that the future of urban Aboriginal peoples is tied to the future of Canada's cities and towns, and that new models of creating housing must ensure that the Aboriginal community participates in the larger urban economic life. Like the AFN proposals relating to home-ownership and new financial and policy instruments, urban Aboriginal organization such as NAHA are speaking with a more confident voice and taking a leadership role in the national policy debate on housing.

Urban Homelessness Among the Aboriginal Population

A common theme runs through most analyses of the homelessness crisis in Canada. You are more likely to be homeless, or at risk of being homeless, if you are a younger Aboriginal male or teen mother, than if you belong to any other segment of Canada's population. The reasons are many: lack of income and education, lack of affordable housing, lack of job skills, social dysfunction, and illness. But there are other causes, which affect the Aboriginal population particularly acutely. These include discrimination and lack of a network of community supports.

Discrimination and the denial of access to rooming houses and other low-income housing options is common for Aboriginal people who are new to a city or town, and have little or no income. The lack of a well-developed network of support agencies and services further contributes to the spiral that leads to the young man or woman being forced to live on the street or in an emergency shelter.

One of the most detailed studies of homelessness and the Aboriginal population was conducted for the City of Toronto Mayor's Action Task Force on Homelessness in 1999.[14] Its report, *Taking Responsibility for Homelessness: An Action Plan for Toronto*, noted that Aboriginal people made up a disproportionate part of Toronto's homeless population, representing about 15 percent of the total homeless, or about 4,000 people in 1996. Another 8,000 were at risk of becoming homeless.

The Task Force made 10 recommendations relating to Aboriginal homelessness, including the recommendation to create an Aboriginal Homelessness Steering Committee, which reported to the city in 2001 on health, housing, and employment among this community. The report also stated that because Aboriginal people are more comfortable using services specifically designed for Aboriginal people, new programs to combat homelessness should be run by Aboriginal organizations.

The federal government responded in 1999 to the homelessness crisis by appointing a Minister to co-ordinate efforts and allocating $760 million over three years for projects to combat the causes of homelessness and to construct or expand emergency shelters and support services. As part of this effort, the federal government developed the National Homelessness Initiative (NHI) to foster community-based action on homelessness. The NHI included $59 million in targeted funding for an Urban Aboriginal Strategy for Homelessness to increase services and support mechanisms for urban Aboriginal people who are homeless or at risk of becoming homeless. In addition, the Aboriginal community was eligible to seek funding for projects under the larger Supporting Communities Partnership Initiative (SCPI). The federal government has renewed funding, but at reduced levels under both initiatives.

Consistent with federal housing policy thrusts, the homelessness initiatives were not carefully thought out with respect to the Aboriginal community and its needs. Delivery of the NHI was initially assigned to Aboriginal regional management boards, which had been a highly successful bilateral arrangement between Human Resources Development Canada (HRDC) and Aboriginal communities to deliver job training. The boards had little experience in the housing area, nor did they have the type of networks they could rely upon to give sound housing-related advice and direction. The fact that they succeeded at all is attributable more to the commitment of the boards than to good program design. HRDC is moving away from this approach and using, in some instances, Aboriginal housing providers such as Lu'Ma Native Housing in Vancouver to deliver homelessness funding.

The SCPI initiative was delivered through municipalities, and although urban Aboriginal groups were eligible to apply for grants, and did participate, there was no requirement for the participating cities to work with the Aboriginal communities in developing community plans and funding priorities. More fundamentally, the federal government failed to address the need for capacity-building within the urban Aboriginal community to ensure that it was an equal partner with non-Aboriginal homelessness service providers. As a result, initial take-up by the Aboriginal community was slow.

Learning to compete with large, well-staffed, and highly professional non-Aboriginal service providers at a municipal level and through the competitive Request for Proposal mechanism was often a frustrating and discouraging exercise. Reinventing the wheel each time a new Aboriginal provider proposed a project and a city had a call for proposals was a waste of valuable and limited resources. Setting aside funds for developing best practices and capacity-building by working through existing Metis, Inuit, and First Nation housing organizations would have resulted in a greater take-up under the first SCPI round of funding.

It is a tribute to the urban Aboriginal community's maturing view of itself and its accumulating business and professional acumen, that it succeeded, in spite of the obstacles, in developing new shelters and support services across Canada. These include the construction or renovation of emergency shelters and transitional and supportive housing facilities, the creation of housing services, information-referral/follow-up agencies, training, and employment counselling.

Closing

Federal housing policies have not always been kind or generous to Aboriginal people. Despite more than 30 years of public intervention in Aboriginal housing, high levels of housing need persist among Canada's Aboriginal population, regardless of where they live. Some public programs have resulted in partnerships, which can be built upon in future initiatives. But the overwhelming shortage of affordable housing, persistent high levels of homelessness, and the poor physical condition of much of the existing housing stock supports a continuing and significant societal equity rationale for public funding.

Canada needs a national strategy for dealing with Aboriginal housing and homelessness that learns from the past, builds on success, and recognizes the inherent rights of Aboriginal people and the link between safe affordable housing and well-being. The creation of safe, healthy housing communities, where children have educational stability and a place to do their homework, from where young men and women can pursue higher education and job skills, and where the elderly can enjoy their declining years, is one of the keys to achieving federal objectives in Aboriginal health, early childhood development, and youth.

George Devine's career in housing spans 35 years of Canadian Aboriginal housing policy. He worked on the earliest federal urban native housing programs in the 1970s, and later versions of the urban native programs, as well as the on-reserve and rural and native programs. After retiring from Canada Mortgage and Housing Corporation in 1997, he has worked for many Aboriginal housing providers on day-to-day housing operational issues, as well as with national Aboriginal organizations on housing policy. A former Director of the National

Aboriginal Housing Association (NAHA), he became NAHA's Executive Director in 2002.

Endnotes

1 *Core Housing Need Among Off-reserve Inuit, Metis, Status and Non-Status Indians in Canada,* Canada Mortgage and Housing Corporation, Ottawa, February 1998, Endnote 3, p. 49. A household is considered in core housing need if it meets one or more of the following tests: its housing unit is in need of major repair or does not have functioning bathroom facilities; the unit is overcrowded; or the household pays more than 30 percent of its income for rent.

2 Of the 976,305 people reporting Aboriginal ancestry in Canada, 690,225 live off-reserve, compared to 286,080 who live on reserves. Of the off-reserve population, 28.4 percent live in rural areas; 40.6 percent in urban census metropolitan areas; and 31 percent in urban non-census metropolitan areas (Source: Statistics Canada, 2001 Census).

3 Households based on Aboriginal identity, 2002 Census, from *A New Beginning: The National Non-reserve Aboriginal Housing Strategy,* published by the National Aboriginal Housing Association, March 2004.

4 Of the 19,000 units, approximately 11,000 are in cities and towns, and another 9,000 are in rural and remote areas, but of these, less than 50 percent are occupied by households of Aboriginal ancestry.

5 National Aboriginal Housing Association, *A New Beginning: The National Non-Reserve Aboriginal Housing Strategy,* Ottawa, March 2004.

6 *Report of the Auditor General to the House of Commons,* Ottawa: Office of the Auditor General, April 2003, chapter 6, p. 4.

7 Norbert Koeck, *On-Reserve Housing Policy Impact Assessment, 1996–2000,* Ottawa: Indian Affairs and Northern Development, n.d.

8 Daniel J. Brant, *Successful Housing in First Nation Communities: A Report on Community Case Studies,* offers a series of case studies of successful housing programs on reserves. Ottawa: Indian and Northern Affairs, 2000. (http://www.ainc-inac.gc.ca/ps/hsg/cih/ hs/shf_e.html)

9 Koeck, p. 3.

10 *The National Post,* October 24, 2003, p. A8.

11 *Report of the Auditor General,* p. 1.

12 It has been estimated that had the federal government used the 10 percent allocation formula, it would have resulted in approximately 50,000 units over the same period. Instead, in addition to the 10,000 urban units, another 9,000 rural and Native units were delivered, but most were not intended for households of native ancestry.

13 Charles W. Hill, writing in *Canadian Housing,* notes that buried in the transfer was a major policy shift by the federal government towards non-reserve Aboriginal people. Hill questioned the basis for the federal decision, a decision, he noted, made

only a few months before the final report of the government's Royal Commission on Aboriginal Peoples was tabled in the House of Commons, which was clear about the federal government's fiduciary responsibility to consult where the government makes policies that may affect communities in an adverse way. (See *Canadian Housing*, Fall 2003, vol. 20, no. 2, p. 26.) A challenge to the transfer is before the courts in Manitoba.

14 A special report was commissioned for this study: Obonsawin-Irwin Consulting Inc., "A Planning Framework for Addressing Aboriginal Homelessness in the City of Toronto," October 1998.

Chapter 24

The Role of the Co-operative Housing Sector in Creating Affordable Housing

MARK GOLDBLATT

The co-operative housing sector can help moderate- and low-income households meet their need for affordable housing in a number of ways. The two most important are (a) the unique tenure form of non-profit co-operative housing that gives residents direct control of their housing based on the formula of "one member, one vote," and (b) the co-op housing sector's capacity, drawing on 30 years of experience, to work with government on program design and to deliver programs efficiently.

Beginnings

The non-profit co-operative housing form of tenure was introduced in Canada when Campus Co-op in Toronto bought its first house in 1936. The Co-op was formed to serve the housing needs of University of Toronto students. Several more university student co-ops followed.

In 1965, the first family non-profit co-op housing project, Willow Park, opened in Winnipeg. Three years later, the Co-operative Union of Canada, the Canadian Labour Congress, and the United Church of Canada founded the Co-operative Housing Foundation (now Federation) of Canada. Seven co-op housing pilots across the country were financed in 1971 and 1972 by Canada Mortgage and Housing Corporation (CMHC). These initiatives were followed by an important breakthrough in June 1973, when the *National Housing Act* was amended to include a specific provision for financing non-profit housing co-ops.

Operating Principles

From these modest beginnings, Canada's non-profit co-op housing sector has grown to more than 91,000 units owned by 2,185 housing co-operatives, and housing about 250,000 people.

The unique contribution of co-operative housing, in the context of rental housing in Canada, is that the projects are controlled by the residents on the principle of one member, one vote. Like other types of social housing – government-owned and benevolent non-profits (often referred to as private non-profits) – co-ops operate as near as possible at cost in perpetuity. The properties are not sold and resold, and therefore capital gains are not passed along in higher rents. Capital appreciation remains with the property. But the distinguishing characteristic of co-op housing is that residents are directly in control through their elected boards of directors, whereas with the other two forms of social housing residents live as tenants of the owner under a landlord-tenant relationship.

Another essential characteristic of housing co-ops is that the residents include households at different income levels. Traditional public housing, launched by the then-innovative Regent Park project in Toronto, was designed to serve the poor exclusively. As experience has shown, some public housing projects have come to be seen as low-income ghettos, often dysfunctional as communities and held in low esteem by both residents and neighbours. This perception led to a shift in social housing policy in Canada in the early 1970s to support mixed-income housing.

The non-profit co-op housing sector has always aimed to create mixed-income communities that are open to all, ideally a 50/50 split between those who can pay the full break-even rent and moderate and lower-income households in need of a subsidy. As government program financing requirements have changed, however, the low-income component of co-op housing projects has come to range from a low of 15% to 100% in different co-ops. Although income mixing is rarely emphasized in current social housing policy discussions, the co-op housing sector remains convinced that mixing incomes has distinct benefits. The shortage of affordable housing is not confined to the lowest-income households. Many Canadians do not necessarily need rent-geared-to-income assistance, yet cannot find affordable accommodation in the larger cities.

The co-op housing sector believes that members should be direct stakeholders. Their willingness to get involved in the business of running of their co-op affects the cost and quality of their living environment. Two major evaluations of co-op housing by CMHC (in 1983 and 1992) have clearly demonstrated that non-profit co-ops have the lowest operating costs compared to the other two forms of social housing. This has important financial implications as governments search for the most cost-effective way to subsidize low-income households over the long run. If co-op housing rents fall substantially below market rents, especially after the mortgage is paid off, there may be the capacity to internally subsidize low-income members who have no access to government subsidies.

Social Cohesion

As Canada becomes an increasingly diverse society, we face the challenge of building sustainable communities from people of diverse ethnic and cultural backgrounds. The resident-controlled structure of housing co-ops ensures that residents get to know their neighbours and work together to make the best possible living environment. Housing policy has a vital role to play in supporting Canada's social fabric and housing co-ops have demonstrated that they can contribute to building cohesive communities.

As with other forms of social housing, the co-op housing sector seeks to house a mix of household types, including people of every age group, one-person households, and families of every size. A disproportionate number of single-parent households live in co-op housing because this housing offers a supportive community as well as affordable housing. There are also a significant number of seniors-only housing co-ops. Many housing co-ops are built with barrier-free access design principles that allow people with physical challenges to live independently.

Proposals and Observations

The co-op housing sector has extensive experience working with government to design housing programs, some of which are unique to the co-op housing sector, while others are available to all forms of social housing. These include three unilateral federal programs over a 21-year period (1970–91) and several unilateral provincial programs. In some periods, federal-provincial cost-shared programs were available.

The programs directed at housing co-ops are designed to give households that do not receive rent-geared-to-income assistance a financial incentive to manage their projects efficiently and control operating costs – in short, to create a situation similar to private homeownership, where each dollar saved in operations is a dollar less that that residents have to pay.

In 2003 the co-op housing sector put forward program proposals to both the federal and Ontario governments which, if accepted, would create a co-op stream within the larger federal-provincial affordable housing agreement. These proposals attempt to satisfy government concerns while adhering to the fundamental characteristics of non-profit co-op housing. They are worth reviewing, as they provide a window into the co-op housing sector's approach to housing policy, and reflect the sector's past experience with program design.

The current federal-provincial affordable housing program is based on the premise of 50/50 cost sharing. Although there is no inherent problem with this approach, holes in the housing accord on which the current federal-provincial program is based have allowed the provinces to escape putting up true matching dollars. This problem was particularly acute in Ontario under the Conservative government (1995–2003) but will, it is hoped, be resolved with the Liberal provincial government that was elected in 2003.

Current program design is based on up-front capital grants to make projects financially feasible. The capital grant approach is favoured by governments today over a commitment to ongoing operating subsidies, which were part of the program design under earlier programs. Grants reduce mortgage financing requirements, and lower the project carrying costs to levels that can be financed by a rental revenue stream at market levels. Initial project rents (that is, rents before the introduction of rent supplement assistance) should be established at the low end of the local market. This is to ensure the viability of projects that may, in the future, experience operating difficulties and as a result have to increase operating income to cover, for example, higher-than-expected operating costs. The capital grant mechanism, a feature of earlier co-op housing programs, works well, simplifies the nature of government involvement, and creates equity in the project, giving more security to lenders.

Municipalities are often interested in and able to contribute to project financing by waiving development charges or building fees. In some cases they may make land available to the project. Municipalities should be rewarded for such contributions by making sure that funds budgeted for the municipality by higher levels of government are kept constant and that municipal contributions do not replace funds that would otherwise flow from the federal-provincial program.

Social housing groups need up-front assistance to get their projects to the point at which they are ready for financing. These costs include architectural design fees, the cost of rezoning if needed, legal fees, and remuneration for the social housing developers that put the projects together. In the past, CMHC met this need by providing financing through its Project Development Fund program. Such financing should be a part of all future programs. Social housing groups do not have access to the high-risk funds that private developers often have.

Provinces should provide rent-geared-to-income (RGI) subsidies to enable moderate-and low-income households to live in the projects without paying more than 30% of their household income on rent. Having the provinces remain responsible for the RGI component is consistent with current federal-provincial financial relationships. The co-op housing sector aims to ensure RGI assistance for 50% of the households living in co-op housing projects, with the balance of households coming from people who can afford the break-even rent.

A unique feature of the co-op housing sector's program proposal is that every co-op would be required to pay an enrolment fee towards a Stabilization Fund. The existing Co-op Housing Stabilization Fund was created as part of the 1985–91 Federal Co-operative Housing Program, which was based on index-linked mortgages. This new mortgage instrument, used for the first time in Canada to finance housing, was designed to achieve lower interest rates by protecting lenders from the risk of inflation. At that time, CMHC was anxious that this new mortgage instrument might result in more claims on its Mortgage Insurance Fund (MIF) if co-ops financed under the program failed. The result was a mutual agreement between CMHC and the Co-operative Housing Federation of Canada to create a Stabilization Fund that would intervene to support housing co-ops experiencing serious financial problems, thus preventing claims on the MIF.

This Stabilization Fund has been a success story in turning around projects in difficulty that might otherwise have made claims on the MIF. Since continuing government operating assistance will not be a feature of new social housing programs, CHF Canada aims to mitigate the risk by expanding the current Stabilization Fund as part of future co-op housing programs.

In the past, government social housing program financing was available for the acquisition and rehabilitation of existing rental housing, as well as for new construction. As Canada's existing rental housing stock ages, the purchase and rehabilitation of an older property by a social housing group can both renew the housing and capture it as affordable rental housing in perpetuity. A program that assists in the purchase and rehabilitation of existing rental housing is an excellent alternative to building new social housing in areas experiencing high vacancy rates.

The co-op housing sector also proposes the use of flexible mortgages with long amortization periods. This is to reduce monthly mortgage payments and up-front capital grant requirements. The option of extending the amortization period provides a safety valve in the years to come, should projects need to reduce project operating costs in an economic downturn.

Whenever existing housing co-operatives have the potential for infill (the addition of more housing through the densification of their properties), redevelopment will be strongly encouraged. Adding stock to existing housing co-operatives, where feasible, would take advantage of a land contribution, as well as the base of support provided by an existing, experienced co-operative housing community. This approach has the added benefit of allowing established co-operatives to respond to the shifting demographics of their members through the addition of housing suited to "empty-nester" households, thereby freeing up family units for incoming households that need them.

One feature of the current federal-provincial affordable housing program is that it is open to private developers. In the view of the co-op housing sector, this is not sound public policy. When housing subsidies are limited, the government must take into account the fact that the social housing sector provides affordable rental housing in perpetuity. Even if private developers are enticed into participating by the subsidies, they will do so only if rents are controlled for a fixed period of time.

A further issue is that of public-private partnerships, a prominent trend in recent years. While there is nothing essentially wrong with the idea of a public-private partnership, the private side of the equation should bring something to the transaction that is not otherwise available in the open market. For example, if a private developer sells a piece of land it owns to a social housing group at market value, there is no real value added. If a lender provides a mortgage secured 100% by mortgage insurance, there is no special contribution, since almost all lenders provide financing on this basis.

Program Delivery

Once programs are designed, they must be delivered. Over the years the co-op housing sector has built up a network of resource groups that specialize in the development of co-op housing. These resource groups are not subsidized; rather, they are financed by consulting fees that are included in each project's capital costs. The existence of this network means that programs can move from the design phase to implementation very efficiently.

As with all housing after the development phase, co-op housing must be managed and maintained. The co-op housing sector has created its own system of ongoing management support. Since co-op housing is managed by a volunteer board of directors and committees, the members of which usually do not have previous housing management experience, the co-op housing sector has developed its own system of training. The system includes short courses, manuals in plain language, and a program to train trainers.

The co-op housing sector also has national and regional federations funded by members' dues. Being self-financed, this infrastructure does not depend on government support, which could be withdrawn at any point. If an individual co-op finds itself in operating difficulty, the necessary expertise exists to help it deal with its problems. In addition to this training and support capacity, co-op housing federations offer group purchasing and insurance programs that give individual co-ops the benefits of large portfolios while remaining self-managed entities.

Conclusion

The non-profit co-op housing sector has no magic solutions when it comes to providing affordable rental housing. True, housing co-ops offer at-cost rental housing in perpetuity that in most markets should become more affordable as time goes on. However, each housing co-op must break even financially. For households that cannot afford the break-even rents in co-op housing projects, the only solution is government subsidies.

Although the public must not be misled into thinking that there is some easy solution, ongoing incremental growth in the social housing sector should be able to create a permanent stock of affordable rental housing and the potential for a long-term solution.

The fact that the federal government and most provincial governments withdrew from financing new co-op housing over the last decade was not because of a failure of policy but a lack of political will to maintain spending on an alternative that has been a success story. The co-op housing sector welcomes the fact that in the early years of the new millennium, the federal government and most provinces are getting back into the social housing business.

The non-profit co-op housing sector is part of the answer to meeting the needs of renters, especially low- and moderate-income households. It has the experience to develop and deliver government programs. It has the infrastructure to support the management of its affordable housing over the long run. But its most significant contribution is its unique tenure form based on resident control, and through that control, the capacity to meet the social as well as financial needs of its members. Co-op housing offers the powerful combination of non-profit rental housing in perpetuity and a force for social cohesion.

Mark Goldblatt is senior consultant with the Co-operative Housing Federation of Canada.

Chapter 25

Affordable Housing Policy Challenges in Ontario:
The View from the Non-Profit Sector

DAVID PETERS

What Is the Housing Problem?

Too many people are on the streets

In Toronto alone, more than 30,000 homeless individuals passed through the emergency shelter system during each of the last few years. This is up from 26,000 in 1996, the statistic cited in the report of the City of Toronto Mayor's Homelessness Action Task Force (1999). That report noted that just under 30 percent were female; families represented 46 percent of people using hostels in Toronto, and the fastest-growing groups were youth under 18 and families with children. Between 30 and 35 percent of the homeless were suffering from severe mental illness; 75 percent of homeless women were suffering from some form of mental illness.

Too many people are on housing waiting lists

Across Ontario, more than 135,000 households are on active waiting lists for social housing. If those the system has lost track of are included, the number is closer to 170,000. In the GTA, there are about 70,000 households on active waiting lists. On a permanent basis there just isn't enough housing.

Rents are too high

Rents have also been rising at a much faster rate than inflation. The cumulative inflation rate in Ontario was about 11.3 percent from 1997 to 2002. During the same period, in Toronto the rents went up 30 percent, in Hamilton they rose 20 percent, in Ottawa 27 percent, and in Durham Region 18.5 percent.

Low incomes are too low

In Toronto a cashier's average annual income, according to 2001 census data was $13,875. Someone depending on this income can afford rent of $347 a month. A retail salesperson has an average annual income of $20,602 and can afford a rent of $515.

In other words, we have both demand and supply problem. We therefore need both demand and supply solutions.

An opportunity exists to create housing

Although vacancy rates have risen in Toronto recently,[1] it is likely to be a temporary respite. We see the high vacancy rates as a convergence of temporary factors. Low interest rates and a surge in condo supply mean higher numbers of people moving from rental to ownership. But there is a limit to the number who have enough for a down payment, which for an average-priced home in Toronto is around $30,000. Interest rates are more likely to go up than down over next few years, especially as the staggering appetite for borrowing in the United States drives up demand. And the condos will eventually be absorbed by the housing system and converted back to homeownership. So this temporary respite should not be allowed to mask the underlying problem. In fact, part of the respite is probably due to households abandoning tenancies they can no longer afford and doubling up with friends or family.

Nevertheless the respite offers a tremendous opportunity to put in place long-term policies and programs to create more permanent affordable housing.

What is affordable? What is permanent?

Not many people buy the current federal policy (embedded in the Affordable Housing Framework), which defines affordable housing as housing that remains at an average market rent for 10 years. For as much as $50,000 in public subsidy, the taxpayer gets a project that will only be affordable for 10 years. Even Ontario's former Conservative government felt that was indefensible and extended the limit to 15 years. We don't feel this is a best buy for taxpayers, who for all intents and purposes (and $50,000 upfront), are temporarily "leasing" units from the private sector to provide affordable housing.

At the Ontario Non Profit Housing Association (ONPHA) we have taken a simple outcome-based approach to this issue of defining affordability. Our executive committee settled on the position that any government program supporting new supply must ensure that 50 percent of the units are accessible to households on those long waiting lists. As well, 50 percent of the units in a government program must be affordable permanently, meaning that, for the most part, 50% of the yield will be non-profit housing. We believe that designing for this outcome will give the private sector and the non-profit sector an equal opportunity to create affordable housing.

Our board members are indifferent to as whether this outcome is achieved through rent supplements or capital write-downs. But they were adamant that mixed-income communities must result from government programs to stimulate new supply, and that government support, however delivered, should not go to projects that do not serve this affordability requirement.

This means that in Ontario, at least, rent supplements tied to buildings will be necessary to achieve this outcome. Portable shelter allowances do not allow planners to ensure mixed communities. This is especially true when planning subdivisions or large neighbourhoods. One of the deficiencies of shelter allowances is that they cannot serve the dual policy purpose of being a planning tool and an affordability tool.

What is not enough?

The Report of Ontario's Housing Supply Working Group (2002) noted that "the construction of new rental housing has fallen from 37,000 units a year in the early 70's to well under 5,000 units annually" and that "CMHC data suggests a shortfall of about 14,000 new rental units a year over 1996–2016."

Although rental starts have risen in the last few years, they are for the most part at the high end of the rental spectrum – far from even CMHC's definition of affordability. Also, there are not enough of them to create any trickle-down effect, even if you believe in trickle-down effects. Don Drummond, chief economist at the TD bank, in his report *Affordable Housing in Canada: In Search of a New Paradigm*, was quite clear in saying that the trickle-down theory never really works in practice.

As far as supportive housing is concerned, the best overall estimates we have are from the 1999 Mayor's Homelessness Action Task Force in Toronto, chaired by Anne Golden. At that time, the Task Force estimated a need for 14,000 supportive housing units for Ontario.

About 3,000 have been created since then in Ontario, so we estimate a need for 11,000 units for those who are disabled either physically or mentally. These people constitute some of the hardest to house, and many are still in shelters and other institutions, funded at the rate of $38 dollars a day just for shelter. That's $1,200 a month, about the same as the average rent for a three-bedroom apartment in Toronto. To say the least, this leaves unanswered the question of why policy makers aren't transferring some of the financial support for temporary shelters over to permanent supportive housing! There is no argument against supportive housing. There is no economic debate and there is no ideological debate. And no one argues against it as the almost exclusive domain of the non-profit sector, which has the expertise. Finally, virtually everyone agrees that it is an area that needs significant government support. Even the previous Conservative government maintained a program to develop new supportive housing.

The problem is a lack of clear thinking. Why would you spend more money on temporary shelters when it costs taxpayers more than permanent supportive housing? Why would the federal government through SCPI support only transitional housing for the homeless? Why does the Ministry of Health insist that applicants have a formal mental health diagnosis to be eligible for their projects? Or that only providers already receiving funding from their Ministry will be eligible – despite the fact that good proposals have come forward from "alternative" providers who are serving the same target population? We feel that there are some real improvements possible in this area.

People do not have enough income to pay rent

Average rents have increased 21.4 percent in Toronto over the last five years compared to a 12 percent rise in the overall Consumer Price Index. In Ontario in 2001, the rent increase approved under the *Tenant Protection Act* was 4.1 percent – more than twice the rate of inflation of 1.9 percent.

There is a mismatch between falling or stagnant incomes, which is especially dramatic for those on social assistance. Their overall incomes were reduced 21 percent in the Ontario government's cutbacks of 1995, at the same time rent controls were relaxed. As a result, for most social assistance households, average market rents exceed their total welfare income – never mind their shelter allowance component. In Ottawa, for example, the gap between the shelter allowance and average rent grew from $31 to $376 between 1994 and 2002.

According to Statistics Canada, average tenant incomes for Ontario declined about 3.9 percent from 1990 to 1995, while those of homeowners rose about 5.5 percent.[2]

The number of households paying more than 50 percent of their income doubled between 1981 and 1996, to more than 300,000 households. This number has fallen to 270,000 households in the 2001 census. Still, a huge challenge remains.

There are too many taxes and regulations

The recent report of Ontario government's Housing Supply Working Group, *Creating a Positive Climate for Rental Housing Development* (2002), speaks to this issue. Greg Lampert and Steve Pomeroy did most of the research and found, for example, that the after-tax return for a sample pro forma would be 22 percent higher if taxed according to the 1980 rules than the rules in 2002.

ONPHA has supported most of the recommendations of that report, but on the condition that the goal of a balanced government policy is to maximize the potential of both the private and the non-profit sectors. That means some special provisions in program design to ensure that the non-profit sector can take advantage of current and future programs. We also caution that getting at the potential in the non-profit sector is a more complex and subtle process than it is in the private sector, where the financial capacity and the skills sets are more readily at hand. It could be said that the challenges are opposite – providing support to get the private sector to build affordable housing is easy; contracting with them to keep it affordable for longer than 15 to 20 years is hard. On the other hand, helping the non-profit sector build is a challenge, though once the rental housing is built, it tends to remain affordable forever.

There is not enough government funding

There has been little if any government-supported housing built lately and very little if any private-sector rental housing built in Ontario in the last eight years. Although the federal government is now putting money on the table, the Ontario government for the last two years has taken a very lukewarm approach to creating housing, preferring instead to wait until a less regulated market place responds.

We disagreed with that approach – or perhaps we should call it a belief system rather than an approach. We know of no country in the world where a private rental housing market solves these affordability problems without government help. ONPHA believes that over the next five years, Ontario should match the federal offer of $360 million to build close to 20,000 units (the original $245 million plus the additional $115 added in the 2003 federal budget). We also believe that they should commit an annual $44 million to provide rent supplements for half of those units as well as $250 million to build 11,000 units of supportive housing and $12 million to subsidize the rents for those living with mental illness.

For the most part, the new Liberal Ontario government has an election platform that will allow it to meet most of these expectations, although the $5.6 billion deficit may hamper its capacity. Execution and implementation may also be a challenge. In their initial organization of the government, they have no one ministry as lead for the housing file. They have pieces of the file now scattered through four ministries (Health, Community Services, Municipal Affairs, and Public Infrastructure Renewal). We think that the Liberals have badly underestimated the thickness of those very same silos that always seem to prevent the necessary cooperation that would, for example, be required to negotiate a national strategy with the federal government and execute a relatively seamless version of it in Ontario with the municipalities. How do four separate ministers and four separate ministry staff groups do that?

What is the Political Problem?

The role of housing is misunderstood

It is not a boondoggle, as the Conservatives suggested. It is not a fiscal tool. It is not something that the free market or the non-profit sector or the government can solve by itself.

Families and households paying more than 50 percent of their household income cannot contribute to our society without stable affordable housing. We hear constantly from the specialists in mental health, disease control, education, and immigration settlement that without adequate stable affordable housing, their efforts for their clients are virtually stymied. And the alternatives of homelessness, jail, hospitalization, and hostels all cost the taxpayer more.

The Toronto Summit Alliance, the Toronto Board of Trade, the Toronto-Dominion Bank, and Prime Minister Paul Martin have all pointed out that cities don't work without affordable housing. How can we revitalize our cities if they are not healthy and vibrant? How can they be healthy and vibrant if they are not made up of mixed-income communities? How can you have a healthy downtown tourist industry if the cooks and the dishwashers and the maintenance staff can't afford to live there?

Housing has become an ideological football

There is a fault line between those who believe in stimulating supply and those who believe in stimulating demand. The previous Conservative government of Ontario exemplified one view. The Conservatives believed in limiting government involvement. The thinking went like this: If we lower taxes, eliminate regulation, and give vouchers (i.e., shelter allowances) to people in need, the market will build the housing. (To be fair, the Conservatives did, however, accept a government role in supportive housing for those most in need.)

Liberals and NDPers generally believe that you need to invest directly in social assets such as permanent affordable housing and you need rent controls and directly targeted funding as opposed to less targetable tax incentives.

This deep divide has led to dramatic shifts in support when governments change and a very unstable policy and program environment.

Policies over time have been wildly inconsistent

It is very hard to create any kind of momentum and maintain capacity with continued expertise when the program and policy environment is constantly changing. This creates capacity problems that should not be underestimated.

After the war, the government started getting into public housing and some support for the private sector through intermittent programs. Then, in about 1970, the government decided that public housing was not working. All that capacity and expertise was shuffled aside (and stigmatized) and the non-profit sector was geared up and equipped with programs to supply affordable housing.

In 1995, the non-profit sector approach was dropped (and stigmatized) and the government decided to deregulate and rely on the private sector, which was supposed to work productively in a less regulated market. Again, a huge amount of capacity was lost. Our cumulative heritage is that in 2003 the government, the private sector, and the non-profit sector have very little capacity left for designing programs or building truly affordable rental housing and it is going to take some time to rebuild that capacity.

Rent controls are on. Rent controls are off. Demolitions and conversions are allowed. Demolitions and conversions are not allowed. "On-again, off-again" programs are a wasteful way to deal with a permanent ongoing economic challenge.

The answer is obvious. We need a sustained, carefully managed government role in a system that wisely recruits and relies on the capacity of all sectors and holds them accountable.

Furthermore, stigmatizing private-sector providers as gougers or non-profit providers as "boondogglers" or the government as inefficient is counterproductive to maximizing productivity in the whole rental housing sector.

Housing is a federal-provincial football

Federal-provincial relations trouble much of public policy in Canada. The recent federal matching initiative, now known as the federal-provincial Affordable Housing Framework, was announced in 2000. Three years later, not a single unit had been built in Ontario. Only a couple of thousand commitments have been announced as of December 2003.

Two different political parties, two different political ideologies, and three levels of government take a long time to agree. And if feelings run high, as they did between the federal Liberals and the provincial Conservatives, the needs of the stakeholders get lost in the political infighting.

However, as of late 2003, Ontario has three levels of government committed to working together. Hopefully, this spirit of cooperation will persist, although the pressure and competition for the taxpayer's dollar is at an all-time high and the option of blaming another government lies temptingly close at hand. In any event, the question remains: can Canadians expect effective political leadership only when we elect the same party (or at least like-minded people) at all three levels of government in every province and in all the major cities?

Who Should Do What?

What should the federal government do?

We believe the federal government should be providing overall leadership, setting up and supporting a consistent non-political, non-ideological agenda. Housing should be classified as a non-partisan issue.

The specifics can change from time to time and the degree of funding can change, but the high-level prescription of relying on both the private sector and the non-profit sector and on a mix of supply and demand programs should underlie this approach.

We believe there should be a "new supply" program. It should be designed so that it results at least 50 percent of the product being non-profit and at least 50 percent of publicly supported units being accessible to households on waiting lists. Deals with the provinces should be negotiated to achieve this outcome and the program should be delivered as close to the front lines as possible.

Provinces should be required to bring a housing "business" plan to the federal-provincial negotiating table showing a reasonably organized response to housing needs in their areas. It should be judged on a "pass/fail" basis, and if it fails, the federal government should move to "Plan B." That is, the federal government should deliver resources directly to any municipality (or third party) that is prepared to coordinate a balanced approach to housing need. One level of government should not be able to unreasonably delay or veto the efforts of another level to tackle significant problems in an area of joint jurisdiction.

Program funding commitments should be for at least 10 years. We need to get rid of the "on-again, off-again" program environment. Amounts may be adjusted and programs tweaked to respond to economic realities and absorb lessons learned, but there should be a sense of continuity and an ability by all program participants to anticipate a dependable and predictable delivery and program environment.

The federal *Income Tax Act* should be amended to provide a more encouraging environment for rental housing producers. The Ontario Housing Supply Working Group report offers a good template, provided these changes are made in tandem with the supply program described above.

The federal government should also look at a tax benefit, perhaps along the lines of the labour-sponsored funds that we have in Canada now. Such a benefit would be one of the tools to directly help the non-profit sector raise equity.

The federal government should make a greater effort to get along with the provinces, but should be prepared to deal directly with municipalities if necessary. Also, the federal government should provide direct support to municipalities or provinces to deal with the housing needs of immigrants and refugees.

The federal government should explicitly change the mandate of Canada Mortgage and Housing Corporation (CMHC) so that it is not required to be a profitable commercial agency and should highlight its role in supporting affordable rental housing. Recent changes to CMHC's mortgage insurance programs are a welcome example of the seeds of this type of thinking. However, the financing limitations for non-profit proponents are still greater than the equity and cash-flow-rich private providers. CMHC's mandate should be changed to allow direct support in the form of subsidized mortgage insurance for non-profit providers, in recognition of the fact that extra effort is required to generate production out of the non-profit sector. The resulting assets, of course, should be permanently targeted to the public objective of affordable housing.

Program designs at all three levels should encourage partnerships between private developers and non-profit providers with explicit incentives which make such partnerships attractive to private developers.

What should the provinces do?

The provinces should work cooperatively with the federal government. They should pursue a mix of income-support strategies and supply strategies. If their priorities lie elsewhere, they should permit the federal government to deal directly with the municipal service managers or other third parties. Conversely, if municipal service managers are not prepared to deliver programs to achieve the appropriate outcomes, then the province should be prepared to deliver them directly.

For "new supply," with the federal government offering capital grants that should make both private and non-profit projects feasible, the provinces should focus on the affordability issue. Ontario should be matching federal funding with rent supplements. Given that the Ontario Liberals have committed to $100 million in shelter allowances, they will need to figure out a way to transfer some of this "shelter allowance" commitment to the supply program. The projects receiving the capital support to make them feasible at average market rents must also be affordable and integrated. In our view, that means rent supplements, so that 50% of the units are housing people from the waiting lists.

The program should be redesigned to define the outcomes as I have outlined them. In Ontario there should be less micromanagement by the provincial government. In general, more thoughtful and carefully framed accountability arrangements should be developed between governments and with providers. The system chokes on red tape if accountability arrangements are built on suspicion. It chokes on scandal if they are based on wishful thinking.

The provinces should increase funding for housing those with special needs and the homeless. Their limited programs are working relatively well, but need to include more funding for services for female victims of violence and to support those providers serving street people who do not have formal mental health diagnoses.

The provinces should cooperate in making changes to the *Income Tax Act* and GST provisions and they should make the corollary changes to provincial tax regimes.

The provinces should recognize that housing, along with transit and infrastructure, is one of the pillars of successful cities. Thoughtlessly, Ontario's recent tax-exempt Opportunity Bonds excluded affordable housing as a fundable item. This kind of thinking overlooks the fact that revitalizing our cities is shaping up to be the major policy issue of the next decade.

The provinces should also fix the shelter allowance program for those on social assistance so that the shelter allowance portion varies regionally and is adjusted to median rents in the area.

What should municipal service managers do?

Municipalities should deliver the programs to ensure the desired outcomes are achieved. They should not be micromanaged, but should be held sensibly accountable. Where municipalities are not interested in entering the housing arena, the provincial government should be prepared to do direct delivery. Stakeholders should not be left in the lurch when one level of government has an effective veto over the attempts of another level of government to provide resources to solve problems.

In return for the funding from the senior levels of government, municipalities should be required to create a positive environment for rental housing, particularly affordable rental housing. Property taxes for affordable rental housing and indeed all rental housing should be equalized with those of homeowners. Development permit charges and planning and parks fees should be reduced or eliminated, depending on the level of affordability to be achieved.

Municipalities should not be saddled with any new ongoing funding obligations other than managing the programs. Social programs should not be funded through regressive and inflexible taxes such as the property tax base.

Municipalities should be given additional housing-related funding to help with the transition for immigrants and refugees. Canadians depend on the country's ability to build and sustain a healthy multicultural environment. Ignoring the housing needs of refugees and immigrants is not a sensible policy.

Municipalities should have planning policies that enforce smart growth principles, they should have carefully designed inclusionary requirements for affordable housing in large new developments, and they should encourage other forms of affordable housing such as secondary suites.

Where Does the Non-profit Sector Fit In?

Stigmatizing the not-for-profit sector as the beneficiaries and abusers of some sort of wildly overdone boondoggle was clever politics, but wasn't true – any more than the notions that all private landlords are gougers or that all public housing projects are ghettoes are true. Non-profit housing providers have a lot to offer.

Non-profit housing offers permanent long-term affordability

Non-profit housing is found everywhere in the world. If the regulatory environment is set up properly, it provides permanent affordability. A good percentage of non-profit housing should be an important part of any social portfolio of housing investments. Permanent affordability is the key point of difference from for-profit housing. Non-profit housing cannot be converted to condominiums and is intended to remain affordable forever.

Non-profit housing providers are committed to income mixing and use of long-term rent supplements

Non-profit housing providers have generally accepted the commitment to take households off the waiting lists. This is a big priority of municipal governments in Ontario, where waiting lists were downloaded to municipal governments along with the housing itself. Private-sector providers tend to look to rent supplement programs to provide tenants when demand is soft and to drop out of the programs when demand is high – in other words, when secure supply for those most in need is most important.

Non-profit housing providers are community-based and essential for city revitalization

One of the next key policy focuses will be the revitalizing of Canada's cities. Non-profit housing has always had a bottom-up revitalization role. Toronto's downtown still amazes visitors with its enormously mixed and vibrant housing infrastructure. In the United States (which is currently ahead of Canada in this area), much of the non-profit housing is built by "community development" non-profit groups with multiple agendas, often in partnership with private builders using government programs that encourage such partnerships. You see this kind of thinking being used by the Toronto Community Housing Corporation in the plans to revitalize Regent Park and Don Mount Court. We need to encourage and stimulate more of this cooperation.

Non-profit housing providers are committed to quality

If you talk to bylaw enforcement officers, they deal with few complaints emanating from the non-profit rental projects. This, however, could change if the impending operating funding and benchmarks programs for existing social housing providers are mishandled.

Non-profit housing providers have a long history of providing supportive housing

This is probably the primary point of difference with other sectors. Non-profit housing providers are the main supplier for those most in need.

What are the Housing Solutions?

Use many policy tools

The overall policy should be to make the greatest use of the capacity of all the sectors. This means supporting new supply programs, more income support, less regulation, a more supportive tax and fee environment, and so on. We believe that at any point, one can argue over the mix or the total amount of public support. But, to argue that huge supply programs or income tax changes or shelter allowances should be the only solution is a fundamental, ideology-driven error. *There is no single right answer.*

The TD Bank's recent report showed a fundamental understanding of this. Don Drummond, the bank's chief economist, feels that ultimately, affordability is a problem of incomes that are too low. He would like to see this problem dealt with, but, in the meantime, he agrees that supply programs are needed. Other experienced people, such as Dan Burns, former deputy minister of Housing for both the NDP and the Conservative governments, takes the same view, although he believes a continually improving, continually adjusted mix of policy tools is the only effective way to deliver consistent, manageable progress on the ground. As for the ideal of well-funded income programs eliminating the need for any supply support, he says it will never happen.[3]

Create a consistent, more cooperative, less politicized environment

All levels of government and all sectors should take the pledge on this. We need fewer "on-again, off-again" programs and we need to understand how to encourage government cooperation and private/non-profit partnerships. We need to achieve role clarity with more coordination and less competition. We need less of a "throwaway" policy culture –one that sustains learning. We need more people moving between sectors.

Build up and encourage the partnership capacity between sectors

Support for partnerships is approaching the level of a cliché in public policy. It is a cliché because in government, at least, partnership is a very shallow term. Too often it really means trying to get someone else to pay for something (such as municipalities or private-sector developers).

Nevertheless, despite all the talk, little work has been done on the techniques and technology of partnership. What program designs will encourage partnerships? How do we achieve this outcome? What are the tools? What can we learn from the United States? How can we construct good leasing arrangements? How long should they be for? How do we encourage turn-key developments? How could tax policy be designed to encourage private development and financing married to long-term non-profit ownership and commitment to affordability?

Give more thought and more funding to supportive and alternative housing

We need a more thoughtful approach to this area. There is little dispute over "whether" this kind of housing work, only dispute over "how." There is also a disconnect with the front lines. We need to understand the target groups better. For example, there is no sense in "qualifying" street people by insisting they have a formal medical diagnosis of mental illness before admitting them to supportive housing.

Provide direct funding for affordable housing

Tax changes and deregulation and zoning changes and the marketplace will never adequately meet demand. Nor will broad-based shelter allowances create supply. Some direct supply programs will always be necessary. That is what we see around the world and that is what we see in the United States. That is what I think the history of social housing in Canada tells us.

Face reality: Don't rely on temporary market shifts or ideologies

All western free-enterprise governments have some form of affordable housing policy. For various reasons, the private market has never been able to adequately provide enough affordable housing. Today's glut of rented condos and low interest rates does nothing more than buy us a little time.

And we must get over the notion that one single idea will solve the problem. The answer is not shelter allowances *or* massive, unaffordable supply programs *or* a freer, less taxed, deregulated market place – but some continually adjusted mix of all of these which maxes out the capabilities of all sectors.

And don't deceive yourself that it will not cost a lot of money. Canada has to deal with the consequences of years of no policy and no funding. It will cost a lot of money – but money that is carefully managed in a consistent setting that can generate learning and be adjusted along with overall public sector priorities and economic times.

David Peters *is Special Advisor, Affordable and Supportive Housing, for the Ontario Non-Profit Housing Association (ONPHA).*

Endnotes

1 Sudbury presents an interesting anomaly: there is a relatively high vacancy rate of (5.1 percent in 2002), yet over 22 percent of tenants still pay more than 50 percent of their income on rent. That is higher than Ontario's average.

2 In Ontario we recently had a "near death" experience with a government proposing to bet the farm on mortgage interest deductibility – an expensive, ill-thought-out notion that would stimulate a fast-growing market where interest rates and costs are falling and consumers incomes are rising! The plan at maturity would have involved giving up about 5 percent of Ontario's entire revenue base. Fortunately, the government proposing this measure was defeated.

3 As he noted in a speech to the 2003 ONPHA Conference, Toronto, Canada.

Chapter 26

Ending Homelessness:
The One Percent Solution

NATIONAL HOUSING AND HOMELESSNESS NETWORK

United States Senator Everett Dirksen is reported to have said: "A billion dollars here, a billion dollars there, and pretty soon you're talking about real money."[1]

That's the idea behind the One Percent Solution. An additional 1% of the federal budget devoted to housing would mean $2 billion in new funding for social housing annually. Over time, those dollars would add up to tens of thousands of new affordable homes, sustainable housing-related programs and services, and a sharp drop in homelessness and the housing crisis.

The One Percent Solution was proposed by the Toronto Disaster Relief Committee in 1998 as it launched its Disaster Declaration campaign. The TDRC called on senior levels of government to recognize that homelessness is a national disaster. In November 1998, about one month after TDRC launched its initiative, the mayors of Canada's biggest cities endorsed the declaration. Soon after, many other municipalities, organizations, and individuals joined the campaign.[2]

The housing campaign was adopted by the National Housing and Homelessness Network when it was formed in March 1999 at a national symposium in Toronto. The NHHN has grown to be a network of groups and individuals from Vancouver to St. John's that is one of the four leading national voices on affordable housing issues in Canada.

The One Percent Solution is based on the observation of Dr. David Hulchanski, a leading Canadian housing scholar, that: "Canada spends only about one percent of its budget on programs and subsidies for all the social housing ever built across the country."[3] Total budgetary spending by the federal government was $170 billion in 2002–2003.[4]

Housing program expenses by Canada Mortgage and Housing Corporation, the government's housing agency, were about $1.8 billion in 2002,[5] or about 1% of overall federal spending. However, there have been cuts to housing programs in recent years. For instance, CMHC annual reports note that housing program expenses were $1.9 billion or higher in earlier years. So advocates rounded off the 1% calculation to an even $2 billion – and that's the target of the One Percent Solution.

Starting in 1984 and continuing throughout the 1990s, the federal government and most provinces cut back on housing programs. In 1996, the federal government announced plans to download federal social housing programs to the provinces and territories. The One Percent Solution would reverse this erosion of federal and provincial housing initiatives and support a comprehensive national housing strategy. Local communities, after identifying their particular needs and the most appropriate responses, would be able to use the funding to get the housing built and provide the services that are needed.

Provinces, territories, municipalities, community-based organizations, and the private sector all have a role to play in this new strategy. Each can bring additional money and other resources to the table. But leadership would come from the national government.

Restoring Federal Leadership on Housing

Over the years, there have been constitutional debates within Canada about which level of government should take responsibility for particular policy areas. Housing is not specifically mentioned in the country's original constitution (the *British North America Act*), but there was a move in the 1980s to link housing with property. Responsibility for property-related matters is assigned by the constitution to the provinces and territories.

The Charlottetown Accord of August 1992, signed by federal, provincial, and territorial officials, specifically mentioned housing as a provincial/territorial responsibility: "Exclusive provincial jurisdiction over housing should be recognized and clarified through an explicit constitutional amendment and the negotiation of federal-provincial agreements."[6] The Accord called on the senior levels of government to negotiate a series of bilateral deals to set out the details of the various policy areas.

The Accord was politically controversial and a national referendum was called. The vote was held on October 26, 1992, and Canadians rejected the Charlottetown Accord. Despite that rejection, however, the federal government announced plans in 1996 to transfer administration of federal housing programs to the provinces and territories – despite the fact that this download was part of the rejected Charlottetown deal. The Co-operative Housing Federation of Canada mounted a national campaign and, by 1999, succeeded in removing co-ops from the downloading plans. The rest of the federal social housing programs, however, were transferred to the provinces and territories.

The One Percent Solution would reverse the trend that started with the Charlottetown Accord and the 1996 federal transfer and ensure that housing remains a federal responsibility. There are three key reasons why housing should be a federal responsibility:

- the federal government has the strongest fiscal base, which makes it the best candidate to lead housing policy;
- only the federal government can set national standards for housing policy;
- Canada has signed treaties and other international instruments that recognize housing as a right and place an obligation on the federal government to ensure that this right is upheld.[7]

The need for national standards in a federal country like Canada is recognized in other social policy areas, notably health. Although health care is assigned to provincial jurisdiction under Canada's constitution, the *Canada Health Act* sets national principles and a funding program. The act states:

> It is hereby declared that the primary objective of Canadian health care policy is to protect, promote and restore the physical and mental well-being of residents of Canada and to facilitate reasonable access to health services without financial or other barriers.[8]

Libby Davies, MP for Vancouver East, has proposed a National Housing Bill of Rights that would, in the words of the draft legislation, "provide for adequate, accessible and affordable housing for Canadians."[9] It would set similar goals as the *Canada Health Act*.

The Housing Bill of Rights was introduced for first reading as Bill C-416 in the House of Commons on November 28, 2001. Under the rules of Parliament, a private member's bill must go to a Commons committee (with a majority of members from the governing Liberal party) to determine whether it is "votable." The Housing Bill of Rights was denied this status. After a Parliamentary debate, the bill lapsed without coming to a vote. But advocates have called for the bill to be reintroduced and given proper voting status.

A Comprehensive National Solution

Many national organizations, local groups, and housing advocates have endorsed the One Percent Solution. An enhanced funding envelope (combined with existing housing spending) would allow the federal government to adopt a comprehensive national housing strategy that would address:

- the supply of housing, by increasing the number of rental units;
- affordability, by ensuring that the new units are affordable to the households in the greatest need of new housing;
- housing supports, that is, programs for those who require special services;
- rehabilitation, through funding to maintain housing at a proper standard;
- emergency relief, in the form of special support for people who are already homeless.

The first four are prevention strategies, aimed at ensuring that everyone has access to good quality, affordable housing. The fifth offers relief, aimed at providing a basic level of comfort for those who are on the streets and assistance to help them secure permanent homes. Details of programs aimed at these five elements need to be developed in consultation with public, private, and non-profit experts. New programs would have to be targeted to make sure that the housing and services meet the needs of low and moderate-income households.

Supply

New social housing supply is essential if Canada is to end its housing crisis. While the social housing programs of the 1970s to the 1990s produced hundreds of thousands of good-quality, affordable units that continue to provide good homes to many Canadians, the programs were administratively cumbersome. A large staff was required to oversee complicated capital subsidy formulas. Few governments, and even fewer social housing providers, want to return to these programs. An alternative would be to offer one-time only capital grants to stimulate new supply. These would be administratively efficient while still ensuring proper accountability for public funds.

Affordability

In addition to new supply, there is an urgent need to increase the rent supplements available to low- and moderate-income households. These supplements would be available to both private and non-profit housing providers, based on a contract with the landlord that ensures the property is well maintained and remains affordable over time.

A number of recent major studies on housing and homelessness, including the Federation of Canadian Municipalities National Housing Policy Options Paper and the Toronto Mayor's Homelessness Action Task Force (the Golden report), recommend an expanded program of rent supplements. A rent supplement program to assist about 160,000 tenant households would cost about $500 million annually.

Supports

Some homeless people and renter households require specialized social support services to help them find or maintain housing. Many provinces, including Ontario, maintain modest supportive housing programs for those with special needs. About 10,000 units of supportive housing could be funded with $125 million annually.

Rehabilitation

The federal government's Residential Rehabilitation Assistance Program (RRAP) has been effective over the years in providing funds to upgrade properties and maintain them at appropriate standards. In recent years, the RRAP mandate has been expanded to include rental and homelessness initiatives. RRAP is due to expire, and the federal government has started a consultation process on extending the program. A budget of $125 million would allow the federal government to double the amount of RRAP assistance, which would provide help to 30,000 households annually.

Emergency relief

The federal homelessness strategy is also due to expire, and the federal government has announced a consultation process on renewing this important program. An allocation of $250 million would allow the federal government to double the amount of homelessness strategy money available annually, and increase funding for services and programs that provide immediate relief and transitional housing for homeless people and those at risk of homelessness.

Matching funds from the provinces and territories (an additional $2 billion annually) would double these housing and homelessness initiatives.

Local Delivery of a National Strategy

While the One Percent Solution places the overall leadership for housing policy at the federal level, it recommends that local communities – which are best placed to assess the local situation – have the flexibility to create particular solutions to specific needs.

Housing advocates have succeeded in recent years in getting the government to put in place a patchwork of housing and homelessness funding. The federal homelessness strategy, announced in December 1999, created a funding envelope of $753 million over three years, but assigned the responsibility for delivery to local homelessness communities in ten designated communities across the country. The federal affordable housing program, announced in November 2001, created a funding envelope of $680 million over five years, but assigned delivery to provincial and territorial governments.

The housing program has become snared in a federal-provincial-territorial quagmire, but the homelessness initiative (including a three-year renewal announced in the 2003 federal budget) has been delivered effectively by local communities under national standards and with national funding.

The first stage in local delivery in the homelessness funding was the creation of local committees that included municipal officials, community partners, and – in some cases – private-sector representatives. The local committees consulted and developed community plans for addressing homelessness that identified target groups (such as urban Aboriginal people, youth, single mothers, single adults, seniors, mental health consumer/survivors, homeless) and then developed specific solutions (such as transitional housing, emergency shelters, food programs, mental health services, Aboriginal programs, and prevention initiatives). Then, in most cases, a proposal call was made to solicit specific ideas, which were then assessed to ensure that they met the needs identified in the community plans.

*The **National Housing and Homelessness Network** was formed in March 1999 by community-based housing and homelessness advocates from across Canada. It provides a national forum for provincial, territorial and regional housing groups to share information and collaborate on common campaigns. The One Percent Solution ($2 billion annually from the federal government for a comprehensive national housing strategy) is the key goal of the NHHN. Participating groups include the B.C. Housing and Homelessness Network, Housing and Homelessness Network in Ontario, and FRAPRU and RAPSIM in Quebec, along with regional groups based in more than two dozen communities across the country from Vancouver, B.C., to St. John's, Newfoundland. At the national level, the NHHN works with the National Housing Policy Options Team of the Federation of Canadian Municipalities, the Canadian Housing and Renewal Association and the Co-operative Housing Federation of Canada. Contact: National Housing and Homelessness Network, c/o Toronto Disaster Relief Committee, Telephone – 416-599-8372. Facsimile – 416-599-5445. E-mail: tdrc@tdrc.net.*

Endnotes

1 The senator may never have actually said the famous words attributed to him. See, for instance, research posted at the Dirksen Congressional Center at http://www.dirksencenter.org/featuresBillionHere.htm.

2 For more information, see the TDRC website: www.tdrc.net.

3 Hulchanski, J David, "Housing Policy for Tomorrow's Cities," Discussion Paper F/27, December 2002, Canadian Policy Research Networks, p. iv.

4 Finance Canada, Fiscal Reference Tables, October 2003, p. 15.

5 Canada Mortgage and Housing Corporation, *Opening Doors*, 2002 Annual Report, p. 8.

6 Consensus Report on the Constitution (Charlottetown Accord), August 28, 1992, Final Text, clause 33.

7 These rights were also prominent in *Finding Room: Housing Solutions for the Future*, Report of the National Liberal Caucus Task Force on Housing, 1990, co-chairs, Paul Martin and Joe Fontana. See Appendix E for excerpts from this report.

8 *Canada Health Act*, section 3.

9 The full text of the Housing Bill of Rights, Bill C-416, is in Appendix B.

Chapter 27

Promoting Rental Housing: An International Agenda

ALAN GILBERT

If few governments in developing countries have done much to stimulate rental housing, what can be done to encourage them to do more? This chapter suggests that one significant way is to stimulate more debate about rental housing, particularly as it is easy to demonstrate that so many of the ideas about the sector are misplaced. Also, although the United Nations' recent acceptance that adequate housing is a human right ought to stimulate more governments to think about how to improve the housing conditions of their tenants, the current formulation of what constitutes adequate housing and particularly the campaign for secure tenure is not without conceptual problems. This is particularly true in the area of rental housing, where more discussion of the tenure rights of landlords and tenants is called for.

The chapter also argues that if more governments are to be persuaded to take the housing sector seriously, more is required of the international development banks and national aid agencies. Currently, most are silent about the rental housing issue, even when their investment programs directly affect the tenant population, as in the case of upgrading programs. More research would also help because, although we know much more than we once did about rental housing in poor cities, there are numerous gaps in our knowledge. Nonetheless, enough is known to be able to stimulate the production and improve the quality of rental housing. All that is lacking is the political will to do it.

Stimulating a Debate about Rental Housing

This report does not argue that renting is an ideal tenure for every household or even for the majority. It is certainly not arguing that tenants should be prohibited from becoming homeowners. What it is underlining is that the balance of advantage is currently slanted far too much in favour of homeownership. Too few governments recognize that renting offers many people definite advantages at particular points in their lives. In many cases, renting may be the most appropriate tenancy during both the early years of the housing career and towards the end. It may also offer the only real answer to temporary setbacks like unemployment or divorce. There is absolutely no contradiction between being a tenant today and wanting to be a homeowner tomorrow.

In this sense the report follows Saunders in arguing for "support for the freedom of households to choose for themselves the housing arrangements which best suit them."[1] It also develops the argument made earlier by UN-HABITAT that:

> the first priority in redressing the current crisis in rental housing is to establish tenure-neutral housing policies. Too many governments provide generous incentives for owner-occupation and too few attempt to maintain, let alone, increase the rental housing stock. Governments need to rethink their priorities in the housing arena in the light of the arguments presented in this report. There are strong reasons why rental housing should receive equality of treatment from government vis-à-vis that afforded to owner-occupation.[2]

Unfortunately, in the ten years since that statement was written, little change has occurred in most governments' housing policies. Some inappropriate forms of rent control have been removed here or there, but nothing much has generally been done to offer families a wider tenure choice. Too many governments continue to bribe people to become homeowners, through tax incentives and rising property prices, and to convince them that they have little choice but to buy now. Most governments still encourage homeownership because they believe that homeowners are better citizens and that they are more likely to support the status quo.

The debate is strongly tilted to favour homeownership. Is Krueckeberg's description of the United States of America not relevant to most developing countries?

We are the inheritors of a nasty and pervasive property bias in our society with roots that run deep, just as other strong biases of gender, race, and nationality still do in spite of our efforts to outlaw them. Our institutions and practices continue to embody and perpetuate the property bias, particularly in the tax system – in the subsidies given to owners but denied to renters and in many of the property tax laws that deny that renters are stakeholders in their communities. The celebration of homeownership in the US stigmatizes those who don't, can't, or won't buy property.[3]

Before tenure-neutral housing policies can be introduced, something must be done to generate a tenure-neutral housing debate. As this report demonstrates, many of the ideas about rental housing do not apply consistently across the globe and some are just wrong. As such, the first step in promoting rental housing is to demonstrate to politicians and policy makers that many of their prejudices about rental housing are unjustified. At the very least, they need to be disabused of their belief that any of the following statements are always true:
- "There is a single best housing tenure."
- "Developed countries are societies of homeowners."
- "Every household wants to own."
- "Every household wants to own now."
- "Every landlord owns a lot of property."
- "All landlords are exploitative."
- "Landlord-tenant relations are conflictive."
- "Tenants crave security of tenure."
- "Owners are better citizens than tenants."
- "Rent control is bound to help tenants."

Human Rights and Tenure

The United Nations Housing Rights Programme (UNHRP) was launched in April 2002, as a joint initiative by UN-HABITAT and the Office of the United Nations High Commissioner for Human Rights (OHCHR). The UNHRP aims at initiating actions which ensure that:

governments ... take appropriate action in order to promote, protect and ensure the full and progressive realization of the right to adequate housing.[4]

The realization process of the "right to housing" comprises:

packages of policies and practices rather than a single (ultimately unenforceable) right. Such packages include: ensuring secure tenure, preventing illegal and mass evictions, removing all forms of discrimination, and promoting participation, gender equity and freedom of information, especially with respect to land markets.[5]

To judge from their national constitutions, more and more governments are recognizing the human right to adequate housing. Certainly, "most countries with new constitutions in the last 10–12 years have included the right to housing within them or at least a formal acceptance that the state has a responsibility for ensuring people find housing."[6] In 1998, "the constitution or national laws of more than 70 per cent of countries" promoted the "full and progressive realization of the right to adequate housing."[7] Most importantly, "without exception, every government has explicitly recognized to one degree or another the human rights dimensions of adequate housing."[8]

Of course, "the fact that the right to housing is implicitly or explicitly recognized in state constitutions does not necessarily mean that it is implemented and enforced."[9] Many countries insert housing rights into the constitution and then forget them. As Mwangi remarks with respect to Kenya, "the goal of adequate shelter for all remains more a statement of social and political intention than a feasible objective in the foreseeable future."[10] And as UN-HABITAT/OHCHR admit:

no government could proclaim that housing rights exist as much in fact within their jurisdictions as they do in international (or national) law. Thus, renewed commitments on housing rights and more refined legislative initiatives at the national level on housing rights appear necessary. Such initiatives should lead to action on:

- amending national legislation when existing laws are inconsistent with international human rights law;
- enforcing and implementing existing housing rights provisions with more vigour; and
- ultimately adopting new national and international legislation addressing the under-emphasized human right to adequate housing.[11]

As part of their efforts to ensure the full and progressive realization of the human right to adequate housing, UN-HABITAT and the OHCHR published a joint report entitled *Housing Rights Legislation* in 2002. The report contained a review of housing rights in international and national law, including a discussion of housing rights as progressive legal obligations and reviews of selected adjudication. It illustrates that effective constitutional and legislative measures on the right to adequate housing are not only realistic but have already been in use successfully in a number of countries. The examples presented there provide guidance to the development of a model legislation framework with respect to specific components of the right to adequate housing, and legislative reforms that could be initiated to advance housing rights more effectively.[12]

Those components include the following:
- security of tenure in informal housing;
- protection from forced eviction by State and non-State actors;
- non-discrimination, including gender-based discrimination in customary law;
- provision of affordable housing for the poor;
- accessibility to persons with disabilities;
- housing restitution;
- habitability;
- homelessness;
- land rights.[13]

The key question for this report is what does the human right to adequate housing imply for government action towards landlords and tenants? What in practice are the housing rights of tenants and what is the best way to consolidate those rights? So far this issue does not seem to have been addressed comprehensively in the housing rights literature.

Persuading Governments to Include Renting in their Policy Agendas

The ideology that owners are better citizens than renters is a modern manifestation of a bias hardened in stereotypes that has misguided public policy in many countries. As such, it seems essential to begin the reform of housing policy near the top. Governments have been over-anxious to encourage households to become homeowners. More governments need to be persuaded of the inadequacy of this policy. For this argument to be made, it is useful and essential to convince the relevant international institutions and development agencies to give rental housing a higher profile. At present, very few ever do.

UNECLAC [United Nations Economic Commission for Latin America and the Caribbean] for example, has recently paid more attention to housing than previously but has been virtually mute on the subject of rental housing. Certainly a recent statement does not hold out much hope.

> Housing policies in the region have placed so much emphasis on finance that there has been a tendency to overlook other important modifications that could improve the efficiency and effectiveness of housing programmes. National programmes are almost always geared, either explicitly or implicitly, toward facilitating the purchase of new homes, but do not consider other options, such as the improvement or expansion of existing homes.[14]

Although the opportunity was there to mention rental housing, it was definitely not grasped. The United Nations Development Programme {UNDP] is no different and although rental housing could figure in the agendas of the International Labour Organization, in terms of income generation, or the World Health Organization, in terms of health improvement, little or nothing has ever been said. Even UN-HABITAT (which has addressed the issue seriously in some of its publications) is sometimes rather silent on rental housing.

Silence about rental housing is also characteristic of the multilateral development banks. The World Bank did carry out some important research on rental housing in the past,[15] and its influential policy statement of 1993 did, occasionally, refer to rental housing.[16] However, the Bank has been virtually silent on the issue ever since and has certainly not provided any loans to support the rental housing sector. In fact, the Bank is:

> surprisingly reticent regarding the impact of its tenure proposals on the rental sector, particularly private informal rental housing, which accommodates a large proportion of the urban population and almost all of the poorest households. There is therefore a real danger that a policy approach, which emphasizes the benefits of owner-occupation, and provides various incentives for it, may result in the creation of a large underclass that is denied access to any form of affordable or acceptable housing.[17]

Similarly, the Inter American Development Bank has done far too little to finance rental housing or even stimulate a debate among its member countries on the issue.

Clearly, putting the rental issue onto the agendas of multilateral institutions is essential. If housing loans were premised on at least some recognition of the potential role of rental housing, it might help. Convincing NGOs of the benefits from rental housing would also be helpful, insofar as few of these institutions are currently supporting its development. At present, many NGOs seem to be as hostile to the issues of rental housing as national governments. NGOs involved with tenant organizations, for example, tend to be confrontational, challenging landlords to improve conditions and lower rents. This is largely a consequence of those organizations being most active in central areas, where the different interests of landlords and tenants are most brutally exposed. But NGOs concerned with developing self-help housing options seem to do little to encourage rental housing. They normally only develop programs for owner-occupation and when they do directly address the problems of tenants, most come up with proposals to turn the tenants into owners.[18]

To stimulate debate, it is first necessary to convince housing experts that the rental issue is a critical ingredient in the housing debate. In achieving this task, some mileage can be achieved through better diffusion of research evidence and of examples of best practices. In these days of rapid international travel and of instant access to information on the web, it should be possible to convince some policy makers that alternatives to homeownership are available. Seminars should also be organized to bring together policy makers to demonstrate some of the advantages of rental housing and the disadvantages of homeownership. What advantages do the Germans and Swiss obtain from having such a large stock of rental housing? How does the Dutch experience with social housing help the poor and ethnic minorities? What is the downside of giving homebuyers tax relief on mortgages, particularly when such vast sums are offered, as in the United States of America?[19] How do small-scale informal sector landlords actually operate, and what do they need in the way of policy help?

More should also be done to integrate housing into the mainstream of the debate about poverty alleviation. Renting in most developing countries is an activity predominantly involving two sets of poor people. Poor landlords produce rental housing for poor tenants. Since the rents of one set of poor people help sustain the incomes of another set of poor people, the role that housing plays in income generation and household budgets is very important. However, recent debates about poverty alleviation are all too likely to omit the housing question altogether. This is most regrettable given how important letting is to some women-headed households and to increasing numbers of older people. In an aging world, landlordism is one of the few ways in which some older people can survive.

Research Needs

More is known about rental housing today than was the case a decade ago, but there are still many gaps. In particular we know too little about:
- The nature and characteristics of formal rental housing in developing country cities.
- The impact of upgrading programs on tenants and rental housing.
- The reasons why national and local governments have ignored rental housing.
- The reasons why international agencies have ignored rental housing.
- The impact of rent control reform in less developed countries.
- The contribution of rents to incomes of self-help-sector landlords, particularly women and the older persons.
- How self-help landlords run their "businesses."
- The history behind the emergence of the myth of ownership in less developed countries.
- Economic recession and its impact on tenure.
- The attitudes of cooperatives to rental housing.
- How to develop mechanisms for arbitration and conciliation.
- What happens to low-income families that receive government-housing subsidies and then decide to sell out, or to mortgage defaulters who lose their homes.

The Ultimate Task

The main aim of promoting discussion about the nature of rental housing and incorporating it more into national policy agendas is to help to increase the quality and quantity of the rental housing stock. This is one way of addressing the severe shelter problems currently facing most developing countries. Promoting rental housing is not, to repeat, an attempt to undermine the virtues of homeownership, but a means of supplementing its strengths. The essential links between ownership and renting in most low-income settlements are obvious and, given the difficult employment situations found in most cities, there is much to be said for encouraging poor households to increase their incomes by renting out rooms.

This is not so much an option as a necessity. For, as access to land is becoming harder in the major cities of developing countries, ownership even of the self-help kind is going to get harder in the coming years. Given the number of rapidly growing cities in Africa and Asia, providing adequate shelter is going to pose a major problem unless some rethinking is done. Of course, the uncontrolled expansion of un-serviced self-help housing in the rapidly growing mega-cities of developing countries is one possible scenario. But there are more humane ways of accommodating the masses moving to or being born in these cities. One of these more humane routes is to understand the advantages of promoting rental housing.

Ten years ago, UN-HABITAT concluded that the key objectives of housing policy should be to: stimulate housing production, help produce a mix of housing choices (tenure, location, and quality), and assist those who cannot afford adequate housing to improve their shelter situation.[20] That support for rental housing contributes to this task, is demonstrated by a recent analysis of the rental sector in South Africa, which concluded that rental housing:[21]

- Offers choice and mobility to consumers.
- Provides accommodation for the very poor and for those households that currently do not qualify for the housing subsidy.
- Contributes to economic development through providing business opportunities to entrepreneurial rental property developers and specialist service providers.
- Supports the economic sustainability of ownership through household rental, whereby owners are able to afford and improve their accommodation through income earned from sub-letting. This also improves the rates base and financial sustainability of urban areas and contributes to poverty alleviation.
- Improves the performance of urban areas by increasing densities and facilitating urban renewal in inner cities, slum areas and townships.
- Can have a positive impact on female economic empowerment, as it is often women who manage the household rental process.

The research results included in this report demonstrate how such opportunities can be realized. Many stakeholders around the world, and in particular most researchers, are now convinced that renting should receive higher priority than it has in the past. Arguably there is no real choice. What remains, therefore, is for national and international agencies to get on with the job of effectively promoting rental housing.

The full report from which this edited excerpt has been taken is available at:
www.unhabitat.org/rental_housing.asp

Alan Gilbert *is Professor of Geography at University College London. He has published extensively on housing, poverty, employment, and urban problems in developing countries, particularly those in Latin America. He has written or co-written nine books, edited four others, and written more than a hundred academic articles on these topics. He has also acted as an adviser to numerous international institutions, including the Inter-American Development Bank, UN-HABITAT, United Nations University, UNESCO and United Nations Population Fund, the Woodrow Wilson Center, and the World Bank.*

Endnotes

1 Saunders, P., *A Nation of Home Owners*, Unwin Hyman, 1990, p. 4.
2 UNCHS, *Support Measures to Promote Low-Income Rental Housing*, UNCHS, Nairobi, 1993.
3 Krueckeberg, D.A., "The Grapes of Rent: A History of Renting in a Country of Owners," *Housing Policy Debate*, vol. 10, 1999, p. 26.
4 UN Habitat, The Istanbul Declaration and the Habitat Agenda, Nairobi, para. 61
5 UN Habitat, "Implementing the Habitat Agenda: The 1996–2001 experience, Report on the Istanbul+5 Thematic Committee," 25th Special General Assembly, New York, 2001, p. 32.
6 UN Habitat, *An Urbanising World: Global Report on Human Settlements* 1996, Oxford University Press, Oxford, 1996, p. 351.
7 UN Habitat, *Reassessment of Urban Planning and Development Regulations in Asian Cities*, Nairobi, 1999, p. 33.
8 UN-Habitat and Office of the United Nations High Commissioner for Human Rights, *Housing Rights Legislation: Review of International and National Legal Instruments*, United Nations Housing Rights Programme Report no. 1, Nairobi and Geneva, 2002, p. 24.
9 Durand-Lasserve, A. and L. Royston, "International Trends and Country Contexts: From Tenure Regularization to Tenure Security," in A. Durand-Lasserve and L. Royston (eds.), *Holding Their Ground: Secure Land Tenure for the Urban Poor in Developing Countries*, Earthscan, 2002, p. 249.
10 Mwangi, I.K., "The Nature of Rental Housing in Kenya," *Environment and Urbanization*, vol. 9, no. 2, 1997, p. 142.
11 UN Habitat and Office of the United Nations High Commissioner for Human Rights, *Housing Rights Legislation: Review of International and National Legal Instruments*, United Nations Housing Rights Programme Report no. 1, Nairobi and Geneva, 2002, p. 24.
12 UN Habitat and Office of the United Nations High Commissioner for Human

Rights, "Urban Development and Shelter Strategies in Favour of the Urban Poor," Note by the Secretariat to the 19th session of the Governing Council of United Nations Human Settlements Programme (HSP/GC/19/ 5), Nairobi, 2002, p. 639.

13 UN Habitat and Office of the United Nations High Commissioner for Human Rights, *Housing Rights Legislation: Review of International and National Legal Instruments*, 2002, p. xiv.

14 United Nations Economic Commission for Latin America and the Caribbean and UN Habitat, *From Rapid Urbanization to the Consolidation of Human Settlements in Latin America and the Caribbean: A Territorial Perspective*, Santiago, 2000.

15 Mayo, S.K., "How Much Will Households Spend for Shelter?" *Urban Edge*, vol. 9, 1985, pp. 4–5; Mayo, S.K., Malpezzi, S. and Gross, D.J., "Shelter Strategies for the Urban Poor in Developing Countries," *The World Bank Research Observer*, vol. 1, 1986, pp. 183–203.

16 World Bank, *Housing: Enabling Markets to Work*, A World Bank Policy Paper, 1993.

17 Payne, G., (ed.), *Making Common Ground: Public Private Partnerships in Land for Housing*, Intermediate Technology Group, 1999.

18 Ramaswamy, V. and Chakravarti, M., "Falahak, Inshallah (Flowering-God's Will): The Struggle of the Labouring Poor and a Vision, Strategy and Programme for Tenant-Led Basti and City Renewal," *Environment and Urbanization*, vol. 9, no. 2, 1997, pp. 63–80; Richmond, P., "From Tenants to Owners: Experiences with a Revolving Fund for Social Housing," *Environment and Urbanization*, vol. 9, no. 2, 1997, pp. 119–140; Thurman, S., "Unzumo: Improving Hostel Dwellers' Accommodation in South Africa," *Environment and Urbanization*, vol. 9, no. 2, 1997, pp. 43–62.

19 "In 1989, the amount of federal tax subsidy for owner-occupied housing is estimated at between \$49.7 billion and \$51.9 billion. ... including non-taxation of net implicit income in the measurement of home-owner tax expenditures adds substantially to the estimates of the aggregate tax expenditure on owner-occupied housing," possibly reaching US\$109 billion a year (Megbolugbe, I.F. and Linneman, P.D., "Home ownership," *Urban Studies*, vol. 30, 1993, p. 673). This implies an average annual subsidy of more than US\$ 1,600 per owner-occupied unit.

20 UN Habitat, *Support Measures to Promote Low-Income Rental Housing*, UNCHS, Nairobi, 1993.

21 Martin and Nell (Sigodi Marah Martin and Matthew Nell and Associates), "An assessment of rental housing in South Africa," report for USAID, 2002.

Appendix A
Glossary of Housing Terms

STEVE POMEROY AND PHILIPPA CAMPSIE

ACT: Affordability and Choice Today, a housing program of the Federation of Canadian Municipalities.

Adequacy Problem: A measure of poor physical condition of a dwelling unit. A household has an adequacy problem when the dwelling occupied is in need of major repair and is in an unsafe condition.

Affordability Gap: The difference between the amount a household can afford at a specified percentage of income (e.g., 30 percent) and the actual rent paid or market rent.

Affordability: Not defined as a specific income or rent, affordability refers to a relative situation in which income is deemed insufficient to pay for rent. Typically, the affordability benchmark used in housing analysis is 30 percent of income spent on shelter.

Affordable Housing Framework (AHF): In November 2001, all ten Canadian provinces and three territories signed the Affordable Housing Framework Agreement in Quebec City. The federal government agreed to provide $680 million over five years for new affordable housing. The provinces agreed to match the federal funds, although the deal gives them "wiggle room" to get credit for spending by third parties.

Bonusing: Used by some municipalities as a development incentive to encourage a specific outcome, such as affordable housing. Bonusing refers to the practice of allowing a higher density on a development site in exchange for providing a public or social benefit. Instead of a three-storey building, for example, a developer may obtain a bonus of one additional floor (or some percentage of allowable floor area) to four storeys with the condition that a specified amount of the floor area or units produced meet certain criteria.

Break-even Rent: The rent that would have to be charged to cover all operating costs and mortgage payments related to the cost of building.

Brownfields: formerly industrialized land in urban areas that is available for redevelopment, provided that problems of contamination and environmental liability are settled.

Canada Assistance Plan (CAP): The funding mechanism that the federal government used to contribute financially to the cost of provincial social assistance and social services; created in 1966, repealed in 1995 and replaced with Canada Health and Social Transfer (CHST).

Canada Child Tax Benefit (CCTB): A program announced in the 1997 federal budget that provides equal federal payments to all low-income families.

Canada Health and Social Transfer (CHST): In April 1996, this program replaced the Canada Assistance Plan as the vehicle for federal transfers to provincial governments for social programs. The formula for federal contributions changed from federal-provincial cost-sharing (50-50) to a block fund that now includes health insurance and postsecondary program costs.

Canada Pension Plan (CPP): Mandatory contributory defined benefit indexed pension plan started in 1966 by the federal government for all Canadians.

Capital Cost Allowance (CCA): Tax provision that allows a business to deduct the cost of depreciating capital assets to reduce taxable income.

Census Metropolitan Area (CMA): a category used by Statistics Canada in the census for Canada's largest urban areas.

CESCR: The United Nations' Committee on Economic, Social and Cultural Rights.

CMHC: Canada Mortgage and Housing Corporation is the federal housing agency that implements federal housing policy and programs.

Condominium: A form of ownership tenure associated with a multiple-unit building (apartment or townhome). The occupant owns the individual unit and shares common space such as foyer, halls and outdoor space.

Co-operative Housing: A form of tenure, common in social housing, in which the residents are co-op members and participate in the management and operation of the property. Much of the co-operative housing that has been built in Canada is owned on a not-for-profit basis – the occupants have no or limited equity share. Some equity co-ops also have been built outside of social housing programs.

Core Housing Need: A measure developed by the CMHC to determine housing need.

Debt Service: The monthly or annual payments of principal and interest associated with a mortgage loan.

Demand Approach: An approach that is focused on the consumer/tenant with the objective of increasing ability to pay rent and thus improving effective demand.

Fannie Mae: The Federal National Mortgage Association, a U.S. financial institution created as a government-sponsored enterprise to facilitate residential mortgage lending by creating a secondary market to purchase and securitize mortgage loans from loan originators.

Federation of Canadian Municipalities (FCM): the national association of Canada's municipal governments.

Guaranteed Income Supplement (GIS): Income-tested monthly pension supplement for OAS pensioners who have little other income.

Household: The primary unit of analysis in housing research. The term household is used generically and can include unattached individuals, a group of unrelated people occupying the same dwelling, a family or a combination of these groupings.

ICESCR: The United Nations' International Covenant on Economic, Social and Cultural Rights.

Labour Sponsored Venture Capital Corporations (LSVCCs): Corporations that invest in companies that are starting or expanding their businesses. These venture-capital funds offer individual investors federal tax credits and provincial tax credits as an inducement to invest and to partially compensate for higher risk associated with venture investment.

Leverage: The use of a small amount of capital as a downpayment, to support or obtain the use of a larger amount, usually through a mortgage loan. For example, using future rental income to secure a mortgage loan is often referred to as leveraging the mortgage. Using the value of existing assets to secure a mortgage loan is referred to as leveraging the asset.

Low Income Cut-offs (LICOs): This measurement created by Statistics Canada consists of an income level below which families or unattached individuals spend 20% more than average on food, shelter and clothing. Statistics Canada sets several low income cut-off points for different sizes of families. Although these levels are sometimes called poverty lines, Statistics Canada emphasizes that the LICOs are not measures of poverty, but merely identify those who are substantially worse-off than average.

Mixed Income: The practice of accommodating a range of households with different income layers. Income mix is seen as a way to avoid concentration of very low-income households that can lead to stigmatization or ghettoization of certain projects and residents.

NIMBY: "Not in My Back Yard," a term that refers to the resistance of homeowners and others to unwanted developments in their vicinity.

Non-profit: An incorporated association with the objective of operating without gain or profit for members or board members. Much social housing in Canada is operated by not-for-profit agencies or corporations. These may be private corporations, such as a subsidiary of a faith group or service club, or they might be public nonprofit corporations – an arm's-length subsidiary to a municipality incorporated specifically to own and operate housing for low- and moderate-income households.

Old Age Security Pension (OAS): Pension available to Canadian citizens and legal residents of Canada aged 65 and over, who have lived in Canada for at least 10 years since turning 18.

Ontario Municipal Board (OMB): a quasi-judicial organization in Ontario that rules on matters of land use and municipal policy.

Provider: A non-profit corporation that owns and manages housing (a label for a non-profit landlord or co-operative).

Public Housing: Housing owned and operated by a provincial or municipal agency – formerly used as a generic term for assisted housing, now largely replaced by the more encompassing term "social housing." See below.

Rent Supplement: A form of assistance paid to a landlord to provide units to low-income tenants usually over a contracted term. Payment to landlord is based on the difference between actual negotiated market rent and a rent geared to income (RGI) paid directly by tenant (typically 30 percent of income).

Rental Rehabilitation Assistance Program (RRAP): a federal program that provides funding to upgrade homeowner and rental properties or convert non-residential property to rental property.

RGI: Rent-geared-to-income (usually based on 25–30 percent of gross income, as verified by the administering agency).

Shelter Allowance: A form of assistance paid directly to a tenant, based on the difference between actual negotiated market rent and an RGI rent paid by the tenant. Shelter allowance payments are calculated by formula and often pay only a percentage of the gap (e.g., 75 percent of the difference between full market rent less 30 percent of income).

Shelter Component (of welfare): Portion of income assistance calculation that uses an explicit shelter variable.

Shelter Maximum: Typically, this component represents one part of the income assistance and is paid up to a maximum amount (varying by household size and composition) based on actual verified rent.

Social Assistance: Popularly known as "welfare," social assistance is the income support of last resort for people who do not qualify for or have exhausted other income programs and other sources of income.

Social Union Framework Agreement: Formally known as "A Framework to Improve the Social Union for Canadians," signed in 1999 by the Canadian prime minister and provincial premiers to guide intergovernmental cooperation on social policy.

Stacking: Combination of two different types of assistance or programs. For example, a rent supplement may be stacked with non-profit supply assistance to ensure that rents are affordable at a specified percentage of income.

STIR: Shelter-to-Income Ratio.

Suitability Problem: Term used to define an overcrowded dwelling – CMHC uses very specific criteria to determine an appropriate unit size – based on national occupancy standards. Parents and children have separate rooms and children over age 5 of opposite gender are assigned separate rooms; those under 5 may share up to two per room.

Supply Approach: A program response focused on providing a dwelling – usually involves new construction but may include acquisition and rehabilitation.

Supply Gap: The difference between break-even rent and market level rents. The supply gap reflects the cost or subsidy amount necessary to stimulate or support new supply (since typically break-even rent on new construction exceeds potential market rent).

Supporting Communities Partnership Initiative (SCPI): A federal program launched in 1999 to fund efforts to alleviate and prevent homelessness in Canadian communities.

Supportive Housing: Housing provided along with support services that enable tenants (such as seniors, formerly homeless people, or mental health consumer/survivors) to maintain their housing.

Targeting: Specifying the maximum percentage of units that must be made available to households meeting certain income criteria. Public housing is 100 percent targeted – all tenants are generally below income thresholds and receive subsidized rent. Some non-profit developments cap the number of targeted households at 60 percent to encourage a degree of income mix and avoid concentrations of very low-income households.

Toronto Disaster Relief Committee (TDRC): a group originally formed to have homelessness declared a "national disaster," a designation that would permit for disaster assistance to its victims; now an advocacy group on behalf of all homeless and low-income people

Vacancy Rate: A measure of the availability of rental units. Distinct from a turnover rate (when one tenant moves out and a new one is ready immediately to move in), the vacancy rate (as measured and reported in the CMHC annual rental survey) measures the percentage of units that are vacant and available for rent as of a specific date. Typically, a vacancy rate of 3 percent is accepted as a benchmark of a healthy rental market (sufficient units to meet demand without excess pressure on rents).

Welfare Dependant: A household whose main source of income over a continuing period is social assistance.

Working Poor: Households in which one or both adults are employed, but family income is below Statistics Canada low income cut-offs.

Appendix B

An Act to Provide for Adequate, Accessible and Affordable Housing for Canadians

BILL C-416, HOUSE OF COMMONS OF CANADA

THIRTY-SEVENTH PARLIAMENT

FIRST READING, NOVEMBER 28, 2001

Summary

The purpose of this enactment is to respect the dignity and worth of all women, children and men in Canada by protecting their human rights through the provision of adequate, accessible and affordable housing and security in its enjoyment.

This is to be achieved by the adoption of financial policies and by the establishment of a national housing strategy and programs to put it into effect.

The programs must ensure the supply of such housing to those who cannot otherwise afford it as soon as possible and as a legally enforceable right from January 1, 2003.

The Minister of Public Works and Government Services must convene, within 180 days after the coming into force of the enactment, a conference including officials of the federal government and the governments of all provinces and territories and representatives of the municipalities and aboriginal communities, to develop and plan the national housing strategy and programs, and must report to Parliament on the conference within a further 180 days.

Preamble

WHEREAS the provision of and access to adequate housing is a fundamental human right according to paragraph 25(1) of the United Nations Universal Declaration of Human Rights, which reads as follows:

"Everyone has the right to a standard of living adequate for the health and wellbeing of himself and of his family, including food, clothing, housing and medical care and necessary social services, and the right to security in the event of unemployment, sickness, disability, widowhood, old age or other lack of livelihood in circumstances beyond his control.";

WHEREAS in 1976 Canada signed the International Covenant on Economic, Social and Cultural Rights, a legally binding treaty, committing Canada to make progress on fully realizing all economic, social and cultural rights, including the right to adequate housing, as outlined in paragraph 11(1) of the Covenant:

"The States Parties to the present Covenant recognize the right of everyone to an adequate standard of living for himself and his family, including adequate food, clothing and housing, and to the continuous improvement of living conditions. The States Parties will take appropriate steps to ensure the realization of this right.";

WHEREAS the enjoyment of other human rights, such as those to privacy, to respect for the home, to freedom of movement, to freedom from discrimination, to environmental health, to security of the person, to freedom of association, and to equality before the law are indivisible from and indispensable to the realization of the right to adequate housing;

WHEREAS the immediate action required of State Parties to the Covenant arises out of paragraph 2(1) of the Covenant, which provides that State Parties undertake to take steps to carry out its provisions by all appropriate means, including particularly the adoption of legislative measures;

WHEREAS the United Nations Committee on Economic, Social and Cultural Rights has interpreted this to mean that State Parties are obliged to immediately begin to adopt measures towards the full enjoyment by everyone of the right to housing;

WHEREAS the United Nations Committee has been highly critical of Canada's failure to make progress on the provision of adequate housing for all Canadians, a criticism made most recently in its concluding observations of December 10, 1998:

"The Committee is gravely concerned that such a wealthy country as Canada has allowed the problem of homelessness and inadequate housing to grow to such proportions that the mayors of Canada's 10 largest cities have now declared homelessness a national disaster.";

WHEREAS the United Nations Committee issued a specific recommendation that Canada implement a national strategy aimed at reducing homelessness and poverty, which reads in part:

"The Committee recommends that the federal, provincial and territorial governments address homelessness and inadequate housing as a national emergency by reinstating or increasing, as the case may be, social housing programs for those in need, improving and properly enforcing anti-discrimination legislation in the field of housing, increasing shelter allowances and social assistance rates to realistic levels, providing adequate support services for persons with disabilities, improving protection of security of tenure for tenants and improving protection of affordable rental housing stock from conversion to other uses. The Committee urges the State Party to implement a national strategy for the reduction of homelessness and poverty.";

WHEREAS Canada's wealth and national budget are more than adequate to ensure that every woman, child and man residing in Canada has secure, adequate, accessible and affordable housing as part of a standard of living that will provide healthy, physical, intellectual, emotional, spiritual and social development and a good quality of life;

WHEREAS achievement of improved housing conditions is best realized through co-operative partnerships of government and civil society and the meaningful involvement of local communities;

AND WHEREAS the Parliament of Canada wishes to ensure the establishment of national goals and programs that seek to improve the quality of life for all Canadians as a basic right;

NOW, THEREFORE, Her Majesty, by and with the advice and consent of the Senate and House of Commons of Canada, enacts as follows:

Short title

1. This Act may be cited as the Housing Bill of Rights.

Interpretation

2. The definitions in this section apply in this Act.
   "accessible housing" means housing that is accessible to the individu-

als who are intended to occupy it, including those who are disadvantaged by age, physical or mental disability or medical condition, or by being victims of a natural disaster.

"adequate housing" means housing that is habitable and structurally sound, and that provides sufficient space and protection against cold, damp, heat, rain, wind, noise, pollution and other threats to health.

"affordable housing" means housing that is available at a cost that does not compromise the attainment and satisfaction of an individual's other basic needs of life, including needs for food, clothing and access to education.

"Minister" means the Minister of Public Works and Government Services.

Rights respecting housing

3. (1) Subject to this Act, every individual has the right to secure, adequate, accessible and affordable housing, as defined in this Act.
(2) Every individual has the right to the housing referred to in section 2 without the discrimination referred to in subsection (3).
(3) No person shall make any discrimination in respect of another's right to housing under this Act on the basis of race, national or ethnic origin, colour, religion, sex, age, mental or physical disability, family status, the presence of children, sexual orientation, medical status, citizenship, level of education, employment status, social condition or reliance on welfare or other public assistance.
4. Every individual has the following rights, with respect to housing:

   (a) a right to security of tenure against arbitrary eviction, forced relocation, expropriation or threat of any of them, or against any other form of harassment;

   (b) a right to housing that is appropriate to the individual's special needs, including the availability of attention combined with independence;

   (c) a right for all children, women and men to a home in a safe and healthy environment;

   (d) a right to a home free from violence, threat of violence or other form of harassment, both domestic and from outside the home;

   (e) a right to enjoyment and respect of privacy in the home;

   (f) a right to the economic security that results from protection from rent increases, property tax increases or other housing cost increases that

(i) are sudden or excessive,

(ii) are primarily intended to yield an unreasonable profit or to increase the value of rental property, or

(iii) have the effect of diminishing the other rights established by this Act.

Enforcement, offences and penalties

5. Every individual has the right to bring an action before a court of competent jurisdiction to enforce the rights to which they are entitled under sections 3 and 4 or otherwise under this Act, or under any other laws designed to grant rights to, ensure security in, and prevent discrimination with regard to, access to housing.

(2) Subsection (1) does not reduce or abrogate any other remedy available at law.

6. (1) Every person or legal entity that contravenes any provision of this Act, or takes away or threatens a right of an individual granted by this Act, is guilty of an offence and punishable on summary conviction (a) to a fine of not more than $5000 for a first offence; and (b) to a fine of not more than $10,000 or to imprisonment for not more than six months or to both fine and imprisonment for a second or subsequent offence.

(2) For the purposes of subsection (1), an act or omission that takes away or threatens the rights of more than one individual constitutes a separate offence in respect of each such individual.

Government policies and housing strategy

7. (1) The Minister shall develop and adopt, in cooperation with the governments of all provinces and with representatives of municipalities and the aboriginal communities, which cooperation includes the conference referred to in section 12, policies to ensure that the costs of housing in Canada do not prevent or threaten the attainment and satisfaction of other basic needs, including needs for food, clothing and access to education.

(2) The policies mentioned in subsection (1) must provide for

(a) financial assistance in respect of rent for those who are otherwise unable to afford the rights to rental housing established by this Act; and

(b) availability of finance and credit without discrimination based on a characteristic listed as a forbidden ground of discrimination in subsection 3(3) for those who, with such finance and credit, may be able to purchase housing.

8. (1) The Minister shall develop and adopt, in cooperation with the governments of all provinces and with representatives of municipalities and the aboriginal communities, which cooperation includes the conference referred to in section 12, a national housing conference strategy and programs to carry it out, to ensure the full exercise of the rights granted by this Act.

(2) The national housing strategy must provide for the availability, by January 1, 2003, of housing that meets the requirements of this Act and that

(a) is adequate, affordable, accessible, and not for profit in the case of those who cannot otherwise afford it;

(b) reflects the needs of local communities, including aboriginal communities;

(c) does not cost more than thirty percent of the occupants' pre-tax household income;

(d) is appropriate for different needs and provides reasonable design options, including, in an appropriate proportion, access for the elderly and the disabled;

(e) uses design and equipment standardization where appropriate to accelerate construction and minimize cost;

(f) includes not-for-profit rental housing projects, mixed income not-for-profit housing cooperatives, special-needs housing and housing that allows senior citizens to remain in their homes as long as possible;

(g) includes the housing for the homeless specified in section 11;

(h) includes provision for temporary emergency housing and shelter in the event of disasters and crises; and

(i) complies with standards for the maintenance of existing housing stock or for the construction and maintenance of new housing and appropriate health, security and safety standards.

(3) The national housing strategy described in this section shall be implemented as soon as possible in accordance with section 12 to ensure the fulfillment of subsection (4).

(4) The right to adequate, accessible and affordable housing described in this Act is a right that is legally enforceable from January 1, 2003.

9. The programs developed under section 8 shall ensure that priority in the provision of adequate, accessible and affordable housing is given to:

(a) those who have had not had adequate, accessible and affordable housing over an extended period;

(b) those with special housing requirements because of family status or size or because of a mental or physical disability; and

(c) those who have difficulty obtaining housing because of a characteristic listed as a forbidden ground of discrimination in subsection 3(2).

10. Programs developed under section 8 shall include the provision for the rights of the homeless described in section 11.

11. (1) Every individual who is homeless has a right to the immediate provision by public authorities of adequate, self-contained and appropriate housing.

(2) A hostel, emergency shelter or accommodation that provides only bed and breakfast is not adequate housing for the purposes of subsection (1).

(3) Every homeless individual who is refused the housing provided for in subsection (1) has the right to appeal the refusal in a court of competent jurisdiction.

12. (1) The Minister shall, within 180 days after the coming into force of this Act, convene a conference of the ministers of the Crown for each province responsible for housing and representatives of municipalities and the aboriginal communities.

(2) The conference convened pursuant to subsection (1) shall:

(a) develop standards and objectives for the national housing strategy described in section 8, and programs to carry it out;

(b) set targets for the commencement of the programs;

(c) recommend a time by which an additional one percent of the annual expenditures of the federal and all provincial and municipal governments during the fiscal year ending March 31, 2002, are to be assigned to national housing programs throughout Canada; and

(d) develop the principles of an agreement between the federal and all provincial governments and representatives of the municipalities and aboriginal communities for the development and delivery of the programs.

13. The Minister shall cause a report on the conference, including the matters referred to in paragraphs 12(2)(a) to (d), to be laid before each House of Parliament on any one of the first five days that the House sits following the expiration of 180 days after the end of the conference.

Coming into force

14. Sections 5 and 6 and subsection 11(3) come into force on January 1, 2003.

Appendix C

Defining the Right to Adequate Housing

UNITED NATIONS COMMITTEE ON ECONOMIC,
SOCIAL AND CULTURAL RIGHTS,
GENERAL COMMENT NO. 4, 1991

1. Pursuant to article 11 (1) of the Covenant, States parties "recognize the right of everyone to an adequate standard of living for himself and his family, including adequate food, clothing and housing, and to the continuous improvement of living conditions." The human right to adequate housing, which is thus derived from the right to an adequate standard of living, is of central importance for the enjoyment of all economic, social and cultural rights.

2. The Committee has been able to accumulate a large amount of information pertaining to this right. Since 1979, the Committee and its predecessors have examined 75 reports dealing with the right to adequate housing. The Committee has also devoted a day of general discussion to the issue at each of its third (see E/1989/22, para. 312) and fourth sessions (E/1990/23, paras. 281–285). In addition, the Committee has taken careful note of information generated by the International Year of Shelter for the Homeless (1987) including the Global Strategy for Shelter to the Year 2000 adopted by the General Assembly in its resolution 42/191 of 11 December 1987.[1] The Committee has also reviewed relevant reports and other documentation of the Commission on Human Rights and the Sub-Commission on Prevention of Discrimination and Protection of Minorities.[2]

3. Although a wide variety of international instruments address the different dimensions of the right to adequate housing[3] article 11 (1) of the Covenant is the most comprehensive and perhaps the most important of the relevant provisions.

4. Despite the fact that the international community has frequently reaffirmed the importance of full respect for the right to adequate housing, there remains a disturbingly large gap between the standards set in article 11 (1) of the Covenant and the situation prevailing in many parts of the world. While the problems are often particularly acute in some developing countries which confront major resource and other constraints, the Committee observes that significant problems of homelessness and inadequate housing also exist in some of the most economically developed societies. The United Nations estimates that there are over 100 million persons homeless worldwide and over 1 billion inadequately housed.[4] There is no indication that this number is decreasing. It seems clear that no State party is free of significant problems of one kind or another in relation to the right to housing.

5. In some instances, the reports of States parties examined by the Committee have acknowledged and described difficulties in ensuring the right to adequate housing. For the most part, however, the information provided has been insufficient to enable the Committee to obtain an adequate picture of the situation prevailing in the State concerned. This General Comment thus aims to identify some of the principal issues which the Committee considers to be important in relation to this right.

6. The right to adequate housing applies to everyone. While the reference to "himself and his family" reflects assumptions as to gender roles and economic activity patterns commonly accepted in 1966 when the Covenant was adopted, the phrase cannot be read today as implying any limitations upon the applicability of the right to individuals or to female-headed households or other such groups. Thus, the concept of "family" must be understood in a wide sense. Further, individuals, as well as families, are entitled to adequate housing regardless of age, economic status, group or other affiliation or status and other such factors. In particular, enjoyment of this right must, in accordance with article 2 (2) of the Covenant, not be subject to any form of discrimination.

7. In the Committee's view, the right to housing should not be interpreted in a narrow or restrictive sense which equates it with, for example, the shelter provided by merely having a roof over one's head or views shelter exclusively as a commodity. Rather it should be seen as the right to live somewhere in security, peace and dignity. This is appropriate for at least two reasons. In the first place, the right to housing is inte-

grally linked to other human rights and to the fundamental principles upon which the Covenant is premised. Thus "the inherent dignity of the human person" from which the rights in the Covenant are said to derive requires that the term "housing" be interpreted so as to take account of a variety of other considerations, most importantly that the right to housing should be ensured to all persons irrespective of income or access to economic resources. Secondly, the reference in article 11 (1) must be read as referring not just to housing but to adequate housing. As both the Commission on Human Settlements and the Global Strategy for Shelter to the Year 2000 have stated: "Adequate shelter means ... adequate privacy, adequate space, adequate security, adequate lighting and ventilation, adequate basic infrastructure and adequate location with regard to work and basic facilities – all at a reasonable cost."

8. Thus the concept of adequacy is particularly significant in relation to the right to housing since it serves to underline a number of factors which must be taken into account in determining whether particular forms of shelter can be considered to constitute "adequate housing" for the purposes of the Covenant. While adequacy is determined in part by social, economic, cultural, climatic, ecological and other factors, the Committee believes that it is nevertheless possible to identify certain aspects of the right that must be taken into account for this purpose in any particular context. They include the following:

(a) *Legal security of tenure.* Tenure takes a variety of forms, including rental (public and private) accommodation, cooperative housing, lease, owner-occupation, emergency housing and informal settlements, including occupation of land or property. Notwithstanding the type of tenure, all persons should possess a degree of security of tenure which guarantees legal protection against forced eviction, harassment and other threats. States parties should consequently take immediate measures aimed at conferring legal security of tenure upon those persons and households currently lacking such protection, in genuine consultation with affected persons and groups;

(b) *Availability of services, materials, facilities and infrastructure.* An adequate house must contain certain facilities essential for health, security, comfort and nutrition. All beneficiaries of the right to adequate housing should have sustainable access to natural and common resources, safe drinking water, energy for cooking, heating and lighting, sanitation and washing facilities, means of food storage, refuse disposal, site drainage and emergency services;

(c) *Affordability.* Personal or household financial costs associated with housing should be at such a level that the attainment and satisfaction of other basic needs are not threatened or compromised. Steps should be taken by States parties to ensure that the percentage of housing-related costs is, in general, commensurate with income levels. States parties should establish housing subsidies for those unable to obtain affordable housing, as well as forms and levels of housing finance which adequately reflect housing needs. In accordance with the principle of affordability, tenants should be protected by appropriate means against unreasonable rent levels or rent increases. In societies where natural materials constitute the chief sources of building materials for housing, steps should be taken by States parties to ensure the availability of such materials;

(d) *Habitability.* Adequate housing must be habitable, in terms of providing the inhabitants with adequate space and protecting them from cold, damp, heat, rain, wind or other threats to health, structural hazards, and disease vectors. The physical safety of occupants must be guaranteed as well. The Committee encourages States parties to comprehensively apply the Health Principles of Housing[5] prepared by WHO which view housing as the environmental factor most frequently associated with conditions for disease in epidemiological analyses; i.e., inadequate and deficient housing and living conditions are invariably associated with higher mortality and morbidity rates;

(e) *Accessibility.* Adequate housing must be accessible to those entitled to it. Disadvantaged groups must be accorded full and sustainable access to adequate housing resources. Thus, such disadvantaged groups as the elderly, children, the physically disabled, the terminally ill, HIV-positive individuals, persons with persistent medical problems, the mentally ill, victims of natural disasters, people living in disaster-prone areas and other groups should be ensured some degree of priority consideration in the housing sphere. Both housing law and policy should take fully into account the special housing needs of these groups. Within many States parties increasing access to land by landless or impoverished segments of the society should constitute a central policy goal. Discernible governmental obligations need to be developed aiming to substantiate the right of all to a secure place to live in peace and dignity, including access to land as an entitlement;

(f) *Location*. Adequate housing must be in a location which allows access to employment options, health-care services, schools, child-care centres and other social facilities. This is true both in large cities and in rural areas where the temporal and financial costs of getting to and from the place of work can place excessive demands upon the budgets of poor households. Similarly, housing should not be built on polluted sites nor in immediate proximity to pollution sources that threaten the right to health of the inhabitants;

(g) *Cultural adequacy*. The way housing is constructed, the building materials used and the policies supporting these must appropriately enable the expression of cultural identity and diversity of housing. Activities geared towards development or modernization in the housing sphere should ensure that the cultural dimensions of housing are not sacrificed, and that, inter alia, modern technological facilities, as appropriate are also ensured.

9. As noted above, the right to adequate housing cannot be viewed in isolation from other human rights contained in the two International Covenants and other applicable international instruments. Reference has already been made in this regard to the concept of human dignity and the principle of non-discrimination. In addition, the full enjoyment of other rights – such as the right to freedom of expression, the right to freedom of association (such as for tenants and other community-based groups), the right to freedom of residence and the right to participate in public decision-making – is indispensable if the right to adequate housing is to be realized and maintained by all groups in society. Similarly, the right not to be subjected to arbitrary or unlawful interference with one's privacy, family, home or correspondence constitutes a very important dimension in defining the right to adequate housing.

10. Regardless of the state of development of any country, there are certain steps which must be taken immediately. As recognized in the Global Strategy for Shelter and in other international analyses, many of the measures required to promote the right to housing would only require the abstention by the Government from certain practices and a commitment

to facilitating "self-help" by affected groups. To the extent that any such steps are considered to be beyond the maximum resources available to a State party, it is appropriate that a request be made as soon as possible for international cooperation in accordance with articles 11 (1), 22 and 23 of the Covenant, and that the Committee be informed thereof.

11. States parties must give due priority to those social groups living in unfavourable conditions by giving them particular consideration. Policies and legislation should correspondingly not be designed to benefit already advantaged social groups at the expense of others. The Committee is aware that external factors can affect the right to a continuous improvement of living conditions, and that in many States parties overall living conditions declined during the 1980s. However, as noted by the Committee in its General Comment 2 (1990) (E/1990/23, annex III), despite externally caused problems, the obligations under the Covenant continue to apply and are perhaps even more pertinent during times of economic contraction. It would thus appear to the Committee that a general decline in living and housing conditions, directly attributable to policy and legislative decisions by States parties, and in the absence of accompanying compensatory measures, would be inconsistent with the obligations under the Covenant.

12. While the most appropriate means of achieving the full realization of the right to adequate housing will inevitably vary significantly from one State party to another, the Covenant clearly requires that each State party take whatever steps are necessary for that purpose. This will almost invariably require the adoption of a national housing strategy which, as stated in paragraph 32 of the Global Strategy for Shelter, "defines the objectives for the development of shelter conditions, identifies the resources available to meet these goals and the most cost-effective way of using them and sets out the responsibilities and time-frame for the implementation of the necessary measures." Both for reasons of relevance and effectiveness, as well as in order to ensure respect for other human rights, such a strategy should reflect extensive genuine consultation with, and participation by, all of those affected, including the homeless, the inadequately housed and their representatives. Furthermore, steps should be taken to ensure coordination between ministries and regional and local authorities in order to reconcile related policies (economics, agriculture, environment, energy, etc.) with the obligations under article 11 of the Covenant.

13. Effective monitoring of the situation with respect to housing is another obligation of immediate effect. For a State party to satisfy its obligations under article 11 (1) it must demonstrate, inter alia, that it has taken whatever steps are necessary, either alone or on the basis of international cooperation, to ascertain the full extent of homelessness and inadequate housing within its jurisdiction. In this regard, the revised general guidelines regarding the form and contents of reports adopted by the Committee (E/C.12/1991/1) emphasize the need to "provide detailed information about those groups within ... society that are vulnerable and disadvantaged with regard to housing." They include, in particular, homeless persons and families, those inadequately housed and without ready access to basic amenities, those living in "illegal" settlements, those subject to forced evictions and low-income groups.

14. Measures designed to satisfy a State party's obligations in respect of the right to adequate housing may reflect whatever mix of public and private sector measures considered appropriate. While in some States public financing of housing might most usefully be spent on direct construction of new housing, in most cases, experience has shown the inability of Governments to fully satisfy housing deficits with publicly built housing. The promotion by States parties of "enabling strategies," combined with a full commitment to obligations under the right to adequate housing, should thus be encouraged. In essence, the obligation is to demonstrate that, in aggregate, the measures being taken are sufficient to realize the right for every individual in the shortest possible time in accordance with the maximum of available resources.

15. Many of the measures that will be required will involve resource allocations and policy initiatives of a general kind. Nevertheless, the role of formal legislative and administrative measures should not be underestimated in this context. The Global Strategy for Shelter (paras. 66–67) has drawn attention to the types of measures that might be taken in this regard and to their importance.

16. In some States, the right to adequate housing is constitutionally entrenched. In such cases the Committee is particularly interested in learning of the legal and practical significance of such an approach. Details of specific cases and of other ways in which entrenchment has proved helpful should thus be provided.

17. The Committee views many component elements of the right to adequate housing as being at least consistent with the provision of domestic legal remedies. Depending on the legal system, such areas might include, but are not limited to: (a) legal appeals aimed at preventing planned evictions or demolitions through the issuance of court-ordered injunctions; (b) legal procedures seeking compensation following an illegal eviction; (c) complaints against illegal actions carried out or supported by landlords (whether public or private) in relation to rent levels, dwelling maintenance, and racial or other forms of discrimination; (d) allegations of any form of discrimination in the allocation and availability of access to housing; and (e) complaints against landlords concerning unhealthy or inadequate housing conditions. In some legal systems it would also be appropriate to explore the possibility of facilitating class action suits in situations involving significantly increased levels of homelessness.

18. In this regard, the Committee considers that instances of forced eviction are prima facie incompatible with the requirements of the Covenant and can only be justified in the most exceptional circumstances, and in accordance with the relevant principles of international law.

19. Finally, article 11 (1) concludes with the obligation of States parties to recognize "the essential importance of international cooperation based on free consent." Traditionally, less than 5 per cent of all international assistance has been directed towards housing or human settlements, and often the manner by which such funding is provided does little to address the housing needs of disadvantaged groups. States parties, both recipients and providers, should ensure that a substantial proportion of financing is devoted to creating conditions leading to a higher number of persons being adequately housed. International financial institutions promoting measures of structural adjustment should ensure that such measures do not compromise the enjoyment of the right to adequate housing. States parties should, when contemplating international financial cooperation, seek to indicate areas relevant to the right to adequate housing where external financing would have the most effect. Such requests should take full account of the needs and views of the affected groups.

Endnotes

1 *Official Records of the General Assembly*, Forty-third Session, Supplement No. 8, addendum (A/43/8/Add.1).

2 Commission on Human Rights resolutions 1986/36 and 1987/22; reports by Mr. Danilo Türk, Special Rapporteur of the Sub-Commission (E/CN.4/Sub.2/1990/19, paras. 108–120; E/CN.4/Sub.2/1991/17, paras. 137–139); see also Sub-Commission resolution 1991/26.

3 See, for example, article 25 (1) of the *Universal Declaration on Human Rights*, article 5 (e) (iii) of the *International Convention on the Elimination of All Forms of Racial Discrimination*, article 14 (2) of the *Convention on the Elimination of All Forms of Discrimination against Women*, article 27 (3) of the *Convention on the Rights of the Child*, article 10 of the *Declaration on Social Progress and Development*, section III (8) of the *Vancouver Declaration on Human Settlements*, 1976 (Report of Habitat: United Nations Conference on Human Settlements (United Nations publication, Sales No. E.76.IV.7 and corrigendum), chap. I), article 8 (1) of the *Declaration on the Right to Development* and the ILO *Recommendation Concerning Workers' Housing*, 1961 (No. 115).

4 See footnote 1.

5 Geneva, World Health Organization, 1990.

Appendix D

Canada's Record on Economic, Social and Cultural Rights – UN Report

UNITED NATIONS COMMITTEE ON ECONOMICS,
SOCIAL AND CULTURAL RIGHTS,
GENEVA DECEMBER 4, 1998

1. The Committee considered the third periodic report of Canada on the rights covered by articles 1 to 15 of the Covenant (E/1994/104/Add.14) at its 46th to 48th meetings, held on 26 and 27 November 1998, and adopted, at its 57th meeting held on 4 December 1998, the following concluding observations.

A. Introduction

2. The Committee expresses its appreciation to the Government of Canada for the submission of its detailed and extensive report, which generally follows the Committee's reporting guidelines and for the submission by Canada of comprehensive written answers to its list of issues. While the Committee notes that the delegation was composed of a significant number of experts, too many questions failed to receive detailed or specific answers. Moreover, in the light of the federal structure of Canada and the extensive provincial jurisdiction, the absence of any expert representing particularly the largest provinces, other than Quebec, significantly limited the potential depth of the dialogue on key issues. The Committee notes with satisfaction that the Government of Canada engaged in extensive consultation with non-governmental organizations (NGOs) in the preparation of the report, that it submitted information in the form of a Core Document (HRI/CORE/1/Add.91) and provided supplementary information during the consideration of the report.

B. Positive Aspects

3. The Committee notes that for the last five years, Canada has been ranked at the top of the United Nations Development Programme's Human Development Index (HDI). The HDI indicates that, on average, Canadians enjoy a singularly high standard of living and that Canada has the capacity to achieve a high level of respect for all Covenant rights. That this has not yet been achieved is reflected in the fact that UNDP's Human Poverty Index ranks Canada tenth on the list for industrialized countries.

4. The Committee notes with satisfaction that the Supreme Court of Canada has not followed the decisions of a number of lower courts and has held that section 15 (equality rights) of the Canadian Charter of Rights and Freedoms (the Charter) imposes positive obligations on governments to allocate resources and to implement programmes to address social and economic disadvantage, thus providing effective domestic remedies under section 15 of the Charter for disadvantaged groups.

5. The Committee notes with satisfaction that the Federal Government has acknowledged, in accordance with the interpretation adopted by the Supreme Court, that section 7 of the Charter (liberty and security of the person) guarantees the basic necessities of life in accordance with the Supreme Court of Canada and the Covenant.

6. The Committee notes with satisfaction that the Human Rights Tribunal in Quebec has, in a number of decisions, considered the Covenant in interpreting Quebec's Charter of Rights, especially in relation to labour rights.

7. The Committee notes that in recognition of the serious issues affecting Aboriginal Peoples in Canada, the Government appointed the Royal Commission on Aboriginal Peoples (RCAP), which released a wide-ranging report in 1996 addressing many of the rights enshrined in the Covenant.

8. The Committee welcomes the reinstatement by the Federal Government of the Court Challenges Program, as recommended by the Committee while reviewing the State party's previous report.

9. The Committee welcomes the Canadian Human Rights Commission's statement about the inadequate protection and enjoyment of eco-

nomic and social rights in Canada and its proposal for the inclusion of those rights in human rights legislation, as recommended by this Committee in 1993.

10. The Committee views as a positive development the high percentage of women attending university and their increasing access to the liberal professions traditionally dominated by men. The Committee notes that Canada has one of the highest percentages of population having completed post-secondary education and one of the highest percentages of GDP devoted to post-secondary education in the world.

C. Factors and difficulties impeding the implementation of the Covenant

11. The Committee notes that since 1994 in addressing the budget deficits by slashing social expenditure, the State Party has not paid suficient attention to the adverse consequences for the enjoyment of economic, social and cultural rights by the Canadian population as a whole, and by vulnerable groups in particular.

12. The Committee heard ample evidence from the State Party suggesting that Canada's complex federal system presents obstacles to implementing the Covenant in areas of provincial jurisdiction. The Committee regrets that, unless a right under the Covenant is implicitly or explicitly protected by the Charter, through federal-provincial agreements, or incorporated directly into provincial law, there is no legal redress available to either an aggrieved individual or the Federal Government where provinces have failed to implement the Covenant. The State Party's delegation emphasized the importance of political processes in this regard but noted that they were often complex.

13. While the Government of Canada has consistently used Statistics Canada's "Low Income Cut-Off" as a measure of poverty when providing information to the Committee about poverty in Canada, it informed the Committee that it does not accept the Low Income Cut-Offs as a poverty line, although this measure is widely used by experts to consider the extent and depth of poverty in Canada. The absence of an official poverty line makes it difficult to hold the federal, provincial and territorial governments accountable to their obligations under the Covenant.

D. Principal subjects of concern

14. The Committee has received information about a number of cases in which claims were brought by people living in poverty (usually women with children) against government policies which denied the claimants and their children adequate food, clothing and housing. Provincial governments have urged upon their courts in these cases an interpretation of the Charter which would deny any protection of Covenant rights and consequently leave the complainants without the basic necessities of life and without any legal remedy.

15. The Committee is deeply concerned to receive information that provincial courts in Canada have routinely opted for an interpretation which excludes protection of the right to an adequate standard of living and other Covenant rights. The Committee notes with concern that the courts have taken this position despite the fact that the Supreme Court of Canada has stated, as has the Government of Canada before this Committee, that the Charter can be interpreted so as to protect these rights.

16. The Committee is also concerned about the inadequate legal protection in Canada of women's rights which are guaranteed under the Covenant, such as the absence of laws requiring employers to pay equal remuneration for work of equal value in some provinces and territories, restricted access to civil legal aid, inadequate protection from gender discrimination afforded by human rights laws and the inadequate enforcement of those laws.

17. The Committee is greatly concerned at the gross disparity between Aboriginal people and the majority of Canadians with respect to the enjoyment of Covenant rights. There has been little or no progress in the alleviation of social and economic deprivation among Aboriginal people. In particular, the Committee is deeply concerned at the shortage of adequate housing, the endemic mass unemployment and the high rate of suicide, especially among youth in the Aboriginal communities. Another concern is the failure to provide safe and adequate drinking water to Aboriginal communities on reserves. The delegation of the State Party conceded that almost a quarter of Aboriginal household dwellings require major repairs for lack of basic amenities.

18. The Committee views with concern the direct connection between Aboriginal economic marginalization and the ongoing dispossession of Aboriginal people from their lands, as recognized by the RCAP, and endorses the recommendations of the RCAP that policies which violate Aboriginal treaty obligations and extinguishment, conversion or giving up of Aboriginal rights and title should on no account be pursued by the State Party. Certainty of treaty relations alone cannot justify such policies. The Committee is greatly concerned that the recommendations of the RCAP have not yet been implemented in spite of the urgency of the situation.

19. The replacement of the Canada Assistance Plan (CAP) by the Canada Health and Social Transfer (CHST) entails a range of adverse consequences for the enjoyment of Covenant rights by disadvantaged groups in Canada. The Government informed the Committee in its 1993 report that the CAP set national standards for social welfare, required that work by welfare recipients be freely chosen, guaranteed the right to an adequate standard of living, and facilitated court challenges to federally funded provincial social assistance programmes which did not meet the standards prescribed in the Act. In contrast, the CHST has eliminated each of these features and significantly reduced the amount of cash transfer payments provided to the provinces to cover social assistance. It did, however, retain national standards in relation to health under CHST, thus denying provincial "flexibility" in one area, while insisting upon it in others. The delegation provided no explanation for this inconsistency. The Committee regrets that, by according virtually unfettered discretion in relation to social rights to provincial Governments, the Government of Canada has created a situation in which Covenant standards can be undermined and effective accountability has been radically reduced. The Committee also recalls in this regard paragraph nine of General Comment No. 3.

20. The Committee is concerned that newly introduced successive restrictions to unemployment insurance benefits have resulted in a dramatic drop in the proportion of unemployed workers receiving benefits to approximately half of previous coverage, in the lowering of benefit rates, in reductions in the length of time for which benefits are paid and in the increasingly restricted access to benefits for part-time workers. While the new programme is said to provide better benefits for low-

income families with children, the fact is that fewer low-income families are eligible to receive any benefits at all. Part-time, young, marginal, temporary and seasonal workers face more restrictions and are frequently denied benefits, although they contribute significantly to the fund.

21. The Committee received information to the effect that cuts of about 10% to social assistance rates for single people were introduced in Manitoba; 35% for single people in Nova Scotia; and 21.6% to both families and single people in Ontario. These cuts appear to have had a significantly adverse impact on vulnerable groups, causing increases in already high levels of homelessness and hunger.

22. The Committee notes with concern that in all but two provinces (New Brunswick and Newfoundland), the National Child Benefit (NCB) introduced by the Federal Government which is meant to be given to all children of low-income families is in fact only given to children of working poor parents since the provinces are allowed by the Federal Government to deduct the full amount of the NCB from the amount of social assistance received by parents on welfare.

23. The Committee notes with grave concern that with the repeal of CAP and cuts to social assistance rates, social services and programmes have had a particularly harsh impact on women, in particular single mothers, who are the majority of the poor, the majority of adults receiving social assistance and the majority among the users of social programmes.

24. The Committee is gravely concerned that such a wealthy country as Canada has allowed the problem of homelessness and inadequate housing to grow to such proportions that the mayors of Canada's ten largest cities have now declared homelessness a national disaster.

25. The Committee is concerned that provincial social assistance rates and other income assistance measures have clearly not been adequate to cover rental costs of the poor. In the last five years, the number of tenants paying more than 50% of income toward rent has increased by 43%.

26. The Committee is concerned that in both Ontario and Quebec, governments have adopted legislation to redirect social assistance payments

directly to landlords without the consent of recipients, despite the fact that the Quebec Human Rights Commission and an Ontario Human Rights Tribunal have found this treatment of social assistance recipients to be discriminatory.

27. The Committee expresses its grave concern at learning that the Government of Ontario proceeded with its announced 21.6% cuts to social assistance in spite of claims that it would force large numbers of people from their homes.

28. The Committee is concerned that the significant reductions in provincial social assistance programmes, the unavailability of affordable and appropriate housing and widespread discrimination with respect to housing create obstacles to women escaping domestic violence. Many women are forced, as a result of those obstacles, to choose between returning to or staying in a violent situation, on the one hand, or homelessness and inadequate food and clothing for themselves and their children, on the other.

29. The Committee notes that Aboriginal women living on reserves do not enjoy the same right, as women living off reserves, to an equal share of matrimonial property at the time of marriage breakdown.

30. The Committee notes with concern that at least six provinces in Canada (including Quebec and Ontario) have adopted "workfare" programmes that either submit the right to social assistance to compulsory employment schemes or reduce the benefit of social assistance when recipients who are usually young, assert their right to choose freely what type of work they wish to do. In many cases, these programmes constitute work without the protection of fundamental labour rights and labour standards legislation. The Committee further notes that in the case of the Province of Quebec, those workfare schemes are implemented, notwithstanding the opinion of the Human Rights Commission and the decisions of the Human Rights Tribunal which state that those programmes constitute discrimination based on social status or age.

31. The Committee notes that Bill 22, entitled "An Act to Prevent Unionization," was adopted by the Ontario Legislative Assembly on 24 November 1998. The Act denies to workfare participants the rights to

join a trade union, to bargain collectively and to strike. In response to a request from the Committee, the Government provided no information in relation to the compatibility of the Act with the Covenant. The Committee considers the Act to be a clear violation of article 8 of the Covenant and calls upon the State Party to take measures to repeal the offending provisions.

32. The Committee is concerned that the minimum wage is not sufficient for a worker to have an adequate standard of living, which also covers his or her family.

33. The Committee is perturbed to hear that the number of food banks has almost doubled between 1989 and 1997 in Canada and are able to meet only a fraction of the increased needs of the poor.

34. The Committee is concerned that the State Party did not take into account the Committee's 1993 major concerns and recommendations when it adopted policies at federal, provincial and territorial levels which exacerbated poverty and homelessness among vulnerable groups during a time of strong economic growth and increasing affluence.

35. The Committee is concerned at the crisis level of homelessness among youth and young families. According to information received from the National Council of Welfare, over 90% of single mothers under 25 live in poverty. Unemployment and under-employment rates are also significantly higher among youth than among the general population.

36. The Committee is also concerned about significant cuts to services on which people with disabilities rely, such as cuts to home care, attendant care, special needs transportation systems and tightened eligibility rules for people with disabilities. Programmes for people who have been discharged from psychiatric institutions appear to be entirely inadequate. Although the Government failed to provide to the Committee any information regarding homelessness among discharged psychiatric patients, the Committee was told that a large number of those patients end up on the street, while others suffer from inadequate housing with insufficient support services.

37. The Committee views with concern the plight of thousands of "Convention refugees" in Canada who cannot be given permanent resi-

dent status for a number of reasons, including the lack of identity documents, and who cannot be reunited with their families before a period of 5 years.

38. The Committee views with concern that 20% of the adult population in Canada is functionally illiterate.

39. The Committee is concerned that loan programmes for post-secondary education are available only to Canadian citizens and permanent residents and that recognized refugees who do not have permanent residence status, as well as asylum seekers, are ineligible for these loan programmes. The Committee views also with concern the fact that tuition fees for university education in Canada have dramatically increased in the past years, making it very difficult for those in need to attend university in the absence of a loan or grant. A further subject of concern is the significant increase in the average student debt on graduation.

E. Suggestions and recommendations

40. The Committee recommends that the State Party consider re-establishing a national programme with designated cash transfers for social assistance and social services which include universal entitlements and national standards, specifying a legally enforceable right to adequate assistance for all persons in need, a right to freely chosen work, a right to appeal and a right to move freely from one job to another.

41. The Committee urges the State Party to establish officially a poverty line and to establish social assistance at levels which ensure the realization of an adequate standard of living for all.

42. The Committee recommends that federal and provincial agreements should be adjusted so as to ensure, in whatever ways are appropriate, that services such as mental health care, home care, child care and attendant care, shelters for battered women, and legal aid for non-criminal matters, are available at levels that ensure the right to an adequate standard of living.

43. The Committee calls upon the State Party to act urgently with respect to the recommendations of the RCAP. The Committee also calls upon the State Party to take concrete and urgent steps to ensure respect

for Aboriginal economic land and resource base rights adequate to achieve sustainable Aboriginal economies and cultures.

44. The Committee recommends that the National Child Benefit Scheme be amended so as to prohibit provinces from deducting the benefit from social assistance entitlements.

45. The Committee recommends that Canada's Employment Insurance Programme be reformed so as to provide adequate coverage for all unemployed workers in a benefit amount and for a duration of time which fully implements their right to social security.

46. The Committee recommends that the federal, provincial and territorial governments address homelessness and inadequate housing as a national emergency by reinstating or increasing, as the case may be, social housing programmes for those in need, improving and properly enforcing anti-discrimination legislation in housing, increasing shelter allowances and social assistance rates to realistic levels, providing adequate support services for persons with disabilities, improving protection of security of tenure for tenants and improving protection of affordable rental housing stock from conversion to other uses. The Committee urges the State party to implement a national strategy for the reduction of homelessness and poverty.

47. The Committee calls upon the State party, in consultation with the communities concerned, to address the situation described in paragraph 29 with a view to ensuring full respect for human rights.

48. The Committee recommends that the Government of Canada take additional steps to ensure the enjoyment of economic and social rights for people with disabilities, in accordance with in the Committee's General Comment No. 5.

49. The Committee urges the Government to develop and expand adequate programmes to address the financial obstacles to post-secondary education for low-income students, without any discrimination on the basis of citizenship status.

50. The Committee urges the federal, provincial, and territorial governments to adopt positions in litigation which are consistent with their obligation to uphold the rights recognized in the Covenant.

51. The Committee again urges federal, provincial and territorial governments to expand protection in human rights legislation to include social and economic rights and to protect poor people in all jurisdictions from discrimination because of social or economic status. Moreover, enforcement mechanisms provided in human rights legislation need to be reinforced to ensure that all human rights claims which are not settled through mediation be promptly determined before a competent human rights tribunal, with the provision of legal aid to vulnerable groups.

52. The Committee, as in its previous review of Canada's report, reiterates that economic and social rights should not be downgraded to "principles and objectives" in the ongoing discussions between the federal government and the provinces and territories regarding social programmes. The Committee consequently urges the Federal Government to take concrete steps to ensure that the provinces and territories are made aware of their legal obligations under the Covenant and that the Covenant rights are enforceable within the provinces and territories through legislation or policy measures and the establishment of independent and appropriate monitoring and adjudication mechanisms.

53. The Committee encourages the State Party to adopt the necessary measures to ensure the realization of women's economic, social and cultural rights, including the right to equal remuneration for work of equal value.

54. The Committee also recommends that a greater proportion of federal, provincial and territorial budgets be directed specifically to measures to address women's poverty and the poverty of their children, affordable day care, and legal aid for family matters. Measures that will establish adequate support for shelters for battered women, care-giving services and women's non-governmental organizations should also be implemented.

55. The Committee urges the federal, provincial and territorial governments to review their respective "workfare" legislation in order to ensure that none of the provisions violate the right to work freely chosen and other labour standards, including minimum wage, rights which are not only guaranteed by the Covenant but also by the relevant ILO Conventions on fundamental labour rights and labour standards.

56. The Committee calls upon the federal, provincial and territorial governments to give an even higher priority to measures to reduce the rate of functional illiteracy in Canada.

57. The Committee recommends that the State Party should request the Canadian Judicial Council to provide all judges with copies of the Committee's concluding observations and encourage training for judges on Canada's obligations under the Covenant.

58. The Committee also recommends that since there is generally in Canada a lack of public awareness about human rights treaty obligations, the general public, public institutions and officers at all levels of Government should be made aware by the State Party of Canada's human rights obligations under the Covenant. In this regard, the Committee wishes to make specific reference to its General Comment No. 9 on the domestic application of the Covenant.

59. The Committee recommends that the Federal Government extend the Court Challenges Programme to include challenges to provincial legislation and policies which may violate the provisions of the Covenant.

60. Finally, the Committee requests the State Party to ensure the wide dissemination in Canada of its present concluding observations and to inform the Committee of steps taken to implement those recommendations in its next periodic report.

Appendix E
Adequate Shelter: A Fundamental Human Right

CHAPTER 2 OF
FINDING ROOM: HOUSING SOLUTIONS FOR THE FUTURE
REPORT OF THE NATIONAL LIBERAL CAUCUS
TASK FORCE ON HOUSING, 1990
BY PAUL MARTIN, M.P. AND JOE FONTANA, M.P.

Chapter 2: Adequate Shelter: A Fundamental Human Right

Shelter is a basic human need – in our climate a matter of life and death. In more prosaic terms, adequate and secure housing is a fundamental requirement for acceptable levels of health and comfort, for normal family life, and for ensuring that all New Brunswickers can access and contribute to the social and economic life of the Province. We believe that the federal government should acknowledge decent, affordable housing to be a basic right for all Canadians.

–Habitation New Brunswick, Moncton, New Brunswick, October 10, 1989

Towards Defining Rights

The unique distinguishing feature of a genuine democracy is the rights and freedoms that its inhabitants share, a feature Canada shares with other democracies. Individual rights are the cornerstone of our system of government and adherence to such rights is crucial to maintaining a healthy, tolerant society. In the words of well known Canadian political scientist, Donald V. Smiley:

The protection of human rights is the final end of government and the degree to which human rights are safeguarded is the final test by which any polity should be judged.

A right can best be described as a claim or advantage possessed by a person (individual rights) or persons (collective rights), which is conferred or protected by law and implies a corresponding duty or responsibility on the part of the other. The relationship between right and duty is fundamental to the democratic state: for example, an individual has a "right" to an education until a certain age and there is a corresponding duty on the part of the state or some other authority to provide that education.

It should also be noted that the particular rights being claimed or established by societies change over time. Prevailing attitudes towards rights and their ranking in importance change; new rights are demanded and recognized in law. There can be various opinions in society over the relative values which should be given to certain rights and how to resolve conflicting claims to rights. In Canada, aboriginal rights, mobility rights and the rights of the handicapped have recently been given increased emphasis. All of these discussions have taken place within the vibrant healthy democracy which is Canada. Arguments to establish new rights, protected in the Constitution, are part of the evolution of our country and its constitution.

Towards Housing as a Right

(i) Rights and Obligations Placed on Government

As we begin the 1990s, can we say that Canadians should have a constitutionally guaranteed right to housing? How could such a right be phrased? Would it be contained in the Charter of Rights and Freedoms? How would it be enforced?

Rights as we know them, certainly the majority of those set out in the Charter of Rights and Freedoms, are "negative" rights. People or the State are to refrain from interfering with one's right to speak. In other cases, people are to refrain from aggressive behaviour that interferes with another's freedom of movement. There are no positive obligations on the State.

This has been the situation with respect to rights from early time. However, since the middle of the Great Depression and particularly from the end of World War II, we have moved into an era where government decides not only that certain rights are available but also undertakes an obligation to provide the means whereby the rights may be enjoyed. In Canada, the most obvious example of those types of rights and corresponding obligations can be seen with respect to minority language rights, health care and education.

The Task Force believes that it is a healthy sign in a democracy for new rights to be created. It is therefore not unusual at this time in our history to have positive rights creating a State or government obligation. The question then becomes how best can a right to housing, or even to shelter, be expressed.

(ii) International Covenants and Housing Rights
In order to find a definition and legal description of housing rights, it is instructive to look at specific international covenants to which Canada is a signatory. These covenants are also significant in that they highlight the fact that Canada, as a member of the international community, has recognized the universal need for a rights declaration dealing with adequate housing.

The Universal Declaration of Human Rights, adopted by the United Nations General Assembly in 1948, made the first explicit reference to housing as a fundamental human right. Article 25(1) states:

> Everyone has the right to a standard of living adequate for the health and well-being of himself and his family, including food, clothing, housing and medical care, and necessary social services.

Future international declarations on the implementation of housing rights would include emphasis on the physical structure such as the provision of drinking water, sewer facilities, access to credit, land and building materials as well as the de jure recognition of security of tenure and other related issues.

Thus the process of recognizing human rights began forty years ago. The rights enshrined in the Universal Declaration became binding obligations in 1966. Article 11 of the International Covenant on Economic, Social and Cultural Rights expanded on Article 25(1) of the Universal Declaration. It further codified the right to housing by stating:

> The States Parties to the present Covenant recognize the right of everyone to an adequate standard of living for himself and his family, including adequate food, clothing, and housing, and to the continuous improvement of living conditions.

Though Canada is a signatory to these international covenants, some of the matters contained in them, such as housing, tend still to be looked upon only as worthy goals of social and economic policy rather than legally enforceable rights.

In 1987, the International Year of Shelter for the Homeless, the United Nations spoke of the right of all individuals to:

> a real home ... one which provides protection from the elements; has access to safe water and sanitation; provides for secure tenure and personal safety; is within easy reach of centres for employment, education and health care; and is at a cost which people and society can afford.

Current building codes and similar legal guarantees in Canada address questions such as structural soundness, the provision of clean water and the adequacy of sanitation facilities among other matters, and provide legal avenues for redress.

The Task Force also recognizes that there are provincial anti-discrimination laws in effect regarding housing. However, they do not provide any protection from discrimination on the basis of income. It is a fact of life in Canada that people are routinely denied access to adequate housing simply because they have low incomes or no credit rating. Housing Help of Ottawa told the Task Force that:

> Discrimination due to inadequate income and social prejudice is widespread against disadvantaged groups (including low-income families, families with children, social assistance recipients, visible minorities, women, disabled persons and Native people). This greatly increases their difficulty in finding adequate housing.

The Task Force believes that those searching for adequate, affordable housing may be better served by giving them some form of constitutionally guaranteed right to shelter. This would help them combat the weak or inadequate anti-discrimination laws as well as make governments face, and begin to resolve the desperate shortage of adequate, affordable housing. This constitutional guarantee would force governments to deal in a positive manner with these problems or be subject to legal claims brought forward by those disadvantaged by a lack of access to adequate housing.

Constitutional Recognition of the Right to Adequate Shelter

Our market housing system has not responded adequately to all of society's needs. Canadians living in poverty do not generate market demand nor in many cases, can they pay market rents. In fact, the gap between those who can afford housing and those who cannot has widened significantly in the past five years. Access to adequate, affordable housing is more than ever determined by economic status.

The Task Force believes that housing is a fundamental human right: all Canadians have the right to decent housing, in decent surroundings, at affordable prices. Shelter is a necessity of life and adequate shelter must be viewed as both an individual and collective right for all Canadians. Such a right would impose an obligation on governments and therefore make them accountable to their citizens to create the conditions necessary to ensure an adequate supply of shelter.

The Task Force recognizes that many people have advocated the inclusion of property rights in the Constitution. The right to shelter is much more specific and narrow than a "right to the enjoyment of property." The Task Force believes it is necessary to be specific so that the primary objective will be accomplished. The inclusion of a housing right within the Charter of Rights and Freedoms, however, does not inhibit or prevent the addition of the recognition of property rights in the Charter at some future time.

Based upon the evidence of the current situation, the Task Force does not believe that it is sufficient for Canadians to be guaranteed equality of access to existing housing under various provincial and federal human rights codes. We must go farther and recognize the necessity to provide sufficient adequate shelter so that those in need are provided with units that they may occupy and at a price that they can afford. This objective may be assisted by guaranteeing housing as a Charter Right. This perspective is shared by many of the groups which appeared before the Task Force, including the Social Planning Councils of Metropolitan Toronto and Ottawa-Carleton, the Housing Concerns Group of Winnipeg, the Saint John Housing Coalition, the Affordable Housing Action Group of Ontario, the Canadian Housing and Renewal Association and the Co-operative Housing Federation of Canada.

Obviously, such a right cannot be included in the Constitution without provincial consent. At the same time, it is vital that the concept of shelter be defined in the context of the Constitution and that this definition reflects a social consensus on this matter.

Recommendation

The Task Force recommends that the Conservative government place the issue of shelter rights on the list of items to be discussed at the next First Minister's Conference.

Index